Studies in Eighteenth-Century Culture

VOLUME 21

EDITORIAL BOARD
for
Studies in Eighteenth-Century Culture
Volume 21

James G. Buickerood
Washington University

J. Paul Hunter
University of Chicago

J. A. Leo Lemay
University of Delaware

Lawrence A. Lipking
Northwestern University

Studies in Eighteenth-Century Culture

VOLUME 21

Edited by

Patricia B. Craddock
University of Florida
and
Carla H. Hay
Marquette University

Published for the
American Society for Eighteenth-Century Studies
by COLLEAGUES PRESS

Published 1991

Colleagues Press Inc.
Post Office Box 4007
East Lansing, Michigan 48826

Distribution outside North America
Boydell and Brewer Ltd.
Post Office Box 9
Woodbridge, Suffolk IP12 3DF
England

Copyright © 1991
American Society for Eighteenth-Century Studies
All rights reserved

First printing

Printed in the United States of America

LC 75-648277

ISBN 0-937191-42-6
ISSN 0360-2370

Editorial Policy

>The editors of *Studies in Eighteenth-Century Culture* select papers of the highest quality and broadest intellectual interest in eighteenth-century studies. Papers presented at regional and national meetings of the American Society for Eighteenth-Century Studies must be submitted by August 1 each year to be considered for publication in the current volume. Papers written for oral presentation require revisions and the addition of scholarly apparatus. Contributions will be judged according to the highest standards of scholarship. Papers should be written in English, but quotations in foreign languages are permissible. Papers have usually averaged about 20 to 25 pages, but the editors encourage articles of greater length.

Current editorial practice follows the *Chicago Manual of Style*, 13th edition. The entire paper, including block quotations and footnotes, should be double-spaced. Footnotes should be numbered consecutively and typed on separate sheets following the text. Submit FOUR copies of the paper. Photocopies of illustrations should also be submitted in quadruplicate. Please accompany the typescript with a self-addressed envelope and enough loose stamps to cover the cost of returning one copy of the paper.

Editorial Readers for Volume Twenty-One

W. BARBARA ALLEN / History / Siena College
PAULA BACKSCHEIDER / English / University of Rochester
CAROL BLUM / French / State University of New York at Stony Brook
PATRICK BRADY / Romance Languages / University of Tennessee
LESLIE ELLEN BROWN / Music / Pennsylvania State University / Beaver
MARY CAMPBELL / English / Brandeis University
CHARLES MICHAEL CARROLL / Music / independent scholar
JAMES K. CHANDLER / English / University of Chicago
GREGORY CLAEYS / History / Washington University
THOMAS CLAYTON / English / University of Minnesota
LEOPOLD DAMROSCH / English / Harvard University
HELEN DEUTSCH / English / Northwestern University
MARGARET DOODY / English / Vanderbilt University
ROGER L. EMERSON / History / University of Western Ontario
DARIN FIELDS / English / University of Delaware
BERNADETTE FORT / French and Italian / Northwestern University
MARCIA FOUNTAIN / Music / University of Texas at El Paso
CHRISTOPHER FOX / English / Notre Dame University
JUDITH FRANK / English / Amherst College
ELISSA GELFAND / French / Mount Holyoke
KERRY S. GRANT / Music / University of Nebraska / Lincoln
WILLIAM W. HAGEN / History / University of California, Davis
JEAN HAGSTRUM / English / Northwestern University
PHILLIP HARTH / English / University of Wisconsin
ROBERT B. HAY / History / Marquette University
RAYMOND HILLIARD / English / University of Richmond
ROBERT HOPKINS / English / University of California, Davis
MYRA JEHLEN / English / University of Pennsylvania
KATHARINE JENSEN / French / Louisiana State University
J. W. JOHNSON / English / University of Rochester
LAWRENCE S. KAPLAN / History / Kent State University
ANN CLINE KELLY / English / Howard University
GWIN KOLB / English / University of Chicago
JOAN B. LANDES / Social Science / Hampshire College
DEIRDRE LYNCH / English / State University of New York at Buffalo
RACHAEL LYNCH / English / Boston University
ELIZABETH J. MacARTHUR / French / University of California, Santa Barbara

vi / *Editorial Readers*

SARAH MAZA / *History / Northwestern University*
WILLIAM McCARTHY / *English / Iowa State University*
WILLIAM McNEILL / *University of Kansas*
JEFFREY MERRICK / *University of Wisconsin, Milwaukee*
ELLEN MESSER-DAVIDOW / *English / University of Minnesota / Twin Cities*
MARJORIE MORGAN / *History / Southern Illinois University at Carbondale*
FELICITY NUSSBAUM / *English / Syracuse University*
HUGH ORMSBY-LENNON / *English / Villanova University*
PETER PARET / *History / Institute for Advanced Study / Princeton*
CATHERINE PARKE / *English / University of Missouri, Columbia*
JEAN A. PERKINS / *French / Swarthmore College*
RICHARD G. PETERSON / *English and Classics / St. Olaf College*
J. G. A. POCOCK / *History / Johns Hopkins University*
MARTIN PRICE / *English / Yale University*
DAVID RAYNOR / *Philosophy / University of Ottawa*
BRUCE REDFORD / *English / University of Chicago*
KATHARINE M. ROGERS / *English / American University*
EDWARD W. ROSENHEIM / JR. / *English / University of Chicago*
BARBARA BRANDON SCHNORRENBERG / *History / independent scholar*
GORDON SCHOCHET / *Political Science / Rutgers University*
SAMUEL F. SCOTT / *History / Wayne State University*
STUART SHERMAN / *English / University of Chicago*
SEAN SHESGREEN / *English / Northern Illinois University*
DAVID SHIELDS / *English / The Citadel*
JEFFREY SMITTEN / *English / Utah State University*
PATRICIA MEYER SPACKS / *English / University of Virginia*
BARBARA STAFFORD / *Art / University of Chicago*
KRISTINA STRAUB / *English / Carnegie-Mellon University*
ALBRECHT STRAUSS / *English / University of North Carolina, Chapel Hill*
GREGORY SYMCOX / *History / University of California, Los Angeles*
JAMES TULLY / *Political Science / McGill University*
DALE VAN KLEY / *History / Calvin College*
PHEROZE WADIA / *Philosophy / Rutgers University*
WILLIAM B. WARNER / *English / State University of New York at Buffalo*
HOWARD D. WEINBROT / *English / University of Wisconsin*
JAMES WINN / *English / University of Michigan*
JOHN W. YOLTON / *Philosophy / Rutgers University*
ROSE ZIMBARDO / *English / State University of New York at Stony Brook*
EVERETT ZIMMERMAN / *English / University of California, Santa Barbara*

Contents

Preface xi

The Literary Revolution of 1789
ROBERT DARNTON 3

Anna Barbauld's Criticism of Fiction — Johnsonian Mode, Female Vision
KATHARINE M. ROGERS 27

Versions of Female Nature in John Gay's Fan
JACOB FUCHS 43

Eroticism in Graphic Art: The Case of William Hogarth
HANS-PETER WAGNER 53

Swift and the 'Conjectural Histories' of the Eighteenth Century: The Case of the Fourth Voyage
CHARLES H. HINNANT 75

A Dance in the Mind: The Provincial Scottish Philosophical Societies
  KATHLEEN HOLCOMB   89

"See Locke on Government": The Two Treatises and the American Revolution
  STEVEN M. DWORETZ   101

Another Turn of the Screw: Prefaces in Swift, Marvell, and Genette
  JON ROWLAND   129

"This was a Woman that taught": Feminist Scriptural Exegesis in the Seventeenth Century
  MARGARET OLOFSON THICKSTUN   149

History, Genre, and Insight in the "Characters" of Lord Chesterfield
  ALAN T. MCKENZIE   159

Historical Fiction: David, Marat, and Napoleon
  HEATHER MCPHERSON   177

Swift and Patronage
  DUSTIN GRIFFIN   197

Nationality and Knowledge in Eighteenth-Century Italy
  JAMES L. FUCHS   207

From Clarens to Hollow Park, Isabelle de Charrière's Quiet Revolution
  NADINE BÉRENGUIER   219

The Origins and Significance of Gossip about Princess Augusta and Lord Bute, 1755–1756
    JOHN L. BULLION   245

Did Minnesota Have an Eighteenth Century, and If So, When?
    PAUL ALKON   267

Contributors   289
Executive Board 1990–91   291
Institutional Members   293
Sponsoring Members   295
Patrons   299
Index   301

Preface

One keynote of this volume of *Studies in Eighteenth-Century Culture* is struck by the Clifford Lecture of Robert Darnton with which it begins: heresy. Many of the essays collected here attack or revise orthodoxies old and new, explicit or implicit. Beginning with Darnton's audacious recharacterization of the French revolution, and concluding with Paul Alkon's Presidential Address of 1990, which requires reformulation of "the eighteenth century" itself, our contributors not only propose new material for consideration, but reconsiderations of received perspectives. Typically, they derive impetus from the other common feature of this diverse collection of essays, true and responsible interdisciplinarity. Almost every essay draws on expertise in at least one other discipline; every essay is thoroughly grounded in its own discipline. Thus, like ASECS itself, *SECC* is also multi-disciplinary. Disciplines represented include anthropology, art, classical studies, economics, political science, religion, and, of course, history of several kinds and literature in several languages. I think readers from many disciplines will find, as I have, much that is new, much to respect, perhaps some things to question or reject. Editing this volume has been, in the fullest and best sense, an enlightening experience.

I wish to thank the members of the Editorial Board for outstanding service, under the difficult conditions of being short-handed and having an editor away from her home base, and also two helpful and ingenious persons at the University of Florida, my graduate assistant Chuck Gobin, and Louise P. Stephenson, my secretary when I am functioning as departmental chair there. Both of them have coped ably and patiently not only with the usual chores connected with the annual, but with the unusual problems created by my absence. Mr. Gobin also compiled the index for Volume 21.

I wish also to thank those who created the happy occasion of that absence, the faculty of the School of Historical Studies, Institute for Advanced Study, Princeton, who have supported my research on Gibbon xii / *Preface*

during 1990-1991 and incidentally the final preparations of this volume, and members of the library and secretarial staff of the Institute who have been helpful to me, especially Margaret Van Sant. And finally I wish to acknowledge the support of the University of Florida, which has made possible my work on this and (as associate editor) prior volumes, and initial support for my associate editorship from Boston University.

—Patricia Craddock
December, 1990

Studies in Eighteenth-Century Culture

VOLUME 21

The Literary Revolution of 1789

ROBERT DARNTON

I have divided this lecture* into two parts: one part sociology, one part heresy. Since heresy is more interesting than sociology, I will concentrate on part two; and I will announce its central proposition right away, so that you can prepare objections while I work my way through some preliminary statistics. My thesis goes as follows: one of the most important tasks of the French Revolution was to rewrite Molière.

Now to the sociology. It concerns a set of related questions about the facts of literary life under the Old Regime — questions so seemingly simple that you would think they had been answered long ago:

How many writers were there in eighteenth-century France?

Where did they come from?

And how did they fit into the social order?

Those questions soon turn into an inquiry about sources. There is a great deal of information about individual authors scattered about the world, but it is so disparate and uneven that it resists any attempt to create a coherent series of statistics about authors in general. Short of enlisting an army of graduate students to run a dragnet through all the archives and libraries of France, the only way I can imagine to form a picture of the literary population as a whole is to study one exceptionally rich source: *La France littéraire*, an informal guide to writers and writing published at regular intervals throughout the second half of the eighteenth century.

La France littéraire began as an almanac, tiny enough to fit into the daintiest vest pocket, and ended as a multi-volume reference work, part biographical dictionary and part bibliography. In the course of its metamorphoses through a dozen editions and supplements, it became a fixture of literary life, a kind of *Who's Who* consulted by anyone who wanted to locate anyone else within the Republic of Letters.

It has defects, of course. In fact, it was a hack work produced by a hack writer, the abbé Joseph de La Porte. La Porte was a defrocked Jesuit who took up writing as a way of life and actually managed to make a living from it—one of the very few writers under the Old Regime who actually lived from his pen. He did so by producing a great deal—at least 214 volumes by my count—on every conceivable subject, from the economy of China to the domestic lives of English women. Not that he wrote everything he printed. "The important thing," he reportedly remarked, "is not to write but to publish." La Porte compiled, abridged, digested, and anthologized. He was the supreme scissors-and-paste man, the king of the hacks, in an age when hack writing first came into its own.

Given the character of its author, one should not expect *La France littéraire* to be a great work of literature. It is not, but it is a remarkably exhaustive one. La Porte knew how to compile information. He kept files, issued appeals for help, received reports from provincial *savants* everywhere in the kingdom, and improved his book as it progressed from edition to edition. By 1757, it can be taken as a reasonably accurate guide to France's literary population. And its later editions, especially those of 1769 and 1784, show how that population evolved throughout the second half of the century.

Now, that information, I submit, is important, because we do not have the foggiest notion, not even a ballpark estimate, of how many writers existed at any time in eighteenth-century France. By reworking La Porte's data—tricky business, since every entry must be checked for duplications and errors—one can sketch the outline of a literary demography.

The number of living writers who appear in the three main editions of *La France littéraire* can be summarized as follows:

1757	*1769*	*1784*
1,187	2,367	2,819

For various reasons having to do with the inferior quality of the 1784 edition, which was published after La Porte's death, I think the last figure is much too low. I would estimate the number of writers in France at the outbreak of the Revolution as at least 3,000 and probably many more. The literary population had more than doubled since the middle of the century.

Literary Revolution / 5

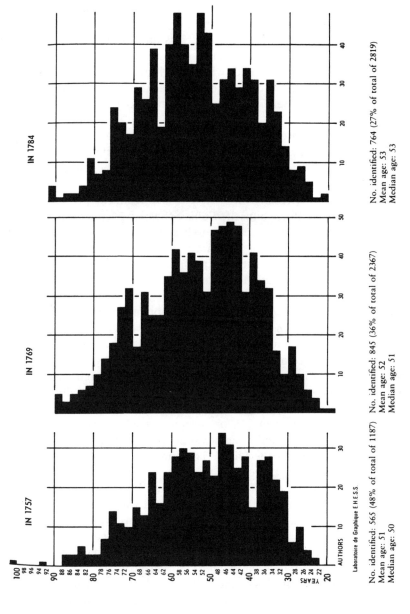

Figure 1. Age of Authors.

What should we make of those figures? Three thousand writers in a country of twenty-six million: were they a burden on the economy? a sector of social unrest? a source of ideological discontent? The numbers don't mean much by themselves, and they raise all kinds of definitional difficulties. La Porte defined a "writer" as anyone who has published a book (and he did not specify what he meant by a book). Very arbitrary, you will object. But not so bad, when you think of it. At least La Porte's definition is workable, and it avoids the anachronism built into the modern notion that a writer is someone who somehow makes a living from writing.

Conditions in eighteenth-century France made that kind of professionalism almost unthinkable. The lack of effective copyright, the prevalence of pirating, the non-existence of royalties, the cumbersome constraints of the censorship system, and the monopolistic practices of the booksellers' guild made it virtually impossible to live from the pen—with a few exceptions like La Porte himself. Louis-Sébastien Mercier estimated that only thirty writers supported themselves from writing in the 1780s—thirty of three thousand, or one in a hundred. The Republic of Letters was suffering from a population explosion on the eve of the Revolution, and it offered nothing but misery for anyone who tried to rise through its ranks without an independent income.

What were the characteristics of this population? Figure 1 shows its demographic profile in 1757, 1769, and 1784. Having expected to find youth, I was surprised to discover a middle-aged bulge in the center of the bar graphs. The average age of the writers in 1784 was fifty-three, and there were more of them in their sixties and seventies than in their twenties and thirties. This pattern may be something of an optical illusion, however, because many aspiring writers published a volume at an early age, failed to gain any recognition or income, gave up writing in order to pursue another career, and nonetheless continued to appear in *La France littéraire* for the rest of their lives. The number of these inactive authors cannot be determined. It probably was large enough to mitigate the population pressure. But I doubt that France could have supported two thousand or even one thousand active writers. And whatever their number, it seems likely that the inactive ones identified themselves, at least to some degree, with "literary France." They belonged to the Republic of Letters in spirit, even if they could produce little more than a brief entry in *La France littéraire* to substantiate their claim to citizenship.

The geographical origins of the writers can be studied on the adjoining maps (Figures 2 through 4). They fall into a pattern like that on other maps of cultural life under the Old Regime—maps showing variations in literacy rates, in the density of schools, and in subscriptions to the *Ency-*

Figure 2. Birthplaces of Authors, 1757. Number identified: 778, or 66 percent of a total of 1187. Number born in Paris: 190, or 24 percent of the identified.

clopédie. In each case, a fertile north-northeast stands out in contrast to an underdeveloped south-southwest. The exceptions are scattered along the commercial arteries leading from Lyon to Marseille and from Toulouse to Bordeaux. In 1784 four-fifths of the identified authors came from the provinces, mainly from small towns and villages; and most of them probably lived in Paris at some point in their lives. I don't have figures on emigration to the capital; but if they were available, I suspect they would bear out some standard themes in the literature of the time: Paris soaked up talent from the provinces, and it may well have corrupted some of the country boys who arrived with the dream of scoring hits in the Comédie française and *bons mots* in the salons.

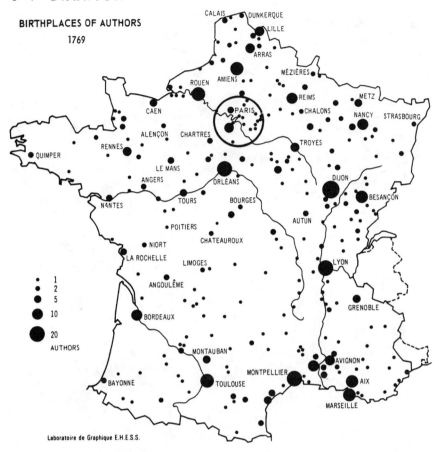

Figure 3. Birthplaces of Authors, 1769. Number identified: 990, or 42 percent of a total of 2367. Number born in Paris: 211, or 21 percent of the identified.

Figure 5 shows the socio-occupational positions of the authors. Like any sociological grid, it raises problems about defining categories and sorting out data; but I think it works quite well. It certainly illustrates the relative importance of the three estates, which can be summarized as follows:

	1757	1769	1784
Clergy	32%	24%	20%
Nobility	9%	12%	14%
Third Estate	55%	59%	59%
Unidentified	4%	5%	7%

Figure 4. Birthplaces of Authors, 1784. Number identified: 860, or 31 percent of a total of 2819. Number born in Paris: 170, or 20 percent of the identified.

The privileged orders occupied a disproportionately important place in the Republic of Letters. Although the clergy and nobility together represented less than five per cent of the population, they made up one third of all the authors on the eve of the Revolution. True, the percentage of priests declined from 1757 to 1784, but the percentage of noblemen increased. If we must characterize literary France by some formula, it would be more accurate to invoke the "mixed elite" favored by revisionist social historians than the "conquering bourgeoisie" of the Marxists.

When examined more closely, the writers of the third estate include a high proportion of professional men: engineers, architects, lawyers, and especially doctors. By contrast, the commercial and industrial bourgeoi-

	1757		1769		1784	
	Number	Percent	Number	Percent	Number	Percent
Upper Clergy, secular	7	1	15	1	13	1
Upper Clergy, regular	4	0	1	0	1	0
Lower Clergy, secular	120	14	194	12	196	13
Lower Clergy, regular	151	17	168	11	91	6
Titled Nobility, no office	9	1	21	1	50	3
Officer, upper administration	8	1	20	1	17	1
Officer, military	38	4	85	5	109	7
Officer, sovereign courts	17	2	64	4	42	3
Officer, high finance	8	1	23	1	1	0
Officer, lower courts	6	1	17	1	20	1
Lower administration	42	5	63	4	51	3
Lawyer, Attorney	67	8	169	11	162	11
Law personnel	2	0	3	0	3	0
Doctor, Surgeon	106	12	231	15	244	16
Apothecary	1	0	13	1	13	1
Engineer/Architect	17	2	30	2	35	2
Rentier	3	0	2	0	0	0
Lower Finance	4	0	5	0	6	0
Merchant	2	0	9	1	14	1
Manufacturer	1	0	2	0	0	0
Bookseller, Master Printer	5	1	26	2	295	20
Intellectual trades	198	23	309	20	295	20
Professor	93	11	165	10	167	11
Private Teacher	26	3	44	3	38	3
Journalist	9	1	0	1	5	0
Librarian	7	1	19	1	23	2
Interpreter	5	1	8	1	12	1
Secretary	15	2	15	1	12	1
Scribe	2	0	8	1	8	1
Sinecure	26	3	15	1	14	1
Actor, Theater personnel	8	1	15	1	21	1
Musician	7	1	11	1	4	0
Protestant Clergy	18	2	7	0	8	1
Student	0	0	1	0	1	0
Employee	4	0	8	1	1	0
Shopkeeper	1	0	1	0	4	0
Artisan	8	1	17	1	15	1
Servant	1	0	1	0	0	0
Women, no profession	14	2	42	3	49	3
Other	6	1	30	2	29	2
	868	99	1577	100	1393	98
	73% of total of 1187		67% of total of 2367		53% of total of 2819	

Figure 5. Socio-occupational Position of Authors.

sie is almost non-existent: only fourteen writers were merchants and none at all were manufacturers in 1784. The largest group of them belonged to what I would call the "intellectual trades": teachers, secretaries, scriveners, librarians, journalists, and actors. They congregated in cafés and garrets at the heart of the Republic of Letters; and they provided most of its energy as well as its prose and poetry, in contrast to the more casual varieties of writers scattered throughout the provinces—the country doctors who published papers on cures and epidemics and the parish priests who put out collections of their sermons.

It would be misleading, however, to consider these Parisians as "professionals," even if writing itself can be construed as a profession. They supported themselves by intellectual odd jobs, not by selling their wares on the literary market place; and most of them lived in misery. A tiny minority penetrated into the world of the salons, where they picked up pensions, sinecures, and seats in the academies. But most writers without an independent income sank into Grub Street, where they lived like Rameau's nephew, on whatever scraps they could find. It is impossible to calculate the population of Grub Street, because hack writers had no "état," no clearly defined estate or occupation, which could be attached to their name in *La France littéraire* and provide them with a social identity. They probably made up the bulk of the unidentified writers in the statistics, forty-seven percent of the total in 1784. So if I may hazard a guess, I would estimate that France contained 1,000 hungry hacks when the Revolution exploded in 1789.

Did the literary population include many writers from the lower classes? A few, like Restif de la Bretonne and Jamerey Duval, were born in the peasantry. But I could find none living among the common people in the country and only nineteen, one per cent of those identified, living as shopkeepers or artisans in the 1780s.

Were there many women? The question has some urgency, now that feminist scholars are reworking literary history and rediscovering women writers. La Porte, like many defrocked priests, had a sharp eye for women, especially literary women. In 1769 he published a four-volume *Histoire littéraire des femmes françaises*. But he found very few among his contemporaries: only fifty-one in 1784, or less than two per cent of the total. In an earlier attempt to study the social history of authorship, I extracted statistics from a remarkable survey of the literary population of Paris conducted by the police from 1748 to 1753. The police tracked down every "author" they could find (they used the term "auteur" without defining it, but it can be taken broadly to mean anyone who ever published anything). They came up with five hundred one, but only sixteen were women. Of course women had great influence on literary life as readers, leaders of salons, and arbiters of taste. Statistics do not provide an adequate measure of their importance. But insofar as quantification can produce a sociological profile of writers as a whole, I think the conclusion is clear: only a tiny proportion of "literary France" was female.

With those caveats about statistics in mind, it should now be possible to venture a few more conclusions of a sociological sort. Most writers under the Old Regime belonged to a mixed elite, which consisted of a great many members of the privileged orders, an equal number from the professional bourgeoisie, and a large contingent from the intellectual trades. Their share of industrialists, workers, peasants, and women was disproportionately small. And they lacked writers of the modern variety—the kind who live from their pen as independent intellectuals. To be sure, an intelligentsia of sorts had begun to emerge by 1750. It grew up around Voltaire, Diderot, and the other *philosophes*. But it did not yet have a clear social identity and a firm economic base. In fact, it shaded off into Grub Street, the marginal element of the Republic of Letters, which lay outside the categories of civil society.

* * *

It would be nice if I could stop at this point as if we had the subject firmly nailed down. But there is something unreal about all these graphs, maps, and socio-occupational grids. Nothing could be further from the writers' sense of their experience. Yet they lived through the phenomena that we cut apart and rearrange according to the conventions of our sociology. What would those phenomena look like if translated back into terms used by the writers themselves? To cope with that question, we need to shift the mode of study. Having attempted to produce a macro-sociological photograph of the literary world in general, I now propose to go to the other extreme and to try some microscopic analysis of texts.

Fortunately, eighteenth-century authors produced an enormous literature about authorship. Much of it merely vented squabbles and lamentations of a parochial sort, but some can be read as a commentary on the facts of literary life, which I have already tried to summarize statistically. I would like to discuss two pairs of such works: two literary almanacs by Antoine Rivarol and two plays by Fabre d'Eglantine. In each case, one work was written just before and one just after 1789; so the double pair of texts provides a neat, comparative, before-and-after view of literature and revolution.

At first glance, Rivarol's almanac, *Le Petit Almanach de nos grands hommes* (1788), looks like a sequel to La Porte's. It presents itself as a survey of all the authors in France, or at least all the poets, for Rivarol generally restricted his coverage to belles-lettres and promised to provide entries on the least known authors of the least memorable madrigals. In fact, the poems are so trivial and the poets so obscure that one soon realizes the "almanac" is a joke, an elaborate send-up of literary life at a time when the supply of *sensiblerie* had far exceeded the demand. By combing through all the ephemera of his day, Rivarol produced a stupendous roll call of mediocrities. He turned the literary world upside down, burying the most famous writers in silence and exposing the smallest fry to the grossest praise.

For example:

> Rigoley de Juvigny: A writer who is completely unknown, thanks to the power of his eloquence, his poetry, his philosophy and erudition.

> Pons de Verdun: A literary Hercules. He has not feared to sign about 10,000 epigrams or vignettes in verse and to send them to all the almanacs and reviews.

> Perrot, master poet and tailor in Paris: He favors the tragic muse. Here are two of his best known and most pathetic verses:
>   Alas, alas, alas, and four times alas,
>   He cut right through his neck with a stroke of his cutlass.

The burlesque almanac conveyed a kind of satirical sociology; and the satire worked, because it cut deep into literary life—life as it was actually lived by most French writers, not in a rarefied Republic of Letters but in garrets, cafés, and the columns of fifth-rate periodicals. To be sure, Rivarol made his victims look so absurd that one may suspect him of inventing everything in their mock biographical notices, including their existence. But he usually documented his assertions, and I have confirmed his references by tracing a sample of them into the obscure poetry reviews, the *muses* and *étrennes* and *almanachs*, that proliferated everywhere in prerevolutionary France and have since been forgotten. I felt skeptical when I found Rivarol linking two particularly ridiculous *beaux-esprits*, a M. Briquet and a M. Braquet. But the two can be found, exactly as he noted, in the *Muses provinciales* of 1788, Briquet as the author of an ode based on Psalm 129, Braquet as the author of an allegory. Every character in *Le Petit Almanach*, no matter how laughable, seems to have actually existed.

In fact, Rivarol did his research so thoroughly that it has some relevance to the question of literary demography. He identified 672 poets—672 poets in a society about to explode in the first great revolution of modern times! It gives one pause. It amounts to something that might be called the literarification of public life, if that were not such an unliterary way to put it—a tendency that was pointed out by Tocqueville and is still going strong in France, where the prestige of letters is invoked in political campaigns and Chamber of Commerce propaganda. In quantitative terms alone, *Le Petit Almanach* demonstrated the severity of the population problem in literature.

Rivarol's rhetoric, for all its tendentiousness, shows how that problem entered into contemporary discourse about literature. In a facetious preface, Rivarol claimed that his book originated from a parlor game devised by two Parisian wits. Weary of discussing the great authors of the past, they decided to concentrate on "la petite littérature" of the present. One named a minor writer and challenged the other to identify him. After meeting the challenge, the other riposted with an equally unknown name. The competition warmed as the names flew back and forth. It was the world's first trivia contest. "Mérard de Saint-Just," called out the first wit. "Joli de Plancy," answered the second. "Lourdet de Santerre" came the reply, and "Regnault de Beaucaron," the counter attack. It was "Briquet" here and "Braquet" there; "Guinguenet," "Moutonnet," "Fricot," "Pistolet," "Mitraille," "Cathala-Cotire" — an "army of Lilliputians" on either side with salvos of titles so unfamiliar that the onlookers finally protested. The contestants had to be making it up. Certainly not, they retorted indignantly. There really was a writer named Levrier de Champrion and another known as Delormel de la Rotiere. They could prove it, given an adequate supply of *almanachs* and *étrennes*. So the parlor game turned into a research project, and the result was *Le Petit Almanach de nos grands hommes*.

There was also a sub-text. Rivarol described "low literature" as a world of insects. In his preface, he promised to "descend from those imposing colossi [great writers] to the smallest insects; and you will feel your admiration for nature increase when I arrive at that vast throng of families, of tribes, of nations and empires hidden beneath a blade of grass." This theme came from Voltaire, who a generation earlier in *Le Pauvre Diable* had also treated "la basse littérature" as a population problem: "Egypt of old had fewer locusts."

Rivarol picked up the theme where Voltaire had left it. In fact, he remarked facetiously that Voltaire would have used *Le Petit Almanach* as a reference work, had it been available while he was writing *Le Pauvre Diable*. But in Rivarol's version, the picture of low literature as an underworld of insects looked more menacing. The creatures swarming in obscurity might appear ridiculous, but they could scratch and claw. Thus, Jean-Louis Carra: "After having written fifteen or sixteen volumes of physics about the atom, the apatom, and the exatom, which everyone knows by heart, he has not disdained to fall on M. de Calonne. Armed with invincible eloquence, he delivered the last blow to the dying lion." Rivarol was referring to Carra's *M. de Calonne tout entier*, a crucial pamphlet in the barrage of radical propaganda that helped to drive Etienne de Calonne, the Controller General, from the government and finally from France during the crisis surrounding the Assembly of

Notables. *Le Petit Almanach* appeared in 1788. In it, the first rumblings of the Revolution can already be heard, and literature has already spilled over into politics.

Two years later, Rivarol published a sequel: *Petit dictionnaire des grands hommes de la Revolution* (1790). He used the same format, style, and satirical technique as in his earlier almanac, but now he completed the transition from literature to politics. His little great men were all leaders of the French Revolution. Many of them had appeared in the first book, because they were also little great men of letters: Fabre d'Eglantine, Collot d'Herbois, Desmoulins, Fréron, Manuel, Mercier, Gorsas. They turned up again in the sequel, along with others of the same stripe: Sieyés, Brissot, Danton, Garat, Marat, and Pétion. In a particularly well placed barb, Rivarol hailed Robespierre as the author of a madrigal, "which was the despair of Voltaire in his old age." The Incorruptible appeared as a puffed-up little scribbler from the provinces, a fifth-rate *littérateur*, who took advantage of his position in the National Assembly to lecture all of France on how to make a revolution. Rivarol's Robespierre was already Poor Bidos.

And Rivarol's satire had turned into counter-revolutionary propaganda. Almost every figure in his pantheon of clowns represented the same theme: the mediocrities of the Old Regime had taken over the Revolution; they were compensating for their frustrations and failures under the old order by careers in the new. In fact, the demographic tensions of the Old Regime's Republic of Letters had become transformed into the politics of the Revolution: they were a prime source of the Revolution's leadership. Rivarol's mockery of the leaders operated as a kind of pop sociology à la Taine. Yet Rivarol continued to view politics from the perspective of literature. Here is how he described the National Assembly: "What miracles patriotism works! The dullest spirits of literature have proven to be the profoundest of the Assembly. The most illustrious ignoramuses of France's youth have not appeared to be embarrassed or out of place before the Parisian mob. In a word, the enemies of the language have suddenly become the defenders of the nation." The little great men of the Revolution sinned in the same way as those of the Old Regime: they sinned against language. Rivarol concentrated most of his fire on radical journalists and orators, and he objected less to the substance of what they said than to the way they used words. Thus his article on Desmoulins: "It is in the street that M. Desmoulins has set himself up and exercised his eloquence, and he has all the passers-by as his admirers. With three learned words — nation, lantern, and aristocrat — he has succeeded in putting himself on the same level as the valiant butcher's apprentice, the shy fish-monger, and all the new readers produced by the Revolution. Only such pens are capable of leading the people and of accustoming it to having ideas." Rivarol condemned Prudhomme's *Révolutions de Paris* for fomenting sedition with the same vulgarity: "In order for a mere journal to have such a great effect, its style must correspond to its purpose and it must succeed in charming the most barbarous reader."

It hardly seems surprising that the author of the celebrated essay *De l'Universalité de la langue française* (1784) should have shown a concern for language. But after 1789 Rivarol defended esthetic standards as if they were social and political distinctions. He noted with satisfaction that the members of the Académie française did not support the Revolution, except for a few deviants like Bailly, who had been misled by "the noble simplicity of his character." It was the hack writers who rallied to the cause of the common people. In doing so, they destroyed high society and elevated taste at the same time; and they also produced a social revolution within the world of letters: such was the mischief wrought by the freedom of the press. "What a noble source of abundance is the liberty of the press! It has merely destroyed talent and good taste, and ruined a few individuals who stood out as the opprobrium of a million poor scribblers. So equality of the mind ['l'égalité d'esprit'] can be counted as one of the greatest achievements of the National Assembly."

Seen at a distance of two hundred years, Rivarol's bitterness may look odd. We expect social distinctions to be expressed in terms of social consciousness and politics to be political. But Rivarol's categories do not coincide with ours. He saw politics through literature, and he understood literature in the broadest sense as a force that shaped a way of life. When he sided with the counter-revolution, he took up a stand for good taste, pure language, elegant manners, and even Enlightenment, for he always wrote in the spirit of Voltaire. He developed an esthetic view of the social order and depicted the Revolution as a battle between an older, patrician civilization and a vulgar, vandalistic, plebeian culture.

Rivarol's chain of associations was peculiar to his time, but it has not come completely apart. Insofar as we still associate snobbery with the Right and vulgarity with the Left, we draw on distinctions that he helped to embed in the revolutionary process, along with more fundamental divisions like the opposition of Left and Right itself, which derived from the seating plan of the National Assembly. The Revolution was a time of rearranging affinities and of sorting things out into new configurations. Literature was part of this process, and Rivarol succeeded in defining its part—at least from the viewpoint of the Right.

For a view from the Left, we should turn to Fabre d'Eglantine. He exposed the social and political sides of literature in two plays, *Les Gens de lettres*, performed at the Comédie italienne on September 21, 1787, and *Le Philinte de Molière*, which opened at the Comédie française on February 22, 1790. Unlike the works of Rivarol, they are almost unreadable today. So instead of discussing them in detail, I will be merciful and limit myself to an overview of their main themes.

Les Gens de lettres is actually a fascinating work, despite its heavy-handed plot and its arthritic alexandrine verse, because it provides a picture of the literary world from the perspective of someone on the bottom. That was Fabre's place. He had spent fifteen years as an actor and hack writer in just the sort of obscurity that was satirized by Rivarol. In fact, he was in *Le Petit Almanach*, where Rivarol had dispatched him in one sentence: "The success of his plays. . . is balanced by the prodigious rage for his couplets, which have charmed everyone in the salons."

The hero of *Les Gens de lettres*, an obscure poet from the provinces named Clar, writes masterpiece after masterpiece in a Parisian garret but remains frozen out of a successful career by the villains of the play, who make up most of the cast of characters. They include salon dandies, fashionable playwrights, exploitative publishers, mercenary journalists, and an assortment of *beaux-esprits*, who have taken over literature and turned it into a monopoly of the *beau monde*. While they shut off access to the top of the literary world, hordes of ambitious young writers flood the bottom; for Fabre treats overpopulation as a basic fact of life: "There are as many poets in Paris as stones in the street." At every turn in the plot, Clar runs into an insurmountable obstacle. He cannot get any payment from his publishers, a hearing in the salons, or a sinecure from the dispensers of patronage. His genius counts for nothing, because protection is everything and literature itself is merely a social system, closed to all except the privileged few.

These conditions are about to overwhelm Clar, when he is saved by a deus ex machina. A virtuous, bourgeois millionaire arrives from the provinces, recognizes Clar's talent, and carries him off to a country estate, where he writes masterpieces happily ever after. The text is bathed in Rousseauism. It has all the catch words — pity, virtue, nature, equality, *bienfaisance* — and it invokes Rousseau himself at one point as the pure genius who refuses to compromise with the system and therefore gives up writing and withdraws to a garret, where he lives by copying music. In short, Fabre describes the same world as that in Rivarol's *Petit dictionnaire*, but he does so from the opposite point of view. He presents it as a *comédie larmoyante* instead of as a subject of ridicule. And he invokes Rousseau instead of Voltaire. Also, I should add, Fabre failed miserably. The reviewers all heaped scorn on the play, the public hooted it off the stage on opening night, and it has never been performed since.

Two years later, in *Le Philinte de Molière*, the Rousseauism was even more explicit. Fabre opened the play with a prologue in which an actor advanced to the front of the stage, pulled a copy of Rousseau's *Lettre à d'Alembert sur les spectacles* from his pocket, read an excerpt from it, and announced that Jean-Jacques had inspired everything that was to follow. The inspiration would have been obvious to most of the audience in any case, because Fabre wrote a sequel to Molière's *Misanthrope* according to the formula in the *Lettre à d'Alembert*. He made Alceste the hero and Philinte the villain. Then, continuing the action from the point where Molière had left it, he turned the plot into a moral lesson about virtue confounding vice. Nowhere does the text betray the slightest hint of humor. Instead, it is one long declamation against the hypocrisy and wickedness of high society (*le monde*).

This time Fabre scored a hit. Virtue was the height of fashion in 1790; and Fabre's defense of it produced enthusiastic applause from the public and unanimous praise from the reviewers—including some, like La Harpe, who had panned the earlier play. The strongest and longest review came from Camille Desmoulins, who celebrated *Le Philinte de Molière* as, in effect, the collective triumph of the Cordelier District.

Desmoulins's reaction seems especially interesting to me, because it indicates the sociological and ideological lay of the land occupied by the extreme Left during the first year of the Revolution. In February 1790, Desmoulins had emerged as the principal spokesman for the radicals associated with the Cordelier Club, and Fabre, his close friend, was president of the Cordelier District. The district had a peculiar place in the new political geography of Paris, because it included an extraordinary number of literary institutions: the old Académie française, the old Comédie française, the theatres of the Foire Saint-Germain, the Café Procope, and the Musée de Paris, a literary club frequented by fifth-rate poets and pamphleteers—that is, by exactly the kind of writers whom Rivarol had satirized. In fact, Rivarol had singled out the Musée for mockery by dedicating his *Petit Almanach* to its horde of geniuses in 1788, and in 1791 the Cordelier Club set up headquarters in the Musée's assembly hall on the rue Dauphine. Everything seems to fit. The political radicals moved into the space occupied by the marginal intellectuals as if they were acting out a script composed by Rivarol.

Yet the fit seems almost too good, and I for one find it puzzling. *Le Philinte de Molière* was a period piece. It presented Molière's characters in a seventeenth-century setting without making the slightest overt allusion to the Revolution. But while the actors exchanged alexandrines in costumes from the reign of Louis XIV, the population outside the theatre was tearing down the most important institutions from the France of

Louis XVI and constructing a whole new world. The French were locked in a deep, desperate struggle to determine the character of the new regime—its constitution, religion, property rights, administrative structure, law codes, and even its weights and measures. How could they take time off for Molière? Why, aside from his personal friendship for Fabre, did Desmoulins drop his usual political commentary in order to produce a long review of this literary revisionism, as if it were perfectly natural for the Cordeliers to be concerned with *Le Misanthrope*?

Moreover, it all seems so involuted. We have Desmoulins's version of Fabre's version of Rousseau's version of Molière's version of the conflict between moral absolutism and worldliness. It is like a game of mirrors. But why was this literary game so important to the French? Why was it played at all?

We are back to my heresy. And to make it more heretical still, let me, by way of an answer, try to formulate it in a more extreme manner: the French Revolution was a literary revolution.

Now, that is a very wicked thing to say, so I hasten to add that I think the Revolution involved a great deal more than literature. It was an attempt to destroy a whole way of life and to create a new one. It was opposed by its very nature to the cultural system of the Old Regime. And insofar as it transformed French culture, it revolutionized French literature—not merely literature as a set of texts but literature as a social system and the very notion of literature itself. The revolutionaries freed the press, disbanded the booksellers' guild, abolished the monopolies of the Comédie française and the Opéra, destroyed the academies, scattered the salons, and smashed the system of court patronage. They demolished the world that Fabre had dramatized in *Les Gens de lettres* and that Rivarol regretted in *Le Petit Dictionnaire*. And while they dismantled the institutions of the literary old regime, they made their new variety of literature into an ingredient of a new, revolutionary culture. Molière lay at the heart of the old literary system, so the revolutionaries redid Molière. They repossessed their past and remade literary history. To carry "literarification" so far was not to play a game at all; it was to contribute to the social reconstruction of reality.

That may sound excessively abstract, so let me try to explain. Unlike some revisionists today, I do not understand the Revolution as a political phenomenon derived from the "discourse" of theorists like Rousseau and Sieyès. I think it was a total revolution, in its programs and often in its practice—a revolution in time, space, and personal relations as well as in politics and society; a revolution so big that it could not be comprehended by the people who made it. The twentieth century has accustomed us to mass upheavals, and our history books have laid out revolutions with such clarity—"crisis of the old order," "insurrection," "radicalization," "terror," and "reaction"—that we find it difficult to appreciate the scale and the confusion of the events that took place in France two hundred years ago. To the people in the midst of it, the French Revolution numbed the senses and staggered the mind. It tore their world apart. And when things fell apart, they felt an overwhelming need to make sense of things, to find some order in the new regime that was confusedly coming into being. That job fell to the intellectuals—that is, to the people who had a way with words and who had played with words for years among the ranks of the three thousand writers under the Old Regime. Fabre, for example, did not merely rework *Le Misanthrope*; he helped to reorder time by producing a nomenclature for the new, rational, natural, revolutionary calendar. To rewrite Molière and to redesign time belonged to the same task, the social reconstruction of reality.

But one cannot remake reality *ex nihilo*. The intellectuals naturally fell back on their experience and worked with themes that they had inherited from the Old Regime. They opposed Rousseauistic moralizing to Voltairean satire, and they framed their remarks in familiar genres: the *drame bourgeois* vs. the burlesque almanac, the Ciceronian declamation vs. the *bon mot*. The form was as important as the content, because the radical journalists and orators did not distinguish style from substance. They hated satire the way they hated high society, and they distrusted wit as a sign of an aristocratic disposition.

Their attitudes varied, of course. Some made use of popular strains of humor: hence the belly laugh of the Père Duchesne and the mockery of the Vieux Cordelier. But even these seemed treasonous to Robespierre. When he looked back at the literature of the Old Regime, he saw an alien world of refinement and corruption. Although he acknowledged the importance of the Enlightenment as a "preface to our Revolution," he smashed the bust of Helvétius in the Jacobin Club and vilified the Encyclopedists: "The high priests [of the Encyclopedist sect] sometimes declaimed against despotism, but they received pensions from despots. On some occasions they wrote books against the court but on others they penned dedications to kings, speeches for courtiers, and madrigals for aristocratic ladies. They were proud in their writings and obsequious in the antechambers of the great."

"Men of letters" in general seemed suspicious to Robespierre. Having guillotined a heavy proportion of writers amongst the Girondins, the Hébertistes, and the Dantonistes, he deplored their role in the Revolution and singled out only one writer from the Old Regime for praise: Jean-Jacques Rousseau.

One man, by the greatness of his soul and the grandeur of his character, proved himself worthy to be the educator of the human race. He attacked tyranny openly; he spoke with enthusiasm of the divinity; he used his virile, righteous eloquence to portray virtue in flaming colors. . . . The purity of his doctrine, inspired by nature and by a profound hatred of vice, and his invincible scorn for the intriguing sophists who had usurped the title of philosopher, drew upon him the hatred and persecution of his rivals and false friends.

On October 24, 1793, Fabre presented his project for the revolutionary calendar to the Convention. When he listed the patriotic festivals to be celebrated at the end of the year, he put Genius first and Virtue third. Robespierre objected. Virtue must come first, he insisted. It was a moral force essential to a republic, whereas Genius was nothing more than a literary quality, possessed by men like Voltaire: "The author of Brutus had genius, but Brutus was more worthy than Voltaire." A few months later, Robespierre denounced Fabre as an artful intriguer who used his experience on the stage to cabal and corrupt "on the stage of the Revolution." When Robespierre reworked Rousseau's ideas, he took them off the stage and into the street. He marched them about Paris in the Festival of the Supreme Being. And he turned them against Fabre himself, who went to the guillotine as a kind of Philinte, the essence of corruption in the eyes of the Incorruptible.

The revolutionaries used Rousseau in different ways at different times and often against one another. I do not mean to imply that they spoke with one voice or that the literary revolution was simple and unanimous. I am arguing, rather, that it belonged to a common task, which arises in all great revolutions and which was so enormous after 1789 that historians have rarely recognized it—the task of remaking reality from the rubble of an old regime. As products of the literary system peculiar to the Old Regime in France, the writers of the Revolution revolutionized through literature. They began in 1789 by capturing the sacred center of the old literary system—the space shaped by Molière—and they ended in 1794 by working it into the core of a new political culture.

* * *

Such, at least is my thesis. To demonstrate it, I would have to make a long detour through literary history—that is, through territory you might call the "old historicism." I have no time for that now, but if you will grant me a few more minutes I will try to explain what I think was at stake in the opposition between Voltaire and Rousseau, which was what ultimately lay behind the opposed positions occupied by Rivarol and Fabre.

And if I may inject a theoretical component into the argument, I would like to steal a leaf from Pierre Bourdieu. I think it is helpful to imagine the literary system of the Old Regime as what Bourdieu calls a "field" of power relations, organized around two opposing "poles" or "habitus": the ideological and esthetic positions embodied by Voltaire and Rousseau. There were also intermediate positions—Diderot's, for example—but the opposition of Voltaire and Rousseau defined the struggle to dominate the "symbolic goods" peculiar to that field—not merely the wealth, status, and power conferred on the most prestigious writers, but the very conception of literature itself.

Consider the way "literature" figures in the most important works of these two writers.

First, Voltaire. His long, complex, and changing oeuvre can hardly be reduced to a formula, not even "écrasez l'infâme"; but I will be so bold as to suggest that a key word lies at the heart of it: *politesse*. In 1730 Voltaire was overwhelmed by an incident, which haunted him for the rest of his life. His beloved mistress, the great actress Adrienne Lecouvreur, suddenly died after playing the lead in his tragedy *Oedipe*. Voltaire had sat by her bed in her last agony, and he may well have witnessed the disposal of her body, which was thrown into a common ditch, without the slightest ceremony. Death struck Adrienne Lecouvreur before she had time to renounce her profession and to receive the last sacraments. Actors and actresses were excluded from the rites of the Church, so the body of Adrienne Lecouvreur could not be buried in hallowed ground. It was dumped in a ditch and covered with quicklime to speed its decomposition.

This obscene act obsessed Voltaire right up to the moment of his own death, when he feared that his body would receive the same treatment. It appears in some of his most impassioned poetry, in the *Lettres philosophiques*, and even in *Candide*. In chapter 22, Candide visits Paris and is told the story in all its horror. He then remarks: "That [was] very impolite." Not what we would expect by way of a comment on a barbarism that had set a lover's blood to boil.

The first characteristic Candide noticed among the inhabitants of the utopian society of Eldorado was their "extreme politeness." He marveled at their good manners, elegant clothing, sumptuous housing, exquisite food, sophisticated conversation, refined taste, and superb wit. The king of Eldorado epitomized these qualities. He "received them with all imaginable grace and invited them politely to supper." Utopia is above all a "société polie" or "policée," which is the same thing.

I think the discussion of Voltaire's politics has turned around a "question mal posée": Was he a liberal? A champion of enlightened despotism? A man of the Left, or the Right, or the Center? In fact, Voltaire understood politics according to categories that antedated all those terms and that no longer exist. "There are only three ways of subjugating men," he wrote. "To police them by proposing laws to them, to employ religion to buttress those laws, and to slaughter one part of a nation in order to govern the other." The three methods really came down to two: politics was a matter of tyranny and superstition on the one hand, or an "Etat policé" on the other.

The eighteenth-century notion of "police" could be translated roughly as rational administration. It belonged (conceptually, not etymologically) to a series of interlocking terms—*poli, police, policé, politique*—which extend from culture to politics. For Voltaire, the cultural system of the Old Regime shaded off into a power system, and the code of polite society belonged to the politics of enlightened absolutism.

The interpenetration of culture and politics is the main theme of Voltaire's most ambitious treatise, *Le Siècle de Louis XIV*. This was a crucial work for eighteenth-century writers, a book that defined the literary system of the Old Regime and that created literary history in France, rather as Johnson's *Lives of the Poets* established literary criticism and history in England. In *Le Siècle de Louis XIV* Voltaire argued, in effect, that all history is literary history. Kings, queens, and generals do not count in the long run, although they attract most of the attention of their contemporaries and occupy a good deal of Voltaire's narrative. What matters above all is civilization. So, of the four happy ages in the history of mankind, the greatest was the age of Louis XIV, when French literature reached its zenith and the politeness ("la politesse et l'esprit de société") of the French court set a standard for all of Europe.

By civilization, Voltaire meant something akin to Norbert Elias's "civilizing process." It is the moving force in history, a combination of esthetic and social elements, manners and mores ("moeurs"), which pushes society toward the ideal of Eldorado, a state in which men are perfectly "poli" and "policé." So Voltaire understood *politesse* as power, and he saw an essential connection between classical French literature and the absolutism of the French state under Louis XIV. This argument underlies the key episodes of *Le Siècle de Louis XIV*. Louis masters the French language by studying the works of Corneille. He controls the court by staging plays. And he dominates the kingdom by turning the court itself into an exemplary theatre. That idea may be a cliché now, but Voltaire (with help from Saint Simon) invented it. He saw power as performance—the acting out of a cultural code. The code spread from Versailles to Paris, to the provinces, and to the rest of Europe. Voltaire does not deny the importance of armies, but he interprets the supremacy of Louis XIV as ultimately a matter of cultural hegemony.

Playwrights, academicians, the masters of the French language, and the molders of the beaux-arts played a crucial part in the creation of this theatre-state; and their leader was Molière. Voltaire presents him, of course, as the creator of the Comédie française, the supreme institution in the absolutist system of culture. But he also makes him out to be a "philosophe" and even a force in politics. For it is Molière who writes the script of the new court culture. The performances of his plays set a tone for the court as a whole; and because the court is also a theatre, they operate as plays within a play, spreading their influence in ever-widening circles. Voltaire describes the court production of *Tartuffe* in 1664 as the high point of a fête, which was the high point of a reign, which was the highest point in history.

In short, Voltaire presented the literary system of the Old Regime as a power system, a crucial ingredient of the Louisquatorzean state, and he placed Molière at the very heart of it—as the "legislator of the code of conduct in polite society."

How does this highly inaccurate and anachronistic vision of history apply to Rousseau? Curiously, in light of the later antagonism between him and Voltaire, he accepted it. He subscribed to Voltaire's version of cultural history, but he saw it negatively rather than positively. Rousseau took culture to be the force that holds society together, the essence of politics, and therefore the source of all the evil in the current social order. When he traced inequality back to its origins, he found it connected with the origins of language. When he followed the development of language, of literature, of the arts and sciences, he discerned a process of ever-increasing enslavement. The chains that bound mankind in the present had been forged by the finest artists in the world. To break those chains, therefore, the oppressed would have to turn against their culture; and they could not choose a better target for a cultural revolution than the classic French theatre.

This theme runs through all Rousseau's writing. It was the essence of his illumination on the route to Vincennes. You remember the famous episode: Rousseau, an unknown scribbler living down and out in Paris, was walking to the prison on the outskirts of the city in order to visit Diderot, his friend and fellow hack, who had been locked up for publishing unorthodox and illegal books. Rousseau's path took him past the Enfants trouvés, where he had abandoned his illegitimate children, and onto an open road. As the sun beat down upon him, he pulled a journal from his pocket and read an announcement of a contest sponsored by the

Academy of Dijon for the best essay on the topic, "Has the restoration of the sciences and arts tended to purify morals?"

The question, as he described it later in his *Confessions*, literally knocked him off his feet and into a delirium. When he awoke, he found that it had cut to the heart of his existence. It had forced him to ask another, more troubling question: "Who am I?" And to face the answer: a Grub Street hack, an intellectual tramp, a literary flim-flam man, living off handouts and odd jobs, trying to get operas performed and fiction published, working the salons in search of patrons and the cafés for contacts, living with a semi-literate, plebeian wench, and abandoning the children to the orphanage—that is, to almost certain death. What had happened to him? What had become of the innocent boy who had begun life among the honest artisans of Geneva? He had been corrupted. How? By trying to win a place for himself as a man of letters—that is, by literature, by culture, by internalizing the code of the salons.

So, when Rousseau wrote his answer to the question of the academy, he lashed out at culture itself—not just the arts and sciences, but culture in the broadest sense, as a way of life peculiar to the dominant classes of the Old Regime, or as he put it, "this uniform and perfidious veil of politeness ("politesse") that we owe to the Enlightenment ("lumières") of our century." Enlightenment, the cause of the philosophes and the favorite game of the salons, was therefore bound up with the cultural system. When Rousseau pursued this thought to its logical conclusion a few years later, he broke with the philosophes; he drove a great wedge through the cause that he had joined; and he split his century in two.

How did he make the break? By an act of literary criticism, in his *Lettre à d'Alembert sur les spectacles*. This was the first and greatest act of deconstruction in the history of literature—greater than the deconstruction of Rousseau wrought by Jacques Derrida and Paul de Man. Rousseau took apart Molière's *Misanthrope* and transformed it into a manifesto for a cultural revolution. He accepted Voltaire's notion that the theatre was the keystone to the culture of the Old Regime; then he turned it against the regime itself. Behind d'Alembert's article in the *Encyclopédie* proposing that a theatre be erected in Geneva, he (rightly) spied Voltaire. Behind Voltaire, he perceived the entire literary system of France. And behind the literature, he saw a system of power—power imbedded in language, in social codes, and in the behavior patterns of everyday life.

In short, Rousseau invented anthropology, and he did so as Freud invented psychoanalysis—by doing it to himself. Out of his introspection, his autobiographical obsession, he drew the insight that political systems are held together, are made to stick, by the force of culture. He transformed Voltaire's patrician view of literature into democratic political theory; and he crowned his analysis of politics with a proposal for a civil religion, with republican festivals of the kind that he placed in his imagination on the shores of Lake Geneva, at the opposite extreme from the sophisticated theatricality of the court of Louis XIV, but not so far from what would soon take place in the streets of revolutionary Paris.

As it happened, the Revolution had room for both Voltaire and Rousseau. It put both of them in the Pantheon. Voltaire provided it with weapons against the Church, Rousseau with weapons against the aristocracy. But at the high point of the Revolution, from August 1792 to July 1794, the Rousseauistic current swept everything before it. The Jacobins denounced Voltairean wit as a sign of "the aristocracy of the mind," and Robespierre banished laughter from the Republic of Virtue. They knew what they were doing, and it was serious business, nothing less than the reconstruction of reality. So they began with the task left to them by Rousseau, a task so strange that we can barely understand it — the rewriting of Molière.

NOTE

* The following is the text of the Clifford Lecture delivered at the ASECS convention in New Orleans on 1 April 1989. Because it was written as a lecture, it does not include footnotes or bibliographical references. For information on the sources, see a preliminary study, "The Facts of Literary Life in Eighteenth-Century France," in *The Political Culture of the Old Regime,* ed. Keith Baker (Oxford: Pergamon Press, 1987), 261-91.

Anna Barbauld's Criticism of Fiction—Johnsonian Mode, Female Vision

KATHARINE M. ROGERS

Anna Barbauld is credited with writing an exceptionally good imitation of Samuel Johnson's critical style in her early essay "On Romances." Her mature criticism continues to show a Johnsonian moral concern, a Johnsonian ability to fix on the significant issues, a Johnsonian clarity of analysis and realistic understanding of human nature. Take, for example, her opinion that "all fictions have probably grown out of real adventures"—based on the Johnsonian belief that rational beings have a preference for truth—which she supports convincingly by showing how fantastic adventures could have been developed from actual events. The effects of scientific knowledge and inventions would naturally seem magical to societies that lacked them; written communications "were easily turned into talismans by illiterate men, who saw that a great deal was effected by them, and intelligence conveyed from place to place in a manner they could not account for."[1]

But her voice is distinctively different from Johnson's, and the difference has much to do with her gender. She wrote her best criticism on the novel, a new form particularly associated with women—as readers from the beginning, and as writers from the middle of the eighteenth century. Like Clara Reeve before her and Jane Austen after, Barbauld thought the fiction-writer deserved to be closer to the poet in the temple of fame *(The Progress of Romance*, Evening I; *Northanger Abbey*, ch. 5; "On the

Origin," 2). Although the most exciting and significant generic development of the eighteenth century was the rise of the novel, it got little attention from male critics. Even male novelists were mainly concerned with legitimizing their own particular works by emphasizing differences from others of their kind. Samuel Richardson called *Clarissa* a history and pointedly distinguished it from "a *light Novel*, or *transitory Romance*" (Preface to 1759 edition, xix, xxi). In the Preface to *Joseph Andrews* (1742), Henry Fielding's first concern was to separate his work from the tradition of fiction; seeking about for a respectable affiliation, he seized upon epic.[2] Frances Burney, in contrast, presented *Evelina* (1778) as a novel, deplored the disparagement of the genre, and traced a tradition of illustrious novelists (Preface).[3] Reeve and Barbauld took up Fielding's comparison to defend the genre as a whole: Barbauld claimed that "A good novel is an epic in prose" ("On the Origin," 3).

Johnson wrote about even minor poets rather than major novelists. His only published work on fiction, *Rambler* 4 (1750), focuses exclusively on its moral effects. Because novelists portray everyday life and, supposedly, address "the young, the ignorant, and the idle," they are under a particular obligation to convey wholesome morality. Johnson proceeds to define this morality with a narrowness he did not apply to other writers, such as Shakespeare; for he would not allow ambiguity or complexity. He cautions that mixed characters will corrupt readers of novels: the hero must be as virtuous as is humanly credible, and the immoral characters altogether odious. By not naming a single novelist, Johnson suggests that not one is distinguished above the others or worthy of being considered except as a more or less innocent purveyor of light entertainment. Apparently it did not occur to him to mention his friend Richardson as an exception or positive example, even though he admired the morality and knowledge of human nature shown in Richardson's novels. Johnson's disparagement of novels and excessive emphasis on their potentially dangerous moral effects was typical of male critics, such as Vicesimus Knox, who feared that some of Fielding's and Richardson's scenes might "corrupt a mind unseasoned by experience." Critics who accepted the prevalent assumption that novel readers were predominantly young women were even more worried about moral consequences, since women's purity was considered more important than men's and at the same time particularly at risk because of their liability to sexual stimulation: Henry Pye warned that novel reading "excites and inflames" erotic passion in "the gentler sex."[4] Women were not so worried about female sexuality.

Johnson's disparaging attitude led him to devalue *Tom Jones* and to see in the hero nothing more than a pernicious example. Although Barbauld also had moral qualms about Tom, she evaluated him in a more balanced way. Agreeing that characters who combine significant faults with amiable qualities can set a dangerous example, she could still see the difference between Tom and the crude, callous heroes presented as virile patterns by Smollett: Jones "has an excellent heart and a refined sensibility, though he has also passions of a lower order" (introduction to Fielding, xxiv). Barbauld wrote the criticism of the great eighteenth-century novelists that we might wish Johnson had written.

Barbauld had few precursors as a serious critic of the new genre. Closest in time and value is Clara Reeve, whose *Progress of Romance* (1785) is the first serious defense and history of fiction in English.[5] Although Reeve discusses all prose fiction, what presumably prompted her work was the urge to defend the new form of her time, the realistic novel. There are radical aspects to Reeve's book: she refuses to tie worth to genre and raises the possibility that the canon has been arbitrarily formed (similarities between *The Odyssey* and the tale of Sindbad the Sailor prove "that there is frequently a striking resemblance between works of high and low estimation, which prejudice only, hinders us from discerning" [1:23-24]); and she puts her ideas into a conversation in which a woman instructs a man on literary theory. But she shows little literary insight: her treatment of individual works is sketchy and often reflects narrowly conventional views. Her wide reading, however, may have supplied the outline and names of little known works for Barbauld's own essay on the origins and development of the novel.[6]

Barbauld, on the other hand, developed perceptive analyses of many issues and works that Reeve merely listed, and she applied the commonly accepted generalizations in an original way. Barbauld saw, for example, that, if realism is the essential characteristic of the novel, *Robinson Crusoe* should be included in *The British Novelists*, despite its lack of the sentimental appeal that would have been expected at the time; and she recognized that Defoe's realism was akin to Richardson's: "They were both accurate describers, minute and circumstantial," although Defoe was concerned with things and Richardson with "persons and sentiments" (introduction to Defoe; introduction to *Correspondence*, xx). Moreover, although Barbauld measured novels in terms of her perception of the world and human nature, she acutely developed the difference between the expectations reasonable in life and those of fiction. In life, Tom Jones's "parents would either never have been found, or have proved to be persons of no consequence," Jones himself "would pass from one vicious indulgence to another, till his natural good disposition was quite smothered under his irregularities," and Sophia would have either married him clandestinely and become poor and unhappy, or "conquered her passion and married some country gentleman with whom she would have lived in moderate happiness, according to the usual routine of married life." But in the context of Fielding's fiction, of course, such conclusions would be unthinkable ("On the Origin," 54).

Richardson was less judicious, she believed, when he suggested that Lady Clementina (in *Sir Charles Grandison*) would ultimately accept her second choice in marriage. Although it is realistic and moral to show a woman successfully overcoming a hopeless passion, it is not artistically sound, because common-sense moderation is inconsistent with the strength and exaltation of Clementina's passion as Richardson has drawn it. A moral is not properly enforced where it destroys the artistic coherence of the novel (introduction to *Correspondence*, cxxii-cxxiii).

Although Barbauld shared her contemporaries' concern with the moral effects of literature, she forthrightly acknowledged, as Aphra Behn had before her, that its primary purpose (at least, the primary purpose of novels or comedies) is to entertain—not, that is, "to call in fancy to the aid of reason, to deceive the mind into embracing truth under the guise of fiction . . . with such-like reasons equally grave and dignified" (Behn, preface to *The Dutch Lover* [1673], 1; "On the Origin," 44). Barbauld analyzed the pleasure novels afford as Johnson might have, had he been more sympathetic to them: "It is pleasant to the mind to sport in the boundless regions of possibility; to find relief from the sameness of every-day occurrences by expatiating amidst brighter skies and fairer fields; to exhibit love that is always happy, valour that is always successful; to feed the appetite for wonder by a quick succession of marvellous events; and to distribute, like a ruling providence, rewards and punishments which fall just where they ought to fall" (45).

Barbauld's finest criticism was inspired by Richardson, who first adequately expressed female sensibility in the English novel and created the form that women novelists could use. In her edition of his *Correspondence* (1804), she identified him as "the father of the modern novel of the serious or pathetic kind," which she incisively defined as a form that combined "the high passion, and delicacy of sentiment of the old romance, with characters moving in the same sphere of life with ourselves, and brought into action by incidents of daily occurrence" (xi, xvii).

Barbauld responded fully to the greatness of *Clarissa*. She represents Richardson's success in sustaining interest without underplots or surprises with an architectural image worthy of Johnson: "We do not come upon unexpected adventures and wonderful recognitions, by quick turns and surprises: we see her fate from afar, as it were through a long avenue, the gradual approach to which, without ever losing sight of the object, has more of simplicity and grandeur than the most cunning labyrinth that can be contrived by art." As we draw near the mansion, our eyes and imaginations are filled "with still increasing ideas of its magnificence. As the work advances, the character rises; the distress is deepened; our hearts are torn with pity and indignation; bursts of grief succeed one another, till at length the mind is composed and harmonized with emotions of milder sorrow; we are calmed into resignation, elevated with pious hope, and dismissed glowing with the conscious triumphs of virtue" (*Correspondence*, lxxxiii-iv). Barbauld's metaphor clarifies our response to Richardson's narrative process by converting it into visual terms and establishes the impressiveness of his novel by identifying it with a noble building.

As Barbauld shared Johnson's generous appreciation of literary greatness, she also shared his belief in the critic's responsibility for noticing faults, while always retaining a charitable recognition of human limitations and a desire to excuse them as much as she honestly could. She concedes, for instance, that it is improbable that Lovelace's confidant, Belford, would tamely acquiesce "in a villainy which he all along so strongly disapproves"; but she explains that "Belford is a being, created in order to carry on the story, and must not be made too strictly the object of criticism. A novel writer must violate probability somewhere, and a reader ought to make all handsome and generous allowances for it. We should open a book as we enter into a company, well persuaded that we must not expect perfection" (*Correspondence*, cvi).

On the other hand, she found no sufficient reason for the inordinate length of *Sir Charles Grandison*. Contemporary readers' requests for another volume of *Grandison* did not indicate that it was too short, but that Richardson had failed to terminate it at the proper time; that is, with the hero's marriage. Having passed the point where the story came to its natural end, Richardson might as well have continued it indefinitely. Perhaps *Clarissa* also "runs out into too great a length, but bold were the hand that should attempt to shorten it. Sir Charles, on the contrary, would be improved by merely striking out the last volume, and, indeed, a good part of the sixth, where descriptions of dress, and parade, and furniture, after the interest is completely over, like the gaudy colouring of a western sky, gives symptoms of a setting sun. But it is ungrateful to dwell on the faults of genius" (cxxxii-cxxxiii). Without overemphasizing minor faults in a major novel, she acutely notices Richardson's self-indulgent long-windedness and his excessive preoccupation with expensive material objects.

Like her contemporary critics, Barbauld recognized that realistic fiction had particular power to move readers; but, unlike them, she saw this influence as positive and ennobling: by filling the reader's heart "with the successive emotions of love, pity, joy, anguish, transport, or indignation," a realistic novelist can more effectively inculcate "virtuous and noble sentiments" than can a writer who portrays only idealized figures (*Correspondence*, ix-x). Although we may find her too much preoccupied with moral effect and moral teaching, her understanding of morality was broad and sophisticated, raising her above the platitudes of her day. While Reeve unreservedly admired the morality of *Pamela*, Barbauld shrewdly pointed to its defects. Once Pamela begins to entertain hopes of marrying Mr. B., "we can only consider her as the conscious possessor of a treasure, which she is wisely resolved not to part with but for its just price" (lxiii-lxiv). Richardson would have us believe that Pamela married Mr. B. because he had won her affection, but is it likely that a virtuous girl's affection could be won by bribery and bullying? Such insults would be easier to overlook, Barbauld points out, by a woman marrying for money and position. The Andrews family's gratitude to Mr. B. at the end is excessively humble, since they should have seen that he "married her to gratify his own passions" (lxvi). This assessment of Richardson's limitations recalls Fielding's, but is more judicious than his wholesale debasement in *Shamela*.

Barbauld acutely demolished Richardson's moral equivocations in *Sir Charles Grandison*, such as his attempt to unite Christian principles in Sir Charles with readiness to prove himself virile and gentlemanly by engaging in duels. Richardson's solution, making Sir Charles disarm his opponents and let them go, is not satisfactory; for it makes his principles dependent on his skill at fencing. "In certain cases," she forthrightly concludes, "the code of the gospel and the code of worldly honour are irreconcileable, and . . . a man has only to make his choice which he will give up" (*Correspondence*, cxxviii-cxxix).

On the other hand, Barbauld wholeheartedly admired the moral teaching of *Clarissa*—but she defined it better than Richardson did himself. The lesson that Richardson repeatedly spells out is that young ladies must not place their affections upon libertines—but this maxim "has not dignity or force . . . to be the chief moral" of a great novel. Simultaneously, Richardson implies that he is exhibiting Clarissa "as a rare pattern of chastity"—but that is to concur with Lovelace's conceited and contemptuous belief that all women are seducible. Pamela's virtue was genuinely tried, because of the social distance between her and Mr. B.; but Clarissa had no motive whatsoever to yield to Lovelace as a mistress. Therefore, her virtue "could never have been in the smallest danger." What, then, is the moral of the book? "The real moral of Clarissa is, that virtue is triumphant in every situation; that in circumstances the most painful and degrading, in a prison, in a brothel, in grief, in distraction, in despair, it is still lovely, still commanding, still the object of our veneration, of our fondest affections" (*Correspondence*, xcix-cii). The novel is virtuous because it inspires enthusiasm for virtue.[7] This moral has the requisite "dignity and force"; it remains valid and valuable today.

Barbauld evaluated Richardson's character, also, with Johnsonian judiciousness—although her verdict was more favorable, perhaps more just, than Johnson's. Johnson saw only a "love of continual superiority" in Richardson's constant care "to be surrounded by women, who listened to him implicitly, and did not venture to contradict his opinions." Similarly, Barbauld demurely remarked on Richardson's "mental seraglio" and acknowledged "that it had a tendency to feed that self-importance which was perhaps his reigning foible. Experiencing no contradiction, and seeing no equal, he was constantly fed with adulation." She qualified this judgment, however, by pointing out "that the ladies he associated with were well able to appreciate his works. They were both his critics and his models, and from their sprightly conversation, and the disquisitions on love and sentiment, which took place, he gathered what was more to his purpose than graver topics would have produced. He was not writing a dictionary, like Johnson, or a history, like Gibbon. He was a novel writer; his business was not only with the human heart, but with the female heart" (*Correspondence*, clxxii; preface to Richardson, xliv-xlv). It does not seem to have occurred to Johnson that a distinctively female perspective could, for some significant types of literature, be more authoritative than a traditionally educated male one.

I have suggested that Barbauld's gender helped to determine her choice of the novel as a subject for serious analysis. Her particular sensitivity as a female reader also led her to inquire into the sociology of literature. Johnson had drawn connections between literature and the state of society in the preface to his edition of Shakespeare (1765), but Barbauld carried such connections further by distinguishing among different groups of contemporary readers—between men and women within the literate class. She looked for social causes and examined effects on a reader in terms of social conditions. This was not altogether new: for example, Germaine de Staël's explicit aim in *On Literature* (1800) was "to examine the influence of religion, customs, and laws on literature, and the influence of literature on religion, customs, and laws" (173). However, de Staël dealt in more general terms than Barbauld and with different factors—nation and class rather than gender. Moreover, despite her plan, de Staël showed the effect of customs on literature, but not the reverse.

Barbauld's specific concern with women readers appears in her first mature critical work, her introduction to *Selections from the Spectator, Tatler, Guardian, and Freeholder* (1804). It is significant that she chose to edit Addison, for he, like Richardson, presented himself and was appreciated as a particular friend to women. She acutely pinpoints why these periodicals were "the favourite volumes in a young lady's library": "From the papers of Addison we [women readers] imbibed our first relish for wit; from his criticisms we formed our first standard of taste; and from his delineations we drew our first ideas of manners" (iii-iv). That is, Addison helped women to shape themselves to the new feminine ideal of the eighteenth century—that of a rational, educated woman who could take her place in cultivated society. His essays reflected his society's changing standards of gentility and culture and, in turn, helped to define them; since these changes affected women more than men, it was women particularly who appreciated his guidance. From the particular example of women, Barbauld generalizes that literature effects changes in "taste and moral sentiment," which in turn whet the appetite for appropriate books (ii).[8] *The Spectator* was universally read because it met this need. When it no longer did so—partly because manners and sentiments had changed, but also because the standards it taught had become internalized—it ceased to be popular. In opposition to the conventional neoclassical belief that artistic merit is absolute, Barbauld declares that such changes affect not only "ephemeral publications," but also works "of the first excellence." Although the latter continue to be respected as classics, they pass out of general consciousness as taste and beliefs change and therefore cease to influence people's thinking and feeling (ii-iii).

At the end of the eighteenth century, this influence had passed to sentimental novels. These display to their readers tender affection, high principle, unshaken constancy, delicacy of feeling, benevolence, and compassion for distress, and in this way have contributed to the increased sensitivity and humanity of later eighteenth-century manners. Barbauld is aware that "it costs nothing . . . to an author to make his hero generous, and very often he is extravagantly so; still, sentiments of this kind serve in some measure to counteract the spirit of the world, where selfish considerations have always more than their due weight" ("On the Origin," 47). She judiciously evaluates the effects of presenting exemplary sentiments, where most of her contemporaries responded to them with exaggerated approval or blame.

Because she carefully considered the effects of novels on women readers, Barbauld was able to refine the stock warnings by pointing out good effects as well as analyzing bad ones. Novels can introduce young women to areas of experience that would otherwise be unavailable to them, and, more significantly, instill "principles and moral feelings." Novels "awaken a sense of finer feelings than the commerce of ordinary life inspires. Many a young woman has caught from such works as *Clarissa* or *Cecilia*, ideas of delicacy and refinement which were not, perhaps, to be gained in any society she could have access to" ("On the Origin," 45–46).[9] On the other hand, novels often present ideals that are harmful because inflated beyond prudence or rationality. The particular danger for women is the novels' overemphasis on romantic love. They suggest to a young lady that love is the most serious occupation of life, that "every thing gives way to its influence, and no length of time wears it out." But when she "comes into the world, . . . [s]he will find but few minds susceptible of its more delicate influences." Even "where it is really felt, she will see it continually overcome by duty, by prudence," or even by mere worldly values. In short, "it has a very small share in the transactions of the busy world, and is often little consulted even in choosing a partner for life" (50–51).[10]

Too sensible to believe that a little earthy realism would corrupt the purity or inflame the sexual passions of the youthful female, Barbauld put her finger on a real danger. Novels raise expectations that will be bitterly let down by "the neglect and tedium of life" which a young lady

> is perhaps doomed to encounter. If the novels she reads are virtuous, she has learned how to arm herself with proper reserve against the ardour of her lover; she has been instructed how to behave with the utmost propriety when run away with, like *Miss Byron,* or locked up by a cruel parent, like Clarissa; but she is not prepared for indifference and neglect. Though young and beautiful, she may see her youth and beauty pass away without conquests, and the monotony of her life will be apt to appear more insipid when contrasted with scenes of perpetual courtship and passion. ("On the Origin," 51–52)

The heroine of a novel, however distressed, is the constant center of attention, as few people in real life can be, especially if they are female. Consciously or not, Barbauld comments on a society that reduced women's lives to monotony and unimportance. Instead of assuming that women read novels because their heads are empty, she recognizes that they read them to escape from empty lives. Accepting Johnson's assumption that possibilities for happy fulfillment are limited for all human beings, Barbauld reminds us that they were more stringently limited for women.

Barbauld also looked for connections between the conditions of women's lives and their writing. Frances Sheridan's *Sidney Bidulph,* a lachrymose account of misfortunes heaped upon an impeccably virtuous heroine, prompted her to inquire why women writers, as well as readers, were so drawn to sentimental distress. She recognized that this was a question to be asked, and she did not resort to the explanation that would have suggested itself to most of her contemporaries: namely, that women are by nature effusive and tender-hearted. Instead, she looked into their social circumstances for an explanation. Is it that women

> suffer more, and have fewer resources against melancholy? Is it that men, mixing at large in society, have a brisker flow of ideas, and, seeing a greater variety of characters, introduce more of the business and pleasures of life into their productions? Is it that humour is a scarcer product of the mind than sentiment, and more congenial to the stronger powers of man? Is it that women nurse those feelings in secrecy and silence, and diversify the expression of them with endless shades of sentiment, which are more transiently felt, and with fewer modifications of delicacy, by the other sex? ("On the Origin," 42)

Apart from the speculation that men have more natural humor than women, her explanation is based on her recognition of the depressing effects of women's circumscribed lives. She perceives the connections among isolation, monotony, depression, and brooding over feelings.

Unfortunately, Barbauld did not pursue similar insights in her introductions to the works by women she included in *The British Novelists*. It is significant, though, that she recognized their contributions—she included twelve novels by women in a total of twenty-eight—and criticized them seriously.[11] She praised with discrimination and enthusiasm the works of Charlotte Lennox, Elizabeth Inchbald, Charlotte Smith, and Frances Burney, devoting the most space to Burney. In accordance with the principle of artistic coherence she had stated in regard to Clementina in *Sir Charles Grandison*, she deplored Burney's inconsistencies in tone—her mixing of genteel comedy with rowdy humor and intense pathos—and the problematic endings of *Cecilia* and *Camilla*. It may be more realistic to limit Cecilia's ultimate happiness (as Burney vehemently argued), but fiction is more agreeable if its ending is definitively happy or tragic, Barbauld believes. She does not speculate, as modern feminist critics have, on possible reasons for Burney's ambiguities. Nor does she examine Burney's moral teaching in depth. She notes that Lionel Tyrold's behavior "presents but too just a picture of the manner in which many deserving females have been sacrificed to the worthless part of the family" (viii), but says nothing about Mr. Tyrold's letter of advice to his daughter, considered by reviewers to be the moral crux of *Camilla*. Barbauld's discussion of this book omits so many of its major themes and characters as to suggest conscious evasiveness: perhaps she could not approve of Burney's apparently repressive moral message, but did not wish to criticize it publicly, particularly as the author was still living. It is tantalizing that Barbauld did not leave more indications of an intelligent female contemporary's reactions to this problematic novel, to guide us among diverging interpretations today.

Barbauld shared the eighteenth-century taste for virtue in distress — Clarissa's dying interviews, Clementina's melancholy madness, Sidney Bidulph's wrongs, Evelina's tearful meeting with her father, Cecilia's mental breakdown. But she did temper her sensibility with Johnsonian good sense. She hinted that Sheridan overdid Sidney's sufferings: "the author seems to have taken pleasure in heaping distress upon virtue and innocence, merely to prove, what no one will deny, that the best dispositions are not always sufficient to ward off the evils of life" ("On the Origin," 41–42). There is a hint of derision in her picture of an author whose highest ambition is "to draw tears plentifully," who "sits down, ... like an inquisitor, to compute how much suffering he can inflict upon the hero of his tale before he makes an end of him," and who, even crueller than the inquisitor, "chooses the most excellent character in his piece for the subject of his persecution" ("An Inquiry into Those Kinds of Distress Which Excite Agreeable Sensations," *Works*, 2:214–16). She sensibly refutes the cherished contemporary view that responding to fictitious distress improves "the tender and humane feelings." In fact, since these novels call forth sensibility that cannot be exerted in virtuous action, they tend to dissociate good feeling from good action, so that the first becomes less and less likely to prompt the second. Moreover, by regularly endowing the objects of pity with beauty and refinement, novels make us less responsive to the objects of pity who are apt to need our help in actual life, who may well be crude and ignorant (2:227–28).

The same clear good sense, together with her particular sensitivities as a woman reader, enabled Barbauld to perceive exploitation and contempt where her contemporaries saw enthusiastic appreciation or urbane instruction. While acknowledging what Addison had done for women, Barbauld also perceived his patronizing tone and even underlying hostility. Although his decorous satire seems opposite to Swift's attacks, she suspected that "Both are perhaps in reality equally severe, and by their pleasantries betray a contempt for a sex they probably considered in a very inferior light"; it is principally the Spectator's "charm of manner" that makes him seem so much more agreeable than Swift (introduction to *The Spectator*, xviii).

Fielding's antifeminism was as clear to her as Richardson's respect for women, and no twentieth-century feminist critic could have defined it more precisely. She pounces on the revealing points and deflates sentimental effusions by exposing them to common sense based on actual life. She notices that "Fielding uniformly keeps down the characters of his women, as much as Richardson elevates his," because the quality he seems to admire most in them is "a yielding easiness of disposition." "Allworthy is made to tell Sophia, that what had chiefly charmed him in her behaviour was the great deference he had observed in her for the opinions of men. Yet Sophia, methinks, had not been extraordinarily situated for imbibing such reverence."[12] Barbauld goes on to make the telling point that "Any portion of learning in women is constantly united in this author with something disagreeable" — if not unchastity, at least mannishness and conceit (introduction to Fielding, xxv). She suggests that the unattractive character of Mrs. Bennet was introduced into *Amelia* "purely to show the author's dislike to learned women," and suspects that jealous pique contributed to this dislike: "Probably the coterie of literary and accomplished ladies that generally assembled at his rival's house had its share in fostering this aversion" (xxx).

Barbauld roundly attacks the sentimental morality of *Amelia*, a morality that often facilitated exploitation of female relatives. After pointing out that the distresses in that novel arise largely "from the vicious indulgencies of the husband," she characterizes Amelia as "such a wife as most men of that stamp would deem the model of female perfection, such a one as a man, conscious of a good many frailties and vices, usually wishes for. Faithful, fond, and indulgent, the prospect of immediate ruin cannot draw from her one murmur against her husband, and she willingly sacrifices to him her jewels and every article in her possession" (introduction to Fielding, xxviii). She is an amiable and touching character, but she displays the irrationally extreme compassion that Barbauld had mentioned among the misguided ideals held up by sentimental novelists ("On the Origin," 50). Although the book presents "many tender touches of conjugal affection and domestic feeling," Booth shows "no great merit, . . . in receiving graciously the endearments of a beautiful woman who is always in good humour with him, even when he is most faulty. He is pleased with her; he could not well be otherwise; but he denies himself nothing for her sake or his children's" (introduction to Fielding, xxxi).

Women had been publishing criticism throughout the eighteenth century, although their right to judge was still in dispute. Elizabeth Inchbald, a successful playwright and novelist, adopted a defensive, self-deprecatory tone when she responded to an attack by George Colman the Younger on her presumption in writing critical prefaces for her anthology *The British Theater* (1808; preface to *The Heir at Law)*. These critics occasionally reveal a specifically female point of view: Inchbald anticipated Barbauld's criticism of *Amelia* when she demolished the sentimental morality of Edward Moore's *The Gamester* (1753), which idealizes a marriage in which the hero shamelessly exploits his wife. But no one before Barbauld came close to systematic feminist criticism. Focusing her attention on literature for and by women, she thought about the needs and interests that it met, about why women read and the effects their reading had upon them. Reading self-consciously as a woman, she was sensitive to covert attitudes. Inquiring why women writers luxuriated in sentimental distress or speculating upon the reciprocal influences of literary models and social attitudes, she raised issues that are being explored by feminist critics today.

NOTES

1 "On the Origin and Progress of Novel-Writing," in her edition, *The British Novelists; with an Essay, and Prefaces Biographical and Critical*, 50 vols. 2nd ed. (London: F. C. and J. Rivington et al., 1820), 1:7.

   Anna Laetitia Aikin Barbauld (1743-1825), a friend of Johnson and the Bluestockings, was well educated by her father and encouraged by her brother, John. In 1773 she published *Poems*, and her first independent critical essays—"On Romances: An Imitation" (of Johnson) and "An Inquiry into Those Kinds of Distress Which Excite Agreeable Sensations"—appeared in a joint publication with John, *Miscellaneous Pieces in Prose* (1773). After her marriage to the Reverend Rochemont Barbauld, a schoolmaster, she devoted herself to teaching and writing books for children. Repressive governmental actions in the 1790s moved her to write stirring political tracts in favor of religious and political liberty. In her later years, she became a professional editor. Her most important criticism appears in the prefaces to her editions: *Selections from the Spectator, Tatler, Guardian, and Freeholder, with a Preliminary Essay*, 3 vols. (London: J. Johnson, 1804), *The Correspondence of Samuel Richardson, with a Biographical Account . . . and Observations on His Writings*, 6 vols. (London: Richard Phillips, 1804), and *The British Novelists* (1810). Her *Works*, in two volumes, were edited, with a memoir, by her niece Lucy Aikin (London: Longman et al., 1825).

2 In the preface to *Sir Charles Grandison* (1754), Richardson referred to his three novels as his first, second, and third collections of letters. Tobias Smollett was the only major male writer of the period to call his work a novel, but his definition in the dedication to *The Adventures of Ferdinand, Count Fathom* (1753) could fit any narrative. Geoffrey Day has shown that the terms novel and romance were not stabilized during the eighteenth century. Although the genres were clearly separate, the terms were often interchanged (*From Fiction to Novel* [London: Routledge and Kegan Paul, 1987], 6-16). Barbauld, however, generally uses "novel" consistently to mean "realistic fiction."

3 It must be admitted that Burney insisted that *Camilla*, a more pretentious novel, was not a novel but "sketches of Characters & morals, put in action" (*The Journals and Letters of Fanny Burney (Madame d'Arblay)*, ed. Joyce Hemlow et al., 12 vols. [Oxford: The Clarendon Press, 1972-78], 3:117).

4 "On Novel Reading" (1778) and *A Commentary Illustrating the Poetics of Aristotle* (1786), respectively, in *Novel and Romance 1700-1800: A Documentary Record*, ed. Ioan Williams (New York: Barnes and Noble, 1970), 304-5, 336-37.

5 Clara Reeve, *The Progress of Romance* (Colchester: W. Keymer, 1785; rpt. New York: Garland, 1970).

6 Reeve also anticipated Barbauld in suggesting that the chivalric romances might have influenced manners by inspiring men to live up to high ideals of courage and honor, in warning that novels arouse false expectations by leading young women readers to expect adventures and romantic courtship that they will not encounter in their lives, and in identifying Richardson and Addison as pro-woman writers (1:97, 102, 135; 2:78).

7 Compare "Essay on Fictions," in *An Extraordinary Woman: Selected Writings of Germaine de Staël*, trans. Vivian Folkenflik (New York: Columbia University Press, 1987), 73.

8 In her *Remarks on Mr. Wakefield's Enquiry into the Expediency and Propriety of Public or Social Worship* (1792), she drew a similar connection between religion and manners: as religion, well understood, improves our manners, "manners, as they advance in cultivation, tend to correct and refine our religion." "The age which has demolished dungeons, rejected torture, and given so fair a prospect of abolishing the iniquity of the slave trade, cannot long retain among its articles of belief the gloomy perplexities of Calvinism, and the heart-withering perspective of cruel and never-ending punishments" (*Works*, 2:469-70).

9 Here Barbauld sheds light on the exasperating perfection of almost all later eighteenth-century heroines. It was not only that authors, particularly female authors, had to avoid any possible pretext for charges of impropriety (as I have argued in *Frances Burney: The World of "Female Difficulties"* [New York: Harvester Wheatsheaf, 1990], 170-71). They also felt an obligation to educate readers who were, typically, limited in education and experience, by presenting them with models of female excellence in models of cultivated social settings.

10 Like Johnson in his *Preface to Shakespeare*, Barbauld disapproved of literature that gave romantic love more importance than it has in actual life. But where Johnson contrasted Shakespeare's diversity with other dramatists' excessive preoccupation with one passion, Barbauld contrasted the novelists' overemphasis on love with the drabness of a daily life that lacks any exhilarating passions.

11 Catherine E. Moore discusses Barbauld's recognition of the contributions of women to fiction-writing in "Ladies . . . Taking the Pen in Hand," in *Fetter'd*

or Free: British Women Novelists, 1670–1815, ed. Mary Anne Schofield and Cecilia Macheski (Athens: Ohio University Press, 1986).

12 Although the character of Sophia was widely criticized in the eighteenth century, especially by Richardson's admirers, Barbauld alone complains of her lack of intellectual distinction and the repressive idea of female excellence she represents. Richardson indeed described Sophia as "so fond, so foolish, and so insipid," but he was chiefly objecting to her "trapsing after [Jones], a Fugitive from her Father's House." He charged that she revealed Fielding's ignorance of "how to draw a delicate Woman—he has not been accustomed to such Company" (letter to Astrea and Minerva Hill, August 4, 1749). The anonymous Orbilius reprehended Sophia's immodesty, evidenced by "her Partiality to the well-known Debaucheries of Jones, and in her Elopement from her Father's House, on *Pretence* [my emphasis] of avoiding a disgustful Match with Blifil" *(An Examen of the History of Tom Jones, a Foundling,* 1750). (For both comments, see Lynn C. Bartlett and William R. Sherwood, eds., *The English Novel: Background Readings* [Philadelphia: J. B. Lippincott, 1967], 3, 11.) Barbauld mentions Sophia's alleged indelicacy, but it is not her main stress.

Versions of "Female Nature" in John Gay's Fan

JACOB FUCHS

"John Gay may be coming into his own." With that sentence Arthur Sherbo began his "John Gay: Lightweight or Heavyweight?", published in 1975. Only three years later, Dianne S. Ames, referring to Sherbo's essay, expressed concern that Gay might not be coming into his own.[1] Now, as the nineties begin, younger scholars may wonder why anyone ever imagined that Gay might some day be recognized as a heavyweight. Compared to the established contenders, such as Pope or Swift or Defoe, he seems to enter the ring at 112 pounds, dripping wet. If not for *The Beggar's Opera*, he might not even be reckoned a flyweight, and even that beloved play fails to bring him significant attention. The latest *Scriblerian* reviews two articles about Gay, one of them only one page in length, compared to eleven articles on Pope, sixteen on Swift, and nine on Defoe. To my knowledge, only one conference, held at Durham University, marked the tercentenary of Gay's birth in 1985.

His rank as a poet, which chiefly concerns me here, is low, but it isn't easy to see why. It never is in these cases. Perhaps he has suffered lately because of his reputation, formerly quite enviable, as a poet of allusion. Professor Ames, for example, praised him as a "master of the poetry of classical allusion." However, Irvin Ehrenpreis is far from the only critic to have been repelled by the excesses of source-hunting scholars in the sixties and seventies.[2] To study Gay's poetry is also to study his uses of allusion, and to many, perhaps, these may seem less interesting and more treacherous than they once did. If so, *The Fan* must be considered a work unlikely to elevate Gay's status, since it largely consists of passages echoing Virgil and Ovid. Nonetheless, this mock-epic will reward readers who come to it unburdened by prejudice against allusive verse, or this poet, or this particular example of his allusive work.

Unfortunately, it may be difficult to be thus unburdened where *The Fan* is concerned, since no one has ever thought much of it from Samuel Johnson ("of little value") to Patricia Meyer Spacks ("unutterably trivial and almost unreadable"). Moreover, both of these critics, writing well before the current reaction against Wassermania, objected to Gay's use or misuse of allusion. Johnson, generally impatient with classical mythology when it appeared in English poems, wrote that "the attention naturally retires from a new tale of Venus, Diana, and Minerva." Spacks has only contempt for what she finds in the poem: a "series of Ovidian episodes [set] in a pseudo-mythological framework."[3]

I agree, of course, that it is a tale of Venus, Diana, and Minerva (but would add that Momus, who will be discussed, is just as important), and certainly its framework is mythological or pseudo-mythological. In fact, the whole poem is; it is an odd example of mock-epic in being, as its latest editors point out, "almost all machinery": that is, almost all gods and goddesses, primarily the latter in this case.[4] But I think the machinery works. It is amusing to watch, but it also generates meaning, for, as this paper will seek to show, within *The Fan* Gay opposes different versions of what he calls "female Nature" (2.192). In my reading *The Fan* is particularly interesting because he never decides which version of female nature is correct.[5]

The poem's action, which is nearly all talk, may be easily reviewed. In the first of the three books, young Strephon, spurned by Corinna, asks Venus for a gift to win Corinna's favor. Flying to her grotto, where a work force of cupids produces love's bows and arrows, as well as female ornaments and cosmetics, Venus commissions the construction of the first fan. As the scene shifts, Book 2 presents an Olympian debate in heaven concerning the scenes to be painted on the presently blank fan ("What Story," Venus asks, "shall the wide Machine unfold?" [2.42]). Diana urges depictions of women betrayed by men—Theseus, Aeneas, Paris—to teach maids to be chaste; but Momus, the personification of fault-finding, sneers at what he considers her hypocrisy and sarcastically urges a panorama of goddesses, including Diana, shown seeking or enjoying physical love. In Book 3, however, swiftly gaining the assent of the others, wise Minerva covers the fan with examples drawn from ancient myth and poetry of the bad effects on women of pride, suspicion, delight in male finery, and vanity concerning their own beauty. Venus then delivers the fan to Strephon, who — as the poem's final scene begins — "offers the Present, and renews his Vow" (3.194) to Corinna, at that moment enjoying the attentions of a rival swain, Leander.

"The Present" affects Corinna differently, very differently, according to which edition of Gay's mock-epic one happens to be reading. In the revised version of 1720, she examines the fan and immediately realizes how foolish and self-destructive are her pride, suspicion, delight in masculine "Show" (3.204), and vanity, all of which would prevent her from experiencing true love "e'er [her] Blossom dies" (3.210). Humbled now, she is spiritually ready to fulfill what the eighteenth century generally thought to be a woman's proper destiny, marriage and a lifetime of submission to her husband.[6] Accordingly, the revised *Fan* concludes with this epithalamial couplet: "Thus *Pallas* taught her. *Strephon* weds the Dame, / And *Hymen's* Torch diffus'd the brightest Flame" (3.211-12). However, in Gay's original edition of 1714, when Strephon gives Corinna the fan, she greedily "Snatches" it away, then turns to Leander, and, in the very last line, "Smiles on the Fop, and flirts the new Machine." The polar difference between the two endings — between modest bride and callous coquette — allows room for yet other conceptions of female nature and signals Gay's indecision regarding what seemed to him a baffling quiddity indeed.

Of course, in either edition of *The Fan* many of Gay's verses present the traditional, condescending, male opinion that — until and unless reformed by the wise advice of someone like Gay's Minerva or Pope's Clarissa in *The Rape of the Lock* — women can easily be both trivial and vain. As the patroness of female charms and wiles, Gay's Venus, who is similar in character to Ariel in the *Rape*, is the proper deity for such women. Her grotto workshop, staffed by cupids, produces such trifles as "The Patch, the Powder-Box, Pulville, Perfumes, / Pins, Paint, a flatt'ring Glass, and Black-lead Combs" (1.129-30).

Grotto, cupids, and products make an obvious contrast to Vulcan's imposing cave, described in *Aeneid* 8, with his crew of cyclops and their output of war chariots and thunderbolts. Asked by Venus to fashion weapons for Aeneas, Vulcan, chief engineer, brusquely orders the cyclops: " 'Tollite cuncta' (8.439: "Drop everything"); " 'Arma acri facienda viro' " (8.441: "Arms must be made for a brave man"). With this heavily masculine business going on in the background, Gay's Venus seems even more to incarnate the trivial, the foolish, the frilly aspect of female nature. Instead of a rough and manly "tollite cuncta," she cajoles her cupids: "industrious *Loves*, your present Toils forbear" (1. 151) and then instructs them on the manufacture of a paper fan.

Thus Gay employs what Ellen Pollak calls (and finds in his work) the "comic deflation of the threat of female deviancy." Comic, because men really need fear nothing from any action a woman could take and can therefore afford an attitude of "urbane tolerance."[7] However, Gay also seems to imply, through Venus's actions and intentions, that coquetry conceals real dangers for men. In this poem, in which Gay seems generally unsettled on the subject of women, he not only deflates the "threat of female deviancy," as I have shown, but also inflates it.

To understand that Gay can take coquetry seriously requires only that one recognize the obvious connection between Strephon and Aeneas, Venus's son, whom in the *Aeneid* she does her best to support and protect. Thus, in 8.608-731, she provides him with arms, forged in Vulcan's cave, including the shield which both protects him in battle and, because of the prophetic historical scenes pictured upon it, serves as an emblem of Rome's ultimate prosperity. In contrast, the loyalties of Gay's Venus are mixed at best. In one version of the poem, by giving Corinna the fan Strephon wins the battle for her heart, but it is hard to believe that Venus cares whether her "son" (adopted by allusion) wins or loses. To her the fan signifies (as much as it can signify anything while still blank), not a triumph for a power that Strephon represents, as Aeneas represents Rome, but a future of conquest of men by women.

Up in heaven in Book 2, while Strephon waits hopefully on earth, Venus boasts to the Olympians of having designed the fan as one more weapon to assist women "to subdue Mankind" (2.25). It is a means of concealment, for blushes, and of ambush, from which to dart swift glances, but she seems to think of it as an offensive weapon. Indeed, her cupids have constructed the prototype she exultantly displays out of the sticks and points of arrows (1.179-84). "Unhappy Lovers!" exclaims the poet, "how will you withstand, / When these new Arms shall grace your Charmer's Hand?" (1.195-96). In the original ending, of course, Strephon's gift has an effect exactly opposite from that which he, but not she, intends. Mother betrays son, Gay implies, and all men along with him, to advance the power of women.

But other deities have plans for the fan besides Venus, who becomes a minor character after the beginning of Book 2, where Gay's subject becomes the heavenly debate concerning the scenes to be inscribed upon it. Diana, who speaks first, suggests three tales of betrayal to teach young women that men "vow but to Deceive" (2.104). Were the fan decorated with scenes of Ariadne and Theseus, Dido and Aeneas, Oenone and faithless Paris, then would (she claims)

> . . . the Nymph, when e'er she spreads the *Fan*,
> In his true Colours view perfidious Man,
> Pleas'd with her Virgin State in Forrests rove,
> And never trust the dang'rous Hopes of Love.
> (2.123–26)

However, while Diana paints some appealing word-pictures, Gay probably does not intend his readers to take her seriously. "Never" (in line 126) is too long. Although all unmarried women were supposed to spend their time in Diana's forests, to most eighteenth-century minds, virginity, as Pollak succinctly explains, was a "prelude, not an alternative, to marriage."[8] The "Celestial Synod" (2.27) does not embrace Diana's decorative scheme. In fact, Momus arises to laugh at it. But more of Momus later.

It is Minerva, finally, who in Book 3 takes up her "creating Pencil" and "bid[s] the Paint express her great Design" (3.10, 3.8) upon the fan. The story of Niobe, whose children were slain by the gods as her punishment for boasting, counsels against pride; that of Procris, who spied on her husband and died when he mistook her for a deer and shot her, against suspicion; that of Camilla, the spoils-seeking warrior queen in the *Aeneid*, against caring about the tawdry trifles of male dress; that of Narcissus against vanity. In the 1720 ending, every lesson takes. For example,

> When [Corinna] the fate of *Niobe* beheld,
> Why has my Pride against my Heart rebell'd?
> She sighing cry'd: Disdain forsook her Breast,
> And *Strephon* now was thought a worthy Guest.
> (3.195–98)

Corinna is transformed. Rendered properly passive, she enters into matrimony.

In the 1714 ending every lesson fails. This outcome seems, to me at least, far more logical and satisfying. First, Corinna's instantaneous conversion is not only unlikely, given her carefree spirit, but also simplistic; imagine the dulling effect in the fifth canto of *The Rape of the Lock* if, after hearing Clarissa's "good Humour" speech, Belinda had simply said, "Yes dear, you're right." More importantly, Minerva's examples would probably fail to persuade Corinna if she thought about them (instead of simply falling into the blessed state of submissiveness), for she would realize, as will the thoughtful reader, just how remote these examples are from any non-mythological reality. Their unpersuasive character, as we shall see, would support the unconventionality of the 1714 ending; their retention in 1720 indicates Gay's continuing ambivalence despite his ostensible commitment there to the conventional view of female nature.

First, the punishments the mythological women suffer are so drastic, and so bloodily described, that application to modern women becomes very awkward. After Diana and Apollo slaughter every one of the fourteen children of Niobe, "Fixt in Astonishment she weeping stood, / The Plain all purple with her Children's Blood" (3.67–68). As for poor Procris, "purple Gore her snowy Bosom dies [sic])" (3.88), and mortally wounded Camilla, the "bloody Ground, / Floats with a Torrent from the purple Wound" (3.105–6). These horrifying examples are supposed to warn women against follies that would lead them to remain unfortunately single for life; but, although spinsterhood was not an enviable condition, nothing in it could have seemed equivalent to these ghastly consequences. Clarissa's warnings to Belinda, it will be remembered, are much milder and therefore more realistic.

Second, three of the applications seem wholly or partially inappropriate. Narcissus was a boy. More importantly, Niobe was a wife and a mother, who, although she boasted of her beauty, was much prouder of having had seven daughters and seven sons; moreover, Niobe stupidly scorned Latona, also a mother, and it is Latona's divine children, Apollo and Diana, who, obeying their outraged mother's request, punish Niobe by killing her children. But Corinna, of course, is unmarried and has no children. Thus, after recounting the whole Ovidian tale (*Met.* 6), in giving the moral, Minerva can only warn the "haughty Fair" against taking "lofty Pride" in "Beauty's Pow'r" (3.75–77). Most of the power of the example is lost. The example of Camilla has even less application.

In *Aeneid* 11, Virgil says that Camilla "femineo praedae et spoliorum ardebat amore" (11.782: "burned with a female's lust for spoils and plunder"); but she was a steadfast warrior and a responsible commander, adept at strategy. Camilla really takes little interest in spoils, and when she does, rather than finding their possessor alluring, she seeks to kill him; Virgil speculates, moreover, that she may not even want them for herself.[9] In any case, it is ludicrous to think of her as Minerva insists we do: as an ancient version of a "raw Maid," ready to succumb to a fop's "tawdry Coat," "snowy Feather," "bright Sword-knot," etc. (3.109–14).

Like the contrast between *The Fan*'s two endings, the tutorial inadequacy of Minerva's "great Design" suggests that Gay, perhaps like Swift, could not easily accept the eighteenth-century myth of the passive woman, fulfilled only by marriage and a lifetime of happy subservience and spirituality.[10] Unlike Swift, however, who imaged women as grotesques, in *The Fan* Gay is willing to consider that sexual ardor may be natural in women. Even merely recognizing this possibility would shake one's belief in "passive womanhood"; and Gay, through Momus's address to the "Celestial Synod," seems almost to celebrate the feminine "pleasure-seeking" which, somewhat before his time, Restoration wits found so appealing.[11]

Leda, for example, certainly pursues her pleasure in one scene that Momus proposes for the fan:

> Here let dissolving *Leda* grace the Toy,
> Warm Cheeks and Heaving Breasts reveal her Joy;
> Beneath the pressing Swan she pants for Air,
> While with his flutt'ring Wings he fans the Fair.
> (2.161-64)

Although Leda lies beneath her partner, her passion is certainly as great as his; and he, great Jove himself, seems subordinate in a traditionally feminine way, "flutt'ring" and servilely fanning. She masters him.

In Momus's proposed design, Diana to sleeping Endymion's "soft Embraces . . . Steals, / And on his Lips her warm Caresses seals" (2.137-38). Aurora places the "modest Hand" of boyish Cephalus "upon her Bosom" (2.158). Of course, Venus and Mars both wind up as objects of ridicule in Vulcan's trap (2.189-90), and Cephalus rejects Aurora's unsubtle gambit "with Disdain" (2.160). Gay has Momus point out that women have strong sexual desires, not that they should feel free to act on them. Nonetheless, it is significant that through plain-speaking Momus he can show women as sexual beings, rather than as passive objects, without distorting their bodies in the way of Swift or, when not turning them into passive objects, Pope.

Curiously, in the one vignette in Momus's speech in which a female is not shown having sex or trying to, the goddess in question does become grotesque. While playing the pipe, Minerva, of all people, is disgusted by her own image, which she sees reflected in a brook: "Her bloated Cheeks, worn Lips, and shrivell'd Eyes" (2.174). Perhaps this satiric description, by demeaning Minerva, who will sermonize in Book 3 on behalf of the ideal of feminine passivity, indicates in advance Gay's uneasiness about it. In the context of Book 2, however, the effect of her bizarre, unnatural reflection is to emphasize, by contrast, how natural sex is.

If an active sexuality is natural and even attractive in women, passivity, the eighteenth-century feminine ideal, may not be. This implicit bit of reasoning lies, like a seismic fault, at the center of Gay's *Fan* and keeps it in an unsettled state. The mock-epic machinery works, even though its product, the debate on female nature, is not smoothly finished, for the debate is never resolved. In fact, the machinery works all the better for that reason. In the end, Gay isn't sure about female nature. Unwilling or unable to accept fully the mythical ideal of passive womanhood, he rose above the smooth certainty that might well have rendered *The Fan* an "unutterably trivial" product by a featherweight poet, and created a poem that remains alive.

NOTES

1 Sherbo, "John Gay: Lightweight or Heavyweight?" *Scriblerian* 8 (1975): 4; Ames, "Gay's *Trivia* and the Art of Allusion," *Studies in Philology* 75 (1978): 199.

2 Ames, p. 199. For Irvin Ehrenpreis on the value of detecting and commenting on allusions, see his *Literary Meaning and Augustan Values* (Charlottesville: University of Virginia Press, 1974), 8-20. Cf. my "Women, 'Learned Lumber,' and English Neoclassical Poetry," *Pacific Coast Philology* 15 (1980): 27-34, which supports Ehrenpreis's ideas, and Robert Folkenflik's " '*Homo Alludens*' in the Eighteenth Century," *Criticism* 24 (1982): 218-32, which opposes them. See also Ellen Pollak, whose influence on this essay will soon become apparent, concerning the "distortions of traditional formalist and allusion-tracing analyses" (*The Poetics of Sexual Myth: Gender and Ideology in the Verse of Swift and Pope* [Chicago: University of Chicago Press, 1985], 8).

3 Johnson, *Lives of the English Poets*, ed. George Birkbeck Hill, 3 vols. (Oxford: Clarendon Press, 1905), 2:283; Spacks, *John Gay* (New York: Twayne, 1965), 29.

4 John Gay, *Poetry and Prose*, ed. Vinton A. Dearing with the assistance of Charles E. Beckwith, 2 vols. (Oxford: Clarendon Press, 1974), 2:499. While the notes to *The Fan* are printed in volume two, the poem itself appears in volume one, which will be used here as the source for all quotations; book and line numbers will be indicated in my text.

5 Opinions differ interestingly among those who have considered Gay's attitude toward women. To Susan Gubar, Gay, like the other Scriblerians, creates "female grotesques" ("The Female Monster in Augustan Satire," *Signs* 3 [1977]:380); answering her, Ellen Pollak claims that while Swift indeed creates female monsters who "often overwhelm and repel," Pope and Gay, who comfortably accept the "myth of passive womanhood," find women quite unthreatening and therefore unmonstrous ("Comment on Susan Gubar's 'The Female Monster in Augustan Satire'," *Signs* 3 [1978]:731, 729). More recently, in "The Migrant Muses: A Study of Gay's Later Drama," in *John Gay and the*

Scriblerians, ed. Peter Lewis and Nigel Wood (London: Vision Press; New York: St. Martin's, 1989), Carolyn D. Williams finds him sometimes capable of "sympathy," sometimes apparently convinced, like the other Scriblerians (in Williams's opinion), "that every woman was at heart a Whig . . . an unscrupulous Walpolean Whig, venal from her laced shoes to her powdered hair" (174, 177). But Yvonne Noble's "Sex and Gender in Gay's *Achilles*," in the same volume, supposes Gay in his *Achilles* aware of "how, in a society with a double standard, women are forced to destroy each other" and even interested in "undermin[ing] . . . male dominance" (200–201, 185).

6 On the submissiveness expected of women in marriage, see Pollak's chapter, "The Eighteenth-Century Myth of Passive Womanhood," in *Poetics*, chapter two.
7 Pollak, "Comment," 729.
8 Pollak, *Poetics*, 55.
9 Camilla attacks Chloreus, but Virgil, briefly considering her motive, leaves it uncertain "sive ut templis praefigeret arma / Troia, captivo sive ut se ferret in auro" (11.778–79: "whether she wanted to hang his Trojan arms up in the temples," her motive being a combination of martial pride and patriotism, or "to put on his captured golden [armor]"). Moreover, the subject, which appears in the next line, of "se ferret" is "venatrix" ("huntress"), so Camilla's possible desire to have Chloreus's armor for herself seems closer to a huntress's desire for the pelt of a prey than a putatively female lust for finery.
10 On Swift's inability to accept the myth of passive womanhood, see Pollak's *Poetics*, 16–17.
11 See Katharine M. Rogers, *Feminism in Eighteenth-Century England* (Urbana: University of Illinois Press, 1982): the Restoration "court wits . . . extended to women the right to plain-speaking and pleasure-seeking they claimed for themselves" (54). Similarly, Pollak refers to an "aristocratic tolerance for, nay even attraction to, the sexual exuberance and gamesmanship of women . . . in Restoration drama" (*Poetics*, 3).

Eroticism in Graphic Art: The Case of William Hogarth

HANS-PETER WAGNER

William Hogarth's engravings that allude to, or comment on, aspects of human sexuality contain a decidedly moral if ironic pictorial discourse satirizing the titillations of eroticism. This is most obvious in the early series on the rake and the harlot and in the ambiguous prints on marriage, which were first discussed by Lichtenberg (1784) and have since then received ample critical attention, but it can also be seen in less discussed works, on which I shall focus here.[1]

Hogarth was concerned with the shocking reality behind the glittering facade of prostitution, revealing it as a horrible and, more often than not, deadly trap. He could never have celebrated sexual joy in the character of a harlot in the way John Cleland did in *Fanny Hill*, for Hogarth was averse both to the phony world of the whore and to sex as mere pleasure. Like Jonathan Swift, Hogarth worked and argued in a satirical tradition that combined Protestant Christian moral principles with the critical and pessimistic views of love and lovers portrayed by such classic writers as Juvenal and Ovid.[2] In addition, he integrated into his iconography the popular bawdy satires that shaped the "mentalité" of his day. Hence his engravings associate the sexual drive with disorder, animal lust, scatology, illegitimacy and even criminality.[3]

In several of Hogarth's prints the erotic motif plays a role only apparently marginal while actually supporting his major moral argument. In

Figure 1. William Hogarth. *The Sleeping Congregation* (1736; revised in 1762. Third State, 1736).

The Sleeping Congregation of 1736 (revised in 1762; fig. 1), for instance, Hogarth presents a comic and essentially moral juxtaposition of the absence of God and the presence of lust. In the top corner on the left, Hogarth has "deconstructed" the royal coat of arms to illustrate his message both literally and emblematically: while the inscription merely shows "ET MON DROIT," excising "GOD" and thus hinting at the selfishness of the sleeping congregation, the sexual organs of the royal lion have been grotesquely exaggerated. God's absence in this Anglican meeting house is again suggested by the missing eye in the upturned triangle below the angel, whose figure is as risible as that of the lion. The symbolic moral message of the top corner is reflected symmetrically and thematically, as it were, in the scene in the lower corner on the right. There, a lustful clergyman secretly eyes the exposed bosom of the dozing girl beside him. Like the rest of the congregation, she has fallen asleep because of the preacher's obvious tedium. Hogarth suggests that religious worship has been replaced by idolatry. To underline the implication of sinful adoration Hogarth turns the pretty young woman into a somnolent figure resembling a classical statue. God has been displaced by a new idol, and it is this tempting idol that is being worshipped by the ogling clergyman who literally turns a blind eye to the Word of God before him.[4]

The expression on the girl's face is rather ambiguous, suggesting both dreams and rapture. Hogarth seems to imply that she might be dreaming of the erotic pleasures "OF MATRIMONY," which is the title showing on the open page in her copy of the prayer book. A contemporary observer of the print would have immediately understood Hogarth's implicit reference to popular satiric writings. Eighteenth-century satirists—especially Swift and Fielding—invariably portrayed religious "enthusiasts," such as Methodists, as affected bigots with secret sexual desires bordering on perversion.[5] Hogarth adopted this cliché, toying with it in double entendres and puns. Thus he plays on the religious and sexual meanings of such terms as "matrimony" in this print, or "regeneration" in plate 2 of *Marriage à la Mode*.[6] "OF MATRIMONY"—which also appears, with the same ironic function, in plate 5 of *A Rake's Progress* (1735; third state 1763)—is, in fact, an allusion to a large body of works on marriage and procreation which were read because they promised instruction, but were potentially erotic because they provided titillation as well. Nicolas Venette's *Mysteries of Conjugal Love Reveal'd* (1703 and later), Defoe's *Conjugal Lewdness or Matrimonial Whoredom* (1727), and the best-selling sex guide *Aristotle's Master-Piece* are just three examples of an important and highly ambiguous pseudo-instructional literature that shaped the eighteenth-century English *mentalités*.[7] The emblematic and ironical allusions to sexuality in this print enforce the central argument about idolatry, i.e., that Eros is an idol replacing God. It is summed up in the biblical inscription on the pulpit and applies to the parson as well as to his sleeping parishioners: "I am afraid of you, lest I have bestowed upon you labour in vain Galats 4th 11." It is characteristic of Hogarth's view of human sexuality that he perceives and represents it as dangerous and illicit. When God is absent, the print seems to suggest, Eros creeps in

Figure 2. William Hogarth. *Noon* (Plate 2 of *The Four Times of the Day*. First State, 1738).

in the form of new and preferably female idols. But for William Hogarth, at least in his graphic art, Eros is not a god who can replace the god of bourgeois English Puritanism.[8]

A similar symmetrical arrangement, with sexuality removed to the margin, as it were, can be found in *Noon* (fig. 2), the second engraving of the series *The Four Times of the Day* produced in 1738. In this work, Hogarth juxtaposes two groups of Londoners, contrasting the modish superficiality of the Huguenots on the right with the sensual brutishness of the English group on the left. Again the engraving is rich in double meanings and ironical allusions (note, for instance, the head of John the Baptist as an ambiguous sign for an eating house, and the other sign, on the tavern, showing a woman without a head). The gutter in the middle of the picture separates the refined from the vulgar, the spiritual from the physical, and the civilized from the savage. But Hogarth does not present the scene with a simple dualism that would prefer English vitality to French artificiality or vice versa. Instead, he criticizes both forms of behavior. What is important here, however, is the repeated pictorial allusion to sexuality. These allusions are made in the form of emblematical encodings of an essentially repressive discourse on sexual behavior. Significantly, the two sides of the print are connected by the carcass of a cat, a symbol of unbridled lust and vitality—the fact that the cat is dead indicates Hogarth's attitude toward uncontrolled sex. In the right half of the picture, sex is subdued but nevertheless present. Hogarth conveys its negative aspect by stressing affectation, falsity, and narcissism. The lady and her lover on the right represent artificial or false lovemaking in its eighteenth-century sense. Perhaps, as Lichtenberg suspected, the lady's wide petticoat is not an expression of contemporary fashion but hides her (illegitimate) pregnancy (*Erklärung*, 1:177). Both her lover and the boy in front of the couple, probably her son, introduce the theme of self-love. The overdressed gallant behind the boy is apparently as enamored of his own person as he is of the beautiful lady beside him. The boy's gesture recalls satirically the tragic myth of another youth who fell in love with his own image; like Narcissus he admires his reflection in a puddle while stroking his chest. Hogarth also ridicules the French custom of kisses of greeting; in this case two old women render the potentially erotic aspect of kissing ludicrous by their very age.

On the other side of the gutter, the allusions to sex are cast into much cruder images suggesting savagery, even cannibalism.[9] The iconography of the print draws on sexual symbols and emblems that had been part of sexist and misogynist satire for centuries, including "The Silent Woman" (the sign showing a woman without her head) and the food represented.[10] In the upstairs window of the tavern, a man and a woman fight over a piece of meat. The shape of the platter and of the meat itself suggests sexual organs and intercourse. The general mood of passionate hunger for both food and sex is further reinforced by objects referring to penetration and spillage, i. e., ejaculation: note the spear-shaped bar of the sign-board entering the woman's head from behind (where her male adversary is positioned), and the liquid running out of the girl's pie beneath the sign as she is being fondled by a black man also standing behind her. It is this couple (left) who are most explicitly erotic in the print, the black man's "hunger" exposing one of the girl's nipples to public view.[11] David Dabydeen has argued that "Hogarth's black is . . . a positive figure, for the group he belongs to, though they exist in dirt and passion, are preferable to the aristocrats, their shared animal energy, however squalid, and their naturalness, being in positive contrast to the reserve, polish and ostentation of the latter group."[12] I argue rather that Hogarth presents the observer with two behavioral patterns of which neither is to be preferred. As Dabydeen has to admit himself, the eighteenth-century (white) English conception of the black man associated him with animal drives, i.e., lust, cannibalism, and savagery. In the context of this print, one should also consider Hogarth's general satirical intention, directed not only against aristocratic (French) behavior, but also against the traditional, classical way of showing "les points du jours" as against the squalid and barbarian aspect of low life in London. Thus the entwined lovers on the left, the cook-maid and her paramour, represent Hogarth's humorous interpretation of the mythological meeting of Europe and Africa, of Apollo and Venus.[13] Venus's nakedness indicates her carnality. Like the pretty milkmaid in *The Enraged Musician* (1741), her beauty stands in sharp and deliberate contrast to the ugly low-life figures around her. Since she is so beautiful, showing the typical Hogarthian serpentine lines of a desirable young woman, her toleration of sexual advances must be all the more shocking to the observer.[14] The unacceptable nature of this primitive passion is further expressed by her choice of a primitive—African—lover. If the cook-maid represents a part of England, then England—and this seems to be an important point in Hogarth's encoded pictorial discourse—unashamedly and even willingly gives in to savage lust and hunger.

Moving sexuality, and the signs or icons representing it, to the periphery, is a part of Hogarth's satiric strategy. It permits an implicit argument, eventually, that the margin controls and informs the center. Other examples of this ironic marginalization of sexuality include Hogarth's *Masquerade Ticket* (1727) and plate 2 of *The Analysis of Beauty* (1753). The emblematic *Masquerade Ticket*, for instance (fig. 3), product of a phase in which Hogarth still identified with, and even defended, the cultural values of the dominant aristocratic class, overwhelms the ostensible center with its peripheral material, referred to also in the legend of the engraving. Dominating the frame is the central clock, itself framed by two masturbating animals; and two sacrilegious altars dominate the sides of the picture, where Priapus (on the left) and Venus (on the right) are to be worshipped. Amor's arrow seems to come straight from Venus's pudenda. If one adds to these symbols and emblems the Bacchanalian

Eroticism in Hogarth / 59

Figure 3. William Hogarth. *Masquerade Ticket* (First State, 1727).

picture on the back wall (another "margin" of the room), and the obscene punning signs, "Supper below," on each side, one realizes how Hogarth subverts the apparently innocent center of the engraving through the marginalization of sexuality.

This strategy is most convincingly applied in the plate of *The Analysis of Beauty* showing a dancing assembly (fig. 4). In fact, one might at first overlook in the print the more than decorative significance of the Samaritan Woman looking at the couple on the left, and of Sancho Panza commenting on the assignation taking place in front of his eyes. In this case the marginal figures, including the portrait of Henry VII on the wall, as well as the subtexts they stand for (the story of the Samaritan Woman in the Bible; Sancho Panza's role in *Don Quixote* as the normative, realistic figure who sees more clearly than his deluded master), cast doubt on the moral integrity of the dancing couples.[15] The various references to sex in these engravings, like those in *Noon*, although often ambiguous and even erotic, assert Hogarth's essentially moralistic view

Figure 4. William Hogarth, *The Analysis of Beauty* (Plate 2. First State, 1753).

of sexuality as a dangerous force that needs controlling and policing. This view is conditioned by the popular sexual *mentalité*.

The same view is most obvious in his most erotic prints, the series entitled *Before and After*. The engravings were preceded by two series of paintings that are importantly related to the engraved version. With the original outdoor scene of the paintings *Before and After* (Fitzwilliam Museum, Cambridge, England; figs. 5 and 6), Hogarth significantly produced a pair of pastoral works dealing comically rather than realistically with the fall from innocence. Although done in the French manner, they are far from stressing the joy of sex and of sensuousness in the style of Boucher or Fragonard. From a modern perspective, Paulson is right when he terms them "indecent," for Hogarth reduces erotic love to lust and frustration on the part of the actors, and therefore the viewer to a voyeur.[16] The indoor version of the paintings, produced a few years later (J. Paul Getty Collection), displaces voyeuristic realism in favor of the allusive symbolism that is also typical of Hogarth's graphic art. Significantly, he used this latter series, which is more "readable" because of its emblematic discourse, as a model for the engraved moral works.

Eroticism in Hogarth / 61

Figure 5. William Hogarth, *Before*, painting (outdoor scene; 1730–31). Reproduced by permission of the Syndics of the Fitzwilliam Museum, Cambridge.

Figure 6. William Hogarth, *After*, painting (outdoor scene, 1730–31). Reproduced by permission of the Syndics of the Fitzwilliam Museum, Cambridge.

Figure 7. William Hogarth, *Before* (First State, 1736).

In 1736, immediately after the completion of *A Rake's Progress*, when Hogarth was engraving *Before and After*, he was also working on a religious painting in the grand manner, *The Pool of Bethesda* (1735-37).[17] Thus he never lost sight of his moral and social concerns, even though he was creating a new version of an age-old erotic theme in art. Beyond its criticism of sexual lust, Hogarth's engraved version of *Before and After* (figs. 7 and 8) has several targets: the engravings revise his own paintings, adding "wit and satiric bite to his conception,"[18] and also mock the contemporary French genre of "scènes galantes." In fact, a first "reading" of

Figure 8. William Hogarth, *After* (First State, 1736).

the prints as separate pictures discloses Hogarth's subtle and ironical play with the French tradition by way of allusion. In *Before*, a number of symbols refer to imminent seduction and sex, but also to the hypocrisy, vanity, and essential ludicrousness of the couple: the painting on the wall, struck by the sun from above, shows Cupid lighting a rocket; and the dog, as in similar French indoor scenes, is on his hind legs, reflecting symbolically the arousal of the characters in front of the beckoning bed. The mobcap fastened to the curtain on the right resembles the face of an onlooker,[19] probably as a satirical allusion to the customary voyeur in contemporary French engravings.[20] The lady is characterized indirectly by her personal objects and books that reveal her resistance to be mere conventional bashfulness if not hypocrisy. In this instance, Hogarth employs the old literary technique of evaluating characters by associating them with their belongings, a method which Pope had perfected in *The Rape of the Lock* (1712, 1714) where the beautiful Belinda is described indirectly by her "Puffs, Powders, Patches, Bibles, Billet-doux" (canto 1, line 138). In Hogarth's print, the lady's pretended shock at her paramour's advances is ironically contrasted with the nature and arrangement of her books: *The Practice of Piety*, a devotional book which is said to have influenced Bunyan, lies unread but ostentatiously in the drawer; beside it, however, are love letters and novels. She seems to have been reading a copy of Rochester's notorious poems, which is placed beneath the mirror. At the time the prints were made, "Rochester's poems," like Grébillon's *Le Sopha* a few years later, which serves a similar function in plate 4 of *Marriage à-la-Mode*, were synonymous with pornography—especially for the middle class—since, at least in the public sphere, the aristocratic libertine *mentalité* was being rapidly displaced.[21] The fact that the lady has already taken off her corset (now on the chair in the corner on the right) and has put on a nightcap *before* receiving her lover, indicates that she is "ready for action" but wants to keep up appearances. Other elements in the picture, such as the table and mirror which are about to tilt over, refer not to pleasure or joy but to an impending disorder and disaster, including the biblical fall from innocence into sexual experience. The outdoor version of the paintings shows falling apples; in the engraved version Hogarth changed them into pills, perhaps aphrodisiacs, which the lovers may have tasted and which have spilled from a box beside the dog. Hogarth even adds a scatological symbol that demonstrates both his closeness to the Swiftian vision of love and his indebtedness to the popular comical tradition: the chamber pot, quite visible under the bed, is deliberately placed in the middle of the picture.

Constantly undermining any kind of sexual tension that might be building up in the observer, Hogarth is clearly interested in developing a comical atmosphere—which is of course anathema to eroticism. In addition to the scatological detail, note, for instance, the fact that the male is about to lose his wig and that he is apparently bald.

If the first picture is dominated by comical and ambiguous symbols that debunk rather than reinforce eroticism, the *After* engraving provides an impression of disorder, exhaustion, frustration, and depression. The sun on the wall is now a little lower, indicating the passing of time and revealing a second picture that depicts Cupid laughing at the spent rocket. The table has been turned over, and a number of symbols refer to the loss of virginity: the mirror is broken, and so is the chamber pot—

broken pots being symbols of lost maidenheads[22] — while the curtain has been torn at one end. The man is obviously in a state of postcoital depression — the open page of the book of Aristotle at his feet reads "omne animal post coitum triste." Significantly, this apothegm traditionally ascribed to Aristotle is from his book treating *Of the Generation of Animals* — both humans in the print, especially the male, are now being shown in an "animal" state. The reaction of the woman, suggesting both shame and the wish for more, is less easily determined.[23] The total impression of this picture is summed up not only by the quotation in the book of Aristotle but also by the sleeping dog symbolizing the waning of lust: passion is over, and the participants in the war of love, having now lost their innocence, are tired and disillusioned.

I believe, however, that *Before and After* should also, perhaps even exclusively, be examined as a series, for the two pictures complement each other and can be better understood when read as a "story," as it were, in which Hogarth, with his tongue in his cheek, asks the reader to imagine the most "exciting" part.[24] The series can be read either as a sequence or as a juxtaposition, each reading yielding a slightly different interpretation. Thus Frédéric Ogée perceives a sequential plot in the pictures, arguing that Hogarth was here interested in the movement of time and that the perception is therefore oriented like that of reading, from left to right. Ogée believes that the two engravings, when put side by side, point toward the space between them, to the present tense as it were, between the future and the past. Ronald Paulson, however, interprets the prints on the basis of a juxtaposition that still leaves a causal, temporal relation but also drives home another important idea: "the opposition of desire and fulfillment."[25] Both readings bring out the moral message of the prints, which was Hogarth's major concern. If the two pictures suggest that there is a third one that cannot be shown, one can at least imagine it. But Hogarth makes sure that the observer's imagination is not free, for the satirical aspect of the scenes we are allowed to witness suggests that "Now" must be even more ludicrous than "Before" or "After." By way of satiric emblems, supported by the relationships between the two scenes, Hogarth thus tries to prevent the observer's imagination from straying into pornographic dimensions. As a juxtaposition, especially, the engravings demonstrate not only the opposition of desire and fulfillment, but specifically the immoral complementarity of lust and sexual satisfaction: both are animal desires, and both must therefore be controlled. Those who fail in this Christian-Puritan enterprise will be reduced to the physical and mental state of animals and must appear ludicrous.

As a pair, *Before and After* also represents Hogarth's attack on the tradition, in French erotic graphic art, of creating two versions of an amorous scene: the first state ("Before"), usually produced in a small edition for libertine connoisseurs, showed the female unclothed, whereas in the "After" state, available to a larger public, there was no nudity. With the titles of his engravings Hogarth alludes, tongue in cheek, to this tradition, only to deconstruct erotic expectations with his typical moral irony, so reminiscent of Jonathan Swift's poetry concerned with love-making.

A final dimension to Hogarth's didactic iconographic strategy is its employment of eroticism as a lure for the (male) observer in order to teach him a moral lesson. We tend to ignore it today because it derives from a "world which is lost" (or rather, a world that scholars more interested in the culture of the élite have tended to ignore): the popular eighteenth-century discourse on sex, which cut through all genres and varieties of discourses and, more often than not, mocked and subverted the "official" discourse.[26] Like Swift in his satiric "love poems," such as "A Beautiful Young Nymph Going to Bed" (1734), Hogarth relies on the reader's knowledge of contemporary erotica and the popular discourse on prostitutes. For it is to the sexist male who makes "goddesses" or idols out of ordinary (female) human beings that both Swift and Hogarth want to teach an iconoclastic lesson.[27] Such an erotic, popular subtext frequently contributes to Hogarth's graphic palimpsests, for example, in *Masquerade Ticket*, discussed above; in plate 4 of *Marriage à-la-Mode*, in *The March to Finchley*, which relies on the observer's knowledge of contemporary ribaldry concerning bawds and prostitutes, and, most suggestively and artistically, in plate 1 of *The Analysis of Beauty* (1753, fig. 9). On the left, we see the statue of Antinous (catamite of the emperor Hadrian) and a dancing master. A contemporary observer, familiar with the popular bawdry on dancing masters and homosexuals, would have chuckled at the scene, as the helpless classical statue is propositioned by the gay dancing master. Such a reading is corroborated by the contemporary popular discourse on sex. Hogarth appeals, then, to a sexual *mentalité* shared by both plebeians and members of the middle class.

Two examples will suffice to demonstrate how Hogarth relies on this *mentalité*, including its repressive features and stereotypes, even though he makes it subservient to his satirical aims. Both examples allude to what (in popular eighteenth-century writings) was called "onanism," i.e., the manual stimulation of genitals. In plate 1 of *A Harlot's Progress* (1732), which Hogarth entitled "Her Coming to Town,"[28] the notorious libertine and rapist Colonel Francis Charteris appears in the doorway together with his pimp (fig. 10).[29] Hogarth casts him as an extremely negative character, and, in Paulson's view, as part of an implicit satire on "great men," thus underlining the political context (*Hogarth's Graphic*

Figure 9. William Hogarth, *The Analysis of Beauty* (Plate 1. Third State, 1753).

Works, 78; *Breaking and Remaking*, 174). But it seems to me that the sexual context is equally important here. As in *The Sleeping Congregation*, Hogarth uses an iconographic strategy that removes obscenity and illicit forms of sexuality to the seemingly less significant periphery. In my view, he casts Charteris as a masturbator: his right hand is thrust deeply into his pocket, and he is leering at the virgin in the center of the picture. In the popular sexual discourse, masturbation was synonymous with (sexual and moral) perversion. From the very beginning of the eighteenth century, popular, para-medical, and medical writings associated "onanism" with mental and physical diseases. The combined efforts of both medical and moral writers produced a massive, and essentially repressive, literature on masturbation. The prime example is the best-selling treatise entitled *Onania* (first published in 1708), which grew from a short booklet of about 60 pages to 194 pages and sold close to 38,000 copies, receiving a supplement (of ambiguous readers' letters obviously meant for voyeurists) of 142 pages in the sixteenth edition. The errors and myths of *Onania* (e. g., that masturbation produces venereal diseases) were taken up and developed by subsequent authors, notably Tis-

Figure 10. William Hogarth, *A Harlot's Progress* (Plate 1. First State, 1732).

sot and Bienville, and were continued into the nineteenth century, if not beyond. If Hogarth suggests that Charteris is masturbating, the association, at least for nonaristocratic viewers, clearly marks him as a pervert or as an abnormal and hence despicable character who is unable, or refuses, to restrict himself to "normal" (or "natural") sexual intercourse.

The theme of illicit or "unnatural" masturbation also appears in the final plate ("Her Funeral") of the Harlot series (fig. 11). In the typical Hogarthian ironic manner, sexual activities—which are here part of the satiric strategy of mocking "les passions"—are again removed to the margin, as if they were unimportant. The masturbator, a parson, appears on the left. Lichtenberg compares him to Charteris, the rapist and masturbator in plate 1.[30] The parson's posture makes it difficult to ascertain what his right hand is up to. But the point is not whether he stimulates the (unperturbed) prostitute beside him—the only figure, incidentally, casting a direct and tempting look at the (male) observer of the scene—or (less likely) pleasures himself: for Hogarth, following the popular sexual *mentalité*, manual stimulation of anyone's genitals is "unnatural" and hence illicit and immoral. This scene within a scene is predominantly

Figure 11. William Hogarth, *A Harlot's Progress* (Plate 6. First State, 1732).

humorous. In addition to the prostitute's come-on look at the observer, note, for instance, the emblematic treatment of orgasm in the spilling of the parson's brandy; and the sprigs of yew and rosemary, held by the woman and at the parson's feet, which were thought to prevent infection at funerals and which gain another meaning in this tableau. But Hogarth's humor does not detract from his moral message about masturbation, which is in complete accordance with the *mentalité* of his day and class. As we have already seen in the case of *Noon*, it found expression in popular bawdry and in sexual symbols and types from medieval misogyny, and for his graphic art, Hogarth drew on this discourse as well as on the old iconography.

Hogarth could not and did not want to abandon the kind of moralism which had its roots in the Puritan middle class. His vision is not exceptional. In fact, it is noticeable as a manifest current in English pictorial erotica from Hogarth to the late eighteenth-century caricaturists Rowlandson, Gillray, and Newton, and even in the works of Turner and Fuseli.[31] Although the English painters and engravers occasionally produced works for aristocrats who were known for their amoral attitudes and libertine lives,[32] the artists seemed to have been too class-conscious to ignore the English bourgeois tradition of didacticism in art and literature. Significantly, even English pornographic prints, mostly book illustrations engraved by anonymous artists for libertine magazines, are not frank or downright obscene like the French examples from the same period: they retain an element of the forbidden and the secret, indicating the moral confinement in which artists had to work in England.[33]

As the works of Hogarth and of his successors demonstrate, English artists worked in an atmosphere dominated by a *mentalité* that prevented the development of the amoral "genre galant" as it was known in contemporary France (fig. 12). If Frederic Antal is somewhat inclined to exaggerate the moral aspect of Hogarth's art, he is nevertheless entirely right in saying that it is "unthinkable divested of moral teaching."[34] There was no need of a public censor in England, for the English engravers who felt and thought in Christian moral terms censored themselves. Paradoxically, the remarkable increase of pictorial discourse on sex during the eighteenth century was, in the final analysis, repressive rather than liberating. Age-old stereotypes and traditional roles remained virtually unchanged; and with the growing influence of the middle-class *mentalité* the notion of the illegitimate and the immoral gained in importance. Graphic erotica constitute an area of symbolical discourse on sex that mirrors the erotic and sexual preoccupations of an age that is only selectively to be called "enlightened."

Figure 12. Pierre-Antoine Baudouin, *Le carquois épuisé*, engraved by Nicolas de Launay (undated).

NOTES

1 See Georg-Christoph Lichtenberg, *Ausführliche Erklärung der Hogarthischen Kupferstiche* (Göttingen, 1784; repr. Göttingen: J.C. Dieterich, 1795-1796); English translation *Lichtenberg's Commentaries on Hogarth's Engravings*, ed. Innes and Gustav Herdan (Boston: Houghton Mifflin, 1960). In addition, see the discussion of the two series in John Nichols and George Steevens, eds., *The Genuine Works of William Hogarth*, 2 vols. (London: Longman et al., 1808-1840), and vol. 3 published by Nichols in 1817. See also Ronald Paulson, *Hogarth's Graphic Works*, 3rd revised ed. (London: The Print Room, 1989) and *The Art of Hogarth* (Oxford: Phaidon, 1975); and Joseph Burke and Colin Caldwell, *Hogarth. The Complete Engravings* (London: Thames & Hudson, 1974).

2 Swift, in particular, drew on the Bible and on a satiric tradition that reaches back to Juvenal's sixth satire and Ovid's *Remedia amoris* but included also the authority of such Church Fathers as Jerome, Cyprian, and Tertullian. On Swift's sources see Felicity Nussbaum, *The Brink of All We Hate: English Satires on Women, 1660-1750* (Lexington: The University Press of Kentucky, 1984), 94-117; and Ronald Paulson, *Breaking and Remaking. Aesthetic Practice in England, 1700-1820* (New Brunswick: Rutgers UP, 1989), 25-47. As Paulson has pointed out, Hogarth made clear his closeness and indebtedness to Swift in his own portrait (1748-49) that shows him standing in front of books by Shakespeare, Swift, and Milton.

3 Hogarth also drew on and constantly alluded to a neglected tradition, the popular satire on love and lovers. For a survey see chapters 5-8 in my *Eros Revived. Erotica of the Enlightenment in England and America* (London: Secker & Warburg, 1988; repr. paperback Paladin Grafton Books, 1990).

4 See Paulson, *Breaking and Remaking*, 149-56, and *Hogarth's Graphic Works*, 98-99, for discussion of this print in the context of Hogarth's aesthetic theory.

5 Lichtenberg, for instance, recognized Hogarth's double entendre when he termed "OF MATRIMONY" a "Copulationsformel," adding a bawdy joke about prayer books and girls that "unfold," automatically, once they are "put on their backs." *G. C. Lichtenberg's Erklärung der Hogarthischen Kupferstiche* (Göttingen: H. Dieterich, 1808), 10:79, 82.

6 In this plate, a book protrudes from the coat pocket of the estate steward who is a Methodist. The title, REGENERATION, refers to George Whitefield's most famous sermon, published in 1737, but also to the sexual proclivities ascribed to Methodists. For more details see Paulson, *Hogarth's Graphic Works,* 118, and Lance Bertelsen, "The Interior Structures of Hogarth's *Marriage à la Mode*," *Art History* 6 (1983): 136.

7 See my "The Discourse on Sex—or Sex as Discourse: Eighteenth-century Medical and Paramedical Erotica," in *Sexual Underworlds of the Enlightenment*, ed. G. S. Rousseau and Roy Porter (Manchester: Manchester University Press, 1987; and Chapel Hill: U of North Carolina Press, 1988), 46-69, and two articles by Roy Porter, " 'The Secrets of Generation Display'd': *Aristotle's Master-Piece* in Eighteenth-Century England," in *Unauthorized Sexual*

Behavior During the Enlightenment, ed. Robert P. Maccubbin, *Eighteenth-Century Life* 9 (special number, 1985): 1-21, and "Love, Sex and Medicine: Nicolas Venette and his Tableau de l'amour conjugal," in *Erotica and the Enlightenment*, ed. Peter Wagner (Frankfort and New York: Lang, 1990), 90-123.

8 For discussions of this print, see especially Ronald Paulson, *Breaking and Remaking*, 149-156, and *Hogarth's Graphic Works*, 98-99. See also Berthold Hinz and Hartmut Krug, eds., *William Hogarth. Das vollständige graphische Werk*, (Giessen: Anabas, 2nd ed. 1986), 107-8; and Herwig Guratzsch, *William Hogarth. Der Kupferstich als moralische Schaubühne* (Stuttgart: Hatje, 1987), 86-87.

9 For persuasive discussions of Hogarth's emblematical allusions to food and sex in this part of the print, see David Dabydeen, *Hogarth's Blacks. Images of Blacks in Eighteenth-Century English Art* (Kingston-upon-Thames: Dangaroo Press, 1985), 62-64; and Sean Shesgreen, *Hogarth and the Times-of-the-Day Tradition* (Ithaca and London: Cornell University Press, 1983), 110-11, and 116-18.

10 See Malcolm Jones, "Folklore Motifs in Late Medieval Art II: Sexist Satire and Popular Punishment," *Folklore* 101 (1990): 70-87, especially 71 and 73. See also part I of the same study, *Folklore* 100 (1989):201-17.

11 In Hogarth's painting of the same scene, which was produced for an elite (aristocratic) audience, both nipples are visible.

12 Dabydeen, 64.

13 See Shesgreen, 111.

14 See Ronald Paulson's comments on the milkmaid in *The Enraged Musician* and on Hogarth's serpentine line of beauty, in *Representations of Revolution (1789-1820)* (New Haven and London: Yale University Press, 1983), 133. On the crucial role of the beautiful young plebeian woman as a mediator in Hogarth's engravings see Paulson, *Breaking and Remaking*, 176-187.

15 See Paulson, *Hogarth's Graphic Works*, nos. 108 and 196.

16 *Hogarth: His Life, Art, and Times*. Abbrev. ed. (New Haven: Yale University Press, 1974), 101-102. See also Dabydeen, 111, and David Bindman, *Hogarth* (London: Thames and Hudson, 1981), 42-43, 48-49.

17 Shesgreen, 150, argues that these works are "disparate kinds of productions." Such a reading considers only the titles. The common theme of these pictures is a moral, bourgeois view of human behavior.

18 David Kunzle, *The Early Comic Strip. Narrative Strips and Picture Stories in the European Broadsheet Tradition from c. 1450-1825* (Berkeley: University of California Press, 1973), 302.

19 Burke and Caldwell, no. 165, n.

20 Some are reproduced in my *Lust and Love in the Rococo* (Nördlingen: Greno, 1986), 33-79. A voyeur (hidden in the roof) is visible in Hogarth's *Strolling Actresses. Dressing in a Barn* (1738).

21 See Roy Porter, "Mixed Feelings: the Enlightenment and Sexuality in Eighteenth-Century Britain," in *Sexuality in Eighteenth-Century Britain*, ed. Paul-Gabriel Boucé (Manchester: Manchester University Press, 1982), 1-28;

and James G. Turner, "The Properties of Libertinism," *Eighteenth-Century Life* 9 (1985): 75-88.
22 See, for instance, Greuze's picture, *La cruche cassée*, and the bawdy, anti-aristocratic satires on "crack'd pots" quoted in *Eros Revived* (chap. 3).
23 Whereas in the painting the woman looks simply exhausted, the print version shows her "wheedling her distressed lover for more," as Ronald Paulson puts it in his recent edition of *Hogarth's Graphic Works*, 99.
24 Few commentators pay attention to the serial aspect of the two prints. Notable exceptions are Paulson (1974), 173, 186; Kunzle, 302-304; and Frédéric Ogée, "L'oeil erre: les parcours sériels de Hogarth," *Tropismes* No. 5 (Fall, 1989).
25 *Hogarth* (1974), 186.
26 I have discussed this issue at length elsewhere; see "Anti-Aristocratic Erotica Before and During the French Revolution," in *Evolutions et révolutions*, ed. Paul-Gabriel Boucé (Paris: Presses de la Sorbonne, 1990); and "Introduction," *Erotica and the Enlightenment*.
27 Readings that see Swift's attack as directed against women, as opposed to false idealization of women by men, seem to me misguided. A more convincing reading of the poem can be found in Felicity A. Nussbaum, *The Brink of All We Hate*, 105-11. On Hogarth's similar attack on idolatry of females, see Paulson, *Breaking and Remaking*, 35-48, 149-203.
28 See Robert L. S. Cowley, "Hogarth's Titles in His Progresses and other Picture Series," *Notes & Queries* 228 (1983): 46-48. For general information about the details of the print see Paulson, *Hogarth's Graphic Works*, 76-78.
29 In 1730, Charteris had been condemned to death for the rape of Anne Bond; but his powerful friends (including the prime minister, Walpole) contrived to obtain a pardon for him. Charteris figured in the newspapers and in trial reports and was attacked by several writers, including Pope and Fielding.
30 *Erklärung*, 2:304.
31 For Gillray, Rowlandson, and Newton, see my *Lust and Love in the Rococo*, 194-202. For Turner's erotica, *Eros Revived*, 291. For Fuseli's erotica, see David H. Weinglass, "'The Elysium of Fancy': Aspects of Henry Fuseli's Erotic Art," in *Erotica and the Enlightenment*, 291-350.
32 Hogarth is said to have painted the indoor version of *Before and After* for the Duke of Montague; and Rowlandson made several erotic drawings for his temporary friend, the Prince Regent.
33 See the illustrations in my "The Pornographer in the Court Room: Trial Reports About Cases of Sexual Crimes and Delinquencies as a Genre of Eighteenth-Century Erotica," in *Sexuality in Eighteenth-Century Britain*, 120-141. Note, for instance, that most of the prints in the trial reports illustrating crucial scenes from cases of adultery have a kind of theatrical frame, with a devil's head at the top, and with a cloak or curtain surrounding the pictures. These "marginal" details argue by implication that the content being shown is illicit or immoral.
34 "The Moral Purpose of Hogarth's Art," *Journal of the Warburg & Courtauld Institutes* 15 (1952): 171.

Swift and the 'Conjectural Histories' of the Eighteenth Century: The Case of the Fourth Voyage

CHARLES H. HINNANT

The Fourth Voyage of *Gulliver's Travels* embodies an underlying anthropological opposition, the opposition between hunter-gatherers (the Yahoos) and agriculturists (the Houyhnhnms). This opposition can throw light on the familiar debate between the "soft" and "hard" schools of interpretation of the Fourth Voyage.[1] For the most part, this debate — as aptly termed and outlined by James L. Clifford in an essay published in 1974[2] — has always been cast in uniformitarian or essentialist terms. That is, it has invariably been preoccupied with supposedly universal truths, truths which have their foundation in the notion of an essential human nature. It is to be expected, of course, that the Fourth Voyage would produce very different interpretations, according to whether it was being studied from the vantage point of the hard school, basically in terms of the entire race, or from the angle of incidence of the soft school, in terms of the solitary individual. What is enlightening is that the same essentialism was manifested on both sides of the argument. According to the hard school, Swift's target is the pride and pretensions of that animal called man; the soft school, also preoccupied with man, shifted attention from the collective aggregate to Lemuel Gulliver. As the one actual human being present in the first nine chapters, Gulliver, it was argued, was the obvious target of Swift's satire on human pride. The soft school also contested the claim of the hard school that the Houyhnhnms embody the utopian ideal of a true life of reason. If the Houyhnhnms are to be justified at all, it is because they, like the Yahoos, represent an extreme against which human behavior may be measured. By insisting that "the proper life for man is not that of Yahoo or of Houyhnhnm, for he has in something of both, and in the blending of passion and reason, body and mind, something different from these simple, natural creatures," Kathleen Williams, to cite perhaps the most familiar example, argued that the Fourth Voyage was dramatizing a timeless, universal truth, the notion of a *via media* or golden mean.[3]

It would be wrong to represent this debate as still dominant in Swift studies. On the contrary, it appears, if bibliographical entries are any indication, to have been losing steam for some time. Perhaps one reason for the gradual diminution of interest among scholars in this dispute lies in the way in which it has usually been framed. This essay will argue that, in one respect at least, essentialism was the unperceived and uncontested common ground of both the hard and soft schools. To the extent that the hard school envisaged the Houhynhnms as an ideal of pure reason and the Yahoos as an emblem of human depravity and sinfulness, it seemed bound, like its more benign counterpart, to encourage a complacent attitude toward the existing social order. If "human nature" is viewed in wholly pessimistic terms, it goes without saying that social and political conditions will be seen in a similar manner. This difficulty is what has led to the attempt, implicit also in the argument of the present essay, to redefine the hard school interpretation of the Fourth Voyage in a somewhat more flexible way. Instead of ascribing Swift's satire to a conception of natural depravity or original sin, I want to locate it within an iconoclastic critique of the emerging eighteenth-century sciences of man, especially the science of anthropology.

There is at least one way in which the hard school appears to resemble the soft school: it mystifies evil and invests human depravity with a quasi-transcendental status. Swift, by way of contrast, appears to take considerable precaution to avoid doing either of these things. Indeed, throughout his career, Swift consistently repudiates essentialism. In *A Tale of a Tub* the adjective "universal" is inscribed in a linked group of phrases devoted to a parodic deflation of the pretensions of the Modern hack.[4] It is from the same perspective that Swift pokes fun in "The Preface" at the kind of misanthropic satire that allows the reader to set aside its attack, to deflect it onto the other: "Tis but a Ball bandied to and fro, and every Man carries a racket about Him to strike it from himself among the rest of the Company" (51). This possibility is sufficient to render ineffectual any satire directed at general human depravity and vice; Swift holds that in England at least this kind of satire could all too easily be transformed into an ideological legitimation of the *status quo*: "Here, you may securely display your utmost Rhetorick against Mankind, in the Face of the World; tell them *'That all are gone astray; That there is none that doth good, no not one; That we live in the very Dregs of Time; That Knavery and Atheism are as Epidemick as the Pox; that Honesty is fled with Astraea'*; with any other Common Places *equally* new and eloquent" (51–52). These "Common Places" possess a common feature: they are opposed to the exposure of a particular individual, to the exposure of the corruption of the individual, and above all to the exposure of the corruption of an individual in power or public prominence. Referring to the Attic stage, Swift insists that "it was the Privilege and Birth-right of every Citizen and Poet, to rail aloud and in publick, or to expose upon the Stage by Name, any Person they pleased, tho' of the greatest Figure, whether a *Creon*, an *Hyperbolos*, an *Alcibiades*, or a *Demosthenes*" (51). The scope of this kind of raillery cannot be limited to essentialist notions of universal depravity. Otherwise, it would lack the shock value, the scandal of the specific indictment: "a single Hint in publick, How *such a one* starved half the Fleet, and half-poison'd the rest: How *such a one*, from a true principle of Love and Honour, pays no Debts but for Wenches and Play: How *such a one* has got a clap and runs out of his Estate . . . whoever, I say, should venture to be thus particular, must expect to be imprisoned for *Scandalum Magnatum*" (53). Human depravity is not an abstraction, separable from the actions of such indivduals as these, but, on the contrary, can only be manifested by their actions.

Swift's critique of essentialism in A *Tale of a Tub* has of course been noticed, but it has never been linked to his later satire, perhaps because this critique seems to have been meliorated in subsequent letters and poems. Yet there is no evidence that Swift's later comments challenge the underlying premise of his earlier polemic. The substitution of *"animal rationis capax"* for *"animal rationale"*[5] can be taken to suggest that the Stoic definition of man as *animal rationale* might be the effect of a kind of naiveté and that this suspicion is sufficient to suspend belief in that definition. But what remains suspended is not only the status of rationality as the *differentia* of the definition. Suspended also is the very form of a definition of the essence of human nature, the classical assumption concerning the dominating authority of this definition of essence, and a corresponding belief in the consistency of its application to particular individuals and groups. In place of this metaphysical determination, Swift substitutes a material preoccupation with power and authority. Thus when he writes to Pope that "I have ever hated all Nations professions and Communityes [sic], and all my love is toward individuals" (*idem*), he appears to be shifting the focus of his earlier remarks on satire in *A Tale of a Tub* from the individual to the group. Yet he may also be indicating as well his detestation of the quasi-metaphysical representations, the universalizing mystifications that perpetuate such collectivities. By the same criteria, it may be wrong to assert that Swift's satiric apologia in the "Verses on the Death of Dr. Swift" necessarily represents a softening of his earlier stance. By insisting that "His Satyr points at no Defect, / But what all Mortals may correct" (lines 467–68),[6] Swift may not simply be affirming an optimistic notion of corrigibility. He may also be insisting, crucially, upon the limitation of a misanthropic and corrosive satire that is pointed at universal human corruption. Ultimately, such a linkage encourages the conviction that man is powerless to effect change and thus must accept as axiomatic for humans and their societies, the biblical teacher's claim that "what is crooked cannot be made straight" (*Ecclesiastes* 1:15).

The Fourth Voyage reflects another dimension of Swift's critique of essentialism. This critique is perhaps most instructively revealed by placing it in the context of the newly emerging discipline of anthropology. This science has often been traced back, as is well known, to the matrix of travel literature that provided the cultural context and intertext for *Gulliver's Travels*. Swift's voyages combine two modes of discourse that were soon to become separated. One mode, exemplified in the chapters on the customs and manners of the peoples that Gulliver visits, lies at the center of each voyage; the other mode is embodied in the accounts of the adventures and incidents that occupy the outward journey and return. Where the former mode was to become the basis for the disciplines of anthropology and historical sociology, the latter was to become the groundwork for the modern literature of travel. Defoe's *Tour Through the Whole Island of Great Britain* might be said to anticipate the former disciplines in its emphasis on systematic description based on actual contact and in its absence of any real interest in the particular details of the tour. *Robinson Crusoe*, by contrast, anticipates the latter genre not only in its exploitation of the fictional potential of its subject matter but also in the heightened attention it devotes to the personal experiences of the voyager. In *Robinson Crusoe*, the deserted island also comes to rest in the place customarily occupied by the depiction of a savage society as seen by a "true witness." The virtual disappearance of savages from this emptied place is not merely an aspect of Crusoe's narrative; it is the very condition of its possibility. What cannot be represented except through direct observation is what disappears from view.

In its initial, eighteenth-century phase, the science of anthropology offers an alternative to essentialism. To the extent that it sought to account for differences between cultures, it turned attention from the problem of human unity to the problem of the genesis and development of human societies.[7] This is perhaps most evident in its notion of a unilinear yet unequal social development based on modes of food production: all societies, it argued, must pass through a series of four distinct stages whose past moments are represented in the contemporary world by savage and barbarous peoples. These stages are hunting and gathering, pastoralism, agriculture, and the formation of cities and states. This idea was a basic element in the "conjectural histories" and "histories of civil society" of the Scottish *philosophes*—Adam Smith, Lord Kames, John Millar, Adam Ferguson and Lord Monboddo—and their French counterparts. In *Sketches of the History of Man*, for example, published in 1774, Lord Kames projects a total history of the human race, tracing its progress from savagery to the highest level of civilization and improvement. The most primitive stage is that of hunting, fishing, and gathering of the natural fruits of the land; in this stage, there is little property and scarcely any evidence of subordination or government. The next stage is that of herders who possess property and hence rudimentary distinctions between rich and poor, masters and servants. Kames's theory is both comparative and uniformitarian, in the sense that it postulates a theory of evolution by which the level of material culture of all societies can be measured and derives that theory from an analysis of stages of production that are accompanied by certain types of political institution and certain distinctive cultural traits.[8]

Such a developmentalist conception of anthropology reached its zenith in the mid and late eighteenth century, but it had its roots in earlier eras. In fact, Swift could have found adumbrations of the theory of four stages of culture in a variety of Greek and Roman sources, from Plato and Aristotle through the Epicureans and Stoics. Plato's theoretical reconstruction of the development of any society from its earliest phase produced a division into the four stages of family, village, town and polis *(Laws,* 676–682a). Aristotle distinguished hunters, shepherds, cultivators, and traders (*Politics* I.8, 1256a.30–1256b.5). In *De Re Rustica* Varro traced the four stages of man in the following manner: "the earliest stage was a state of nature, when men lived on those things which the virgin earth bore; from this life they passed into a second, a pastoral life, . . . Finally in the third stage, from the pastoral life they attained the agricultural, in which they retained many of the features of the two earlier periods, and from which they continued for a long time in the condition which they had reached until that in which we lived was attained" (*De Re Rustica*, II, 1, 3ff.)[9] The specific components of this essentially Epicurean and Lucretian view were the notion of progress, a sharp division between different levels of material culture, and a perspective in which the earliest stage was seen as primitive and impoverished.

There were more recent articulations of a unilinear conception of society that Swift might also have known. Bishop Bossuet's *Discours sur l'Histoire Universelle* (1681) belongs to a tradition that sought to accommodate the history of nations within the six thousand years of biblical chronology. Yet Bossuet's *Discours*, which Johannes Fabian has characterized as an anticipation of the enlightenment genre of "philosophical history," described the evolution of the arts after the Flood essentially in developmentalist terms: "The earth, but an immense forest in the beginning, takes on a new form: clearings make room for fields, pastures, hamlets, villages, and, finally, towns."[10] To a certain extent, the arguments of the "conjectural historians" were also anticipated, as Robert Nisbet has argued, in the rationalistic political theories of Hobbes, Locke, Pufendorf, and others. Their conception of a prehistoric state of nature was a response to the belief, fostered by travel narratives, that the customs and values of other present-day peoples could be used to understand the origin of all civil societies.[11]

In a similar manner, Sir William Temple contended in essays of the 1670s and 1680s, especially the "Essay upon the Origin and Nature of Government" and "Upon the Gardens of Epicurus" that, in spite of differences in climate and culture, all societies evolve in pretty much the same way: "In the first and most simple ages of each country, the conditions and lives of men seem to have been very near of kin with the rest of the creatures: they lived by the hour, or by the day, and satisfied their appetite with what they could get from the herbs, the fruits, the springs they met with when they were hungry or dry, then, with what fish, fowl, or beasts they could kill."[12] What distinguishes more advanced societies from this rudimentary state of hunting and gathering, Temple argued, can be found in man's capacity to emancipate himself from the present moment. In later ages, according to Temple, man "cast about, how by sowing of grain, and by pasture of the tamer cattle, to provide for the whole year." In Temple's patriarchalist rather than contractarian account, the most advanced age, characterized by the introduction of money, arose not from advances in the arts and sciences but from the father's wish to keep part of his family's increase: "dividing the lands necessary for these uses, first among children, and then among servants, he reserved to himself a proportion of their gain, either in the native stock, or something equivalent, which brought in the use of money" (3:203). The developmentalist hypothesis was thus given attention long before the middle of the eighteenth century, and it was the widespread circulation of reports of primitive societies abroad that led to its revival.

What links Swift's satire to this developmentalist hypothesis is its identification of different groups of the Fourth Voyage with different stages in the development of human culture: the Yahoos are portrayed as hunter-gatherers, the Houyhnhnms as herdsmen and farmers, and Western European society is presented as the most advanced stage of human culture. Within this context, the satire of the Fourth Voyage unfolds in an unusual way. It does not contest the system of classification, on which cultural anthropology continues to rest even today, nor does it challenge the basic economic criteria by which the different stages are distinguished. What it does do is to take issue with the ethnocentrism and celebratory teleology that sustained and propelled the evolutionist hypothesis. By establishing an implicit parallel between the Yahoos and Western Europeans, the Fourth Voyage upsets the logic implicit in eighteenth-century travel literature and "conjectural history": it makes it possible for an advanced form of human culture—the development of cities and states—to be envisaged as a masked reformulation of the most primitive and impoverished level of human culture. This development is seen as implicit in hunting-gathering from its very beginning. It is an inevitable consequence of its underlying structure and logic.

The rudimentary state of the Yahoos is captured most tellingly in the attention devoted in the Fourth Voyage to their promiscuous methods of hunting and gathering food. When Gulliver first enters the Houyhnhnm compounds, he sees three "of those detestable Creatures . . . feeding upon Roots, and the Flesh of some Animals," which he "found to be that of Asses and Dogs, and now and then a Cow dead by Accident or Disease."[13] Much later, the Houyhnhnm master confirms Gulliver's initial perception, insisting that "there was nothing that rendered the Yahoos more odious, than their undistinguishing Appetite to devour every thing that came in their Way, whether Herbs, Roots, Berries, corrupted Flesh of Animals, or all mingled together" (261). That the Houyhnhnms, who tend milk cows and raise oats, belong to a much higher stage of culture is made obvious by the fact that the Houyhnhnm master is unable to comprehend why the Yahoos prefer hunting to farming: "it was peculiar in their Temper," he tells Gulliver, "that they were fonder of what they could get by Rapine or Stealth at a greater Distance than much better Food provided for them at home. If their Prey held out, they would eat till they were ready to burst, after which Nature had pointed out to them a certain *Root* that gave them a natural evacuation" (261–62).

The question might immediately be raised whether Swift meant this primitive state to be understood as a specific stage in the development of culture. There is no evidence, so far as I am aware, that Swift ever formulated an explicit theory of historical development. Yet a positive answer to this question still might be provided in the *Answer to the Craftsman* where Swift appears to invoke an implicit theory of stages when he ironically proposes that "the profitable Land" of a now depopulated Ireland "be wholly turned to Grazing" and its remaining inhabitants be converted to "shepherds and cowherds." To emphasize that this supposedly idyllic state is actually a reversion to a more primitive form of society, Swift describes the inhabitants of Ireland as descendants of the *Scythians*.[14] In this identification, Swift is probably alluding to Book IV of Herodotus's *Histories* where the contrast between the barbarian and the city-dweller is given its earliest systematic articulation.

It might also be objected that what I propose as an analogy with human culture is, in fact, a simple identification of the Yahoos with Christian symbols of sin. This is, in essence, the argument advanced by Roland M. Frye, who convincingly demonstrated that the Yahoos violate Biblical prohibitions against eating the carcasses of dead animals.[15] But this argument fails to recognize that savage and barbarous hunter-gatherers were frequently described in early voyage literature as violating the same prohibitions. Johannes Laetius's mid-seventeenth-century description of the American Indians and Asiatic Tartars as unclean eaters as well as nomadic hunter-gatherers is one example Swift might have known.[16] It is true, of course, that the Yahoos are portrayed as degenerate nomads whose ancestors wandered into a settled area and became at least partially domesticated, yet the lineaments of a more rudimentary pattern of behavior can still clearly be discerned. The fact that the Houyhnhnms are unable to discipline the unruly Yahoos is evidence not only of their natural depravity but also that the Yahoos, like the other "backward" tribes described by travellers and ethnographers, are seen as resistant to any kind of cultural assimilation or adaptation.

Such considerations can help us to define more carefully the significance of the link between the Yahoos and Western European culture. Clifford observed that "no one today accepts the older identification of the Yahoos with mankind, or assumes that they represent a crazy slander on human beings," but his conclusion that "for the most part, current theories accept them as descriptions of the limits to which man may degenerate if his passions are unrestrained, or, using biblical and theological symbols of sin, as the orthodox representation of the natural depravity of man" (40-41) seems equally limited. All these explanations are guilty of the same drawback: they isolate Swift's satire from any kind of political or cultural context. The more particular and detailed the satire, the less likely is it to be directed at an essentialist identification of the Yahoos with man, unrestrained passion, or natural depravity. A much more provocative and historically-specific identification would link a debased form of hunting and gathering—much more depraved, as Maximillian Novak observed, than any ethnographic account of the Hottentots[17]—with what Gulliver terms "the whole State of *Europe*" (245). In pursuing the implications of this identification, we should note Swift's central preoccupation with power and violence. Warfare and military technology seem to be a dominant aspect of European culture: the Yahoo propensity "to hate one another more than they did any different Species of Animals" and their readiness to engage in "*Civil War* among themselves" are assessed by the yardstick of the Wars of the Spanish Succession. In a similar manner, the structure of political power embodied in "*Courts, Favourites,* and *Ministers of State*" is traced back to the rudimentary form of despotism that Gulliver and the Houyhnhnm master observe in the Yahoo herds. Behind and parallel to the prominence of money, commerce and luxury in Europe, can be detected the primitive Yahoo fascination with "shining Stones" of which they are said to be "violently fond" (260). A proto-Marxist distinction between exchange value and use value, the use value that governs the political economy of the Houyhnhnms, lies at the root of this analogy. It is true, of course, that the Houyhnhnm master devotes some attention to the essentialist commonplace that animals are physically superior to men, who are born barefooted, naked and defenseless. Yet he also concedes that the Europeans have advanced beyond the Yahoos in point of "Cleanliness." Moreover, even though the Houyhnhnm master observes that "as to Learning, Government, Arts, Manufactures, and the Like . . . he could find little or no Resemblance between the *Yahoos* of that Country and those in ours," he immediately proceeds to draw Gulliver's attention to "some Qualities remarkable in the *Yahoos*, which he had not observed" Gulliver "to mention." These qualities, he reluctantly concedes, provide the basis for an analogy that extends beyond the general "Parity" in the "Natures" of the two groups (262–63). What had appeared to be the common ground linking the Yahoos and all mankind turns out to be guided by considerations that are regional and culturally limited.

From this perspective, it seems apparent that Swift is mounting an attack upon the most advanced form of modern culture, the conception of the sovereign state as the center of power and authority. His satiric conception of state power, needless to say, is essentially negative, even exploitative ("A *First* or *Chief Minister of State* . . . makes use of no other Passions but a violent Desire of Wealth, Power, and Titles"); and is parasitic rather than grounded upon any kind of legitimating authority, whether natural or contractualist ("That, these *Ministers* having all

Employments at their Disposal, preserve themselves in Power by bribing the Majority of a Senate or great Council") (255, 262). As such, the nation-state is clearly unjust and despotic. The only alternative to this system is at once represented and not represented by the Houyhnhnms. The fact that they are sharply distinguished from humans by their animal natures is an indication that Swift's procedure may no longer be governed by the reassuring logic of the exemplum. Generic "difference" is what might be said to upset the logic implicit in all essentialist identifications; it is what makes Gulliver's later attempts to emulate the virtues of the Houyhnhnms seem like an absurdity, hardly worthy of serious consideration. Yet if attention is shifted from ideal virtues to material practices, the situation may be different.

In an essay that represents a notable exception to the general trend of recent scholarship, Louis Landa has suggested that the rudimentary mode of production of the Houyhnhhnms clearly embodies "a localized, idealized agrarian provincialism": "although specific details are few and the pictures is shadowy," writes Landa, "Houyhnhnmland is recognizably a simple agrarian society which in sharp contrast to Gulliver's England and Swift's Ireland poses no problems in providing food and shelter."[18] Even if the virtues of the Houyhnhnms are prelapsarian, their political arrangements conform to this agrarian ideal. Without in any way intending to be exhaustive, one can suggest that these arrangements include a material relation to the environment that renders technological innovation unnecessary; a community that creates strong social obligations through reciprocity and kinship ties; and a structure of authority that minimizes domination through the avoidance of exploitative relationships. In all these respects, Houyhnhnm culture sustains Xenophon's account of agriculture as a process that does not involve "knowledge" or "the discovery of some wise or unwise contrivance," but rather virtue and a simple capacity for attention to the matter at hand (*Oeconomicus* 20.2, 5)[19].

The advantage of viewing the Houynhnms as the embodiment of an agrarian ideal is that it enables us to avoid the suggestion that Swift is consciously turning back to a seventeenth-century theory of cultural degeneration in *Gulliver's Travels*. In such a theory, the classification of the world's cultures in an arrangement from the simple to the complex might actually mark a retrogression rather than a development: agriculture and advanced cities and states might appear to represent a decline from a golden age of pastoralism or hunting-gathering. Yet there is at least one difficulty with this interpretation. It appears to condemn Swift to rehearsing, yet again, all the clichés about pessimism and original sin that he ridicules in *A Tale of a Tub* (e. g., "*That we live in the very Dregs of Time*" [269]) and alludes to in *Gulliver's Travels* when Gulliver refers to the "usual Topicks of *European* Moralists" in Glumdalclitch's little treatise (e. g., "that Nature was degenerated in these latter declining Ages of the World" [137]).

Fortunately there is another alternative. It is possible to argue that what Swift's satire amounts to is a historically qualified theory of degeneration. Unlike seventeenth-century theories of cultural decline, Swift's narrative implicitly concedes the notion of technological progress implicit in the concept of material development, but it implies that the third, not the fourth stage, actually represents the highest level of human culture: "nostalgia for agrarian paradises," Pierre Bourdieu has suggested, is "the principle of all conservative ideologies."[20] The fourth stage, the stage of cities and states, is also an advance, but it is an advance that borrows from what it has supposedly overcome, from that which appears as its heart of darkness, its other — to wit, the Yahoos as its other, the Hottentots, the archaic and degenerated hunter-gatherers as its other. In this, Swift may be following the biblical identification of the hunter — exemplified by Cain or Nimrod — with the builder of cities (*Genesis* 4.18; 10.9-10). Yet so long as this kind of identification is not made — as it was not made, apparently, by John Wesley, who opposed the condition of the Hottentots, the Laplanders, and other debased hunter-gatherers to the more advanced "state of civilization" of "the inhabitants of Europe"[21] — these concepts remain mystified or dogmatic. In contrast, whatever makes the parallel of the Yahoos and Europeans more continuous, more immanent, and more natural also makes it more scandalous as concerns a teleology of progress and development.

There is at least one other reason for supposing that Swift was affirming an identification of the Yahoos, as a culture, with European culture. This is the striking fact that Kames's argument converges on at least this one point with that of Swift. We might not be surprised that Kames, like Swift, associated the earliest stage of hunting-gathering with an appetite for hoarding. We might equally suppose that he would contend that the "calm and sedentary life of a shepherd tends to soften the harsh manners of hunters," that agriculture "improves benevolence," and that "industrious nations, . . . all the world over, are the most cleanly."[22] Yet what is unexpected is that Kames resembles Swift in believing that these improvements are still threatened in the most advanced stage of human culture, for "here the hoarding appetite starts up to disturb that auspicious commencement of civilization": "Fine houses, splendid gardens, and rich apparel, are desireable objects; the appetite for property becomes headstrong, and to obtain gratification tramples down every obstacle of justice or honour. . . . Differences arise, fomenting discord and resentment: war springs up, even among those of the same tribe. . . . Inequality of rank and fortune foster dissocial passions; witness pride in particular" (345). In this passage, at first glance little more than a conventional eighteenth-century indictment of luxury, Kames goes on to make it clear that he regards this state not merely as a regression, but also as a reversion to the most primitive stage of human society: "In the progress of manners, men end as they began; selfishness is no less eminent in the last and most polished state of society than in the first and most rude state" (401). This reversion to hoarding and selfishness, moreover, does not lead to a moral parity between the first and the last stages, for while the "selfishness" of savages is "rough, blunt, and undisguised," the selfishness of humans in "an opulent kingdom" is "smooth, refined, and covered with a veil" (414). Something very much like the Houyhnhnm master's argument thus reappears in Kames's theory of the development of human culture, and this theory, it seems clear, envisages a decline as well as an improvement.

That Kames's teleology should resemble the Houyhnhnm master's is not so paradoxical as it might initially seem, for both appear to be subscribing to an obscure tradition in which cultural history is seen as involving both progress and degeneration. A. O. Lovejoy and George Boas, citing Varro as an example, somewhat awkwardly characterize this tradition as a combination of "cultural primitivism" and "chronological anti-primitivism" (369). In tracing the sequence of the stages of culture, Varro places agriculture after hunting-gathering and pastoralism, yet he also regards the beginning of urban life as a degeneration: "not only is farming more ancient, it is also better; wherefore our ancestors with good reason sent their citizens from the town back to the land" (*De Re Rustica*, III, 1, 4).[23] Despite the fact that Varro, unlike Swift and Kames, does not identify the last stage with the earliest one, his argument reflects the kind of thinking that shaped their profoundly ambivalent conception of the historical process.

One final reason for supporting this interpretation of the Yahoos is afforded by Gulliver's encounter with thirty natives immediately after his departure from Houyhnhnmland. Even though Gulliver does not remain long enough to give a precise description of these natives, the fact that they possess fire and bows and arrows suggests that they belong to an advanced phase of hunting and gathering. In the light of the argument I have been advancing in this essay, Gulliver's comment that he would rather "trust" himself among these "Barbarians" than live among "*European Yahoos*" is a striking statement (285). It suggests, among other things, that Gulliver is distinguishing these "Barbarians" from the hated Yahoos. It also indicates that he is not thinking here of a general identification between the Yahoos and all mankind but rather the more specific linkage I have been suggesting, a linkage that, paradoxically, joins the most advanced stage of human culture to the most degenerate one.

NOTES

*An earlier version of this essay was delivered at the annual meeting of the Midwestern American Society for Eighteenth-Century Studies at Ohio State University in November, 1989. I am grateful to many members of the audience for their helpful questions and suggestions.

1 On this distinction, see my *Purity and Defilement in Gulliver's Travels* (London: Macmillan and New York: St. Martin's Press, 1987), 72-91.
2 "Gulliver's Fourth Voyage: 'Hard' and 'Soft' Schools of Literary Interpretation," in *Quick Springs of Sense: Studies in the Eighteenth Century*, ed. Larry Champion (Athens: Ohio University Press, 1974), 33-49.
3 *Swift and the Age of Compromise* (Lawrence: University of Kansas Press, 1958), 205.
4 *A Tale of a Tub, To which is added The Battle of the Books and the Mechanical Operation of the Spirit*, ed. A. C. Guthkelch and D. Nichol Smith, 2nd ed. (Oxford: Oxford University Press, 1958), 38, 96, 109, 125, 181, 184, 186.
5 *The Correspondence of Jonathan Swift*, ed. Harold Williams, 4 vols. (Oxford: Oxford University Press, 1963), 3:103.
6 *Swift: Poetical Works*, ed. Herbert Davis (London: Oxford University Press, 1967), 512.
7 For critical studies of the "conjectural histories" of the eighteenth century, see Sir Edward Evans-Pritchard, *A History of Anthropological Thought* (New York: Basic Books, 1981), 3-40; and George W. Stocking, Jr., *Victorian Anthropology* (New York: Free Press, 1987), 8-45. For an extensive selection of early anthropological excerpts, see *Readings in Early Anthropology*, ed. J. S. Slotkin (London: Aldine Publishing Company, 1965); hereafter cited as Slotkin.
8 Henry Home, Lord Kames, *Sketches of the History of Man*, 2nd ed., 4 vols (Edinburgh: Creech, and London: Strahan and Cadell, 1778).
9 Quoted from A. O. Lovejoy and George Boas, *Primitivism and Related Ideas in Classical Antiquity* (Baltimore: Johns Hopkins University Press, 1935), 369.
10 *Time and the Other: How Anthropology Makes Its Object* (New York: Columbia University Press, 1983), 3.
11 Robert A. Nisbet, *Social Change and History: Aspects of the Western Theory of Development* (New York: Oxford University Press, 1969), 193-94. See also John Linton Myers, "The Influence of Anthropology on the Course of Political Science," *University of California Publications in History* 4 (1916): 22-33. To these seventeenth-century examples may be added the extensive passage

dealing with cultural evolution from Juan Luis Vives, *On Education*, 1. 1, 2 (1531), in Slotkin, 49-52.
12 "Upon the Gardens of Epicurus," *Works*, 4 vols. (London: F. C. and J. Rivington, 1814), 3:203.
13 *Gulliver's Travels*, ed. Herbert Davis. Revised ed. (Oxford: Oxford University Press, 1959), 229.
14 *Irish Tracts: 1728-1733*, ed. Herbert Davis (Oxford: Oxford University Press, 1955), 175, 178.
15 "Swift's Yahoos and the Christian Symbols for Sin," *Journal of the History of Ideas* 15 (1954): 201-17.
16 Don Cameron Allen, *The Legends of Noah: Renaissance Rationalism in Art, Science, and Letters* (Champaign-Urbana: University of Illinois Press, 1963), 124.
17 Maximillian E. Novak, "The Wild Man Comes to Tea," *The Wild Man Within: An Image in Western Thought from the Renaissance to Romanticism*, ed. Edward Dudley and Maximillian E. Novak (Pittsburgh: University of Pittsburgh Press, 1972), 212.
18 "The Dismal Science in Houyhnhnmland," *Novel* 13 (1979): 49, 39.
19 See Xenophon of Ephesus, *Minor Works*, trans. J. S. Watson (London: G. Bell & Sons, 1888), 140.
20 *Outline of a Theory of Practice*, trans. Richard Nice (Cambridge: Cambridge University Press, 1977), 115.
21 John Wesley, *Sermons on Several Occasions*, 2 vols. (New York: B. Waugh and T. Mason for the Methodist Episcopal Church, 1833; orig. pub. 1760), 2: 122.
22 Kames, 343, 327-328. I am indebted to George W. Stocking, Jr., "Scotland as the Model of Mankind: Lord Kames' Philosophical View of Civilization," *Toward a Science of Man: Essays in the History of Anthropolgy*, ed. Timothy H. H. Thoresen (The Hague and Paris: Mouton, 1975), 78-79, for the original source of several of these citations.
23 See Marcus Terentius Varro, *On Farming*, trans. Lloyd Storr-Best (London: G. Bell & Sons, 1912), 241.

A Dance in the Mind: The Provincial Scottish Philosophical Societies

KATHLEEN HOLCOMB

The Enlightenment in Scotland is to a very great extent the product of the clubs and societies that attracted the energies and loyalties of men all over the country. In Edinburgh, especially, the societies can be seen as channeling the forces of the Enlightenment; the opinion of Lord Kames, that they "contributed greatly to the improvement and diffusion of literature and of science," was shared by the members of the Edinburgh philosophical clubs. The evolution of the Society for Improving Arts and Manufactures into the Philosophical Society of Edinburgh and finally into the Royal Society of Edinburgh emphasizes the active purpose of the clubs in the capital. Kames's biographer approvingly notes their goal: "the cultivation of every branch of science, erudition, and taste."[1]

The Edinburgh model is not altogether appropriate to other Scottish philosophical societies, however. There were such societies in Glasgow and Edinburgh, just as there were improving societies in those towns and in smaller ones. But the philosophical and the improving functions were kept separate; the philosophical societies were designed for speculation, not necessarily to produce social change or to improve arts, agriculture, or manufacture.

The provincial societies did share with the Edinburgh groups some characteristics listed by Roger Emerson: "They related their members to the European world of learning and certified them as citizens of the

Republic of Letters . . . A society like the Edinburgh Philosophical Society . . . provided Scots with an opportunity to contribute to European science and letters while retaining a sense of regional consciousness. Astronomical observations made in the north were useful, plants and animals were still to be discovered." But other characteristics noted by Emerson are less true of the Aberdeen and Glasgow groups. "The articulation of a Scottish viewpoint and the improvement of Scots' culture was an unstated purpose of most of the eighteenth-century Edinburgh clubs."[2] Life was improved in Aberdeen and Glasgow, certainly, and by the men who belonged to the Glasgow Literary Society and to the Aberdeen Philosophical Society—but that improvement can be traced to their personal commitment or to improving societies of which they were also members rather than directly to any design of the local philosophical societies. These were instead designed to produce thinking on natural philosophy, mental science, social science, as these could be understood universally or at least related to the larger European intellectual context. In the papers which survive, social questions are discussed in universal terms, with sparse reference to action and with rare reference to Scotland. Economic and demographic questions are placed in a European context, even when they begin as a consideration of Scottish issues. The provincial philosophical societies were not functional improving societies. They did not articulate a Scottish viewpoint. They gave no medals.

In Aberdeen, organizations related to the Enlightenment began long before the establishment of the Aberdeen Philosophical Society in 1758; a 1736 Philosophical Club enjoyed a brief existence; some discussions are recorded in Reid's papers. Perhaps a more important precursor was a Theological Club, founded in 1742 by George Campbell and a few other divinity students for their personal improvement as ministers. This group subsisted "a good many years"; Campbell "recommend[s] the practice of forming such small societies," noting that "when there is a proper choice of persons, an entire confidence in one another, and a real disposition to be mutually useful, it is one of the most powerful means of improvement that I know."[3] Campbell was one of the founders of the Philosophical Society, whose small size allowed the kind of intensely personal interaction Campbell preferred. Though the Theological Club developed a theory of discourse that Campbell incorporated in his work for the Philosophical Society and later in *The Philosophy of Rhetoric*, neither of these early societies had any major impact on culture in Aberdeen.

Aberdeen could hardly be classed a cultural backwater, however. For instance, its population of about 15,000 at mid-century could support a newspaper, several "friendly" societies, a Masonic lodge, and even a Musical Society supported by "gentleman amateurs." This group appears to have generated some smaller ones; David Skene, then a young physician, was a founding member (1760) of a Musicall Club that, according to its Institution, was to meet monthly with the purpose of "performing a Concert of Instrumental Music." Skene was also a founding member of a Physicall Club (1750), whose members read Dissertations "for their mutuall Improvement in their Profession." By mid-century, Aberdeen had supported "a continuous line of printer-publishers," the Aberdeen Infirmary and Robert Gordon's Hospital.[4] Perhaps because Aberdeen already had a variety of cultural institutions, the members of the Philosophical Society declined to make that body an improving one.

It is true that the members suggested topics related to improvement. Dr. John Gregory asks "What are the good & bad effects of the provisions for the poor by poors rates, infirmarys, hospitals & the like?" but whatever the answer, the debate could hardly have been as effective as Gregory himself was in promoting medical education and health care in Aberdeen. Gregory and Skene "attempted a College of Medicine in Aberdeen,"[5] Gregory lecturing students in pre-medicine, and Skene instructing young women in midwifery. This work did not have its origin in the considerations of the philosophical society.

Similarly, though many members of the society proposed questions about soil chemistry and fertility, the minutes show no attempts to do any actual work. What work was done toward agricultural progress was the province of the Gordon's Mill Farming Club, to which Thomas Reid and Thomas Gordon belonged. That organization investigated several different types of plows, for instance; Reid was charged with the development of a method of accountancy for the use of farmers, a project he submitted to the Club in 1761.[6] Skene, not a member of Gordon's Mill, was another agricultural improver, instructing Lord Kames in the design of moss dunghills.[7]

The Society heard a series of Questions on educational reform, but the practical work in education was being done in other contexts by Alexander Gerard, William Ogilvie and others of the professoriate (though this story is neither clear nor happy). In the practice of education, however, the Philosophical Society did have an effect. Direct evidence of a connection between the Philosophical Society work and the lectures of the King's and Marischal College members can be found. Reid's Optics lectures provide material for his discourse on seeing—or vice versa.[8] Gregory's Edinburgh medical lectures repeat material to be found in his discourses.[9] Gerard made important changes in his Pneumatology lectures between 1758 and 1768, specifically in the discussion of the function of genius, which his discourses were then examining.[10] And practical

James Dunbar refers his King's College classes to his own book, *Essays on the History of Mankind in Rude and Cultivated Ages*.[11]

It would be a distortion to deny that intellectual improvement resulted from the books which the members adapted from their discourses. Moral advancement is harder to assess, but if James Beattie can believed, the demolition of David Hume would have to be the most important single moral advance anyone could make, and he was of the opinion he had achieved it.[12] Reid, Campbell, Gerard, Gregory and Dunbar also published their work for the Society; Reid's and Campbell's had wide and lasting influence. All mention the encouragement to publish they received from the Society, but this was not the primary purpose of the Society.

An interest in science is frequently cited as one of the marks of the Scottish Enlightenment, and the Philosophical Society was certainly interested in science. Lewis Ulman counts 22 Questions on Natural Philosophy, second only to Moral Philosophy with 23.[13] Many members shared an interest in botany—Reid, Skene, Campbell, Ogilvie. The group's mathematicians were Stewart and Reid, who had worked their way through Newton's *Principia* as students. Important astronomy questions were proposed by Gordon, Robert Traill, and Reid. But though some were very competent scientists, and at least one did original work, that competence never had a wide audience and that work was never published; thus we cannot say the Society influenced science either by performance or by popularization, functions Steven Shapin claims for the Edinburgh society.[14] The Aberdeen group's most solid scientific effort was an attempt to observe and measure the transit of Venus predicted by Halley for June of 1761. Truly, here we see participation in the European world of learning. A Question (Question 3) by Robert Traill in 1758 brought to Aberdeen the global excitement over the expected transit. The mechanical astronomer James Ferguson published a pamphlet early in 1761 offering "A Plain Method of determining the Parallax of Venus by her Transit over the Sun: and from thence, by Analogy, the Parallax and Distance of the Sun, and all the rest of the Planets" (London, 1761). The Royal Society's *Philosophical Transactions* eagerly awaited reports from the field. On the morning of June 6, Reid and three or four members of the Society were on hand to make observations, like volunteer astronomers all over Europe.

Reid's report on the observations is very brief. Calculations had been made in advance; good equipment had been set up; but the morning was cloudy. The group was able to make only two observations of the planet as it crossed the sun. Nevertheless, from these Reid was able to derive some conclusions: either Halley's tables were incorrect or the maps which placed Aberdeen "seven minutes in time west of London" were.[15] The remarks that accompany the report are lengthy and technical. If the Society followed Reid's explanations, the quality of their astronomical and mathematical understanding was high.

It is possible that Reid had anticipated sending a report to the Royal Society. In the very bulky material gathered with the Transit of Venus paper are reports of observations made by European astronomers. These reports are taken from the *Aberdeen Magazine*, August 1761, which had reprinted them from the *London Magazine*. They appear as well in the *Philosophical Transactions*.[16] Reid's results were inconclusive, but not necessarily more so than some of the Royal Society's correspondents. The Aberdeen group's inconclusive results can be blamed on the weather, not on the quality of the design or of the experiment. Science in Aberdeen was capable of making its contribution to the international brotherhood. But the contribution was in fact not made. As will be shown later, the Glasgow Literary Society, or some of its members, was more persistent with its observations of the 1769 transit.

The disinclination to enter the public world of science was not Reid's alone. The same is true of the most original scientific work done for the Philosophical Society, David Skene's discourses on natural history. Skene's early biographer, Alexander Thomson of Banchory, is enthusiastic in his assessment: "Skene pursued the study of nature to an extent and with an accuracy previously unknown in Scotland; and . . . it is evident that his merits were thoroughly recognized by his contemporaries. . . . it is impossible to say how much science in Scotland may have been indebted to his personal exertions, and to the stimulus to inquiry which he gave to all with whom he associated or corresponded" (3).

Certainly Skene belongs to the international scientific brotherhood. He corresponded with European scientists, notably Linnaeus, who cited Skene as an authority on certain corallines, and with British naturalists.[17] Skene was very much interested in the fauna and flora of Northeast Scotland; he collected and classified fossils and botanical specimens and was sent specimens by others. The discourses on natural history are clear and interesting.[18] But he did not publish them, though he could have, despite Reid's friendly urging, "Can you find no time, either when you are laid up in the gout, or when the rest of the world is in good health, to bequeath something to posterity?"[19] Skene died early, without writing a book on coal, or on fossils, or on invertebrates, or on the fauna and flora of the north of Scotland.

If the audience for science requires a critical mass, as Shapin suggests,[20] we can suppose that the numbers in Aberdeen were simply not there. The science that the Society practiced could be formidable, but it had no impact outside the Society. A letter of James Beattie's (to his friend R. Arbuthnot? written about 1791?) offers a supplementary insight into the discontinuity between the Aberdeen Philosophical Society and its culture: "A club, with which I was formerly connected, once had thought of making up a firm for purchasing such new books as are not commonly found in publick libraries; and [one of the members] sketched out a plan (which was printed) for regulating the operations of the society. . . . There were in it so many precautions for preventing abuses, and so much about committees, balloting, &c that . . . . [t]he project of the library soon came to nothing: the theory being too refined and too complex to be applied to practice."[21]

Several circumstances operated to make the Glasgow Literary Society rather less refined and complex, though it had as little of the improving spirit as did the Aberdeen group. As in Aberdeen, the appearance of the Literary Society was preceded by other evidence of healthy intellectual life: the Political Science Club and the Foulises' printing establishment and Art Academy, for example. The university was readier to accept innovations and to respond to urban and commercial pressures.[22] The Society itself was different from the Aberdeen group. The membership was much larger and much more varied. It sent more of its members into the larger world of the European Enlightenment: Adam Smith, Joseph Black, William Cullen, the Foulises.[23] The audience for science was larger in Glasgow, partly because technological innovation was supported by the university. Certainly the second transit of Venus, which occurred in July 1769, generated more interest in Glasgow than its predecessor had in Aberdeen. This experiment was directed, not by Reid, but by Alexander Wilson, Professor of Astronomy. Technically it ought not to be credited to the Literary Society, as it seems not to have been officially noted by them and as Wilson had resigned his membership in 1765, but many members did take part. Indeed, the citizens of Glasgow could also make a claim for participation. The astronomer had advertised by newspaper, begging them to put out their fires the afternoon of the transit. "The politeness of the inhabitants of Glasgow, in complying with this request, was far greater than could well be expected, insomuch that there was not a spire of smoke to be perceived in that quarter from which the observations could be incommoded."[24] The audience for science in Glasgow must truly have been dependable. Wilson did request and obtain an invitation from the Literary Society to read his observations on a less spectacular astronomical event, sunspots.

If the audience for science was broader in Glasgow, it is true, also, that the Glasgow group was less removed from its national context than its Aberdeen counterpart. The Discourses and Questions listed in the parts of the Minutes still extant (Nov. 1764-May 1779, with long interruptions) are both more varied and more specific than those of Aberdeen. More are on law and commerce; more mention Scotland specifically, and more deal with matters of public policy. These include Reid's question on the warehousing of grain (January 30, 1778), its predecessor, John Millar's discourse on restraining the importation of grain (Nov. 28, 1777), an item by John Anderson, "What is the conduct proper to be observed by G. Britain with regard to the Colony of N. England" (November 11, 1769), one by Andrew Foulis, "In order to an equal representation of Property and People ought not the power to be taken from decayed Burghs and given to those which have increased" (April 28, 1769). But a large number could be treated only speculatively. Archibald Arthur read a series on beauty; James Moor several on the fine arts.[25]

The Literary Society was also able to fit itself into the life of the town. A former student of James Beattie's describes a meeting of the group which he apparently attended as a visitor: "The last point disputed was, Whether the repeal of the penal laws respecting Popery, would be attended with good, or bad consequences, to the kingdom in general? Dr. Reid maintained mildly, that the Repeal would be attended with no bad consequences. Mr. Anderson &c, that it would. — The Nat. Philosopher [Anderson] compared the Papists to a Rattle-Snake, harmless when kept under proper restraint: but dangerous like it, when at full liberty; and ready to diffuse a baleful poison around." Anderson's opinion was apparently shared by the clergy of the Synod, who proclaimed a public fast "principally on account of the apprehended growth of Popery."[26] The interchange recorded in this letter seems to have been typical. Unlike the Aberdeen society, the Glasgow group allowed participation by non-members. Although the structure of the meetings was designed to discourage heated debate, both Anderson and John Millar disputed with Reid. "The heat of these battles was, however, never allowed to rankle long . . . after the debates were concluded."[27]

Reid's Glasgow discourses have been rediscovered in the last few years. They do not reflect heated battles, although some of them are on topics that had generated such battles. For example, Reid offered his question "On the Warehousing of Grain" as a supplemental question, presumably in response to a discourse Millar had read a few weeks earlier and in the context of public debate. Several "Glasgow Theorists" (Sir James Steuert's phrase) had published pamphlets on the topic, prompting an irritated letter from the political economist. Reid's paper is very similar in matter and structure to a treatment of the subject in Adam Smith's *Wealth of Nations* to which Steuert objected;[28] additionally, both Smith and Reid are less polemical and less hysterical than most Corn Law pamphleteers. The topic later became urgent when the famine worsened, but Reid's paper is more speculative than practical.

The speculative bias permeates other apparently topical questions on issues such as interest rates and recoinage. Even the French Revolution is treated abstractly in Reid's Literary Society work, though it is known that he was deeply committed to the Revolution, especially when it was young. Millar, who could never have been accused of neutrality on this subject, would have taken almost an identical stand.[29] The members of the Literary Society apparently did not regard their group as a forum for comment on the Revolution.

Certainly Revolutionary sentiment in Glasgow before 1792 was well known; the Beattie letter cited above continues: "I am told that republican (I should rather say *levelling*) principles are very prevalent in the College of Glasgow."[30] Several of Reid's colleagues in the Society, notably Millar and Anderson, were active in support of the Revolution, even when such support became unpopular.[31] Reid had been an active supporter at least through 1791. A letter from that year illustrates the depth of his commitment: "I have been very long persuaded, that a Nation, to be free, needs onely to know the Rights of Man. I have lived to see this Knowledge spread far beyond my most sanguine hopes, and produce glorious Effects. God grant it may spread more and more & that those who taste the Sweets of Liberty may not turn giddy but make a wise and sober Use of it." Reid remarks that some persons mistakenly associate admiration for the French Revolution with an aversion to the British constitution, but denies this is his case. To show his good faith, he reports, he has allowed his name to be used in an advertisement for a meeting of Friends of the French Revolution, and has received a vicious anonymous letter as a consequence. "[D]o you think it more odd that an old deaf Dotard should be announced as a Stewart of such a Meeting, or that it should give any Man such offense."[32]

Whatever his motives, the "old deaf Dotard" is assumed to have come to dissociate himself from the movement toward which he had earlier extended his praise. Reid ended his career in practical politics with one of his last discourses to the Literary Society, "Some Thoughts on the Utopian System," read 28 November 1794. An excerpt from it was printed in the *Glasgow Courier* after his death, with the title "On the Danger of Political Innovation." It has usually been interpreted as a retraction of Reid's former views on the French Revolution as events became bloodier and as professors came more and more under attack for their "whiggish treason."[33]

The *Courier* excerpt is, however, disproportionately topical. By far the greater part of Reid's discourse has as its purpose the abstract consideration "of that form of political Society which seems to be best adapted to the Improvement and Happiness of Man." Admitting that the point is speculative, Reid defends his method:

> I answer that Speculative points ought not to be excluded from the Circle of human knowledge. They tend to enlarge our Conceptions & to strengthen our Faculties. Speculation has a like Effect with regard to our intellectual powers as bodily Exercises have, with regard to the health strength and agility of the Body. Besides, when political Discussions have come to be so much in fashion among all Ranks, it may perhaps be as profitable to most men, to employ their thoughts upon what is merely speculative, as upon what may influence their practice.[34]

Speculative discourse, then, can be as valuable as urgent calls to action, especially when those calls become shrill. Such discourse offers a chance to consider theoretical issues aside from practical considerations and must not be discounted.

The philosophical societies in Glasgow and Aberdeen excelled in such speculation, and their members valued the advantages it gave to their other activities. The leading members of the provincial societies wrote books that were both popular and permanently influential. They taught students who developed their ideas. They were involved in the rage for improvement that probed governments and plows. But they did these things as actors in other contexts, because they were civic humanists or owners of farms or passionate believers in the Rights of Man. Their membership in philosophical clubs was a matter of character, not action.

Much earlier, in Aberdeen, Reid had prepared a question for the Society: "On what does the character of men depend?" Almost as an aside, he described the phenomenon to which the philosophical clubs owed their existence:

> Discourse or Disputation upon any Subject, quickens all the faculties for canvassing it farther. It does as it were muster all the furniture of the [mind] upon that Subject. So that the Ideas that before came Slowly & with Difficulty to present themselves to the Memory Imagination or Reason, do now readily offer themselves. It is as if a Variety of Ideas related to the Subject which formerly lay still in the Mind perhaps covered with the dust of Oblivion, by discoursing earnestly or hear[ing] with fixt attention a discours upon any Subject were called up and set into a kind of Dance in the Mind.[35]

There were meetings of the Friends of the French Revolution throughout Europe and meetings of the Friends of the People throughout Scotland.

Agricultural improvement, technical innovations, economic transformations were exciting and concrete; such achievements must not be denied. But what produced much of the distinctive work of the Scottish Enlightenment was the speculative thinking in the meetings of provincial philosophical societies, thinking that had no immediate purpose but to clear a space for the dance in the mind.

NOTES

I am grateful to Aberdeen University Library (hereafter cited as AUL) for permission to quote from manuscripts in their care.

1 [Alexander Fraser Tytler, Lord Woodhouselee], *Memoirs of the Life and Writings of the Honourable Henry Home of Kames*, 2 vols. (Edinburgh: William Creech; and London: T. Cadell and W. Davies, 1807), 1:175 and 1:185 n.
2 Roger Emerson, "The Enlightenment and Social Structures," in *City and Society in the Eighteenth Century,* ed. Paul Fritz and David Williams (Toronto: University of Toronto Press, 1973), 120-21.
3 Thomas Reid, Aberdeen University Library MS. 2131/6/I/17 and a few others; George Skene Keith, "Some Account of the Life and Writings of the Author," in *Lectures on Ecclesiastical History by George Campbell,* 2 vols. (London: J. Johnson; and Aberdeen: A. Brown, 1800), 1: viii-ix; Campbell, *Lectures on Systematic Theology and Pulpit Eloquence* (London: Cadell and Davies, 1807), 348.
4 William Kennedy, *Annals of Aberdeen, from the Reign of King William the Lion, to the End of the Year 1818; with an Account of the City, Cathedral, and University of Old Aberdeen* (Aberdeen: A. Brown and Co.; Edinburgh: W. Blackwood; London: Longman, Hurst, Rees, Orme, and Brown, 1818), 2: 171-72 and 2:121; David Skene papers, A U L MS. 37; R. H. Carnie, "Scholar-Printers of the Scottish Enlightenment, 1740-1800," in *Aberdeen and the Enlightenment,* ed. Jennifer J. Carter and Joan H. Pittock (Aberdeen: Aberdeen University Press, 1987), 304; Kennedy, *Annals,* 2:146, 141.
5 Question 50, Minutes of the Philosophical Society of Aberdeen, A U L MS. 539/1,2; A U L MS. 3107/26.
6 J. H. Smith, *The Gordon's Mill Farming Club, 1758-1764,* Aberdeen University Studies No. 145 (Edinburgh: Oliver and Boyd, 1962); Minutes of the Gordon's Mill Farming Club, A U L MS. 49; Reid, A Short System of Book-Keeping, A U L MS. 2341.
7 Alexander Thomson, *Biographical Sketch of David Skene, M. D., of Aberdeen* (Edinburgh: Neill and Company, 1859), 10. Skene's letter to Kames is in A U L MS. 38 (19 Nov. 1766).
8 Reid A U L MS. K. 160; Thomas Gordon A U L MS. 3061/1/1.

9 John Gregory, *Observations on the Duties and Offices of a Physician; and on the Method of Prosecuting Enquiries in Philosophy* (London: Strahan & Cadell, 1770); Gordon A U L MS. 3061/1/4.

10 Gerard, Lectures A U L MS. M. 2052, and MS. Dc. 5.61-62, Edinburgh University Library; Gordon A U L MS. 3061/1/3.

11 A U L MS. 3107/5/2/6.

12 James Beattie, "On the Nature and Immutability of Truth . . .," in *Essays* (Edinburgh: William Creech, 1776). See especially Beattie's Preface.

13 Lewis Ulman kindly allowed me to use the draft of his edition of the Aberdeen Philosophical Society minute book. *The Minutes of the Aberdeen Philosophical Society*, ed. H. Lewis Ulman. (Aberdeen: Aberdeen University Press, 1990).

14 Steven Shapin, "The Audience for Science in Eighteenth Century Edinburgh," *History of Science* 12 (1974): 95-121.

15 A U L MS. 2131/2/1/7. Reid had made "a good many observations" of the latitude of Old Aberdeen (2131/7/III/12). He is inclined to assume that Halley's tables might be slightly inaccurate and mentions that the 1769 transit would enable astronomers to determine this with greater certainty.

16 See especially 52 (1761-62): 173-257. Reports were read to the Royal Society as early as June 11, five days after the transit.

17 Thomson, 8.

18 A U L MS. 37 includes most of these discourses.

19 Reid to Skene, July, 1770. Many of Reid's letters are published by Sir William Hamilton, ed., in *The Works of Thomas Reid*, 8th ed., 2 vols. (Edinburgh: MacLachan and Stewart, 1880).

20 Shapin, 96-98.

21 Beattie to (?) R. Arbuthnot (?) 1791, A U L MS. 30/1/330. Conjectural identification by compiler of AUL summary list for the Beattie collection (MS. 30).

22 See Emerson, 112-13.

23 "Notices and Documents Illustrative of the Literary History of Glasgow During the Greater Part of the Last Century," presented to the President and Members of the Maitland Club by Richard Duncan (Glasgow, 1831), lists the members of the club and occasionally their professions.

24 Alexander Wilson, "Observations . . .," *Philosophical Transactions* (1769), 333-37.

25 Records of the Literary Society of Glasgow. National Library of Scotland MS/245/73, National Library of Scotland. The original (not contemporary) of this manuscript is held in the Procurators' Library. Robert and Andrew Foulis's discourses and questions are listed in the Maitland Club publication, 134-35; James Moor's on p. 131. Archibald Arthur's *Discourses* were edited by William Richardson (Glasgow: J. & J. Scrymgeour, 1803).

26 Alexander Peters to Beattie, December 8, 1778. A U L MS. 30/2/322. I am grateful to Dr. Dorothy Johnston for pointing out this letter to me.

27 W. C. Lehmann, *John Millar of Glasgow 1735-1801: His Life and Thought*

and his Contributions to Sociological Analysis (Cambridge: Cambridge University Press, 1960), 53.

28 Sir James Steuart, *An Inquiry into the Principles of Political Oeconomy,* 2 vols., ed. and intro. Andrew S. Skinner (Edinburgh and London: Oliver and Boyd, 1966), Appendix; Adam Smith, *An Inquiry into the Nature and Causes of the Wealth of Nations*, 2 vols. (London: W. Strahan and T. Cadell, 1776). "Digression concerning the Corn Trade and Corn Laws," 2:105-130.

29 Lehmann, 54 n.

30 A U L MS. 30/I/330.

31 Lehmann, 54; H. W. Meikle, *Scotland and the French Revolution* (Glasgow: James Maclehose and Sons, 1912), 155-56.

32 A U L MS. 2131/3/III/8.

33 See Meikle, 156; A. Campbell Fraser, *Thomas Reid* (Oliphant Anderson & Ferrier, Edinburgh & London, 1898), 115; Lehmann, 54.

34 "On the Utopian System," A U L MS. 3061/6, p. 6.

35 A U L MS. 2131/6/IV/2.

"See Locke on Government": *The* Two Treatises *and the American Revolution*

STEVEN M. DWORETZ

Had the Tercentenary celebration of the publication of John Locke's *Two Treatises of Government* occurred in the first half of this century, a discussion of the reception of the *Two Treatises* in eighteenth-century America would have been brief indeed. One could simply cite Merle Curti's discussion of "the Great Mr. Locke, America's Philosopher"; or Vernon Parrington's adoption of Locke's *Second Treatise* as "the textbook of the American Revolution," or John C. Miller's assertion that the political thought of the American Revolution could be summarized as "an exegesis upon Locke," whose *Second Treatise* served as the Revolutionists' " 'party line.' " In sum, the prevailing scholarly consensus suggested that we needn't go beyond the *Second Treatise* in order to understand American Revolutionary thought.[1]

If, however, the Tercentenary had occurred sometime after 1970, a discussion of the reception of the *Two Treatises* in eighteenth-century America would have been equally brief—not because of Locke's unchallenged importance, but because of his irrelevance (or worse) in the American Revolutionary context. Scholars like Bernard Bailyn and J. G. A. Pocock had transformed the historiographic landscape.[2] Once again you could capture the essence of the (new) prevailing scholarly consensus with a few judicious citations: for example, Stanley Katz, who insisted that Locke had been "a negligible influence upon American political

101

thought before 1776"; or John Dunn, who declared that "in few cases" could the Revolution "possibly have been thought to have been in any sense about the Two Treatises of Government of John Locke."[3]

Indeed, by 1975 the interpretation of the role of Lockean ideas in the development of American Revolutionary thought had shifted 180 degees from Miller to Pocock. Miller called Locke "the guide and prophet" of the Revolution; his *Second Treatise* furnished " 'the principles of 1776.' " Pocock, however, helped to redefine Revolutionary thought in terms of an anti-liberal, "republican," or "civic humanist," tradition. He argued that Locke "does not contribute directly" to that tradition and even suggested that we should "allot [Locke] a place, and debate its magnitude, among that tradition's adversaries." In what must surely represent the most dramatic reversal of fortunes in the history of political thought, the "guide and prophet" of the Revolution had thus become the Revolution's foremost ideological nemesis (Miller, 170-71; Pocock, 424).

I have written elsewhere about this historiographic revolution and the historical and theoretical relationship between Locke's political theory and American Revolutionary thought.[4] In the present essay, I shall concentrate on the *Second Treatise* in the Revolution. In general, the writings from the Revolution—pamphlets, broadsides, newspapers, sermons, official documents, etc.—do not support the revisionists' claims of historical hostility to Locke and reverence for civic republicanism.[5] Consider the most crucial topics of Revolutionary discourse: religious liberty, taxation, consent, the limits of civil authority per se, the right and duty of revolution, the ultimate sovereignty of the people. When the Revolutionists discussed these issues, they consistently framed their arguments in the language and theory of "Locke on Government" (as they called the *Second Treatise*). These were Lockean issues, and the Revolutionists took Lockean positions on them. Indeed, from 1760 to 1776, from pulpit to pamphlet, the Revolutionists cited (and otherwise employed) Locke far more frequently than any other non-Biblical source. The sources of American republicanism, on the other hand, did not even come close to Locke in this regard.

How then did the revisionist position gain any credence? Primarily, as we shall see, by means of specific—and problematic—interpretations of political theory. In some cases these interpretations cannot withstand close analyses of the relevant texts; at other times, they are historically inappropriate for the period under investigation. For example, the exclusion of Lockean liberalism from American Revolutionary thought depended theoretically upon a hostile interpretation of Locke, seeing his liberalism at its worst, as "possessive individualism" and the corrupt apology for the "spirit of capitalism." This is the Locke who emerges from the curiously convergent interpretations of C. B. Macpherson (from the left) and Leo Strauss (from the right).[6] It is this "bourgeois Locke" — the Locke who is associated exclusively with "commerce" — who plays the ideological villain in Pocock's paradigmatic reinterpretation of eighteenth-century Anglo-American political thought as the struggle between other-regarding virtue (civic republicanism) and self-regarding commerce (Lockean liberalism). The revisionists, moreover, do not consider the highly controversial status of this interpretation among Locke scholars. They seem to take it for granted, without pausing to consider 1) alternative interpretations of Locke, or 2) the possibility that twentieth-century scholars troubled by the consequences of three hundred years of capitalism and eighteenth-century colonists interested in revolution might not read and interpret Locke's seventeenth-century text in the same way. In judging the role of the text in the American Revolution, it is the reading of the revolutionaries that is relevant, even if it were shown to be erroneous. But by and large, the revisionists have not sought to identify that reading.[7]

If the revisionists' reading of Locke has been uncritically hostile, their reading of the textual sources of American republicanism has often been equally uncritical, or unrigorous, though far from hostile. *Cato's Letters*, the acknowledged primary textual source of American republicanism, has been presumed to express ideals rooted in the ancient polis, but it reads more like a prospectus for *Leviathan*. Cato, the virtuous alternative to Locke, allegedly believes "that all men are naturally good and that citizens became restless only when oppressed."[8] The textual Cato, however, insists that "the making of laws supposes all men naturally wicked."[9] Virtue is a nice ideal, especially appealing to our contemporaries, both of the left and of the right, who are troubled by the commercial egoism of modern American culture. But it is insufficient for Cato: in the text that is said to have been "of the utmost importance in the creation of American republicanism" (Shalhope, 58),[10] only "fear and selfish considerations can keep men within any reasonable bounds" (Letter 75, 3:76). As with Hobbes, civil society depends upon "the terror of the laws" (Letter 40, 2:54).

The revisionists have tended to treat republicanism itself uncritically, indeed reverently. The purifying doctrine of communitarian virtue promised historiographic redemption of what John Patrick Diggins has so aptly called "the lost soul of American politics"[11] from the hedonistic clutches of liberalism. Yet American republicanism has its dark side, about which its contemporary proponents have thus far been largely silent. The conflict relevant to American republicanism is not between virtue and commerce, but between virtue and liberty. Indeed, Judith N.

Shklar has pointed to a serious "threat to personal freedom and justice" in republicanism's "emphasis on martial discipline, social cohesion, political agreement, and conformity as requirements for public policy."[12] Pocock himself respects the hazards of virtue. In the penultimate paragaph of *The Machiavellian Moment*, after having elevated "Machiavelli at the expense of Locke" in the American founding doctrine, he warns that "the ideal of virtue is highly compulsive" and thus hostile to individual liberty.[13] This warning, however, seems to have been missed by scholars whose hostility to Lockean liberalism, as they understood it, left them vulnerable to Machiavellian temptation.

In sum, the revisionists purged Locke from the doctrine of the American Revolution, thus rewriting a chapter in the history of political thought, in part by failing to take political theory seriously. Introduce the interpretative discipline of political theory, however, and the impressive structure of the republican revision appears to rest precariously upon a questionable, hostile interpretation of Locke's political theory and some wishful thinking about the principal source of American republicanism. It reveals also a tendency, perhaps unconscious, to seek historical legitimacy for contemporary policies and programs in the founding political ideology, a tendency that makes the interpretation of American Revolutionary thought more than merely an antiquarian concern. For if, as I believe, Locke's liberalism, properly understood, is the only political philosophy to justify and *require* — as an *integral* (and not merely ad hoc) component of a comprehensive world-view — limited government, religious toleration, and resistance to tyranny, then a founding doctrine without Locke cannot serve as a source of legitimacy for liberty in the present. Whether or not that interpretation is accepted, however, it is obvious that we cannot understand the political ideology of the American Revolutionists without understanding how they understood "Locke on Government," the source they identify as most significant for their writings.

In the remainder of this essay, I shall try to show exactly how Locke's political theory informed the Revolutionary argument, especially the way the *Second Treatise* was used in the secular writings of the American Revolutionists. Many important aspects of Locke's philosophy were widely known and highly esteemed in North America for decades prior to the Revolution, however.[14] The New England clergy, in particular, began the ideological preparation of the people well before the "long train of abuses" began to unfold. The ministers had read, understood, and sympathized with Locke; and they had been preaching the fundamentals of Lockean political theory for many years before Parliament tried its hand at tax reform.[15] As Clinton Rossiter put it, the New England ministers, who "gave the first and most cordial reception" to Locke's arguments, regularly fed their congregations "doses" of Locke's political theory in a "scriptural spoon" (53, 237). I believe we can trace the ministers' striking propensity to cite "Locke on Government" not merely to the circumstantial utility of Locke's argument, but also to their philosophical affinity for the theistic world-view in which that argument is integrally embedded. I call that Lockean world-view "theistic liberalism"—as distinguished from "bourgeois liberalism"—and I believe it emerges from their careful study of Locke's writings on politics, epistemology, toleration, and religion. "Locke rode into New England on the backs of Moses and the Prophets" (Rossiter, 40), and not as a venture capitalist.

As we turn to the role of the *Second Treatise* in the Revolutionary argument and in the "secular" literature, we shall continue to note the conspicuous absence of the bourgeois Locke from the discourse. Chapter Five ("Of Property") of the *Second Treatise* is the *locus classicus* of possessive individualism, the stronghold of the bourgeois Locke. Yet I have found only two citations of Chapter Five in the American writings, secular or clerical, and only one of these (*Boston Evening Post*, #764, April 2, 1750) was correct in its citation. John Lathrop, a minister, quoted Locke in a sermon, also citing "Locke on Government, Chapter Five" as the source. But the transcribed passage was actually from Chapter Eleven ("Of the Extent of the Legislative Power").[16] So the bourgeois Locke did not inform the Revolutionary argument. The sections of the *Second Treatise* most often cited, quoted (with or without quotation marks or attribution), or very closely paraphrased in the Revolutionary writings dealt instead with the extent of legislative power, the difference between tyrants and magistrates, the right, duty, and competence of the people to judge the conduct of government, and the dissolution of government and consequent reversion of sovereignty to the people. The Revolutionists appealed to Locke as an authority on constitutional politics and revolution.

This was true even though they frequently argued about property itself—or, more precisely, about the "inseparable" issues of "liberty and property." As the Reverend Gad Hitchcock warned in 1774, "Our contention is not about trifles, but about liberty and property."[17] Or as the Reverend William Gordon put it later that year, "It is not conquest, but liberty and property that are at stake!"[18] But the issue in dispute was not the right of the subject to appropriate from nature, but the right of the government to expropriate the subject. Accordingly, the Revolutionists did not call upon the bourgeois Locke to justify unlimited appropriation; they used Locke's political theory to define the inherent moral limits of civil authority with respect to liberty (civil as well as religious) *and* property, and to justify armed resistance and revolution when government exceeds, or threatens to exceed, those limits. Republican ideology, we should note, could not furnish effective theoretical shelter against Parliament's assault upon the liberty and property of the colonists or, for that matter, against the dangerous principle of illimitable Parliamentary sovereignty upon which the Stamp Act and other revenue policies were explicitly based. To defend liberty and property, then, the opposition to Parliament turned to Locke, not to Cato.

Indeed, by 1747 "Locke on Government" was already being cited to justify organized and even violent political protest in disputes over liberty and property. In East New Jersey, "land-rioters," known also as the "Jerseymen," challenged the power of the large proprietors who had benefitted from the contradictory seventeenth-century grants issued by the Stuart regime. The Jerseymen assembled a large, well-armed, organized movement whose activities included a serious attempt to establish a "counter-government." When charged by their adversaries with "libel," "sedition," and "inbred malice to authority," the Jerseymen (who were hardly anarchists) sought theoretical legitimacy in "Locke on Government." In a lengthy written justification for their actions, they explicitly invoked the authority of Locke on the relationship between property and government; to drive the point home, they transcribed verbatim twenty-five lines from sections 138 and 139 of Chapter Eleven ("Of the Extent of the Legislative Power") of the *Second Treatise*.[19]

Appeals to Locke are fundamental not only in particular cases, but in the entire case against the British Parliament's tax initiatives. The offensive "innovations" (as John Dickinson called them) in England's colonial policy began in 1763, taking the initial form of Parliamentary measures "for the purpose of raising a revenue" in the colonies.[20] These measures amounted to an assault on liberty and property because they disrupted a special relationship between taxation and consent, a relationship that for a century had been institutionalized in colonial politics through the mechanism of representation. Basically, the political equation looked like this: Liberty and property are inseparable; one cannot be sustained without the other. Consent, moreover, is the *sine qua non* of property; if you do not control the disposal of an object by granting or withholding consent, it is not your property in the first place. In a large political community, however, where the population is dispersed over extensive territory, representation becomes the necessary institutional mechanism for registering consent. Without representation, then, there is no consent and, therefore, no liberty and no property.

By 1764, "no taxation without representation" had been a fact of political life in the colonies for nearly one hundred years.[21] The sovereignty of the colonial legislatures rested upon their monopoly on the power to tax. But the new revenue policy changed all that; it involved the imposition of taxes upon the colonists by a distant legislative body in which they were not, and practically could not be, represented. This threatened an existing condition of self-government, in which the colonists actually enjoyed the "essential British right that no person shall be subject to any tax but what in person or by his representative he hath a voice in laying."[22] It also directly challenged the authority of the colonial political establishments. The revenue measures (particularly the Stamp Act, which affected the press) thus roused the British colonies in North America from the long slumber of "salutary neglect" and occasioned the first concerted political challenge to the authority of Parliament.

In Revolutionary political thought, the term "property" denoted a relationship between an individual and some object, not the object itself. That is, X becomes my property — or, I have property in X — if and only if I alone control the disposal of X. This control over the disposal of X can be called my liberty (or right) to dispose of X as I please, and in this sense liberty itself is involved in the definition of property. The right of disposal constitutes the defining condition of property and, indeed, the "substance of liberty." By 1767, this was said to have "fled to a distant country."[23]

The colonists and English politicians who opposed Parliament's "innovations" in revenue policy established their arguments on this conception of property. Property, as such, necessarily implied an "exclusive right of disposal. Property without this is but an insignificant name."[24] And here, at the very foundation of the central argument in Revolutionary polemics, the opposition adopted Locke's distinctive language and appealed directly and explicitly to his authority. At the very least, the Revolutionists used the language that Locke himself had used, in order to make arguments that were essentially consistent with the arguments in the *Second Treatise*.

John Dickinson, in his celebrated *Letters from a Farmer*, borrowed "the words of Mr. Locke" from section 140 of the *Second Treatise* to ask the question that had captured the political attention of the colonists: "What property have they in that which another may, by right, take when he pleases to himself?" (Letter 7, 35). "Hampden," in one of his broadsides, asked precisely this question, attributing it to "Mr. Locke."[25] "A Virginian" repeated the question, verbatim, in a letter to the *Pennsylvania Gazette* (Postscript to #2075, September 29, 1768); he also quoted the opening lines from section 138 of the *Second Treatise*. The same question (in quotation marks, but unattributed) opens an important official communication from The Sons of Liberty of New York.[26] William Hicks quoted these words from "Locke on Government" in his pamphlet, *On the Nature and Extent of Parliamentary Power*,[27] as did John Lathrop in a sermon preached nearly ten years later, in 1774 (cited above). And in a speech that was reprinted in several colonial newspapers, Charles Pratt, First Baron Camden, read these (and other) "words of that consummate reasoner and politician, Mr. Locke," before the House of Lords to support the colonists in their opposition to Parliamentary taxation.[28] The Revolutionists and their friends also favored Section 138 of the *Second Treatise* because it, too, went straight to the heart of the matter. This section begins with Locke's insistence that "the supreme power cannot take from any man any part of his property without his own consent." And it includes the statement that "no body hath a right to take their substance or any part of it from them, without their own consent; without this, they have no property at all. For I have truly no property in that which another can by right take from me, when he pleases, against my consent."

Other lines from this section found their way into an issue of the openly seditious, widely circulated *Massachusetts Spy* (#41, December 12, 1771); a footnote directed readers to "Locke on Government." The manifesto that marked the establishment of the Boston Committee of Correspondence in 1772 also included an exact transcription of lines from section 138. Recognizing this (and other) evidence of what I call the Lockean connection in that important historical document requires close familiarity with the *Second Treatise* itself, however, since the author(s) neither cite Locke nor enclose the transcribed passage in quotation marks.[29]

Another writer in the *Massachusetts Spy* (#217, March 39, 1775), who signed his work "From the County of Hampshire," praised the "immortal Mr. Locke" and then transcribed the first seventeen lines of section 138, calling them "lines which ought to be written in letters of gold and sunk to the center of every man's heart."[30] John Allen, in a pamphlet entitled *The American Alarm* (Boston, 1773), closely paraphrased this passage from "the great Mr. Locke" (32, 8). And Camden, America's champion at Westminster, in the speech of March 7, 1766, already cited, reminded the Peers of the essential limits of the legislative power by reading aloud the first two lines of this section during the debate on the Declaratory Act.

An observer of this historic debate recorded Lord Mansfield's reply to Camden. Mansfield forcefully asserted Parliament's right to tax the colonies. "As to Mr. Locke," he argued, "though he had said that money could not be raised in a free government without your own consent, yet it was no more than a general proposition never intended to extend to all particular circumstances whatever."[31] But this obviously interested interpretation notwithstanding, Locke certainly intended for his general proposition to extend to, and even to define, "free government" as such. In fact, he presented it as a moral limitation on "the legislative power of *every* commonwealth, in *all* forms of government" (section 142, emphasis added). As for particular circumstances, Camden also reminded the Lords that Locke's proposition was "drawn from the heart of *our* constitution, which he thoroughly understood" (emphasis added).

Both Camden and the Declaratory Act that he opposed figure prominently in our story. The latter, which I shall consider later in this essay, is especially important, since it lay at the heart of the constitutional issue that had come between the colonies and the mother-country after 1764, namely, defining the limits of the legislative authority. Camden himself, according to Samuel Adams, thoroughly understood the Lockean nature of that issue. In a letter to Camden in 1768, Adams praised him for his "great knowledge of the constitution and the law of nature, of the extent of parliamentary authority and the rights of British subjects."[32] Camden had furnished plenty of evidence of this knowledge in his eloquent speeches on behalf of the colonists. Speaking for the first time before the House of Lords on February 3, 1766, Camden cited Locke and issued this warning: "The sovereign authority, the omnipotence of the legislature, my lords, is a favorable doctrine, but there are some things they cannot do."[33]

This may be the most concise statement of the constitutional principle in the writings from the American Revolution. It prompted Randolph G. Adams, writing in 1922, to describe Camden as "one Englishman who had read his Locke . . . and who seems almost like a voice crying in the wilderness of parliamentary sovereignty and supremacy" (144). Ernest Barker, too, called Camden "a solitary figure in England, however much his view," which "corroborated" Locke's, "might be acclaimed across the Atlantic."[34] And Van Tyne noted that "men who thought with Lord Camden . . . were in the minority in England, while those who agreed with [Samuel] Adams were in the majority in America," that is, presumably in their interpretation of Locke as well as in their general politics.[35] In short, Locke's political theory was apparently more highly esteemed and indeed more relevant in Revolutionary America than in his native land.

Specifically, the colonists' conception of property, which we have already examined, was distinctively Lockean insofar as it essentially contained the notion of consent. Locke himself had propounded this notion of the relationship between property and consent in section 139 of the *Second Treatise*: "The prince or senate . . . can never have a power to take to themselves the whole or any part of the subjects' *property*, without their own consent. For this would be in effect to leave them with no *property* at all." Locke reaffirmed his position in section 193, where he held it to be in the nature of property that "without a man's own consent, it cannot be taken from him." Transposing this formulation into the American Revolutionary context, Joseph Warren of Boston asked how the colonists in North America could "be said to have property" if the British government could, whenever it pleased, take all or any part of it from them "without even asking their consent?"[36] Consent thus provided the only legitimating connection between taxation and property. Parliament, however, severed that connection when it enacted the new revenue measures. As the Connecticut House of Representatives complained in its Resolves of 1765, "The consent of the inhabitants of this colony was not given to the said Act of Parliament."[37] In its petition to the King, the Stamp Act Congress objected to "statutes by which your Majesty's Commons in Britain undertake absolutely to dispose of the property of their fellow subjects in America without their consent."[38] And in Parliament itself, Lord Chatham (Pitt the elder) demanded that "the sacredness" of the colonists' property "remain inviolable" and "taxable only by their own consent, given in their provincial assemblies; else it will cease to be property."[39]

We should not underestimate the significance of consent in the colonists' argument. "The consent of the people is the only foundation" of civil government; "therefore, every act of government . . . against or without the consent of the people is injustice, usurpation, and tyranny." Thus spoke the Massachusetts General Court (in words attributed to John Adams) in January, 1776, in a proclamation that was read aloud in churches, courts, town halls, and taverns throughout the Commonwealth.[40]

Not only did property require consent: the person without property was nothing more than a slave. Property was "inconsistent" with slavery — at least one colonial writer actually quoted Locke on this point.[41] Locke himself had described the person who was "not capable of property" as "being in the *state of slavery*" (*Second Treatise*, sections 85 and 192). And for the colonists, "liberty, which distinguishes a free man from a slave, implies some sort of right and/or property of his own, which cannot be taken from him without his consent."[42] Consent creates, or at least preserves, property, and thus stands between liberty and slavery. A government that takes an individual's property without his consent "commits a robbery" and "destroys the distinction between liberty and slavery."[43] As John Tucker put it, in an election sermon, liberty demands that "no man shall have his property taken from him, but by his own consent." Otherwise, Tucker asked, citing "Locke on Government," "what is he . . . but a perfect slave?"[44]

With this in mind, we should be careful not to misconstrue an early and representative description of the Stamp Act as "that mark of slavery" as simply a piece of rhetorical hyperbole, or as a literary manifestation of some generalized paranoia that was distorting the colonists' political perception.[45] From the Lockean theoretical perspective of the colonial opposition, this described precisely the inescapable consequences of Parliament's revenue initiative. Silas Downer, a Rhode Island Son of Liberty, eloquently summarized the distinctively Lockean position: "The common people of Great Britain very liberally give and grant away the property of the Americans without their consent, which if yielded to, must fix us in the lowest bottom of slavery; for if they can take away one penny from us against our wills, they can take all. If they have such power over our property, they must have a proportional power over our persons; . . . hence . . . they can take away our lives whensoever it shall be agreeable to their sovereign wills and pleasure."[46] Without respect for the principle of consent, liberty would give way to slavery and life itself would be insecure. Parliament's "innovations" in revenue policy thus struck directly at the indivisible Lockean triad of life, liberty, and property (estate).

From here we can put the issue of representation into perspective. The familiarity of the slogan "no taxation without representation" suggests that this was the focus of Revolutionary agitation. Representation was undeniably important (especially to the representatives in the colonial legislatures). In Revolutionary political theory, however, representation was merely the institutional mechanism through which the people could register their consent to the taxes they were expected to pay. As such, it did not enjoy the status of a first principle. The Massachusetts House of Representatives clearly recognized the *derivative* nature of the right of representation while upholding the *fundamental* principle of consent in its Resolves of 1765: "No man can justly take the property of another without his consent . . . . Upon this *original* principle, the right of representation in the same body which exercises the power of making laws for levying taxes . . . is evidently founded." Thus when the House spoke of "certain essential Rights . . . which are founded in the Law of God and Nature, and are the common Rights of Mankind," this meant, in the first place, the "inherent" right to consent to the disposal of one's property. No man could be deprived of this right by any "Law of Society . . . consistent with the Law of God and Nature" (in Morgan, 56; emphasis in original). The right of representation, on the other hand, did not usually receive divine authorization. It was simply an institutional means to a higher end.

Though secondary to consent in this strict theoretical sense, representation for the colonists was indeed a non-negotiable political demand. "Representation . . . in our constitution," wrote "Junius Americanus" (citing "Mr. Locke's doctrine"), is "the mode of giving consent." Thus "representation and taxation are constitutionally inseparable."[47] Camden went even further than this, actually bestowing upon representation the theological sanction that the Massachusetts House of Representatives reserved only for the "*original* principle" of consent. Camden maintained that "taxation and representation are inseparably united; God hath joined them, [and] no British Parliament can separate them." He then declared that "this position is founded on the laws of nature," and "is itself an eternal law of nature" (*Parliamentary History* 16:178).

Nevertheless it was not theology or metaphysics, but tradition and necessity, that made representation the constitutional "mode of giving consent" and thus gave it such a visible and important role in Revolutionary argument. On the one hand, representation was already a cherished institution in American politics by 1760. The tracts from the Andros Affair show that, as early as 1691, representation was already deemed an institution worth fighting for.[48] On the other hand, although only a mechanism, representation was nonetheless the only mechanism, practically speaking, through which consent could be given to proposals affecting a great number of widely-dispersed people. Self-government on a scale larger than that of the small town absolutely depended on it. Thus, in their separate declarations of 1765, the colonial legislatures of South Carolina and New Jersey, as well as the Stamp Act Congress, spoke literally with one voice: "It is inseparably essential to the freedom of a people, and the undoubted right of Englishmen, that no taxes be imposed on them but with their own consent, given personally, or by their representatives" (Morgan 58, 59, 72).

Though Locke himself did not have a systematic political theory of representation, he continued to furnish the Revolutionists with the means of expression by including the concept of representation in his formulations on property, taxation, consent, and the limits of legislative authority per se. In enumerating those essential limits in Chapter Eleven of the Second Treatise, he stated in section 142 that the legislative "must not raise taxes on the property of the people, without the consent of the people, given by themselves or their deputies." Locke recognized the need for taxation in civil society. But "the preservation of property being the end of government, and that for which men enter into society" (section 138), consent constitutes an indispensable condition for legitimacy in the transfer of property from individuals to the government (though apparently not "for the regulating of property between the subjects one amongst another"—section 139). Thus he maintained in section 140 that although "everyone who enjoys his share of the protection" provided by government "should pay out of his estate his proportion for the maintenance of it," the payment (that is, the tax) "must be with his own consent, i. e., the consent of the majority, giving it either by themselves, or by their representatives chosen by them." Without consent, taxation "invades the *fundamental law of property*, and subverts the end of Government." Consent, however, can be given through representatives freely chosen by the people. The people have "reserved to themselves the choice of their representatives, as the fence to their properties."[49] Representation is therefore consistent with civil society, whose chief end is the preservation of property, that is, of property as Locke has already defined it in both sections 87 and 123, in which he makes it clear that property is to be understood not merely as material possessions or "estate," but as "life, liberty, and estate." The position that the Revolutionist took on the vital issue of representation, then, is often explicitly Lockean, and always consistent with these basic tenets of Locke's political theory. Hence it was entirely consistent that Camden formulated his defense of the colonies (discussed above) around the same argument, with explicit appeals to Locke. And it is not surprising that the keynote speaker at the annual meeting of merchants in Philadelphia in 1768 quoted Locke's passages on representation directly as the most succinct way to state the theme of his address. The same speaker so strongly agreed with lines 8 and 9 of section 174 of the *Second Treatise*— "Political power [is] where men have property in their own disposal"— that he quoted them twice.[50]

The issue of representation took a peculiar form during the early stages of the controversy over the new revenue measures, as the debate turned to the notion of "virtual representation." The colonists, of course, demanded representation in the making of any laws that affected them. Supporters of the Stamp Act, on the other hand, argued that the colonists *were* represented in Parliament, virtually if not actually, that is, even though they did not elect and send representatives to Parliament. Thomas Whately, for instance, insisted "that the colonies are represented in Parliament. They do not indeed choose members of that assembly," he conceded; but neither do "nine-tenths of the people of Britain." Each member of the House of Commons represents "all the commons of Great Britain," and not simply his electoral constituency. All are represented, so all are obliged to submit to Parliament.[51] Soame Jenyns, who also invoked the doctrine of virtual representation to defend the Stamp Act, wanted to know why this system of representation did not "extend to America as well as over the whole island of Great Britain." If Manchester and Birmingham can be represented in Parliament without electing members, Jenyns asked, "why are not the cities of Albany and Boston equally represented in that assembly?"[52]

The colonists not only rejected the notion of virtual representation, but also the notion of *actual* representation in the Parliament of Great Britain. Their argument against the latter is at least concordant with the model of representation found in Locke, and their argument against the former is explicitly based on him. The first objection to actual representation in the British Parliament was not theoretical, but pragmatic: The Massachusetts Resolves of 1765 declared that representation in Parliament "is *impracticable* for the subjects in America." The New Jersey Resolves of 1765 stated that "the people of this colony are not, and from their remote situations cannot be, represented in the Parliament of Great Britain." The Stamp Act Congress reaffirmed this principle in its Declarations, as well as in its Petition to the House of Commons (Morgan, 57, 60, 63, 67). Moreover, such an impractical gesture would also "annihilate effectually the power of our assemblies," said a writer in the *Pennsylvania Journal*, a power the Revolutionists were determined to defend,[53] because those assemblies provided effective, actual representation. In fact, the colonists would have flatly rejected an offer to send representatives to Parliament since that would only "secure to the Parliament the right they claim to tax us."[54]

It was in attacking the idea of virtual representation, however—either in the special case of the colonies or in general—that Locke was most valuable to the Revolutionists. Significantly, no proponent of "virtual representation" seems to have cited "Locke on Government"—except to *attack* his theory of government (Dunn, 64). Daniel Dulany attacked the application of the doctrine of virtual representation to the specific circumstances of the colonies. He argued that virtual representation, to be consistent with liberty, presupposed an identity of interests among everyone involved in the political system—the electors, non-electors, and representatives. "The security of the non-electors against oppression," he wrote, "is that their oppression will fall also upon the electors and the representatives."[55] There may indeed have been such an identity of interests in England, where a system of virtual representation could therefore be justified. But a "total dissimilarity of situation" subsisted between the mother-country and the colonies. "There is not that intimate and inseparable relation between the electors of Great Britain and the inhabitants of the colonies which must inevitably involve both in the same taxation" (615-16). A virtual representation of the colonies in Parliament, then, would not be consistent with liberty, because a system without that identity of interests would necessarily become oppressive. This crucial line of argument is clearly Lockean, although Dulany does not cite Locke. But the relevant passage is in the frequently quoted section 138 of the *Second Treatise*: Locke warns against governments which "think themselves to have a distinct interest from the rest of the community, and so will be apt to increase their own riches and power by taking what they think fit from the people." In view of the familiarity of the passage, not only in Locke but in the writings of his fellow Revolutionists, Dulaney may well have had it in mind. The "Virginian," for instance, in his previously cited letter to the *Pennsylvania Gazette*, praises Locke, "that great philosopher and statesman," and offers section 138 of the *Second Treatise* as an argument against virtual representation. And even if Dulany had neither read the *Second Treatise* nor learned about it from his contemporaries, his argument could hardly be regarded as one which Locke would have opposed.

James Otis of Boston took a more radical approach; he attacked virtual representation *per se*. "To what purpose," Otis inquired, "is it to ring everlasting changes to the colonists on the cases of Manchester, Birmingham, and Sheffield? If those now so considerable places are not represented, they ought to be."[56] For Carl Becker, Otis's " 'ought to be' is the fundamental premise of the whole colonial argument," the essentially revolutionary normative impulse. This impulse explains, and is expressed in, the colonists' ultimate recourse to the Lockean abstractions of natural law and natural rights; for "the 'ought to be' is not ultimately to be found in positive law and custom, but only in something outside of, beyond, above the positive law and custom" (*The Declaration of Independence*, 133-34). As Benjamin Wright observes, "an appeal from that which *is* legally established to that which *should* be established almost invariably involves the assertion of principles of a higher validity than those made by human legislatures" (341). For the colonists, the "principles of a higher validity" — the principles from which the fundamental norms of the Revolution were drawn — were the principles of God, divine law, the law of nature. James Otis's preferred source on the law of nature, moreover, was John Locke.

Otis explicitly recommended Locke's ideas over those of Hugo Grotius and Samuel Pufendorf precisely on this crucial subject. John Dunn, in his influential essay discounting the significance of Locke's political theory in Revolutionary thought, claims that in America, his *Two Treatises* "never held the unimpeachable eminence of the works of Grotius and Pufendorf" (70). According to Otis, however, the latter made it "their constant practice to establish the matter of right on the matter of fact" — here Otis cites with approval Rousseau's critique of Grotius. He then directs his readers to "purer fountains" of natural-law theory, "particularly Mr. Locke."[57] Here, in Locke's doctrine, Otis discovered the norms that would animate Revolutionary political thought. The "ought to be" that served as the "fundamental premise of the whole colonial argument" was essentially Lockean. Locke, indeed, would almost certainly have stood with both Dulany and the more radical Otis against the doctrine of virtual representation.

The Revolutionists, of course, did not read "Locke on Government" and consequently decide that representation was a good idea. It was the century of pre-Revolutionary political experience that pushed representation into the forefront of Revolutionary argument and endowed Locke's political theory with such great contemporary significance. As Carl Becker has explained, they turned to Locke because their own governments actually conformed, "in a rough and ready way," to the kind of government "for which Locke had furnished a reasoned foundation." Locke's political theory "assured them that their own governments, with which they were well content, were just the kind that God had designed men by nature to have!" (72–73). Quoting Locke's chapter "Of the Extent of the Legislative Power," Junius Americanus (Arthur Lee) captured the spirit of this synthesis of Lockean theory and colonial political experience in 1772: " '[T]he prince or senate . . . can never have the power to take to themselves the whole or any part of the subjects property without their consent.' Here the American line seems fairly drawn . . . . Representation being in our constitution the mode of giving consent, representation and taxation are constitutionally inseparable. *This is Mr. Locke's doctrine*, it is the doctrine of reason and truth, *and it is*, Sir, *the unvarnished doctrine of the Americans.*"[58]

Given the established political tradition in the colonies, as well as the influence of the colonial representatives whose power was directly threatened by Parliament's "innovations," it is difficult to imagine the Revolutionists taking the non-Lockean, or anti-Lockean, position which revisionist historians have attributed to them. Indeed, what is the non-Lockean, or anti-Lockean, position on representation, consent, and the limits of governmental authority? To find out, let's return to the Declaratory Act, the target of Camden's eloquent Lockean polemics in the House of Lords.

The Declaratory Act asserted the unlimited sovereignty of Parliament over the people of North America. The Act received little attention when news of it first arrived in the colonies.[59] It had been passed as a corollary to the Repeal of the Stamp Act in 1766, on the same day (March 18), and the general jubilation over that apparent victory for liberty and property temporarily drowned out its ominous message, which was essentially a promise (on the American interpretation) to abolish both: "[T]he King's Majesty, by and with the advice and consent of the Lords Spiritual and Temporal, and Commons of Great Britain, in Parliament assembled, had, hath, and of right ought to have, full power and authority to make laws and statutes of sufficient force and validity to bind the colonies and the people of America, subjects of the crown of Great Britain, *in all cases whatsoever*" (Morgan, 155). Parliament thus declared that it was repealing a particular tax law without in any way surrendering its claim to the right to resume taxation at its exclusive discretion.

The Declaratory Act, however, went much further than that. It had the stink of real despotism about it. The British Government did not restrict its claim of legislative authority to economic policy but immodestly extended it to "all cases whatsoever." Obviously taxation was only one form of legislation. In fact, following the repeal of the Townshend Act in 1769, taxation ceased to be much of an issue. The Intolerable Acts, which propelled England and the colonies into armed conflict, had little to do with taxation. In short, the Act proclaimed Parliament's right to do *anything it wished* with respect to the people of North America, even what they feared most.

John Adams clarified the issue for his countrymen and linked their greatest fear to the chilling implications of the Declaratory Act. Adams recognized the centrality of the Act's underlying principle—in Lockean terms, the extent of the legislative power—in the Anglo-American dispute. He called the "authority of Parliament . . . the essence of the whole controversy," and referred to "the power of Parliament" as "the secret, latent principle upon which all encroachments against us are founded." Most fearsome of these was the encroachment upon religious liberty. "If Parliament could tax us," Adams wrote, "it could establish the Church of England" in America. He knew that nothing served to mobilize Revolutionary political thinking more than the dreaded prospect of an army of Anglican bishops landing in America to re-impose the religious tyranny from which the colonists' ancestors had fled in the first place.[60]

Some very able people actually believed this to be Parliament's secret intention. Jonathan Mayhew, the influential clergyman who liked to cite Locke and who had close ties to James Otis,[61] warned that "the stamping and episcopizing of our colonies are only different branches of the same plan of power"; the revenues that Parliament hoped to raise through the stamp tax and other measures were "partly intended to maintain a standing army of bishops" in the American colonies.[62] The Stamp Act had been defeated, but the lethal principle behind it had been enlarged and affirmed, not simply to preserve the honor of Parliament, but to pave the way for a total assault on liberty (civil as well as religious) and property in America, he and others argued.

With so much at stake, it is not surprising that the Declaratory Act and the "annihilating words" of its underlying principle—"in all cases whatsoever"—soon became the "foundation of all our complaints," the "bone of contention" and the "source of all these unhappy differences" between England and the colonies.[63] The colonists understood that "the present dispute . . . turns on the question of Parliamentary power," at the heart of which is Parliament's claim to bind the colonies " 'in all cases whatsoever.' "[64] This "fatal edict" guaranteed "endless and numberless curses of slavery upon us, our heirs, and their heirs forever."[65] It was "so subversive of liberty and so destructive of property" that it guaranteed the delivery of Americans into "the most abject slavery."[66] Concede to Parliament on this issue and we might as well "give up the matter and submit to slavery at once."[67] The colonists, of course, refused to concede; in fact, they insisted upon making repeal of the Declaratory Act a precondition for any reconciliation with the mother country.[68] And when Parliament refused to comply, they took up arms, as they put it, "not . . . merely to drown a chest of tea, but to oppose the dangerous authority" which Parliament had "usurped, pretending a right to bind us 'in all cases whatsoever.' "[69]

The centrality of the principle of the Declaratory Act in the conflict between England and the colonies meant that the theoretical question of the American Revolution was, fundamentally, a Lockean question: "the extent of the legislative power."[70] Locke provided not only the question but the answer. According to Locke, to paraphrase Camden's summary, there are some things that Parliament, or any civil authority, cannot do. Parliament had claimed that its authority over the colonists was, as one anonymous critic put it, "not only supreme but illimitable."[71] Far from supporting the illimitable sovereignty of Parliament, however, Lockean political theory does precisely the opposite. For Locke, the legislature is the supreme organ of government, but its supremacy is contingent; it is neither absolute nor unlimited; and the last word always belongs to the people.

First, there is "natural law, which [according to Locke] is to govern even the legislative itself," and which "stands as an eternal rule to all men, *legislators* as well as others" (sections 134 and 135). Second, legislative power is "only a fiduciary power," which has been established by the people only "to act for certain ends." Thus "there remains still *in the people a supreme power* to remove or *alter the legislative*, when they find the *legislative* act contrary to the trust reposed in them" (sections 149, 240). Moreover, the very things that Parliament was attempting to do—

for instance, taking property without the consent of the people—were specifically proscribed in the *Second Treatise* by both natural law and the fiduciary nature of civil authority (sections 135, 138-40).

In sum, the *Second Treatise* establishes "the *Bounds* which the trust that is put in them by the Society, and the Law of God and Nature, have *set to the Legislative* Power of every Commonwealth, in all Forms of Government" (section 142). Thus Lockean constitutionalism, which we may call the liberal doctrine of limited government, directly contradicts the absolutist position staked out by Parliament in the Declaratory Act. The Revolutionists turned to Locke in opposing the principle of the Declaratory Act. They knew that the question before them was a Lockean question and that Locke had furnished the only answer consistent with liberty. As "A Watchman" put it, on Christmas Eve, 1774: " 'But,' says the famous Mr. Locke, 'whenever a power exists in a state over which the people have no control, the people are completely enslaved.' If this be the case, what shall we say to the claim of Parliament to legislate for us 'in all cases whatsoever'?" (Force, 1:1063-65). This was quite typical. The Revolutionists and their friends in Parliament frequently turned to Locke on this vital issue—sometimes in arguments that attacked the Declaratory Act by name, elsewhere in arguments that challenged its underlying principle of illimitable legislative sovereignty. Some of these arguments were explicitly Lockean, others distinctively so.[72]

To say that Locke had nothing to offer the Revolutionists in their theoretical struggle against the despotic principle of the Declaratory Act[73] or that Locke's arguments supported Parliament's position in that struggle[74] has three regrettable results. First, it portrays Locke as if he were an advocate of absolutism (in its Parliamentary form). It is hard to see how Locke's spirited advocacy of limited, as explicitly opposed to unlimited, government could be overlooked, but apparently this is the case. Second, such claims deprive the Revolutionists of their theoretical voice on the fundamental issue of the Revolution itself. But this position is historically untenable, as we have seen: the colonists did cite Locke, and did make distinctively Lockean arguments, to challenge the "fatal edict." They used Locke correctly, too. Turning Locke into a Tory required extensive textual mutilation—as performed by Joseph Galloway, a loyalist, in *A Candid Examination of the Mutual Claims of Great Britain and Her Colonies* (1775).[75] The Revolutionists described their situation and justified their actions in Lockean terms and often in Locke's own words, or at least in the words that Locke himself had used. Moreover, their use of Locke was faithful to the thrust of his political theory.

Finally, to claim Locke's theoretical irrelevance or ideological hostility to the cause of the American Revolutionists destroys the essential source of historical legitimacy for the defense of constitutional politics in our own age. What other political theory available to the founders inherently imposes limits on political power, in both temporal and spiritual affairs? Would Machiavelli have subjected the prince to the law of nature, or to anything except the survival of the state and the steady growth of its power? A non-Lockean or anti-Lockean founding appeals to historians and political theorists who think of Lockean liberalism only as an apology for bourgeois excess. But a founding doctrine purged of Lockean liberalism, properly understood, could severely impair the struggle against new "encroachments" upon civil and religious liberties in America.

In 1967, when American Revolutionary thought could still be summarized as "an exegesis upon Locke," Bernard Bailyn shifted our attention away from Locke, in part by arguing that the Revolutionists referred to Locke "in the most offhand way, as if he could be relied on to support anything the writers happened to be arguing" (28). In 1989 Oscar and Lilian Handlin literally echoed Bailyn's judgment by asserting that Americans cited Locke "often in the most offhand way, as if to support anything the writers happened to be arguing."[76] So Bailyn's heresy is now conventional wisdom. If, however, we follow up the citations of "Locke on Government" in the Revolutionary writings and relate them to a careful reading of the *Second Treatise*, we discover that in most cases the American Revolutionists correctly understood and competently exploited the substantial theoretical relevance of Locke's argument to their specific circumstances. The conventional wisdom, then, may be vulnerable to a kind of historiography that takes political theory seriously.

NOTES

1 Merle Curti, "The Great Mr. Locke, America's Philosopher," *Huntington Library Bulletin*, No. 11 (1939); Vernon L. Parrington, *Main Currents in American Thought* (New York: Harcourt, Brace and World, 1927), 1:193; John C. Miller, *Origins of the American Revolution* (Boston: Little, Brown, 1943; revised ed. Stanford University Press, 1966), 170–71. See also Carl Becker, *The Declaration of Independence* (New York: Vintage Books, 1958); Louis Hartz, *The Liberal Tradition in America* (New York: Harcourt, Brace and World, Inc., 1955).

2 For the seminal contributions of these scholars, see J. G. A. Pocock, *The Machiavellian Moment* (Princeton: Princeton University Press, 1975);

Bernard Bailyn, *The Ideological Origins of the American Revolution* (Cambridge, Mass.: Harvard University Press, 1967; sixteenth printing, 1982).
3. Stanley Katz, "The Origins of American Constitutional Thought," *Perspectives in American History* 3 (1969): 486. John Dunn, "The Politics of Locke in England and America in the Eighteenth Century," in *John Locke: Problems and Perspectives*, ed. John Yolton (London: Cambridge University Press, 1969), 80.
4. *The Unvarnished Doctrine: Locke, Liberalism, and the American Revolution* (Durham, N.C.: Duke University Press, 1990).
5. My conclusions concerning the "presence" of Locke and of republican sources in the American writings are supported by Donald S. Lutz's survey of that literature, specifically for the period 1760 to 1776, which Lutz defines as the Revolutionary era. Professor Lutz has kindly confirmed my interpretation of his findings in personal correspondence. Lutz, "The Relative Influence of European Writers on Late Eighteenth-Century American Political Thought," *The American Political Science Review* 78 (March, 1984): 196, 192-193.
6. C. B. Macpherson, *The Political Theory of Possessive Individualism* (Oxford: Oxford University Press, 1962; Oxford Paperbacks, 1965). Leo Strauss, *Natural Right and History* (Chicago: University of Chicago Press, 1953; sixth impression, 1968).
7. Winthrop S. Hudson, "John Locke—Preparing the Way for the Revolution," *Journal of Presbyterian History* 42 (March, 1964): 21-22. Modern interpreters, Hudson writes, seem unable to "avoid the temptation to equate references to the 'civil order' and 'natural law' with secularism. But neither John Milton's contemporaries nor those of John Locke would have made this mistake. And certainly the 'pietists' of the Revolutionary generation in America, as heirs of the older Puritan tradition, would not have read Locke in this way." A critic of the ahistorical tendency to read twentieth-century ideas into eighteenth-century heads, Hudson believes that the Revolutionists understood Locke "in terms of his own thought and not in terms of what the rationalists of a much later generation were to make of it."
8. Robert Shalhope, "Toward a Republican Synthesis: The Emergence of an Understanding in American Historiography," *William & Mary Quarterly* 29 (1972): 58. Bailyn, 35-36.
9. John Trenchard and Thomas Gordon, *Cato's Letters*, Letter #31, 1:238. I am using the two-volume Russell & Russell 1969 reissue of the four-volume Third Corrected Edition of 1733, which retains the original four-volume pagination, cited here.
10. See also Bailyn, 35-36.
11. *The Lost Soul of American Politics: Virtue, Self-Interest, and the Foundations of Liberalism* (New York: Basic Books, 1984).
12. "Gone with the Wind," *The New Republic* (March 21, 1988), 41. Professor Shklar's dispassionate analysis of John Calhoun's defense of the slave-holding minority in his Disquisition on Government should persuade the democratic

critics of liberalism to think twice about the virtues of American republicanism.

13 Pocock, *The Machiavellian Moment*, 545.

14 For instance, the epistemological doctrines of the *Essay Concerning Human Understanding*, the arguments for religious toleration and the separation of church and state in the *Letter on Toleration*, the exegesis of Scripture in *A Paraphrase and Notes on the Epistle of St. Paul to the Romans*.

15 *All* of the ministers who delivered the widely-circulated, annual election sermons in Massachusetts and Connecticut between 1710 and 1776 had been educated at Harvard or Yale, where Locke's writings had graced the library shelves and fortified the curriculum since early in the eighteenth century. Locke's "unanswerable" *Letter on Toleration* enjoyed high favor in clerical circles; it received the first American edition of any of Locke's writings, thanks to the senior class at Yale in 1742. Locke's *Essay Concerning Human Understanding*, moreover, was immensely influential throughout the century, a point which Pocock concedes. His writings on theology and religion were also highly esteemed by the ministers. One even "borrowed" Locke's title, *The Reasonableness of Christianity*, for his own distinctively Lockean assault on the purveyors of deism and natural religion. And Ezra Stiles, an influential cleric writing as President of Yale in the critical year 1775, praised Locke's "new method of Scripture commentary, by paraphrase and notes," which had made his "reputation as a Scripture commentator exceedingly high with the public."

See Martha L. Counts, *The Political Views of the Eighteenth-Century New England Clergy, As Expressed in Their Election Sermons* (unpublished doctoral dissertation, Columbia University, 1956), 275-79; Claude M. Newlin, *Philosophy and Religion in Colonial America* (New York: Philosophical Library, 1962), 21, 24-25; Dunn, 69-70; Clinton Rossiter, *Seedtime of the Republic* (New York: Random House, 1953), 491, n. 111; Alice M. Baldwin, *The New England Clergy and the American Revolution* (Durham, N.C.: Duke University Press, 1928), 60; Pocock, "The Myth of John Locke," in *John Locke*, ed. Pocock and Richard Ashcraft (Los Angeles: University of California, 1980), 169-70; Jonathan Dickinson, *The Reasonableness of Christianity* (1732); Ezra Stiles, cited by Herbert D. Foster, "International Calvinism through Locke and the Revolution of 1688," *The American Historical Review* 32 (April, 1927): 475.

16 *A Discourse Preached December 15, 1774* (Boston, 1774), 27.

17 *Election Sermon* (Massachusetts, 1774), in *American Political Writings of the Founding Era*, ed. Charles Hyneman and Donald Lutz (Indianapolis: Liberty Press, 1983), 1:288, 300.

18 *A Discourse Preached December 15, 1774*, in *Pulpit of the American Revolution*, ed. John Wingate Thornton (Burt Franklin, 1970, orig. pub. 1860), 215-216, 210. On liberty and property, see Edmund S. Morgan, "The American Revolution: Revisions in need of Revising," in *The American Revolution: Two Centuries of Interpretation*, ed. Morgan (Englewood Cliffs, N.J.:

Prentice-Hall, 1965), 175; Paul Conkin, *Self-Evident Truths* (Bloomington: Indiana University Press, 1974), 109.

19 The story of the rebellion of the "Jerseymen" is told by Edward Countryman, in "Out of the Bounds of Law: Northern Land Rioters in the Eighteenth Century," in *The American Revolution: Explorations in the History of American Radicalism*, ed. Alfred F. Young (DeKalb: Northern Illinois University Press, 1976), 37-69. The justificatory tract containing the transcription from the *Second Treatise* is in *New Jersey Archives,* First Series, 7 (1746-1751): 30; the transcription itself is on 7:42, where John Locke is referred to as "a very learned and worthy author." I cite the *Two Treatises* from John Locke, *Two Treatises of Government,* ed. Peter Laslett (New York: Mentor Books, revised edition, 1965).

20 In his second *Letter from a Farmer* (8-9). According to Dickinson, "Never did the British Parliament, till the period above mentioned. think of imposing duties in America for the purpose of raising a revenue . . . . This I call an innovation, and a most dangerous innovation." See the preambles to the Revenue Act of 1764 (the "Sugar Act"), the Stamp Act of 1765, and the (Townshend) Revenue Act of 1767, in *English Historical Documents* (New York: Oxford University Press, 1962), 9:543, 656, 701.

21 *Newport Mercury* #316, March 24, 1764. Rhode Island Resolves of 1765 and Connecticut Resolves of 1765, in *Prologue to Revolution*, ed. Edmund S. Morgan (Chapel Hill: Univerty of North Carolina Press, 1959), 51, 55.

22 Oxenbridge Thacher, *The Sentiments of a British American*, in *Pamphlets of the American Revolution*, ed. Bernard Bailyn (Cambridge, Mass: Harvard University Press, 1965), 491.

23 *Newport Mercury*, August 31-September 7, 1767.

24 Judah Champion, *Election Sermon* (Connecticut, 1776), 16. On p. 7, Champion closely paraphrases (without attribution) sections 77 and 123 of Locke's *Second Treatise*. And on p. 8 he transcribes, without quotation marks, section 23 (1-4), where Locke writes: "This Freedom from Absolute, Arbitrary Power, is so necessary to, and closely joined with, a Man's Preservation, that he cannot part with it, but by what forfeits his Preservation and Life together." A footnote at this point in the sermon tells us to consult "Locke on Government."

25 Hampden, "The Alarm" (#5) (New York, 1773), 2.

26 *Newport Mercury*, January 3, 1774.

27 *The Nature & Extent of Parliamentary Power Considered* (Philadelphia, 1768), 2. Hicks claimed to have written this pamphlet prior to the repeal of the Stamp Act in 1766.

28 *Proceedings and Debates of the British Parliaments Respecting North America, 1754-1793*, 2:323 (Speech of March 7, 1766). Thomas Curson Hansard, *Parliamentary History of England* (New York: Johnson Reprint Corporation, i966), 16 (1765-1771):180-81. Camden's speech was reprinted in the *Newport Mercury* #822 (June 6, 1774). It also appeared much earlier, though incorrectly attributed to Lord Chatham (William Pitt), in the *New York Mercury*,

Supplement to #843 (December 30, 1767), and in the *Newport Mercury*, #488 (January 4-11, 1768).
29 *Report of the Record Commissioners of the City of Boston Containing The Boston Town Records, 1770-1777* (Boston, 1887), 98.
30 Arthur M. Schlesinger has called the series of articles signed "From the County of Hampshire" the "ablest sustained reply" to the Tory Daniel Leonard. He suggests that Joseph Hawley, a member of the Massachusetts House of Representatives, might have been the author of these articles. Schlesinger, *Prelude to Independence: The Newspaper War on Britain, 1764-1776* (New York: Knopf, 1958), 221, n.42.
31 Lord Mansfield's Speech of March 7, 1766, in *Proceedings and Debates of the British Parliaments Respecting North America, 1754-1793*, 2:321.
32 Cited in Randolph Adams, *Political Ideas of the American Revolution* (New York: Barnes & Noble, 3rd. edition, 1958; orig. pub. 1922), 148.
33 *Proceedings and Debates of the British Parliaments Respecting North America, 1754-1793*, 2:127.
34 "Natural Law and the American Revolution," in *Traditions of Civility* (Cambridge: Cambridge University Press, 1948), 284, 317.
35 *The Causes of the War of Independence* (Riverside Press, 1922), 233-34.
36 *An Oration Delivered March the 5th, at the Request of the . . . Town of Boston . . . to Commemorate the Bloody Tragedy* (Boston: Edes & Gill, 1772), 10.
37 Morgan, *Prologue to Revolution*, 55.
38 Petition to the King from the Stamp Act Congress, in Morgan, *Prologue to Revolution*, 65.
39 Speech in the House of Lords, January 20, 1775, in *The Political Writings of John Dickinson, Esq.* (Princeton, Princeton University Press, n.d.), 104-5.
40 *American Archives*, Fourth Series, 4:833-34. Edited by Peter Force.
41 *Second Treatise*, section 174 (4-7). "An Address Read at the Annual Meeting of Merchants in Philadelphia, April 25, 1768," in the *Newport Mercury*, June 9-16, 1768.
42 *Essex Gazette*, March 19-26, 1771.
43 *Parliamentary History*, 16:178. Grenville, the Prime Minister, called these words of Camden "a libel upon Parliament."
44 *Election Sermon* (Massachusetts, 1771), in Hyneman and Lutz, 1:162-63.
45 [Anonymous], *A Discourse to the Sons of Liberty . . . in Boston* (Providence, 1766), 6.
46 *A Discourse* (1768), 9-10.
47 *Boston Evening Post*, May 4, 1772. According to Arthur M. Schlesinger, "Junius Americanus" was the pen-name of Arthur Lee, "a crony of John Wilkes and a correspondent of Samuel Adams" (139).
48 Edward Rawson and Samuel Sewall, *The Revolution in New England Justified* (Boston, 1691), 7. See also *A Narrative of the Proceedings of Sir Edmund Androsse and his Complices* ([Boston?], 1691). For a discussion of the Andros Affair—the "Glorious Revolution in New England"—in the American Revo-

lution, see Samuel Cooke, *Election Sermon* (Massachusetts, 1770), in Thornton, 176-78. In the secondary literature, see Theodore B. Lewis, "A Revolutionary Tradition, 1689-1774," *New England Quarterly* 46 (1973): 424-38; Benjamin F. Wright, *American Interpretations of Natural Law* (Cambridge, Mass.: Harvard University Press, 1931), 38.

49 Locke, *Second Treatise*, section 222. De facto representation seems to be a condition for civil society, according to Locke. After noting (section 90) the disadvantages of absolute monarchy, which is "inconsistent with civil society," Locke maintained (section 94) that "the people . . . could never be safe nor at rest, *nor think themselves in civil society*, till the legislature was placed in collective bodies of men, call them Senate, Parliament, or what you please" (Locke's emphasis).

50 *Newport Mercury* #506, May 9-16, 1768.

51 *The Regulations Lately Made Concerning the Colonies and the Taxes Imposed upon Them, Considered* (London, 1765).

52 *The Objections to the Taxation of Our American Colonies . . . Considered* (London, 1765).

53 Jack P. Greene, "The Role of the Lower Houses of Assembly in Eighteenth-Century Politics," in *Reinterpretation of the American Revolution*, ed. Greene (New York: Harper and Row, 1968), 109. Greene writes: "The British challenge after 1764 threatened to render [the] accomplishments [of the provincial representative assemblies] meaningless and drove them to demand autonomy in local affairs and eventually to declare their independence. At issue was the whole political structure forged by the lower houses over the previous century. In this context the American Revolution becomes in form, if not in essence, a war for political survival."

54 [Anonymous], *Pennsylvania Journal*, March 13, 1766.

55 *Considerations on the Propriety of Imposing Taxes in the British Colonies*, (Annapolis, 1765), in Bailyn, *Pamphlets of the American Revolution*, 611-12.

56 *Considerations on Behalf of the Colonists in a Letter to a Noble Lord* (London, 1765), 6.

57 *The Rights of the British Colonies Asserted and Proved* (Boston, 1764), in Bailyn, *Pamphlets of the American Revolution*, 436-37. Lord Mansfield, a staunch advocate of Parliamentary sovereignty, warned the House of Lords that Otis's writings "may be called silly or mad, but mad people, or persons who have entertained silly and mad ideas, have led the people to rebellion and overturned empires" (*Parliamentary History* 16:172). Patrick Riley explains some of the differences between Locke and Grotius on natural law in *Will and Political Legitimacy* (Cambridge, Mass.: Harvard University Press, 1982), 90. Miller called natural law "the first line of defense of colonial liberty." And according to Miller, "what Americans particularly relished in John Locke was his emphasis upon natural law" (173, 171).

58 *Boston Evening Post*, May 4, 1772 (emphasis added). The Locke quotation is from section 139 of the *Second Treatise*.

59 *Pennsylvania Gazette*, June 8, 1774.
60 *The Works of John Adams* (Boston: Little, Brown & Company, 1856), 10:185, 187-188, 288. Lester Douglas Joyce quotes Adams on the fear of an American Episcopate as "a force in bringing about the Revolution: 'It is difficult to this day to realize how much the opposition of the colonists to the Church of England had to do with bringing about the Revolution. But although the fact is not always noticed by historians, *there was probably no other one cause which exerted such an influence*. The feeling of opposition was not so much religious as political. It was proposed to 'Introduce bishops in America to be accepted by the government as they were in England. This meant a hierarchy under foreign domination.' And, according to Adams, it was in discussing this very subject that the colonists were first led to question the supremacy of Parliament." Joyce, *Church and Clergy in the American Revolution* (Exposition Press, 1966), 58-59. See also Baldwin, 91, n.23; Becker, 120.
61 Diggins, 33; Rossiter, 231-33; Baldwin, 90, 92, 169. "It was Dr. Mayhew who suggested to James Otis the idea of committees of correspondence . . . —a thing of vital importance" in the Revolution (Thornton, 44).
62 Jonathan Mayhew, *The Snare Broken* (May 23, 1766), in *The Patriot Preachers of the American Revolution*, ed. Frank Moore (New York, 1862), 25. John Adams called Mayhew a "transcendent genius" (*Works*, 10:288).
63 Ebenezer Baldwin's Appendix to Samuel Sherwood's *Sermon*, delivered August 31, 1774 (New Haven), 57. "From the County of Hampshire, #2," *Massachusetts Spy*, #211, February 16, 1775. *Pennsylvania Gazette*, Postscript #2379, July 27, 1774.
64 *Massachusetts Spy*, #203, December 22, 1774.
65 *Newport Mercury*, #839, October 3, 1774.
66 *Pennsylvania Gazette*, June 8, 1774. *Massachusetts Spy*, #30, October 9, 1770 (reporting the proceedings of the Grand Jury of Philadelphia, September 24, 1770).
67 "The British American, #7" (Williamsburg, July 14, 1774), in Force, 1:541. See also the declaration of the South Carolina Provincial Congress (March 26, 1776), in Force 5:609-615.
68 Charles F. Mullett, *Fundamental Law and the American Revolution* (New York: Octagon Books, 1966; orig. pub. 1933), 170.
69 "To the Inhabitants of Virginia, from a Planter" (April 6, 1776) in Force 5:798-800. The author warns that conceding to the principle of the Declaratory Act "immediately draws after it an endless train of miseries."
70 Locke, *Second Treatise*, Chapter Eleven. Note the literal centrality of the issue in Locke's title for the *Second Treatise*: "An Essay Concerning the True Original, Extent, and End of Civil Government." On the American side, see "From the County of Hampshire, #1," *Massachusetts Spy*, #210, February 9, 1775. The author quotes Parliament's assertion of illimitable authority from the Declaratory Act and says: "This is the Question. And to this claim is our opposition made."

71 *Pennsylvania Gazette*, August 4, 1768.
72 Some examples: Hampden, *The Alarm*, #5 (October 27, 1773), 2 (The author quotes from the Declaratory Act and says, "This Act declares that you have no property of your own, for as Mr. Locke justly observed, 'what property have they in that which another may by right take when he pleases to himself'; and Parliament declares it has this right. This Act, therefore, declares to all the world that you are slaves, the livestock of the people of Great Britain"); "A Friendly Address to the Freemen, from Epaminondas," *Connecticut Courant*, March 27, 1775 (The author transcribes section 136 [1–5] of the *Second Treatise* to denounce the Declaratory Act); "From the County of Hampshire, #2," *Massachusetts Spy*, #211, February 16, 1775, already discussed; "From the County of Hampshire, #7," *Massachusetts Spy*, #217, March 30, 1775 (The author transcribes section 138 [lines 1–17] and section 139 [lines 1–3] to support an argument against the Declaratory Act); Letter of Charles Garth (London, March 5, 1766), reporting the use of Locke by the opponents of the Declaratory Act in the debate on that Act in Parliament, in *Maryland Historical Magazine* 6 (September, 1911): 287–305, especially 291–292; Camden's speech of March 7, 1766, already discussed.
73 Ronald E. Pynn, "The Influence of John Locke's Political Philosophy on American Political Tradition," *North Dakota Quarterly* 2 (Summer, 1974): 53.
74 Esmond Wright, for example, maintains that "the authority Locke supported was that of the British Parliament." Wright, "Men with Two Countries," *The Development of a Revolutionary Mentality* (Washington: Library of Congress, 1972), 153.
75 I have discussed these mutilations in T*he Unvarnished Doctrine*, 46–50.
76 "Who Read John Locke?" *The American Scholar* 58 (Autumn, 1989): 555.

Another Turn of the Screw: Prefaces in Swift, Marvell, and Genette

JON ROWLAND

"Nous sommes au seuil d'une époque paratextuelle, au seuil d'un seuil, stationnés à la frontière d'un moment exégétique, 'dispositionnel' qui privilégie les marges, s'y institue, s'en fait partie," declares Richard L. Barnett, rather grandly, in his "avant-propos" to a recent issue of *L'Esprit Createur* devoted entirely to aspects of "paratextuality."[1] For the following discussion of prefaces in Swift and Marvell, I have used terminology developed by Gérard Genette in his aptly titled *Seuils* (1987)[2] as a part of his "paratextual" emphasis. Genette defines "le paratexte" as "ce par quoi un texte se fait livre et se propose comme tel à ses lecteurs, et plus généralement au public" (7). The paratext is a "seuil," a threshold between the inside ("le texte") and the outside ("le discours du monde sur le texte" [8]), comprised of "épitexte" and "péritexte." The "épitexte" is "tous les messages qui se situent, au moins à l'origine, à l'exterieur du livre" (10); the "peritexte" is all messages "autour du texte" (10). Here I will deal mainly with one aspect of the "péritexte," the preface, as it is described by Genette in *Seuils* and as it appears in Marvell's *The Rehearsal Transpros'd* and Swift's *A Tale of a Tub*.[3]

Genette defines the preface as "toute espèce de texte liminaire (préliminaire ou postliminaire)" (150). It is, both by virtue of its function and its (usual) placement before the text of the book, a threshold (Genette treats it as only one of many "thresholds," like titles, footnotes, endnotes, glosses, etc). While not itself a boundary, or at least no "water-tight" (7) one as Genette remarks, it is frequently concerned with establishing interpretive boundaries and guidelines out of which the reader, like the modern wit in *A Tale*, is warned not to "stray the breadth of a Hair, upon peril of being lost" (43). Even if we choose to ignore such boundaries, in a sense, by the very "choosing," we admit that we cannot utterly ignore them. This is the reason that prefacers often seem to attach such importance to what they say, as if they felt they had to say something and on that something depended interpretive order if not the future of western civilization too. In a sense, in their small but sometimes not-so-modest way, prefacers are staving off interpretive chaos; they are really, and perhaps unconsciously but by no means always unconsciously, registering the fact that if not very much more than some prefaced text is at stake, very much more is at play.

Genette's use of a term like "seuils" for such things as prefaces indicates, I think, the modern realization that such things are *not* distinct from their texts but may, in fact, *be* the text. The attempt on the part of critics like Genette to systematize such things follows naturally from the exploitation of them by significant modern (or postmodern) writers, to expand outward from the text and, as Luiz Fernando Valente says in an article on Guimaraes Rosa's prefaces to *Tutameia*, "open a dialogue with other texts by the author."[4] For Borges the preface in particular represents a kind of ideal: "To compose vast texts is a laborious and diminishing extravagance; that of expounding in five hundred pages an idea whose perfect oral exposition takes a few minutes. A better device is to pretend that those books already exist and to offer a summary, a commentary."[5]

In several collections of prefaces from Henry B. Wheatley's *The Dedication of Books to Patron and Friend* (1887) — which he describes in his own "Preface" as "the first instance of a book being entirely devoted to the history of this topic" (v) — to Guy R. Lyle's *Praise From Famous Men: An Anthology of Introductions* (1977)[6], a common hallmark of the preface is precisely this interpretive anxiety. Wheatley's examples illustrate well how the dedicatee in a prefatory dedication could be used to dispel anxiety in the reader, if not altogether in the writer; clearly the dedicatee was also intended to influence the reading from the start, if only by giving the writer — and his book — a preliminary recommendation. One Dr. Turner, dedicating his *Herbal* to Queen Elizabeth, remarks on just this function, something his printer — typically — suggested: "The Printer had geven me warninge there wanted nothinge to the setting oute of my hole Herbal saving only a Preface, wherein I might require some both mighty and learned Patron to defend my laboures against spitefull and envious enemies to all mennis doyinges saving their owne, and declare my good minde to him that I am bound unto by dedicating and geving these my poore labours unto him" (52). Herbert Grierson, in *The Personal Note* (1946), a collection of prefaces and *post*faces intended to illustrate "personal feelings, which have been kept in check in the effort to be objective or conciliatory," reprints Jonson's dedication of *Volpone*, in which, sounding a very Swiftian note (or does Swift rather sound a Jonsonian?), Jonson protests, "I know, that nothing can be so innocently writ or carried, but may be made obnoxious to construction; marry, whilst I bear mine innocence about me, I fear it not," and complains, "Application is now grown a trade with many; and there are that profess to have a key for the deciphering of everything: but let wise and noble persons take heed how they be too credulous, or give leave to these invading interpreters to be overfamiliar with their fames, who cunningly and often utter their own virulent malice under other men's simplest meanings."[7]

These prefaces, in fact, provide what Genette describes for us as directions "how to read" (194) — here, how *not* to read. There are many other instances, such as Donne's preface to *Biathanatos* (where not judging harshly can be seen in terms of the subject [suicide], the treatment [*Biathanatos*], and Christian charity), and Johnson's famous "Preface" to *A Dictionary of the English Language* (where he, too, wants charity in the reader, but also some fraction of the diligence that went into the writing): "a few wild blunders, and risible absurdities, from which no work of such multiplicity was ever free, may for a time furnish folly with laughter, and harden ignorance into contempt; but useful diligence will at last prevail, and there never can be wanting some who distinguish desert; who will consider that no dictionary of a living tongue ever can be perfect."

The idea of the preface occurs often enough (and usually in vivid, metaphorical language) in *The Rehearsal Transpros'd* to be thematic, if not ubiquitous, and in *A Tale of a Tub* prefatory pieces comprise the first five parts (six if you count "The Introduction"), plus "Section V: A Digression in the Modern Kind," which performs functions "proper in a preface," and "Section X: A Further Digression," which acts like a postface although it is only the penultimate section. Such exaggerated emphasis on the threshold may give "Readers truly learned" of *A Tale* pause, especially if they require (or desire) no instruction. No doubt the "learned reader" above would be appalled to know that even before Marvell's day it was possible to make a career out of reading just prefaces, as Marvell says Archbishop Laud did, when his job was "to look over Epistles Dedicatory and Prefaces to the Reader" and (anticipating

Swift's "true critic") "see what fault may be found" (127). In our day, it is still possible for critics like Gérard Genette (*Seuils*, 184) and Jon Rowland (on the present occasion) to do almost the same thing, at the risk of sounding rather like Swift's hack, "Just come from perusing some hundreds of Prefaces" (45).

Yet in these works the liminal pause is forced upon us. *The Rehearsal Transpros'd* and *A Tale of a Tub* almost present themselves as books only in the bookseller's sense of so many bound paper objects to be sold.[8] In the deeper sense of book as metaphor for wisdom and knowledge, like the Bible or Homer's epics, they do not appear to be books at all, but self-conscious accretions of the conventions of which books are made but which do not make books. The most salient of these conventions, and the one which finally comes to stand, I think, as a metaphor for all the others, is the preface. As Genette remarks, "la préface est peut-être, de toutes les pratiques littéraires [we might say rather, livresque], la plus typiquement littéraire, parfois au meilleur, parfois au pire sense" (270).

The Rehearsal Transpros'd is a hostile paratext (an epitext) to a work claiming status as a book by posing as a preface to another author's work, Samuel Parker's *A Preface Shewing what grounds there are of Fears and Jealousies of Popery* (1672), prefixed to Bishop Bramhall's *Vindication of himself and the Episcopal Clergy from the Presbyterian Charge of Popery*. Marvell's "animadversions" on Parker's "Preface," virtually a reading of it with and through Marvell's eyes,[9] really comprises a satirical preface to Parker's entire oeuvre, devaluing what Parker gave value to, and worse, devaluing Parker himself. The various "lies" criticized in Parker's "Preface" discredit him in the main body of his other works; in Genette's terms, the paratext is made — retroactively — to refute the text: "I am sure our Author had died no other death but of this his own Preface . . . if the swelling of Truth could have choak'd him" (13).

The preface is also, both in Marvell and in much earlier polemicists, closely connected to the issue of religious ceremonies in particular, and religious ridicule in general. The preface can quite naturally be seen as a formal abuse in literature, on the part of those wanting to impose formal abuses in religious matters; moreover, as a kind of dressing of the text it prefaces, it nicely connects with the sartorial nature of some of these abuses. In his "Preface" Parker is seen as not only advocating such abuses in religion but as turning them into absolute requirements for anyone wishing to belong to the state church. When one Matthew Parker (1504-75; formerly Archbishop of Canterbury) seems to rebut Samuel Parker's position successfully, the latter's solution (Marvell supposes) will be to write yet another preface (116); one imagines Parker's prefaces encrusting other mens' works the way the ceremonies they are written to defend encrust Christianity.

In *A Tale of a Tub* the preface comes to represent that awful condition in which literariness and talk about literature have cankered literature itself. The distance between who is talking and what he is talking about ultimately collapses. From the egotistical Parker prefacing the vindication of a dead bishop who comes increasingly to resemble the egotistical Parker himself, to the self-sufficient Hack writing about nothing because all he can write about is what is in himself and he is empty, is a short albeit telling distance.

The preface also is emblematic of what is arguably the central theme of *A Tale*, the relationship (or want of relationship) between container and contained, or, in I.A. Richards's terms, between vehicle and tenor.[10] The same theme is expressed in what Wyrick (and others) have discussed as the main metaphor, the clothes analogy, effectively introduced by the prefaces of *A Tale*, with their inherent sartorialism.[11] Clearly the numerous prefatory pieces of *A Tale* emphasize the "vehicular" side of things, what means over what is meant. This too can be seen as a development of the contentious literature of the seventeenth century and, certainly in Parker's case, of the anxiety of partisans not just to show the meaning of the work but rather to determine how that meaning can be reapplied or enlisted to their cause, mainly by redirecting it in a preface or other paratext. The risk of such a procedure is that with every additional "*re*direction" or "*re*meaning," a bit of the original—which is, after all, the pretext—gets lost.

Genette describes the emergence of the preface, its gradual separation from the text, as a print-related phenomenon (152). It is, moreover, linked to the translation and dissemination of classical texts in the modern era (243), and is therefore an important means of cultural appropriation and assimilation.[12] Genette remarks that this appropriation could be opportunistic, a chance to "déborder quelque peu l'objet prétendu de son discours au profit d'une cause plus vaste, ou éventuellement toute différente" (250).

Opportunism is precisely what Marvell accuses Parker of. The immediate target of Marvell's satire is naturally the preface genre, for the above reasons, and because the book he is attacking presents itself as a preface. Marvell wonders "whether the Author made his Preface for *Bishop Bramhal's dear sake*, or whether he published the Bishop's Treatise for sake of his *own dear Preface*" (9). From Buckingham's play, *The Rehearsal*, Marvell borrows the point that Bayes's prologue could equally be an epilogue: "I do not see but the Preface might have past as wel for a Postscript, or the Headstal for a Crooper" (9). The comparison to the "transposed" saddle of a horse leads to a comparison to an animal whose motion may be directed by the head or the tail, to illustrate the adventitious, opportunistic nature of Parker's preface, the publication of which occasioned the publication of the bishop's *Vindication* rather than vice-versa. Marvell imagines the opportunistic relationship, in its arbitrariness, as potentially a game of leap-frog as, in subsequent editions, the preface and the "Vindication" proper trade places, now Parker first, now the Bishop. The disjunction of the preface and the work is further seen in the remark that it is merely "the Tap-droppings of his Defence" (38). In other words, the preface is not merely unrelated to Bramhall's work, but unrelated to Bramhall's precisely because it is really a thinly disguised postface to Parker's latest book, *A Defence and Continuation of the Ecclesiastical Politie* (1676).

Unluckily for Parker, luckily for Marvell, Bramhall in his "Vindication" had identified a metaphorical "cursed *Bay-tree*" (a metaphor for insistence on transforming indifferent opinions into necessary articles of faith) as the "*cause of all our brawling and contention*" (99). How gratifying, then, to call Parker "Bayes," after the established butt of Buckingham's *Rehearsal*. Thus, ironically, Marvell himself establishes as the basis for the relationship between Parker's preface and its text, one which instead of allowing the "Vindication" to support the policy advanced in the preface, actually subverts it—and by means of the prefacer's very name!

That Marvell is conscious that the kind of opportunism he attributes to Parker has been facilitated by print is made clear by the metaphorical treatment of printing on nearby pages: "O *Printing*! how hast thou disturb'd the Peace of Mankind! that Lead, when moulded into Bullets, is not so mortal as when founded into Letters! There was a mistake sure in the story of *Cadmus*; and the Serpents Teeth which he sowed, were nothing else but the Letters which he invented" (5). Before the printed text the function of the preface ("préface intégrée") was assumed by the first few lines if the work were poetry (as in the classical invocation), or the first few paragraphs if prose (as in Herodotus's *History* or Lucian's *True History)*. The prologue of tragedy (which preceded the chorus) is not a preface in Genette's sense of "avertissement au public" (154).

But the preface does have an oral precursor, the prologue to a comedy like Plautus's *Amphitryon* ("commentaire bonimenteur"—Genette 154). Genette and Swift would have concurred, then, in attributing the "Invention, or at least the Refinement of Prologues" (*Tale*, 101) to the theatre. That Marvell should have been inspired to his parody of Parker's *Preface* partly by Buckingham's comic play, *The Rehearsal*, is no mere coincidence, given that the comic use of prologues—oral prefaces—was part of a dramatic tradition:

> Bayes: Now, gentlemen, I would fain ask your opinion of one thing. I have made a prologue and an epilogue which may serve for either (that is, the prologue for the epilogue, or the epilogue for the prologue)—do you mark? Nay, they may both serve too, I gad, for any other play as well as this . . . . I come out in a long black veil, and a great, huge hangman behind me, with a furred cap and his sword drawn; and there tell 'em plainly that if, out of good nature, they will not like my play, I gad, I'll e'ene kneel down, and he shall cut my head off. (Act I, Scene 1)

A connoisseur of prefaces cannot but recollect Bouilhet's view, cited by Flaubert in his Preface to Bouilhet's *Dernières Chansons*: "Il se serait pendu plutôt que d'écrire une préface" (quoted by Genette, 245).

This transposition of prologue and epilogue is but one of many transpositions in *The Rehearsal*, the first being prose and verse:

> Bayes: I take a book in my hand . . . if there be any wit in't . . . I transverse it: that is, if it be prose, put it into verse (but that takes up some time), and if it be verse, put it into prose.
>
> Johnson: Methinks, Mr. Bayes, that putting verse into prose should be called transprosing. (Act I, Scene 1)

Transposing with its punning connection through transversing to transprosing is fundamental to Marvell's technique in applying the mock-heroics of a play (itself a burlesque of heroic drama) to a burlesque of Parker's *Preface* and a satire of his theology. This transposition of preface and epilogue, back and front, becomes the motive metaphor in Marvell's *The Rehearsal Transpros'd*, generating most of the other mock-heroic ones: "Here you might see one put on his Helmet the wrong way: there one buckle on a Back in place of a Breast. Some by mistake catched up a Socinian or Arminian Argument, and some a Popish to fight a Papist" (120).

Perhaps the most common transposition Parker is seen to make in his *Preface* is that of praise into blame and blame into praise. This amounts to a failure of what Genette sees as the principal function of this type of preface ("préface allographe"), "recommandation" (246). Parker himself seems to be aware that this is his task: "*The ensuing Treatise of Bishop Bramhall's being somewhat superannuated, the* Bookseller *was solicitous to have it set off with some Preface that might recommend it to the Genius of the Age and reconcile it to the present juncture of affairs*" (4). In this kind of recommendation Marvell sees mainly a mistaken and self-serving condescension: "A pretty task indeed: That is as much to say, To trick up the good old Bishop in a yellow Coif and a Bulls-head, that he might be fit for the Publick and appear in Fashion" (4). Worse, Parker fails to heed Aristotle's implicit warning, in his discussion of praise and blame in his Rhetoric, that the difference between vice and virtue, for the hearer or the reader at least, can be entirely a matter of shading or emphasis ("the choleric and passionate man may be spoken of as frank and open, the arrogant as magnificent and dignified"[13]). Here is Parker: "*Tis true, the Ch[ur]ch of* Ireland *was the largest scene of his Actions; but yet there, in a little time, he wrought out such wondrous Alterations, and so exceeding all belief, as may convince us that he had a mind large and active enough to have managed the Roman Empire at its greatest extent*" (12). This praise, or panegyric since while praising it is intended to promote a course of action, ends as unintentional satire. "Mr *Bayes* [Parker] at any time, will make the same thing serve for a Panegyrick or a Philippick" (24), Marvell remarks, recalling again the transposition of epilogue and prologue. Such praise fails at something else very important to its kind of epideictic rhetoric, which is the ethical kind of proof, the creation of a good impression of the speaker's (or the writer's) character. We cannot believe that Bramhall was really what Parker describes (which is just as well), so we suspect that what the description represents is Parker's own ego-maniacal self.

Marvell's subsequent exploitation of the above failure enables him to depict Parker as a madman whose "head runs upon nothing but Romane Empire and Ecclesiastical Policy" (29) and to devastate the panegyric he elsewhere addresses to the King. Marvell himself, of course, uses praise moderately and skillfully to further his cause, writing the kind of deliberative panegyric Aristotle advocates in the Rhetoric ("If you desire to praise, look what you would suggest; if you desire to suggest, look what you would praise" [103]): "And you Mr. *Bayes*, had you lived in the days of *Augustus Caesar* . . . would not you have made, think you, an excellent Privy Counsellour? His Father too was murdered . . . . And His Majesty . . . will in all probability not be so forward to hearken to your advice as to follow their Example. . . . Kings have I doubt, a shrewd understanding with them" (108).

Finally, Marvell transposes Parker's *Preface* in a much more important way than suggesting it "might have past as wel for a Postscript, or the Headstal for a Crooper" (9). He transposes its ideas, which are already topsy-turvy, and so restores order: "Our Author translates Joy to *Chearfulness*, Peace to *Peaceableness*, and Faith to *Faithfulness*: What Ignorance, or rather, what Forgery is this of Scripture and Religion? . . . Joy is not Chearfulness, but that *Spiritual Joy which is unspeakable* . . . Peace is not Peaceableness in his Sense, but *that Peace of God which through Jesus Christ is wrought in the heart of Believers by the Holy Ghost* . . . Faith in God is there intended not faithfulness in our Duties, Trusts or Offices" (87).

This restatement is arguably less transposition than translation, but remembering the myth of Cadmus above, it is apparent that the two are related. Transposing a few letters may result in a significant translation, the letters of the alphabet being relatively few (especially compared to the number of letters in print): "the transposition only of a letter a, another time in the name of a goat, by some called *Crabe*, and by others *Cabre*, was the loss of more men's lives than the distinguishing but by an Aspiration in *Shiboleth* upon the like occasion" (103). One gets from the above and similar passages in *The Rehearsal Transpros'd* the sense of rather few limitations and conventions capable of infinite and infinitely dangerous permutation. In a work intended to explode a particular preface, the preface itself becomes the central metaphor for a synchrony of conventions that extend from the alphabet to God. Of course, if such transpositions are both easier and more dangerous in a post-Gutenberg world, they are also easier to correct (provided that the press is free).

I think it is the sense of access to convention facilitated by print that accounts for Marvell's notable neutrality regarding convention itself. Much of Marvell's argument consists of exposing Parker, the establishment Archdeacon, as an intensely unconventional man ("Why he gives us a new Translation of the Bible, and a new Commentary" [93]). Convention is generally a good thing, and the conventional world of print is no exception. Marvell mocks Parker's complaint against the press ("such is the mischief, that a Man cannot write a Book but presently he is answered" [5]) and defends linguistic convention ("even *Augustus Caesar*, though he was so great an Emperour, and so valiant a man in his own person, was used to fly from a new word" [103]). Finally, the extreme literariness of *The Rehearsal Transpros'd*, in its quotations from classical authors as well as Church Fathers, from plays, etc., seems to belie if not preclude any real contempt for that most literary of conventions, the preface.

The hypocrisy of the print-oriented man who declaims in a preface against other print-oriented men is exploited by Swift in "The Preface" to *A Tale of a Tub*, in the story of the fat man in Leicester Fields. Those who complain about the press of writers should consider that if they would "*bring* [their] *own Guts to a reasonable Compas . . . we shall have room enough for us all*" (46). One difference is that the fat man complaining about the "Press" (the word becomes something of a pun in the context) doesn't stand for an individual like Parker, but for a typical "patron." The difference, though small in itself, is typical of Swift's far greater cynicism about convention. The preface continues to provide a focus and a major (if not the major) metaphor for the discussion, but the treatment of convention is both more exhaustive and more nihilistic than it is in *The Rehearsal Transpros'd*.

Ronald Paulson and others have indicated connections between *A Tale*'s language and "scientific" works like the *Philosophical Transactions of the Royal Society*. We should not be surprised, then, that some of the best examples of the exploitation of the preface in Swift's own time are found in the *Works* of another scientist, Robert Boyle (6 vols., 1772). These *Works*—the very name suggests it—bristle with prefaces, advices, advertisements, and postscripts, as well as occasional digressions and animadversions, just as one imagines Boyle's desk must have bristled with scientific apparatus (like that displayed on the title page, perhaps). The paratextual "apparatus," in particular the liminary texts, are as haphazard and ongoing as the enquiries they attempt to surround. Indeed, such enquiries seem to require an elaborate apparatus, both scientific and literary, as if no less is needed to make the book, than conduct the experiment. If Swift seems indebted to Boyle—and he is, in the same sense that he is indebted to John Dunton—almost as much as to Marvell, Boyle himself is clearly indebted to Marvell and other polemicists. Indeed, his very nervousness in his prefaces about avoiding polemics, betrays the polemical nature of his writing, as well as a preoccupation with religion.

I have no space here to undertake a detailed description of Boyle's paratexts, but a few examples should suffice to indicate the connections between Boyle and *A Tale*. Boyle's *The Excellency of Theology Compared With Natural Philosophy* begins, like *A Tale*, with "The Publisher's Advertisement to the Reader." This piece functions like an apology, the bookseller undertaking to excuse the lack of what we call today "acknowledgement of sources," because the work was written some time before (1665), when there was a plague on (not to mention the Second Dutch War), and the author had "frequently to pass from place to place, unaccompanied with most of his books" (1). The "Publisher's Advertisement" is followed by "The Author's Preface," in which Boyle uses some of that condescending "prefatory [jargon]" that Marvell hated so much in Parker and that Swift satirizes in *A Tale*: "I am not so little acquainted with the temper of this age, and of the persons, that are likeliest to be perusers of the following tract," he begins. He continues by apologizing for his subject, and the fact that he wrote, but ends by establishing the importance of his subject, and that no one could be more qualified for it than himself. He yields to his "fans"—"there are divers persons, for whom I have a great esteem and kindness, who think they have as much right to solicit me for composures of the nature of this, that they will now have to go abroad, as the virtuosi have to exact of my physiological pieces" (2)—with the same gawky grace with which Parker yielded to his bookseller. He also sees that his preface performs the functions appropriate to it, according to Genette's analysis. Thus, we encounter "thème du comment," in "equitable readers will consider, not only what is said, but on what occasion, and with what design it is delivered" (3); "genèse" in "the just indignation I conceived, to see even inquisitive men depreciate that kind of knowledge, which does the most elevate" (4); and "choix d'un public" in "I despair not, that what is here represented, may serve to fortify in a high esteem of divine truths those, that have already a just veneration for them" (4).

One other writer is especially appropriate to illustrate the prefatory conventions that Swift satirizes in *A Tale*—the notorious John Dunton. Robert Adams Day describes him as the more learned Dr. Bentley's equal at writing *scaz*, which he defines after the Russian formalists as "naive, unadorned, idiomatic speech, an idiolect in fact, transferred to paper."[14] Day connects the rise of *scaz* to the rise of print culture and what he calls—with reference both to the visual orientation of print and to the element of egotism it allows—"Eyethink" (135). According to Day, Swift hated Dunton (and satirized him in *A Tale*) for more than Dunton's having hoodwinked him over the Athenian Society; he would have seen in him the shift from discourse with a strong rhetorical sense to discourse more visually oriented, personal and (in a classical sense at least) disordered.[15]

While still pursuing Day's lead, I would like to qualify his ideas a little, and bring them into line with my discussion of prefaces, by considering them in the light of Dunton's prefaces to his own *Life and Errors of John Dunton*. Even the title seems to confirm Dunton's boast that "his own personality was his sole and darling theme" (128). What is curious, and even disturbing about Dunton's prefaces, is not just their degree of *scaz*, but the strange effect of that—essentially non-rhetorical — combined with with a high degree of rhetorical self-consciousness stemming from the author's awareness of the fact that he is, after all, writing a preface. Day remarks that, with printing, "The author need not woo the collective audience with the devices of the classical exordium, nor yet carefully prepare his transitions; he can present his unmediated self instantly" (127), but this is a bit of an overstatement, as well as an oversight, since the preface is itself a kind of exordium, a podium or a platform, but a typographical one which, while it retains some degree of rhetorical place and occasion, allows for a *scaz*-like degree of intimacy as well. Now Dunton can reach privately, in print, such numbers as before could only be reached publicly, in speech; his egotism seems animated by the awareness that he is going "one on one" with multitudes.

Of course, this combination of the private and the public in Dunton's prefaces is disturbing because it creates, or at least aggravates, a confusion of value, a troublesome uncertainty in the reader about how to take what is written, because he is never sure what tone it is written in. It is possible that Dunton was literally mad, yet his excesses exaggerate only slightly the abuses to which prefaces were prone, and the possibility that a madman could so aggrandize himself in a preface argues for its accessibility as a print-created private public podium, a platform that anyone could climb up on and avail himself of.

The very title of Dunton's first prefatory piece seems to glance at Genette's "choix d'un public," "To the Impartial Readers," which precludes many contemporary and perhaps all modern readers. He then writes, in the first paragraph, of the need to "prepare my Reader's mind a little" (xi). Though what follows was written in 1704, it sounds remarkably like the prefatory pieces of *A Tale*. Swift's Hack begins his "Epistle Dedicatory to Prince Posterity" with what sounds like an excuse, if not a complaint: "I here present Your Highness with the Fruits of a very few leisure Hours, stollen from the short Intervals of a World of Business, and of an Employment quite alien from such Amusements as this" (30). Dunton begins similarly: "My retreat from the world and business has given me not only the leisure, but the inclination, to become more thoughtful than before" (xi).

As implied by his title, Dunton, like most prefacers, is concerned about judgment, but he himself seems confused about whether the judge is himself, the reader, or God, or whether the judgment is self-criticism, literary criticism, or the Day of Judgment. He takes pains to establish his good intentions—he says "design," a word that Swift does arabesques on in his "Apology"—but he is never very clear exactly what they are, and one probably wouldn't believe him if he were, because he sounds so dishonest. He insists, in a preface to a book about himself, that "I know very well, and *am satisfied with*, my low obscurity" (xii—emphasis added). Describing the book to follow, he inadvertently suggests a scam—"the burthen of my *New Idea* is no less than the business of the Christian Life"—as if he were really less concerned with the business of life than a life of (constant and rather shady) business. When he allegorizes "Christian Life" in bookseller's terms—"if any have been so unfortunate as to copy after my *real Life*, I here take the opportunity to tell them, that I solemnly disown the original" (xii)—he sounds *worse* than dishonest.

Dunton, conventionally, indicates the originality or novelty of his work, his "New Idea" being a kind of autobiography interleaved with repentence, the life he really lived with the life he wishes he had lived. In his hand, unfortunately, novelty turns immediately into bathos, and bathos into the grotesque. Though speaking in rather commonplace terms of "old life" and "new life," he still finds it necessary to explain to the reader (whom he must suppose is as stupid as himself) that "according to the best evidence he can get, he was living the tenth of October, 1704" (xii), when he wrote this preface. He is like Swift's Partridge, after Swift got through with him. Worse, too delighted with the obvious to leave it alone, he worries it to death and putrefaction: "I confess, six years ago, I printed my *Living Elegy* (or represented John Dunton as dead and buried, in an 'Essay upon my own Funeral'), and perhaps some may think it a little *maggoty*, that I should come again from the Dead to write 'The History of my own Life;' but, Gentlemen, cease to wonder at this, for I have almost finished 'The Funeral of Mankind; or, an Essay proving we are all dead and buried, with a Paradox, shewing what we call Life Is Death, and that we all live and discourse in the Grave,' &c." (xv).

There is a paradox here, but it is that Dunton has nothing to say, least of all in public, and says it in a preface. He is constantly, like Swift's Hack, addressing himself to readers (and only those "impartial" readers) who have had the very same experiences he has—and very scazzy they are, too—while recommending his work as written entirely from experience. He has nothing to impart.

Swift offers us several kinds of preface.[16] The "Bookseller's Dedication" (technically an "épître dédicatoire [fictive] à fonction préfacielle" [181]) is a "préface allographe fictive," the "Dedication to Prince Posterity" is a "préface authoriale fictive," "The Preface" is another "préface authoriale fictive," and the "Apology" Is a "préface authoriale authentique" (and "ultérieure" because it was attached only to the fifth and subsequent editions). Moreover, "A Digression in the Modern Kind" is really a preface dropped into the middle of the book, and "A Further Digression" is a postface (even though the book isn't quite finished yet). What is especially interesting about all these different types of preface is the way each explodes the conventions that Genette sees as peculiar to its type. This suggests both the accuracy of Genette's generalizations and, since Swift must have made his own generalizations two centuries earlier, the rightness of Genette's assertion that the conventions of the preface developed and became fixed very early in the development in the preface itself: "la plupart des thèmes et des procédés de la préface sont en place dès le milieu du XVIe siècle, et les variations ultérieures ne relèvent pas d'une véritable évolution, mais plutôt d'une série de choix divers dans un répertoire beaucoup plus stable qu'on ne le croirait *a priori*" (152).

The disjunction between prefatory piece and prefaced text can be seen, exaggerated, in the disjunction among the prefatory pieces themselves, in particular between the two dedications. The Bookseller dedicates to Somers, over the author's own dedication to Prince Posterity. Wheatley, incidentally, gives us a real-life version of the same thing, when Dryden, at loss of considerable profit, nobly refused to dedicate his *Aeneas* (1697) to King William, only to have Tonson dedicate it for him, by causing every likeness of Aeneas in the engravings to resemble the monarch, so that the wits could say "old Jacob has placed old Nassau's hook-nos'd head on young Aeneas' shoulders" (137).

The problems of praise that were seen by Marvell in Parker's *Preface* remain in Swift's parodic prefaces, if only because they are endemic. The ostensible object of the "Preface authoriale originale" being to obtain a good reading (183), this kind of preface employs a strategy of "giving value to the text" (184) while implicating the author only minimally. In such a preface the author tends to emphasize his subject at the expense of his treatment of it. One way to emphasize the subject is to stress its utility, and we find the Hack doing precisely this in "The Preface." The Swiftian version of the convention is, predictably, slightly askew: the utility celebrated is that of uselessness. "It was decreed, that in order to prevent these *Leviathans* from tossing and sporting with the *Commonwealth* . . . they should be diverted from that Game by a *Tale of a Tub*. And my Genius being conceived to lye not unhappily that way, I had the Honor done me to be engaged in the Performance" (41). The same sort of convention is satirized in "Section V" where the "Endeavours" of the moderns are characterized as "highly serviceable to the general Good of Mankind" (123).

A desire for novelty and originality are also conventions of this kind of valorization. Such a desire perhaps explains what, to my mind, is one of the most "original" prefatory pieces ever penned, Lacy's dedication of *Dumb Lady* (1672) to Lord Limrick, one of Charles's bastards by the Duchess of Cleveland, quoted in Wheatley: "When I began to write this dedication my hand shook, a fear possessed me, and I trembled; my pen fell from me, and my whole frame grew disordered as if blasted with some sudden upstart comet. Such awe and reverence waits on dignity, that I now find it fit for me to wish I had been refused the honour of my dedication, rather than undertake a task so much too great for me" (148). Clearly the desire to write not another "stale bundle of flattery" has induced a state of dementia—but surprise us he does. The distracting shift from the novelty of the work being prefaced to the novelty of the preface itself Genette calls "l'effet Jupien" (89), a tendency to loiter in the vestibule with a too-distinguished servant. According to Swift, "my more successful Brethren the *Moderns* . . . will by no means let slip a Preface or Dedication without some noteable distinguishing Stroke to surprise the Reader at the Entry, and kindle a Wonderful Expectation of what is to ensue" (42). This "stroke" is provided in "A Digression In the Modern Kind" by inserting what is essentially a preface in the middle of the book. Originality has also its pragmatic side, to foil the reader who would "twirl over forty or fifty Pages of *Preface* and *Dedication*, (which is the usual *Modern* Stint) as if it were so much *Latin*" (131).

Perhaps the most interesting convention Swift exploits for his "préface authoriale originale fictive" is what Genette calls (after Aristotle, Quintilian, etc.) "excusatio propter infirmitatem" (193), related to the strategy of valorization because it too, by stressing the author's infirmity, emphasizes the subject at the expense of its treatment. It is also a means of anticipating and thereby frustrating the critics (see "préface paratonnerre" (192). We encounter something of the sort in the Hack's "circumstances and postures of life" of which he remarks, "the shrewdest Pieces of this Treatise were conceived in Bed, in a Garret: At other times . . . I thought fit to sharpen my Invention with Hunger; and in general, the whole Work was begun, continued, and ended, under a long Course of Physic, and a great want of Money" (44). Of course, the change here is that the infirmity has been made out to be a positive thing; moreover, it is combined with another convention, that of advice how to read a book ("thème du comment" [194]), which naturally obviates the question of *why* read that book: "Whatever Reader desires to have a thorow Comprehension of an Author's Thoughts, cannot take a better method, than by putting himself into the Circumstances and Postures of life, that the Writer was in upon every important Passage as it flow'd from his Pen" (44).

A "how to read this book" preface occurs again as late as "A Further Digression," the penultimate section, where it is so late as to be utterly pointless: "I do here humbly propose for an Experiment, that every Prince in *Christendom* will take seven of the *deepest scholars* in his Dominions, and shut them up for *seven* Years, in *seven* Chambers, with a Command to write *seven* ample Commentaries on this comprehensive Discourse" (185). The conventional discussion of the origins (Genette, 195) of the book, the expression of thanks for those who were involved it, and the acknowledgment of sources, are also aspects of valorization, if only because "un auteur qui a tant d'amis et de compagnes ne peut être absolument mauvals" (197). We find versions of these attributes in the relation of the "important Discovery . . . made by a certain curious and refined observer" (40) in "The Preface" and in the acknowledgement in "A Further Digression" of all sorts of people who had nothing to do with *A Tale of a Tub*: "I do here return my humble Thanks to *His Majesty*, and both Houses of *Parliament*; To the *Lords* of the King's most honourable Privy-Council, to the Reverend the *Judges*; To the *Clergy*, and *Gentry*, and *Yeomantry* of this Land" (181).

The most serious implication of the "Preface" regarding praise has to do, oddly enough, with the decline of individual satire and the rise of general satire too sparing in nature. The idea in the "Preface" is that this sparing has hurt not only blame, but praise too; after all, how can one praise effectively, how can praise mean anything, if the praiser is not equally free — and able — to blame? This dilemma is shown, in the conclusion of "The Preface," to have done infinite harm to more than just prefaces (though they are naturally a good beginning) but to what we have come to call today "the fabric of society." It is surely no coincidence that one of the things which one cannot do in the world of *A Tale* is the very sort of thing that Marvell — or someone like him — did so effectively in the "Painter-Poems" (and in *The Rehearsal Transpros'd*), themselves a significant illustration of the importance of individual satire — blame — to individual praise, and praise to blame generally. One may not now, as Marvell did, describe "How such a one, starved half the Fleet, and half-poisoned the rest." The "Preface" expands, then, from a self-manifestation of specific and rather narrow rhetorical problems, to the illustration of those same problems at work at large in society; the decline of a literary kind of social writing — the preface — mirrors the decline of social discourse generally.

The "choix d'un public" (197), oddly enough, occurs in the postface, "A Further Digression," where like the "how to read this book" it is so out of place as to be useless: "Readers may be divided into three Classes, the Superficial, the Ignorant, and the Learned: And I have with much Felicity fitted my Pen to the Genius and Advantage of each . . . . But the Reader truly learned, chiefly for whose Benefit I wake, when others sleep, and sleep when others wake, will here find sufficient Matter to employ his Speculations for the rest of his Life" (185). Clearly Swift knew what conventions went where, and violated such arrangements. Moreover, the uselessness of "A Further Digression" corroborates Genette's argument that the postface is among the rarest variations of the preface (219), for the obvious reason that it comes too late to obtain a good reading. Rather than write a postface, the author might as well wait for a second edition and write a "préface ultérieure," good modern examples of which are also relatively scarce, thanks to the decline of the "critique moralisante" (228) who necessitated it in the first place.[17]

This brings us to Swift's own "préface ultérieure," "An Apology [for the *Tale of a Tub*]." Here, where Swift appears to attempt to assert the positive value of convention, we sense that he has written himself into a corner or (to mix metaphors) pulled the rug out from under his feet in a way that Marvell (narrowly) avoids doing. For here, in "An Apology," Swift attempts to use in earnest many of the very same prefatory conventions he has so thoroughly exploded in the body of his work—he becomes, if not the first, the most conspicuous victim of his own nihilism.

For all the sensitivity to conventions which enables Swift to violate and expose them so effectively, in "An Apology" he comes remarkably close to ignoring the first convention of such a preface (whether "originale" or "ultérieure"), which is never to insist on one's own genius, talent, style, cleverness at composition, etc. (184). He comes too close sometimes to self-praise through self-explanation, to stating the obvious in a way that makes it less clear: "Another Thing to be observed is, that there generally runs an Irony through the Thread of the whole Book, which the Men of Tast will observe and distinguish, and which will render some Objections that have been made, very weak and insignificant" (8).

The principal function of the "préface ultérieure," the "réponse aux critiques" (223), "An Apology" performs adequately enough, but not without employing many of the same conventions he had exploded earlier. We encounter "choix d'un public" in remarks like "those who approve it, are a great Majority among the Men of Tast" (3) and (reminding us of the "Dedication to Prince Posterity") "This Apology [is] chiefly intended for the Satisfaction of future Readers" (9). Similarly we get a great deal about "genèse"—"The greatest Part of that Book was finished about thirteen Years since, 1696, which is eight Years before it was published" (4); "his Discourse is the Product of the Study, the observation, and the Invention of several Years; . . . he often blotted out much more than he left" (10)—and about "how to read this book"—"Had the Author's Intention met with a more candid Interpretation from some whom out of Respect he forbears to name, he might have been encouraged" (5-6); "some have endeavour'd to squeeze out a dangerous Meaning that was never thought on" (8). We even have the assertion of originality, which the Hack himself couldn't have claimed more vociferously: "through the whole Book he has not borrowed one single Hint from any Writer in the World; and he thought, of all Criticisms, that would never have been one. He conceived it was never disputed to be an original, whatever Faults it might have" (13). Finally, Swift's assertion that "He was then a young Gentleman much in the World . . . he gave a Liberty to his Pen, which might not suit with maturer Years, or graver Characters"

(4) resembles the "excusatio propter infirmitatem"—propter iuventum, perhaps.[18]

"An Apology" is inconsistent not only with the main body of *A Tale*, but also with itself. Swift criticizes the language of Dryden's prefaces, where he tells us "that he *possesses his soul in Patience*" (7). This is in dangerous proximity to Swift's own—obviously rather thin—expressions of patience in the "Apology." In similarly dangerous proximity to his injunction against unfavorable or uncharitable applications of his work, he urges the reader to make uncharitable applications: "I believe the Reader may find more Persons to give that Passage an Application" (7). How is his preface any different? Uncharitable applications are welcome, provided they are to parodied authors and not the "real" one, the author of the "Apology," even though it is extremely hard to tell them apart.

Swift is finally left without any ground to stand on, caught up in the very problems of convention he diagnosed so well. Swift's exploitation of conventional forms of valorization and recommendation in *A Tale of a Tub* seems to have destroyed his capacity to assert any positive values directly, least of all conventional ones, and amounts almost to a cancellation of one branch of epideictic rhetoric by another, of panegyric by satire. Swift's own dilemma in "An Apology" is similar to that of his creation, the Bookseller. They have either to invent new conventions, new virtues, which will *ipso facto* be spurious, or to use the old Aristotelian ones that have become counterfeit in print (and which are only introduced by way of parasepiopesis): "But to ply the World with an old beaten Story of your Wit, and Eloquence, and Learning, and Wisdom, and Justice . . . I confess, I have neither Conscience, nor Countenance to do it" (25–26). The predicament is as bad as the Hack's, of having to praise satire because the conventions of panegyric have been exhausted, and so by praising blame, he blames praise and thereby contradicts himself. The screw has been turned once too often and the thread been stripped.

NOTES

1 "En guise d'avant-propos," *L'Esprit Créateur* 27 (1987): 5–6.
2 (Paris: Éditions du Seuil, 1987).
3 Andrew Marvell, *The Rehearsal Transpros'd* and *The Rehearsal Transpros'd The Second Part*, ed. D. I. B. Smith (Oxford: Clarendon Press, 1971). Jona-

than Swift, *A Tale of a Tub*, ed. A. C. Guthkelch and D. Nichol Smith, 2nd ed. (Oxford: Clarendon Press, 1958).

4 Luiz Fernando Valente, "Fiction and the Reader: The Prefaces of *Tutameia*," *Hispanic Review* 56 (1988): 350.

5 Jorge Luis Borges, *Obras completas 1923-1972* (Buenos Aires: Emece, 1975), 429. Quoted as translated by Oviedo, "Borges: The Poet According to His Prologues," *Borges the Poet*, ed. Carlos Cortinez (Fayetteville: University of Arkansas Press, 1986), 121-33.

6 Henry B. Wheatley, *The Dedication of Books to Patron and Friend* (London: Elliot Stock, 1887). Guy R. Lyle, ed., *Praise from Famous Men: An Anthology of Introductions* (Metuchen, NJ: The Scarecrow Press, 1977).

7 Herbert J. C. Grierson and Sandys Wason, *The Personal Note or First and Last Words from Prefaces, Introductions, Dedications, Epilogues* (London: Chatto & Windus, 1946), 9, 39-40.

8 See William Kinsley, "Le Mock-Book" (*Etudes Françaises* 18 [1982]: 43-60), for a discussion of *A Tale of a Tub* as "mock-book."

9 Just as we (reading Marvell reading Parker, to use modern jargon) seem to be on a walk accompanying Marvell through Parker's text (Marvell uses the walk as a metaphor for "animadverting"), we seem to be right with Marvell when he breaks off his reading for the night and resumes the next morning. One paragraph ends, "And so, Mr. Bayes, Good night," and the next begins, "And now Good-morrow" (117). Reading and commentary are signs of authorial presence.

10 See Eugene Korkowski, "With an Eye to the Bunghole: Figures of Containment in *A Tale of a Tub*," *Studies in English Literature* 15 (1975): 391-408.

11 Deborah Baker Wyrick, *Jonathan Swift and the Vested Word* (Chapel Hill and London: The University of North Carolina Press, 1988), especially 132-35.

12 Wheatley noted the same thing in 1887, with particular reference to dedications: "At the revival of learning in Europe, when the grand works of the classic authors were rescued from their long slumber, few of them were published without a dedication" (4).

13 Aristotle, *The "Art" of Rhetoric*, trans. John Henry Freese (The Loeb Classical Library, Cambridge, MA: Harvard University Press and London: William Heinemann Ltd., 1939), 97.

14 Robert Adams Day, "Richard Bentley and John Dunton: Brothers under the Skin," *Studies in Eighteenth-Century Culture* 16 (1986): 125-38.

15 Dunton responds in the preface to his *The Life and Errors of John Dunton, Citizen of London; With The Lives and Characters of More than a Thousand Contemporary Divines, And Other Persons of Literary Eminence, etc.*, 2 vols. (London: J. Nichols, Son, and Bentley, 1818), where he endeavors to turn Swift's satire into compliment: "to use the words of the *scoffing Tub-man*, the History of my *Life and Errors* is 'a faithful and painful Collection,' wholly gathered from my own breast" (xvi).

16 The preface may be described according to "régime" (its order of truth) and "role" (the relationship of the prefacer to the prefaced text [Genette, 169)]:

ROLE ORDER	authorial	other	actorial
authentic	Hugo in *Cromwell*	Sartre in *Portrait d'un Inconnu*	Valery in *Commentaire de Charmes*
fictive	"Laurence Templeton" in *Ivanhoe*	"Richard Simpson" in *Gulliver*	"Gil Blas" in *Gil Blas*
apocryphal	"Rimbaud" *la Chasse Spirituelle*	"Verlaine" in *la Chasse Spirituelle*	"Valery" in *Commentaire de Chamres*

17 Genette remarks that Nabokov was one of the "dernières victimes" of moral critics (228): hence, the "postface ultérieure" to *Lolita*.
18 This autobiographical, even retrospective aspect of the "Apology," resembles what Genette calls the "préface tardive" (228), good modern examples of which would be Borges's prologues to his *Obras completas* of 1974, in which he sometimes expresses a sense of alienation from the prefacer as well as the work prefaced: "I have changed this book very little. It is no longer mine" (55). Borges's preference of "prologue" over "preface" no doubt reflects his appreciation of the theatrical, role-playing potential of the form. Some of Borges's prologues would be closer to the "préface ultérieure" (like the prologue to *El Chacedor* [1960]), but clearly the distinctions between such "seuils" are no more water-tight than the "seuils" themselves.

"This was a Woman that taught": Feminist Scriptural Exegesis in the Seventeenth Century

MARGARET OLOFSON THICKSTUN

In reading contemporary criticism of seventeenth-century women writers, I have noticed that critics tend either to ignore or to misunderstand the feminist implications of women's claim to religious authority as interpreters of Scripture. It seems to me that contemporary scholarship, operating as it does in a secular culture, is not sufficiently aware of the revolutionary nature of a woman's claim to religious authority. I would like to correct this misapprehension by discussing two women writers of the late seventeenth century who attempted a feminist critique of Scripture, Margaret Fell, in *Womens Speaking Justified* (1667), and Mary Astell, in the preface to the third edition of *Some Reflections on Marriage* (1706).[1] But I would also like to distinguish between their arguments in order to identify why Astell's work, which ultimately retreats from claiming women's equality in the Spirit, figures so prominently in recent discussions of early feminism, while Fell's pamphlet defending women's religious authority receives only passing reference.

A brief survey of recent scholarship reveals the intellectual bias that blinds contemporary scholars to the importance of these writers' feminist critique of Scripture. Hilda Smith's *Reason's Disciples: Seventeenth-Century English Feminists* (Urbana: University of Illinois Press, 1982) posits Enlightenment ideas as the efficient cause for a burst of feminist writing at the close of the century: "In rationalism they found the ideology that best answered their desire to assert equality and to develop a framework for questioning the status quo" (60). Ruth Perry, in an essay on Astell in *Women and the Enlightenment* (New York: Haworth Press, 1984) comments that "what strikes one about her life and work as a whole, what marks her as a woman of the Enlightenment, is her unqualified belief in Right Reason and the faith she reposed—both personally and ideologically—in the mind" (15). Katharine Rogers titles one chapter in her book, *Feminism in Eighteenth-Century England* (Urbana: University of Illinois Press, 1982), "The Liberating Effect of Rationalism." Astell's secular arguments appeal to contemporary scholars because she values what they value, education and the exercise of reason, while both her Scriptural criticism and Fell's impassioned claims of inspiration disconcert readers trained to equate religious enthusiasm with either irrationality or fundamentalism.

In their discussions of both writers, scholars reveal their assumption that religious faith and feminist convictions are necessarily antithetical: Smith, for example, says of Astell's *A Serious Proposal to the Ladies* that "the strong religious orientation of her curriculum would not, of course, allow for a genuinely liberating education" (126). Similarly, she dismisses the feminist implications of Fell's pamphlet because Fell does not raise "the issue of women's role in the household or in society in general" (95), asserting that she "asked merely that a Christian woman be allowed to practice her religion as fully and variously as a man" (96). But Margaret Fell's claiming the right to preach is in itself a defiantly and expansively feminist act that transcends any need to pursue an argument about the details of social change that must necessarily follow. Simply by undertaking the task of interpreting Scripture independently of the male clergy, these women threaten the very basis of patriarchy's social control. The continued resistance to women clergy among the more conservative religious bodies today—even though women members of those religions are college professors, corporate presidents, and congresswomen—illustrates the profound connection between religious authority and patriarchal power.

Both Fell and Astell develop hermeneutic practices that allow them to challenge received interpretation of Scripture by establishing an extrabiblical access to divine truth. Fell derives her authority as an interpreter of Scripture from her belief in God's continuing self-revelation in history, an idea that destabilizes the authority of Scriptural texts. Addressing the problem that twentieth-century feminist theologians describe as distinguishing "script from Scripture,"[2] Fell privileges charismatic speaking of God's word over silence: "those that speak against the Power of the Lord, and the Spirit of the Lord speaking in a woman, simply, by reason of her Sex, or because she is a Woman. . ., such speak against Christ, and his Church, and are of the Seed of the Serpent" (116). Passages that exhort silence and order, then, must be interpreted in terms of the overriding command to witness to God's love and power. In the light of this principle, Fell believes she can determine "how God himself hath manifested his Will and Mind concerning women, and unto women" (115).

Mary Astell's hermeneutic practice confronts priestly authority by privileging reason, or common sense, over erudition, "for Sense is a Portion that GOD Himself has been pleas'd to distribute to both Sexes with an Impartial Hand, but Learning is what Men have engrossed to themselves" (78). Common sense leads her to conclude that "One Text for us, is more to be regarded than many against us. Because that One being different from what Custom has establish'd, ought to be taken with Philosophical Strictness" (79). She distinguishes between passages that present divine revelation about women and passages that conform to human practice, arguing that "Scripture is not always on their side who make parade of it, and thro' their skill in Languages and the Tricks of the Schools, wrest it from its genuine sense to their own Inventions" (74). Her subsequent critique of traditional interpretations of Scriptural passages about women asserts her own ability to get at "its genuine sense."

Both writers, then, approach Scripture through what twentieth-century feminist biblical theologians term "a hermeneutics of suspicion." They recognize both the text itself and conventional principles of interpretation as political tools and criticize clergy who use Scriptural authority as an ideological weapon against women. Astell underscores men's power as translators and interpreters when she observes that "women, without their own Fault, are kept in Ignorance of the Original, wanting Languages and other helps to Criticise on the Sacred Text, of which they know no more than Men are pleas'd to impart in their Translations" (74). Without knowledge of the original languages, she asserts, women read not the actual Scripture, but a translation that is necessarily an interpretation of it. The concern which the clergy demonstrates in restricting who can read the original text and how the text can be interpreted "shew[s] their desire to maintain their Hypotheses, but by no means their Reverence to the Sacred Oracles" (74–75). Astell's concern that women be able to test the accuracy of the translation suggests that her religious conviction, at least as much as her reading in philosophy, informs her arguments for women's education. She remarks wryly that "when an Adversary is drove to a Nonplus and Reason declares against him, he flies to Authority, especially to Divine, which is infallible, and therefore ought not to be disputed" (74). As her subsequent Scriptural exegesis demonstrates, an educated female laity would possess the ability to dispute the interpretation of "infallible" Authority.

Fell establishes women's inspired witness as grounds for disputing priestly authority. She not only exposes the hypocrisy of priests who "take Texts, and Preach Sermons upon Womens words, and still cry out, Women must not speak, Women must be silent" (124), but calls into question the completeness of Scripture. Of Jesus's explicit self-revelation to the Woman of Samaria, she comments, "this is more than ever he said in plain words to Man or Woman (that we read of) before he suffered" (117). That parenthetical remark indicates that Fell questions the accuracy of the biblical record itself, not simply its vernacular manifestions. She contests the privileged status of Scripture because she recognizes that the received history of Jesus's ministry is not a full account of the truth, but a telling of the story that serves the political purposes of the priesthood. By claiming an authority derived from a personal experience of the Spirit, Fell is able to ground the legitimacy of her speaking and her message outside received tradition and conventional authority, while at the same time appealing to the ultimate truth it claims to contain.

Both Fell and Astell demonstrate an acute awareness of the historicity of biblical texts, particularly the Pauline epistles. They insist that the Pauline letters be read in their historical, pastoral context. In Fell's discussion of 1 Cor. 14:34 — "Let your women keep silence in the churches, for it is not permitted unto them to speak" — she argues that Paul's exhortation to silence applies to a particular episode in church history, not to the conduct of Christian women throughout all time. Applying her hermeneutic principle that speaking the Gospel takes precedence over social propriety, Fell interprets Paul's subsequent qualification, "as also saith the Law," as further evidence that this command does not apply to women's inspired speaking: "for he speaks of women that were under the Law, and in that Transgression as Eve was" (119). These women who, Fell proposes, had not yet entered the community of grace could not participate as full speaking members in communal worship. Paul's command then does not apply to believing women "that have the Everlasting Gospel to preach, and upon whom the Promise of the Lord is fulfilled" (120). She defends this interpretation by pointing to 1 Cor. 11, which outlines proper behavior for women who are prophesying — such as covering their heads and leaving their hair braided — and Philippians 4.3, where Paul entreats Philemon "to help those Women who laboured with him in the Gospel."

Astell also emphasizes the pastoral context of this injunction. She argues "that tho' he forbids Women to teach in the Church, . . . he did not found this Prohibition on any suppos'd want of Understanding in

Woman, or of ability to Teach; neither does he confine them at all times to *learn in silence*" (77). She points to Priscilla's teaching Apollos, and to Paul's placing her name before her husband's and "giving to her as well as to him, the Noble Title of his *Helper in Christ Jesus*" (78), as evidence that Paul cannot mean this statement to be a universal proclamation. She suggests that he forbade women to teach in the Corinthian church "for several Prudential reasons, like those he introduces with an *I give my Opinion, and now I speak not the Lord*, and not because of any Law of Nature, or Positive Divine Precept" (77). Astell demonstrates through her analysis of this passage not only her sense of the epistles as historical documents, but a careful attention to the uses of language, both by Paul and by his translators, adding "that the words *they are Commanded* (1 Cor. 14.24.) are not in the Original, [as] appears from the *Italic* character" (77). Here, she suggests, ideology determines not only interpretation, but translation.

In the light of this awareness, both writers refute traditional readings of the Genesis story, as well as its manifestations in the Pauline texts on women. Fell privileges the first Creation story in Genesis 1:27—"So God created man in his own image, in the image of God created he him; male and female he created them"—arguing that "God the Father made no such difference in the first Creation, nor never since between the Male and the Female" (116). She reads the punishment and prophecy in Genesis 3 as an allegorical discussion of the enmity between Satan and the Church, an approach which she uses to discredit sexist applications of Ephesians, chapter 5, and 1 Timothy, chapter 2. Astell also reads 1 Timothy, chapter 2, allegorically, remarking that it is "a very obscure place," but that "if it be taken Allegorically, with respect to the Mystical Union between Christ and his Church, to which St. *Paul* frequently accomodates the Matrimonial Relation, the difficulties vanish" (78). She mocks arguments for the subjection of women because of the Genesis story, commenting, that "the Earthly *Adam's* being *Form'd* before *Eve*, seems as little to prove her Natural Subjection to him, as the Living Creatures, Fishes, Birds and Beasts being Form'd before them both, proves that Mankind must be subject to these Animals" (78).

Along with this "hermeneutics of suspicion," both Fell and Astell deploy a "hermeneutics of remembrance," recovering women in Scripture as positive role models for contemporary women. Fell's discussion of Hebrew women stresses their spiritual authority; she includes examples of women teaching and prophesying, followed by the positive response of authoritative figures—patriarchs, elders, and prophets—to their speech. Astell emphasizes Hebrew women's political prominence as leaders of their people. She points to examples where God revealed himself to women rather than to their husbands because of their wisdom, prudence, or superior piety. Like Fell, she emphasizes the positive response of men in authority to women, although her choice of stories singles out pious rather than prophetic women. She also hesitates to use these exceptional women to establish precedents for other women's subverting the social order, commenting of one biblical passage, "I wou'd not infer from hence that Women generally speaking, ought to govern in their Families when they have a Husband" (82).

Both Fell and Astell emphasize the superior devotion of Jesus's female followers, as well as his special attention toward them. Astell lists Mary, Martha, Elizabeth, Magdalen, the Syrophoenecian, and Anna as exemplary women; she points out that "when our Lord escap'd from the Jews, he trusted Himself in the hands of *Martha* and *Mary*" (84), rather than with his male followers. Fell identifies a pattern of special revelation to women in which Jesus reveals himself as the Messiah and in which the women disciples—the woman of Samaria, Martha, and the woman with the alabaster box of ointment—confidently declare their belief. In discussing each story, she emphasizes the intimacy of the conversation, the unusualness of Jesus's blunt speaking, and the confidence expressed in the women's response. Of Martha's ready affirmation of Jesus's divinity—"Yea Lord, I believe thou art the Christ, the Son of God" (117)—Fell comments that "here she manifested her true and saving Faith, which few at that day believed so on him." Both women praise the women at the tomb, who were "so united and knit into him in love, that they could not depart as the men did, but sat watching, and waiting, and weeping about the Sepulchre" (Fell, 119). Both Fell and Astell identify these women's being the first to receive news of the Resurrection as a reward for their superior devotion.

But in her discussion, Fell presses women's prophetic authority more aggressively than Astell does. Astell admits that "GOD Himself who *is no Respecter of Persons, with whom there is neither Bond nor Free, Male nor Female, but they are all one in Christ Jesus* [Gal. 3.28], did not deny Women that Divine Gift the Spirit of Prophecy, neither under the Jewish nor the Christian Dispensation" (83). She identifies Miriam, Deborah, Huldah, and the four daughters of Philip as examples of inspired women and points to Paul's equal treatment of Priscilla as evidence that women did teach with authority. But she refrains from using these models or the events at the tomb as a means to encourage women's preaching, retreating toward more conventional definitions of female spirituality: "And if it is a greater Blessing *to hear the Word of GOD and keep it*, who are more considerable for their Assiduity in this than the Female Disciples of the Lord?" (83). Fell, on the other hand, exploits the revelation at the tomb to clinch her point that Christian witness requires women's active participation: as she asks triumphantly, "what had become of the Redemption of the whole Body of Man-kind, if they had not believed the Message that the Lord Jesus sent by these women [?]" (118). She argues that human redemption requires accepting the authority of women's witness.

Fell's entire discussion insists on a reevaluation of the role of Jesus's women followers as active disciples so that she can reclaim Christian discipleship and religious authority for women. In a striking anticipation of twentieth-century feminist biblical criticism, Fell asserts the prophetic claim of the woman with the alabaster box of ointment who anoints Jesus's head, declaring, "this Woman knew more of the secret Power and Wisdom of God, then his Disciples did, that were filled with indignation against her" (117). This episode has become a central symbol of feminist biblical historical reconstruction of the Christian movement, providing the title for Elisabeth Schüssler Fiorenza's *In Memory of Her*. Fiorenza explains that this woman's anointing Jesus's head not only witnesses to his kingship and messianic status but also asserts the woman's own prophetic power. In the Mark/Matthew telling that Fell quotes, the woman receives from Jesus praise and the promise of continued recognition from the Christian community, which will honor her as a superior disciple: Jesus declares that her action shall be repeated wherever the Gospel is proclaimed "for a memorial of her." In the Lukan source, she is presented as a model of discipleship against Simon, who has not "loved much." Fell uses both versions of the story to underscore her opposition between women's faith and that of the disciples; the disciples become a negative model for priests, who continue to judge the world in terms of the Law, who cannot see beyond physical categories.

Despite the similarities in their arguments, Fell and Astell differ about implications of their biblical criticism on present day life. While Astell claims that "the Bible is for, and not against us, and cannot without great violence done to it, be urg'd to our Prejudice" (84), she does not entirely believe herself, expressing a wish to dismiss the role of Scripture in any discussion of women's equality, to argue instead from the order of Reason: "Our *Reflector* is of Opinion that Disputes of this kind, extending to Human Nature in general, and not peculiar to those to whom the Word of GOD has been reveal'd, ought to be decided by natural Reason only" (74). But it turns out to be natural reason that defeats the practical application of her feminism. Astell may refute the inferiority of woman in the order of Creation, asserting that she "was made for the Service of GOD, and that this is her End. Because GOD made all things for Himself, and a Rational Mind is too noble a Being to be Made for the Sake and Service of any

Creature" (72). But reason tells her that human beings do not behave like rational creatures. She concludes that social hierarchy is a necessary response to fallen human nature: "If Mankind had never sinn'd, Reason wou'd always have been obey'd, there wou'd have been no struggle for Dominion, and Brutal Power wou'd not have prevail'd. But in the laps'd State of Mankind . . ., the Will and Pleasure of the Governor is to be the Reason of those who will not be guided by their own, and must take place for Order's sake, altho' it should not be conformable to right Reason" (75). Believing that there can not "be any Society great or little, from Empires down to private Families, without a last Resort, to determine the Affairs of that Society by an irresistible Sentence" (75), Astell affirms the necessity of hierarchy in general and sexual hierarchy within marriage. A woman may choose not to marry, but once she enters into this social contract, she must honor her voluntarily chosen subordination.

Astell's argument suggests that, while she may believe in women's spiritual and intellectual equality before God, she does not perceive that the realm of the Spirit impinges on temporal reality; she even recommends Christianity as the insurer of domestic tranquility, for "she will freely leave him the quiet Dominion of this World, whose Thoughts and Expectations are plac'd on the next" (128). Her advice to married women offers moral, but not political support. Most tellingly, Astell refrains from claiming for women the religious authority that would validate their interpretations of the Bible. She limits her argument for women's access to Scripture to their need for personal improvement, assuring readers of *A Serious Proposal to the Ladies* (1696) that "We pretend not that Women shou'd teach in the Church, or usurp Authority where it is not allow'd them; permit us only to understand our *own* duty, and not be forc'd to take it upon trust from others" (154). Such a claim concedes authority to men in order to negotiate for women a space in which to pursue their intellectual and spiritual development undisturbed. But this strategy weakens the political effectiveness of Astell's feminist critique of Scripture, because it acknowledges a higher authority to which women have no access, an authority that may at any point contradict their assertions, however reasonable they may appear, and label them as sacrilegious and evil. Fell, on the other hand, uses the authority she derives from her interpretation of Scripture to challenge patriarchal control.

Fell insists on the importance of Scripture not only in defining human nature but in determining social practice. Believing that sexual equality exists both in the Spirit and in the order of Creation, she locates sexual hierarchy in human misunderstanding, misreading, and weakness, for "God the Father made no such difference in the first Creation, nor never since between the Male and the Female" (116). Fell does not recognize sexual hierarchy as a punishment for sin, but as sin itself, for men who oppose women's equal authority are trying to "limit the Power and Spirit of the Lord Jesus, whose Spirit is poured upon all flesh, both Sons and Daughters, now in his Resurrection" (121). Such men revere human custom more than they do God's will for humanity. Fell's argument identifies the suppression of women's voices as an ungodly, anti-Christian activity. Considered in its historical context, Fell's pamphlet does not ask, as Smith contends, "*merely* that a Christian woman be allowed to practice her religion as fully and variously as a man" (Smith, p. 96, emphasis mine); it asserts women's right to speak authoritatively *even* about religion. Fell can take for granted that the acceptance of this fundamental principle will lead to profound changes in the relationships between men and women in everyday life; precisely such changes did occur within the egalitarian religious community that came to be known as Quakers. Fell does not address details of social change because she does not have to.

In privileging the voice of reason over revelation, contemporary feminist scholars unjustly and, I think, unwisely dismiss Fell's contribution to the feminist critique of Scripture because they underestimate the power of religious authority not only in her day, but also in modern life. The task of recovering Scripture and Christian tradition for women's affirmation is enormously important even today in a far more secular culture than the one Fell and Astell inhabited. Traditional religion provides the myths and stories that shape the way our society imagines gender and the way we imagine ourselves; these myths and stories cannot simply be ignored as rubbish, because they remain to poison our environment until we neutralize their effectiveness. In looking at the arguments of earlier feminists, we need to determine which strategies have the most potential for effecting positive social change. Because Astell tries to avoid a confrontation between her personal convictions and the teachings of the established church in which she worships, she allows male interpretations of Scripture and of women to remain authoritative. Fell, on the other hand, confronts sexist interpretations of God's will and activity in human history directly. She is thus able to begin, at least, to wrest the interpretation of Scripture, and therefore of women, from patriarchal control.

NOTES

1 Astell in *The First English Feminist*, ed. Bridget Hill (New York: St. Martin's Press, 1986); Fell in *First Feminists: British Women Writers 1578-1799* (Bloomington: Indiana University Press, 1985).
2 Elisabeth Schüssler Fiorenza, *In Memory of Her: A Feminist Theological Reconstruction of Christian Origins* (New York: The Crossroads Publishing Company, 1983), 16.

History, Genre, and Insight in the "Characters" of Lord Chesterfield

ALAN T. McKENZIE

"Search, therefore, with the greatest care, into the characters of all those whom you converse with."

Readers who know Philip Dormer Stanhope, 4th Earl of Chesterfield, only as one who offered courtly (but candid) advice to his illegitimate son and belated patronage to a proud lexicographer will be surprised at the level of knowledge, wit, and skill in twenty "Characters" of eminent contemporaries left behind in manuscript when he died. In them the Earl brought his considerable intelligence and long experience to bear on persons whom he was especially well qualified to observe and understand, and in a genre that was once both widely practiced and highly regarded. He had worked, dined, conversed, corresponded, and quarreled with the men and women whose "characters" he compiled on terms of civil intimacy for many, many years. Few contemporaries, and fewer writers, had equal access to so many important historical figures.

That access originated in a long and impressive sequence of high political positions: Member of the House of Commons, Gentleman of the Bedchamber, Captain of the Yeomen of the Guard, Member of the House of Lords, Privy Councillor, Ambassador at the Hague, Lord Steward, Viceroy of Ireland, Special Ambassador to the Hague, and Secretary of State.[1] Nor had Chesterfield merely held these positions; he had worked hard and well in them, especially as ambassador and viceroy, as even his numerous rivals and enemies occasionally attested. In every one of them he had sharpened his eye for the foibles of human nature, especially as they were distorted and magnified in the polished lenses of a court. Most of them obliged him to sharpen his pen as well, whether in detailed letters from a distant country, satiric essays in opposition journals, or clever speeches before the House of Lords, where his wit was much feared. The sharp pen and the ready access in themselves entitle these pieces to more attention than they have yet received. The historically accurate and vividly phrased observations, together with thoughtful abstractions and considered opinions, will repay that attention when they do receive it.

It was not until his long and distinguished career was over that Chesterfield found the time to write these "Characters." In 1748, in failing health and weary of objecting to the War of the Austrian Succession and of trying to share the duties of Secretary of State with the Duke of Newcastle, Chesterfield resigned the Seals and devoted himself to building one house, rebuilding another, collecting books and paintings, and cultivating melons and dignified ease. The "Characters" are the product of this period, when he was reading diligently, collecting his thoughts, and distributing them widely in letter after letter. In 1755 he wrote to his friend Dayrolles (the man to whom, from his deathbed some twenty years later, he would offer a chair—one final, courtly, and considerate gesture): "My deafness is extremely increased, and daily increasing; this cuts me wholly off from the society of others, and my other complaints deny me the society with myself, which I proposed when I came here [Blackheath]. I have brought down with me a provision of pens, ink, and paper, in hopes of amusing myself, and perhaps entertaining or informing posterity, by some historical tracts of my own times, which I intended to write with the strictest regard to truth, and none to persons myself not excepted" (10 July 1755, Dobrée #1950).[2] These "tracts of his own times" presumably included the "Characters," the publication of which his family tried to suppress nearly as hard as they did his letters to his son, and with no more success.[3]

The "Characters," then, are informed by a strong sense of real, and very powerful, persons and the actual events those persons had a hand in. They need to be read with an informed sense of history and a discerning (but not necessarily distrustful) attitude toward power. Chesterfield distrusted those he had seen wielding power, without in the least distrusting power itself.[4] Most of all he distrusted the distrust and the wonder of those who had not seen power being exercised from the vantage point he had occupied for so long: "I have been behind the scenes, both of pleasure and business. I have seen all the coarse pulleys and dirty ropes, which exhibit and move all the gaudy machines; and I have seen and smelt the tallow-candles which illuminate the whole decoration, to the astonishment and admiration of the ignorant audience" (23 February 1748, Dobrée #1544).[5] What he had seen was, more often than not, petty as well inconsistent, but a career of encountering pettiness and inconsistency in the highest places never dulled his clear recollection of the major scenes from the show his contemporaries had staged. His eye for characteristic behavior and his mind for larger historical concerns remained unimpaired, as an examination of his "Character" of the Duke of Newcastle will prove.

During the years 1746-1748 Chesterfield had frequent opportunities to look into this fascinating figure from several unique vantage points. As Ambassador to the Hague and Viceroy of Ireland, Chesterfield had corresponded with Newcastle as Secretary of State, regularly and to very good effect. Indeed, Dobrée suspects that it was the quality of his letters that got Chesterfield appointed to the unworkable but established arrangement whereby the two shared, or were supposed to share, the Seals as joint Secretaries of State (1:136).

As long as the two men conducted their business by letter, the clever Fourth Earl could take solace in his own evident superiority over the busy First Duke, and the Duke could ignore both that superiority and its inscriber. But when they had to meet repeatedly in the cabinet, the Duke, who would not share anything, least of all power, was forced to acknowledge what he could not abide. So, with a cunning and insensitivity developed over many years at court, Newcastle drove Chesterfield into the retirement from which, fifteen years later, the latter wrote one of his most historically informed, and one of his best, "Characters."

Author and subject were, as Chesterfield says, "contemporaries, near relations, and familiar acquaintances, sometimes well and sometimes ill together, according to the several variations of political affairs" (463).[6] Their familiarity gave Chesterfield unique and frequent access to Newcastle's actual utterances, which he indicates by underlining, and employs to very good effect: "He was alarmed at so bold an undertaking [Chesterfield's revision of the calendar], and conjured me *not to stir matters* that had been long quiet; adding, that he did not love *new-fangled things*" (464). The genre of the "character," as we shall see, had always relied on "characteristic" utterances, but *these* utterances, while perfectly characteristic, are more: direct quotations, spoken directly to the author. This author was sufficiently a man of his period to employ them as a means of assessing the quality of the mind behind them ("From such weaknesses it necessarily follows, that he could have no great ideas, nor elevation of mind" [464]).

Chesterfield's routine access to Newcastle's person and penetrating insight into his character must have made him a very irritating colleague, however much they contribute to his compositions: "His ruling, or rather his only, passion, was the agitation, the bustle, and the hurry of business, to which he had been accustomed above forty years; but he was as dilatory in dispatching it as he was eager to engage in it. He was always in a hurry, never walked, but always ran; insomuch that I have sometimes told him, that by his fleetness one should rather take him for the courier than the author of the letters" (464). Chesterfield had noticed this characteristic of Newcastle early, and he commented on it to his son: "The hurry and confusion of the Duke of Newcastle do not proceed from his business, but from his want of method in it. Sir Robert Walpole, who had ten times the business to do, was never seen in a hurry, because he always did it with method" (23 February 1748; Dobrée #1544).[7]

All of Newcastle's contemporaries noticed and were inconvenienced by this characteristic; not all of them were diverted by it: "He preferred not to work at the cockpit at Whitehall, the usual office of secretaries, choosing instead an office in Kensington; but he was often on the move, away from the capital, keeping odd hours, and thereby driving his aides to distraction. Charles Delafaye, the duke's undersecretary, wrote that 'His Grace of Newcastle may be at midnight forty miles off at Tyrrel's near Oxford and the next morning at seven at Kensington.' Such bustle, Delafaye added, 'does *deranger* my poor noodle sometimes, as the uncertainty of the time of dining does my stomach.' "[8]

Extravagant as well as busy, the Duke held vast levees to display and consolidate his power. Matthew Bramble and his excessively collegiate nephew attended one of these, as did everyone else in Britain; but their points of view were not as lofty, and their sense of social stratification not as acute, as Chesterfield's.[9] Few people in the eighteenth century (and probably none in any other) had the opportunity, the overdeveloped sense of social scale, and the sharp eye for courtly manner that inform a sentence like: "When at last he came into this levee-room, he accosted, hugged, embraced, and promised everybody, with a seeming cordiality, but at the same time with an illiberal and degrading familiarity" (464). That sentence elevates precise social observation into valid historical insight. It detects and exploits the connections between mind and body that absorbed Chesterfield and his contemporaries, studying the actions of Newcastle's busy body as it exhibited itself in public. Each of the carefully sequenced actions in it conveys the hurried and undiscriminating states of mind behind it, thereby establishing "character." In the process, Chesterfield exhibits and indicts the society within which that character flourished, obliging us to infer the expectations and disappointments of the numerous recipients of Newcastle's attentions and the social and psychological emptiness of those attentions. The concluding phrase, "an illiberal and degrading familiarity," is edged with truth as well as snobbery. It serves as an example of what made Chesterfield such a nuisance at court, but such a valuable recorder of what he saw there: He observed human behavior, he understood human nature, and he was willing to pass informed judgment on both.

When the Duke of Newcastle died in 1768, Chesterfield wrote one of his correspondents as follows:

> My old kinsman and contemporary is at last dead, and for the first time quiet. He had the start of me at his birth by one year and two months, and I think we shall observe the same distance at our burial. I own I feel for his death, not because it will be my turn next; but because I knew him to be very good-natured, and his hands to be extremely clean, and even too clean if that were possible; for, after all the great offices which he had held for fifty years, he died three hundred thousand pounds poorer than he was when he first came into them. A very unministerial proceeding! (21 November 1768; Dobrée #2548).

Not many of his contemporaries gave Chesterfield credit for the cheerful wisdom and informed humanism in that thoughtful and insightful obituary. The artist contemplates his subject and his portrait of that subject without indulging the illusion that he is looking in a mirror. In fact, there are no illusions in that paragraph, illusions of language, illusions of culture, or illusions of self-importance. The same freedom from illusion, reinforced by a sound basis in experience and a strong sense of history, informs the other nineteen "Characters," to the larger historical concerns of which I now turn.

The preoccupation of the first two Georges with their Hanoverian state, commented on by many contemporaries and most subsequent historians, had vexed Chesterfield repeatedly during his years as Ambassador to the Hague (see, for example, Dobrée #s 356 and 381). Some of his pique remains in the "Characters": "His views and affections were singly confined to the narrow compass of his Electorate"; "the Royal dignity shrunk into the Electoral pride" (433, 434). In identifying this concern, if not in resenting it, Chesterfield seems to have been closer to the truth than some subsequent historians. Many of the "Characters" exhibit a concern with "Constitutionality" too well informed and well distributed to be merely a matter of party politics. Frequently Chesterfield will ask, or rather suggest, who had power over the King, and how it was exercised. Thus the reference to a "ruling passion" in George II, in addition to reminding us that Chesterfield was a member of the Opposition (and a close friend of Pope), renders the ascription of a "ruling" passion to a king disturbing. This concern finds extensive expression in the "Characters" of those who provoked and schooled these passions, Queen Caroline and Lord Bute.

Chesterfield's concern for the Constitution was both pervasive and genuine: Hardwicke "loved the Constitution, and maintained the just prerogative of the Crown, but without stretching it to the oppression of the people" (462), while Fox "had not the least notion of, or regard for, the public good or the Constitution, but despised those cares as the objects of narrow minds, or the pretences of interested ones" (467). If this interest must be said to have been somewhat tainted by faction, it usually went beyond that circumscription in both penetration and eloquence.

The ultimate corroboration of the significance and complexity of the term "Constitution" in Chesterfield's informed political vocabulary appears in its application to Scarborough: "He was a true, Constitutional, and yet practicable patriot; a sincere lover and a zealous assertor of the natural, the civil, and the religious rights of his country. But he would not quarrel with the Crown, for some slight stretches of the prerogative; nor with the people, for some unwary ebullitions of liberty; nor with any one, for a difference of opinion in speculative points. He considered the Constitution in the aggregate, and only watched that no one part of it should preponderate too much" (459). Notice that Chesterfield's friend manages, uniquely, to combine the highly desirable attributes of the "Constitutional" with the riskier and more modern ones of the "patriot," without degenerating into a mere courtier.[10] The "Character" of Richard, Earl of Scarborough, becomes more poignant when read with some history and biography in mind. By all accounts (even Hervey's) one of the truly noble figures of this period, and an intimate friend, but not a political ally, of Chesterfield, the melancholy Scarborough, despondent over some matter of courtliness and politics, went home from his friend's library to commit suicide in his own. He left a copy of Temple's *Memoirs* open to the passage he and Chesterfield had been discussing that afternoon.[11]

In addition to these observed particulars and larger concerns that provide an important historical ground for the individual pieces, several thematic designs, humanist conventions, structural devices, rhetorical techniques, and satirical ploys elevate (if one may say so) these pieces from historical information into historical art. For example, subtle indications of Chesterfield's intimacy with his subjects (like the direct quotations mentioned in conjunction with Newcastle) introduce many observations, making them lively as well as valid: "Little things, as he [George II] has often told me himself, affected him more than great ones; and this was so true, that I have often seen him . . . " (435); "I was much acquainted with him [Walpole] both in his public and his private life" (453). The assertions of intimacy with Pope ("I have been with him a week at a time at his house at Twickenham, where I necessarily saw his mind in its undress" [444]) and Scarborough ("for the most secret movements of his soul were, without disguise, communicated to me only" [458]), however, testify to more than historical access.

In compiling these pieces in a genre both long established and well developed, as we shall see in a moment, Chesterfield made frequent and effective use of most of the concerns employed by previous literature devoted to the depicting and assessing of lives: a concern with marriage, friendship, and religion; special attention to the manner in which a character dies; distrust of the professions of those at court and the surmises of those outside it; an eye on posterity and the distribution of fame, and frequent (if somewhat routine) application to the palette of the passions.[12] He made occasional use of allusions ("but when [Pope] died he sacrificed a cock to Esculapius" [445]) and indicative examples (Walpole "had more of the Mazarin than of the Richelieu" [454]). The "Characters," like the letters, often employ or develop maxims (for example, "Men are apt to mistake, or at least to seem to mistake, their own talents" [462]). These concerns and techniques, each with a long history of its own, combine to lock each character into a well established, readily comprehended, framework. That framework rests on the humanist's assumption that there is such a thing as "human nature," that human nature is uniform, or at least widely shared, and that, though full of contradictions, it is capable of being analyzed and understood, and therefore characterized.

It is in this spirit that Chesterfield exploits the satirical topos of scale in several pieces, employing it to discredit mental abilities, national attitudes, political ambitions, sexual appetites, and, occasionally, its customary target, pride. The first two Georges were confined by their abilities and their loyalties to the tight boundaries of Hanover. "England was too big" for George I (433) and "Everything in [George II's] composition was little; and he had all the weaknesses of a little mind, without any of the virtues, or even the vices, of a great one. . . . the Royal dignity shrunk into the Electoral pride. He was educated upon that scale, and never enlarged its dimensions with his dominions" (434). Conversely, George I's appetite for large women provided Chesterfield an opportunity for the exercise of wit, and the historian an occasion for the application of fact: "No woman came amiss to him, if she were but very willing and very fat."

He brought over with him two considerable samples of his bad taste and good stomach, the Duchess of Kendal and the Countess of Darlington; leaving at Hanover, because she happened to be a Papist, the Countess of Platen, whose weight and circumference was little inferior to theirs" (439).[13] The spatial figure recurs with reference to Bolingbroke's imagination, Pulteney's power ("he shrunk into insignificancy and an Earldom" [453]), and Hardwicke's notions, which were clear, but not "great" (462).

One concern that unites Chesterfield with his age and the humanist tradition takes special advantage of his talents and career: the thoughtful assessment of the speaking abilities of nearly every one of the public figures he characterizes. Living in an age when, by all accounts, considerable eloquence was brought to bear on public affairs, Chesterfield displayed his own on numerous occasions, thus establishing his qualifications as a judge.[14] His career gave him many opportunities to judge character from speeches, and his talents made his assessments both searching and discriminating. He heard "some little tincture of the pleader" in Hardwicke's eloquence (461) and found Walpole an "artful rather than an eloquent speaker," able to intuit "the disposition of the House" and state intricate matters clearly so that "whilst he was speaking, the most ignorant thought that they understood what they really did not" (454). This analysis of Walpole's artfulness proves that, like most good speakers and all good critics, Chesterfield combined a strong sense of audience and occasion with attention to technique and content and confidence in his own taste.

This concern with eloquence, like the one with Constitutionality (to which it bears strong and intriguing connections), is constant and thoroughgoing: Pulteney was "a most complete orator and debater . . . eloquent, entertaining, persuasive, strong, and pathetic, as occasion required; for he had arguments, wit, and tears, at his command" (451–52); Granville excelled in both declamation and argument and could quickly seize "the stress of a question, which no art, no sophistry, could disguise to him" (456). Pitt also "excelled in the argumentative as well as in the declamatory way," but "his invectives were terrible, and uttered with such energy of diction, and stern dignity of action and countenance, that he intimidated those who were the most willing and best able to encounter him. Their arms fell out of their hands, and they shrunk under the ascendant which his genius gained over theirs" (468–69).

In these passages Chesterfield admires and characterizes the eloquence of men with whom he did not completely agree. His accounts of the eloquence of Bolingbroke and Scarborough, on the other hand, carry his admiration into his analysis, evoking the fine mind at work in the former—"a flowing happiness of diction, which (from care perhaps at first) was become . . . habitual to him" (441)—and the good heart in the latter—"He spoke so unaffectedly the honest dictates of his heart, that truth and virtue, which never want, and seldom wear, ornaments, seemed only to borrow his voice" (458).

Not all of his subjects were effective orators. George I confirmed his character as a dull, lazy, and diffident ruler by speaking little in public (433), while George II affected the hero in his conversation, which was otherwise sterile, leaving Chesterfield's acute ear little to listen to but his accent (435-37). But even when there was nothing for his ear to hear, his mind was at work. In Chesterfield's age ineloquent statesmen had to find some way to enable their views to take hold in a public forum, and the ways they did so were a means of revealing "character": Townshend was "ungraceful and confused . . ., but always near the stress of the question" (442), and Pelham compensated for his inelegance with candour (457). Chesterfield is silent, perhaps charitably so, on this aspect of Newcastle, who was notorious for his public ineloquence.[15]

Many readers may well need to be informed that Chesterfield expressed a principled concern with the Constitution and exhibited a good ear for Parliamentary eloquence. Few will be surprised that he also saw his way deeply into and behind behavior at court, and that he expressed what he saw vividly and succinctly. His own success in that venue had done much to sharpen his awareness of it, and nothing to diminish his perceptiveness. His "Characters" are full of the insights that he imposed on his son, without the insistent didacticism that makes the reading of much of his correspondence so wearisome. I have already mentioned his shrewd account of Newcastle's behavior at his own levees. George II's graceless yielding of himself to pleasure is another instance of the socially shrewd Chesterfieldian eye pointing the Chesterfieldian pen: "He did it so ungracefully, that both he and the company were mutual restraints upon each other, and consequently soon grew weary of one another" (435-36). Conversely, Scarborough's behavior was precisely what Chesterfield tried to inculcate in his son in letter after letter: "He had in the highest degree the air, manners, and address, of a man of quality, politeness with ease, and dignity without pride" (458; cf. Bolingbroke, 469-70).

One lesson he inculcated was that of "attention," but that inattention in company that he deplored repeatedly to (and perhaps in) his son, he found diverting in Arbuthnot: "As his imagination was always at work, he was frequently absent and inattentive in company, which made him both say and do a thousand inoffensive absurdities" (447).[16] Forgivable in a doctor—at least this doctor, and socially, rather than professionally—such behavior rendered Lord Bute utterly unfit to function at court, for reasons Chesterfield sets forth: "He never looked at those he spoke to, or who spoke to him, a great fault in a Minister, as in the general opinion of mankind it implies conscious guilt; besides that, if it hinders him from being penetrated, it equally hinders him from penetrating others" (474).

Those who congratulate themselves on not having to operate in such a setting may still acknowledge the quality of access to it provided in this text. The insights are social, historical, and psychological; they are conceived with intelligence and expressed with eloquence and efficiency. This is a continuation, and perhaps a polishing and a heightening, of a voice named some time ago and recently celebrated as originating in the Renaissance, the voice of "an English gentleman conversant with affairs."[17]

Chesterfield employed this voice when he had detected something revealing in the behavior he scrutinized: "A hearty kind of frankness, which sometimes seemed impudence, made people think that [Walpole] let them into his secrets, whilst the impoliteness of his manners seemed to attest his sincerity" (455). At its best that voice conveys his sense of the working of the minds of those he characterizes and his ability to articulate those workings. Assuming that one mind works very like another as well as "characteristically," he can take us behind the behavior of, say, Lord Townshend, to the cerebral motions producing it: "His parts were neither above nor below [business]; they were rather slow, a defect of the safer side. He required time to form his opinion; but when formed, he adhered to it with invincible firmness, not to say obstinacy, whether right or wrong, and was impatient of contradiction" (442). Chesterfield allowed himself to penetrate even the remote minds of the lofty: "Within certain bounds, but they were indeed narrow ones, [George II's] understanding was clear, and his conception quick: and I have generally observed, that he pronounced sensibly and justly upon single propositions; but to analyse, separate, combine, and reduce to a point, complicated ones, was above his faculties" (435).

Chesterfield set forth all this history at his disposal along lines laid out by a genre that had been established for centuries. In the seventeenth century that genre had enjoyed a rebirth and great currency, and just before Chesterfield turned to it it had, as genres will, devolved, developed, and complicated itself, absorbing several other genres in the process.[18] Chesterfield cannot have known that he was writing at the end of this long-lived genre, his competence in which is evident in every paragraph. The competence in it of his original readers may be taken for granted.

Its founder, Theophrastus, was a biologist, a student of Aristotle, and his successor at the Lyceum. His "Characters" were all "types," representing a single bad or foolish quality by means of a succession of vivid actions and "characteristic" speech habits. Most of them are nuisances drawn from the streets of Athens: the flatterer, the insincere man, the show-off, the late learner, and so on. "The inner man emerges from this description of externals; there is no abstract analysis" (Smeed, 4). Even in translation it is clear that the style reflects the content in its simplicity and its matter-of-factness. The syntax is highly additive, and the classifications utterly without indignation (Anderson, xii-xix).

All this changed in the hands of Theophrastus's numerous imitators in the English Renaissance, where the character sketch became a device for the display of stylistic ingenuity and moral, social, and political prejudice. The social scope widened, the observation became much less impersonal, and the writing far less laconic—"syncopated conundrums," in Greenough's impatient phrase.[19] Joseph Hall's "Characters," all abstract and didactic, employ antithesis to expose hypocrisy or "a fatal lack of . . . true self-knowledge" (Smeed, 21-22). Sir Thomas Overbury added an emphasis on social, rather than moral, types and a superabundance of those "conceits" that passed for wit in the seventeenth century. John Earle ended most of his "Characters" with some sort of flourish, an element evident in several of Chesterfield's.

Thus, while his subjects are individuals, not types, and his purposes are more psychological, political, and historical than ethical, social, or artistic (and his wit much more urbane than academic and rhetorical), the traditions of the character sketch contributed more than a convenient title to the pieces Chesterfield wrote. They dictated the lines along which these pieces were written and still, I would argue, need to be read.

Other writers incorporated character sketches into other genres. Philosophers, rhetoricians, historians (Tacitus, Clarendon, Halifax, who was Chesterfield's grandfather), dramatists (Terence, Jonson), essayists (Bacon, Addison), and satirists (Horace, Dryden, Pope), among others, scattered "characters" throughout their works—all well known to Chesterfield.[20] Sometimes these inserted characters were historically significant and sometimes socially or morally instructive. Most of these pieces incorporate chronology and a narrative thrust imparted by history; there are hints of both elements in most of the twenty works under discussion.

In some histories, and in many, especially French, memoirs, participants in events recorded their assessments of the personalities of the other participants: "It is a branch of history that flourishes in stirring and difficult times when men believe themselves to have special information about hidden forces that directed the main current of events" (Nichol Smith, xxv). Chesterfield clearly, and rightly, regarded himself as in possession of just such information.

Part "Character" and part *mémoire*, then, these pieces employ the conventions of one other genre and reflect the influence of one other writer. The genre is the prose "Portrait"; the writer, La Bruyère. A vogue for flattering, readily identifiable *"portraits"* of fashionable contemporaries by their intimates swept through the *salons* in the second half of the seventeenth century.[21] This tradition, implicit in the second term in the title of the genre ("sketch"), occurs repeatedly in Chesterfield. The assessment of the person of Lady Suffolk is noticeably painterly (440), and the figure is frequently made explicit: "I may, perhaps, be suspected to have given too strong colouring to some features of this portrait [Pulteney]; but I solemnly protest, that I have drawn it conscientiously, and to the best of my knowledge, from a very long acquaintance with, and observation of, the original. Nay, I have rather softened than heightened the colouring" (453). Chesterfield may be the only artist who can honestly claim, as he does in "George II," that he drew his "character from the life, and after a forty years sitting" (437).[22]

La Bruyère combined all three of these traditions, the character sketch, the memoir, and the portrait, in his translation and imitations of Theophrastus, *Les Caractères de Théophraste traduits du grec avec les Caractères ou les Moeurs de ce Siècle*, a work that Chesterfield had urged upon his son (together with *Les Réflexions Morales de Monsieur de la Rochefoucauld*) as early as 1748.[23] The passage in which he does so demonstrates yet again his own competence in the genre, as well as the tendency to mingle "portraits" and "characters." It also indicates that the reading and the writing of character were, for Chesterfield, by no means merely artistic exercises: "The characters of La Bruyère are pictures from the life; most of them finely drawn, and highly coloured. Furnish your mind with them first; and when you meet with their likeness, as you will every day, they will strike you the more. You will compare every feature with the original; and both will reciprocally help you to discover the beauties and the blemishes" (5 September 1748, Dobrée #1585; cf. #1779).[24]

Sometimes composites, sometimes actual portraits with classical names, La Bruyère's characters are subtly and brightly individualized, but still general and moral, rather than historical figures. Like Chesterfield, La Bruyère comments directly on the contents and workings of the minds of those depicted, while demonstrating the advantages of aphorism over the ornate devices of the English tradition. La Bruyère was also, of course, un-(rather than dis-) illusioned, but Chesterfield needed no model, classical, French, or English, for that.

As the letter assigning the reading of La Bruyère to his son proves, a strong, informed, and workable sense of character is central to the curriculum he set that unfortunate young man. Examples were drawn primarily from the life of the instructor (as the passages above on the Duke of Newcastle attest), but the son will not be excused from doing his own lessons, even while he is on his travels: "The characters, the heads, and the hearts of men are the useful science of which I would have you perfect master: that science is best taught and best learnt in capitals, where every human passion has its object, and exerts all its force or all its art in the pursuit. I believe there is no place in the world where every passion is busier, appears in more shapes, and is conducted with more art, than at Rome. Therefore, when you are there, do not imagine that the Capitol, the Vatican, and the Pantheon are the principal objects of your curiosity" (9 October 1749; Dobrée #1664).

Chesterfield's correspondents were admonished to put his skilled readings of the characters of those with whom he had had dealings to good use: "Lord Holderness, I must acquaint you, has the pride that all little minds have: flatter that, and you may do what you will with him. Far from a jealousy of business, I think he will be very willing that you should do it all, if you please. If I were you, I would tell him . . . " (16 May 1749; Dobrée #1640).

The twenty "Characters" Chesterfield left for posterity are more thorough and more disinterested readings than this one of Lord Holderness (and dozens of others like it). But clearly the years of producing such incidental readings for the benefit of his correspondents had trained Chesterfield's eye, and pen, for the benefit of other, later, readers. His career gave him opportunities to observe his subjects, his own character enabled him to look into the characters of others and record what he saw, and his library had shown him the ways to depict them.

It would be pleasant to conclude this essay with a study of the nature of the entity under scrutiny, answering such questions as: What, exactly, is, or was, "character"? Why was it so much more significant to the writers of the eighteenth century than it is to those of this one? Why did it submit to these deft sketches? And what made so many people then so good at projecting it, and a few so good at analyzing it? Such an investigation would have to discriminate the various senses of the word even in the pieces in question, as Chesterield employs it in a strictly generic sense (456, 461, 463), as a synonym for "reputation" (460), and, most often, in the rich sense illustrated in the following passage: "I think it very possible, considering the unsteadiness and timidity of [Bute's] character, that to some degree he was ['the author and deviser of defeating his own plan']. Might he not fear, considering the imperious character of Mr. Pitt, he had gone too far with him" (481).[25]

Having done all this, such an analysis might well move on to speculate on the differences between "character" and "identity" on the one hand, and "character" and "personality" on the other. It may well be that "character" is a wholly social construct, and both spatial and performative, which can therefore be looked at and into, as well as depicted and fashioned, while "identity," imprisoned in its own interiority, can only be pursued from, and around, its own interior. "Personality" may well be both a construct of, and better left to, the social sciences, which are usually content to classify varieties in bloodless abstractions unlikely to be confused with, or informed by, the insights in the pieces under discussion. Clearly this investigation is another project for another time.

That being the case, I conclude with one last, exceedingly instructive, passage. While he was in Switzerland Philip Stanhope took his eye off the inhabitants of the courts he was visiting to look at and describe the landscape. He should have known better:

> I hope you will be as good a portrait painter, which is a much more noble science. By portraits, you will easily judge that I do not mean the outlines and the colouring of the human figure; but the inside of the heart and mind of man. This science requires more attention, observation, and penetration, than [landscape painting]; as indeed it is infinitely more useful. Search, therefore, with the greatest care, into the characters of all those whom you converse with; endeavour to discover their predominant passions, their prevailing weaknesses, their vanities, their follies, and their humours; with all the right and wrong, wise and silly springs of human actions, which make such inconsistent and whimsical beings of us rational creatures. A moderate share of penetration, with great attention, will infallibly make these necessary discoveries. This is the true knowledge of the world. (2 October 1747; Dobrée #1409)

The author of that letter, and of these twenty "Characters," had such knowledge, and he undertook to put it at the disposal of those who would take the trouble to read his writings. Those who do so with some understanding of the history of the times in which he lived and the genre in which he worked will appreciate the depth of this gentleman's conversancy with affairs and of his insights into the characters of those who conducted them.

NOTES

1 The best biography is Bonamy Dobrée's Introduction, "The Life of Philip Dormer Stanhope, Fourth Earl of Chesterfield," in his edition of *The Letters of Philip Dormer Stanhope, 4th Earl of Chesterfield*, 6 vols. (London: Eyre & Spottiswoode, 1932), 1:1-225. The letters are quoted from this edition and cited as Dobrée. The "Characters" are quoted from *The Letters of Philip Dormer Stanhope, Earl of Chesterfield*, ed. Lord Mahon (London: Richard Bentley, 1847), 2:433-82. The standard bibliography is Sidney L. Gulick, *A Chesterfield Bibliography to 1800*, 2nd ed., published for the Bibliographical Society of America (Charlottesville: University Press of Virginia, 1979).

2 Dobrée suggests that the "Characters" were written in 1768 or 1769 (1:214-15). A slightly different version of "Bolingbroke" appeared in a letter to his son of December 1749 (Dobrée #1677). "Lord Bute" was written while the subject was still in power, though the manuscript evidently says 1764 (470). On this same evidence, Scarborough's was written in 1759, Pitt's in 1762, and Pulteney's and Newcastle's in 1763 (457, 467, 451, 463). Those of George II and Granville were written sometime after their deaths, which occurred in 1760 and 1763.

3 See Sidney L. Gulick, Jr., "The Publication of Chesterfield's *Letters to His Son*," *PMLA* 51 (1936): 165-77.

The manuscript of the "Characters" was for some years in the collection of Arthur A. Houghton, Jr. — see the Gulick *Bibliography*, 5, 207, and the sale catalogue: *Books and Manuscripts from the Library of Arthur A. Houghton, Jr.*, pt. 1 (London: Christie, Manson and Woods, 1979), no. 116, 108-11, which indicates that it was sold for £10,000 to "Arthur." Horace Walpole had a glimpse of it (and of nearly everything else the least bit hidden in the period), and both William Dodd, the clergyman-forger, and J. O. Justamond, an early editor, are suspected of having made surreptitious copies.

Seven of the "Characters" were published in 1777 by W. Flexney; in 1778 the Dillys added nine more, and in 1845 Lord Mahon added the remaining four, evidently from the manuscript just mentioned. Last published in 1892 in an edition of the letters by John Bradshaw (London: Swan Sonnenschein & Co.) and in a Philadelphia reprint of Mahon's edition, they are now available as *Characters [1778, 1845]*, The Augustan Reprint Society Publication nos. 259-260 (Los Angeles: William Andrews Clark Memorial Library, 1990), with an Introduction by the present author.

4 As Viceroy of Ireland, in the tense year of 1745, Chesterfield wielded power with firm and flexible intelligence — see Dobrée 1:120-36.

5 The division between pleasure and business recurs repeatedly in the "Characters," for example, "Pulteney," 451, "Pitt," 467. His constant presence *behind* the scenes prevented Chesterfield from invoking the conventional figure yoking politics and the stage as often as one might expect. Nevertheless, George I was "as unfit as unwilling to act the part of a King" (433) and George II "loved to act the King, but mistook the part" (434), while Pitt "came young into

Parliament, and upon that great theatre soon equalled the oldest and the ablest actors" (468; see also 479).
6 Chesterfield employs an aristocratic sense of "nearness." Anne, the daughter of an Elizabethan Stanhope, married John Holles, first Earl of Clare, from whom the Duke of Newcastle received his title, as Dobrée puts it, "by devious genealogical paths" (1:8).
7 Cf. 10 August 1749; Dobrée #1653, where the example is distilled into a maxim: "Whoever is in a hurry, shows that the thing he is about is too big for him."
8 Reed Browning, *The Duke of Newcastle* (New Haven: Yale University Press, 1975), 45. For Newcastle's aversion to change, mentioned above, see 188. Browning provides ample evidence of the fiscal irresponsibility and the lifelong devotion to lavish entertainment to which Chesterfield refers in the last two paragraphs of his "Character." It is clear from Browning's biography, and from every contemporary account, that Newcastle was, in fact, and in the current sense of the term, a "character"; Chesterfield did not exaggerate. See, for example, Sir Lewis Namier, *England in the Age of the American Revolution*, 2nd. ed. (London: Macmillan, 1966), 67–83; Namier corroborates, employs, and praises Chesterfield's "Character": "There are many brilliant, and even correct, descriptions of Newcastle, and perhaps the best and fairest among them are the sketch by Lord Chesterfield" (67).
9 Tobias Smollett, *Humphry Clinker*, ed. J. L. Thorson (New York: W. W. Norton, 1983), 103–9 (Smollett's Newcastle is primarily a man of blunders).
10 This was not true of Pulteney, whose sense "of shame made him hesitate at turning courtier on a sudden, after having acted the patriot so long, and with so much applause" (452), or of Pitt (469), in both of whom "Patriotism" was theatrically self-conscious.
11 See Dobrée, 1:88–89. For Hervey's extended comparison of the characters of Chesterfield and Scarborough, very much to the advantage of the latter, see John, Lord Hervey, *Some Materials Towards Memoirs of the Reign of King George II*, ed. Romney Sedgwick, 3 vols. (London: Eyre and Spottiswoode, 1931), 1:73–74.
12 The passions abound in the "Characters" of Queen Caroline, Lord Bolingbroke, Pulteney, and Lord Scarborough. See Dobrée #1679, 19 Dec. 1749, which elaborates on them as the keys to character, and much else. For the ways in which Chesterfield's contemporaries construed the passions, see Alan T. McKenzie, *Certain, Lively Episodes: The Articulation of Passion in Eighteenth-Century Prose* (Athens: University of Georgia, 1990).
13 The passage goes on to depict "all those ladies who aspired to his favour, and who were near the Statutable size, strain and swell themselves, like the frogs in the fable." The historical and biographical considerations that intrude into this figure are (1) The first of the two "considerable samples" of George's taste, the Duchess of Kendal, was the mother of Melusina de Schulemberg, Countess of Walsingham and Baroness of Aldborough; and (2) In 1733 Melusina, herself a substantial and inconvenient reminder of George's "good stom-

ach," became Lady Chesterfield. See the *DNB*, under "Schulenburg," and Dobrée 1:72-73.

14 Even Hervey admired Chesterfield's eloquence on occasion; see 3:738-39.
15 See Browning, 44, also 77, where Newcastle is given credit for the "doggedness" of his public speaking.
16 One striking example of this inculcation: "For my own part, I would rather be in company with a dead man than with an absent one; for if the dead man gives me no pleasure, at least he shows me no contempt; whereas the absent man, silently indeed, but very plainly, tells me that he does not think me worth his attention" (22 September 1749; Dobrée #1660).
17 The phrase is Courthope's, who heard it first in Wyatt's assessment of the court; Stephen Greenblatt recovers and extends it, suggesting that it "gradually came to seem inevitable, natural, an object in reality . . . . And the purpose it serves is to free the speaker from any implication in the world he attacks; unlike the court lyrics, here he stands safely apart, in firm moral rectitude" (*Renaissance Self-Fashioning From More to Shakespeare* [Chicago: University of Chicago Press, 1980]), 131.
18 See J. W. Smeed, *The Theophrastan "Character": The History of a Literary Genre* (Oxford: Clarendon Press, 1985). See also R. G. Ussher, *The Characters of Theophrastus* (London: Macmillan & Co., 1960); Warren Anderson: *Theophrastus: The Character Sketches* (Kent, Ohio: Kent State University Press, 1970); Benjamin Boyce, The *Theophrastan Character in England to 1642* (Cambridge, Mass.: Harvard University Press, 1947); and Chester Noyes Greenough, *A Bibliography of the Theophrastan Character in English with Several Portrait Characters*, Harvard Studies in Comparative Literature, 18 (1947—reprinted Westport, Conn.: Greenwood Press, 1970). For an illuminating discussion of the ways genres complicate and perpetuate themselves, see Alastair Fowler, *Kinds of Literature: An Introduction to the Theory of Genres and Modes* (Cambridge, Mass.: Harvard University Press, 1982).
19 See, in addition to Smeed, 19-35, and Boyce, passim, W. J. Paylor, ed., *The Overburian Characters*, The Percy Reprints 13 (Oxford: Basil Blackwell, 1936). Greenough's phrase is from Boyce, 143.
20 David Nichol Smith, *Characters from the Histories & Memoirs of the Seventeenth Century* (Oxford: Clarendon Press, 1920); Benjamin Boyce, *The Polemic Character, 1640-1661* (Lincoln: University of Nebraska Press, 1955). For some of Chesterfield's own incidental "characters" see Dobrée, 1:203-6. For an analysis of what became of the tradition in the hands of the man to whom Chesterfield is too often coupled to his own disadvantage, see Martine Watson Brownley, "Johnson's *Lives of the English Poets* and Earlier Traditions of the Character Sketch in England," *Johnson and his Age*, ed. James Engell, Harvard English Studies, 12 (Cambridge, Mass.: Harvard University Press, 1984), 29-53; Robert Folkenflik, *Samuel Johnson, Biographer* (Ithaca: Cornell University Press, 1978), 101-4; and Jean H. Hagstrum, *Samuel Johnson's Literary Criticism* (Chicago: University of Chicago, 1952), 38-41.
21 Nichol Smith, xxvii-xxviii; Smeed, 48-49, 60-62. Cf. Boyce, *The Theophras-*

tan Character, 83-87. Richard Wendorf, *"Ut Pictura Biographia*: Biography and Portrait Painting as Sister Arts," in *Articulate Images: The Sister Arts from Hogarth to Tennyson*, ed. Richard Wendorf (Minneapolis: University of Minnesota, 1983), 98-124, considers the connections between some of the larger versions of these two art forms.

22 Chesterfield accumulated one of the most distinguished portrait collections in Britain. Most of them were portraits of authors; see David Piper, "The Chesterfield House Library Portraits," in *Evidence in Literary Scholarship: Essays in Memory of James Marshall Osborn*, ed. René Wellek and Alvaro Ribeiro (Oxford: Clarendon Press, 1979), 179-95.

23 For La Bruyère see, in addition to Smeed, 49-56, Jean Stewart's "Introduction" to *La Bruyère: Characters* (Harmondsworth: Penguin Books, 1970), 7-24.

24 He also recommended the characters of Crébillon fils (Dobrée, nos. 1742, 1770) and Cardinal de Retz, among others—the latter in #1746, a letter full of characters and maxims.

25 This sense of "character" is defined in the other book that got Chesterfield in trouble with posterity as "7. Personal qualities; particular constitution of the mind." Samuel Johnson, *A Dictionary of the English Language* (London, 1755, repr. New York: AMS Press, 1967). For the senses in which the word was used in the seventeenth century, see Boyce, *The Theophrastan Character*, 294-96, 302.

Historical Fiction: David, Marat, and Napoleon*

HEATHER McPHERSON

"There are two ways of understanding portraiture—either as history or as fiction"—Baudelaire, 1846.[1]

Portraits have long counted among Jacques-Louis David's most admired works, although the artist and his contemporaries clearly considered them secondary to the history paintings.[2] The portraits, which typically emphasize verisimilitude, rigorous composition, and specific surface detail, appear straightforward and unproblematic in comparison with the didactic, highly referential history paintings. In fact, in the literature there has been a widespread tendency to segregate David's portraits from the rest of his academic production.[3] For example, in his 1907 study of David as portraitist, Prosper Dorbec refers to two artists in total disaccord within David—a hidebound antiquarian and a liberated master enamored of nature and truth.[4] Although it may be convenient to treat David's portraits as a separate aesthetic entity, in the case of official portraits, such as those of Marat and Napoleon, no clear dividing line can be drawn. These public effigies, which demonstrably were painted for ideological purposes, fall midway between portraiture and history painting.

It is this hybrid realm that I am designating *historical fiction*. I have purposely avoided the more usual term, *portrait historié*, which generally denotes fancy dress portraits, like those of Nattier, in which contemporaries parade as gods or goddesses, or ennobled portraits of the type painted by Reynolds, which self-consciously allude to classical prototypes. David's official portraits, in particular those of Marat (fig. 1) and Napoleon (fig. 2), come much closer to historical fiction in the accepted literary sense of the term. The reference here is to Lukács, although I am somewhat subverting his argument by pushing back the concept of historical fiction to the French Revolution rather than the fall of Napoleon.[6] I also reject the contention that David's attempt to collapse art into political ritual ended in 1794.[7] In point of fact, I shall argue, this process reached its apogee under Napoleon; a living legend replaced the cult of the Revolution and its martyrs. Walter Friedlaender rightly insisted upon the profound originality of the revolutionary "martyr portraits" and the Napoleonic commissions (22 ff). In the present article I shall briefly explore that originality, showing how David's most explicitly political (even hagiographic) portrait images—the celebrated *Marat* and the Napoleonic effigies—function ideologically by seamlessly melding together fact and fiction. In the process, they transfigure history.

In the academic hierarchy and eighteenth-century critical discourse, portraiture occupied a poorly defined position below that of history painting. Although the portrait portrayed mankind, unlike history painting it represented a specific individual and was based on imitation rather than invention.[8] This differentiation fostered a patronizing attitude toward portraiture that had already been articulated in the sixteenth century by Michelangelo and his followers. In his *Het Schilderboeck* (1604), Karel van Mander concluded that portraiture was a "bypath of art."[9] But the purported intellectual inferiority of portrait-painting in no way diminished the demand for portraits in Renaissance Italy or eighteenth-century France. Leading portraitists, such as Quentin de La Tour, enjoyed widespread renown and demanded high prices. As Lorne Campbell argues (151), portraitists enjoyed social as opposed to intellectual respectability. Writing in 1747, the critic Lafont de Saint-Yenne decried the overabundance of portraits at the Salons, but admitted that portraiture was the most reliable means of earning a living for artists.[10] And Saint-Yenne's plaint set the pattern for the rest of the century.

Although critics continued to complain of the overabundance of portraits at the Salons, they tended to be more favorably disposed toward portraits of rulers and great men, which could be construed as morally exemplary.[11] The Comte d'Angiviller's policy of commissioning lifesize statues of France's *grands hommes*, like the commissioning of paintings depicting nationalistic subjects, was historic, rational, and patriotic in its aims.[12] But the representation of grandeur was by no means easy.

David and Historical Fiction / 179

Figure 1. J.-L. David, *Death of Marat*, 1793 (Brussels, Musées royaux des Beauxarts). Photo Giraudon reproduced by permission.

Figure 2. J.-L. David, *Bonaparte Crossing the Alps at Saint-Bernard*, 1800 (Malmaison, Musée national).

Houdon, the pre-eminent neoclassical sculptor of the late eighteenth century, specialized in portraits of the leading statesmen of his day, from Voltaire to Washington. Yet ironically, Houdon's contribution to the *grands hommes* series, *Admiral de Tourville*, 1781, is one of his least successful effigies.

Throughout the eighteenth century royal portraits were commissioned from leading artists by the crown and exhibited publicly at the Salons. During the 1780s there was a concerted effort to repair Marie Antoinette's sagging popularity by commissioning edifying portraits of the Queen, notably the Greuzian, maternal image painted by Mme. Vigée Lebrun, which was belatedly exhibited at the Salon of 1787 (fig. 3).[13] Vigée Lebrun, following David's advice, based her composition on a *Holy Family* by Raphael.[14] Although the picture was praised for its decorative qualities, Joseph Baillio has convincingly argued, in a discussion of the instability of the painting's meaning, that Vigée Lebrun's hybrid portrayal of the regal and the maternal failed to coalesce in 1787. Despite this portrait's eloquent rhetoric and distinguished pedigree, it foundered as a piece of political propaganda (Baillio, 59).[15] Ironically, because portraits elevate the individual and emphasize the specific, classicizing critics, such as Lessing and Winckelmann, excluded portraiture from their aesthetic considerations, assuming that a portrait could not easily function as an *exemplum virtutis*.[16] David's official portraits, however, prove the contrary—a lesson that has not been lost on subsequent authoritarian regimes.

Although David's critical reputation rested primarily upon his skill as a history painter, he practiced portraiture throughout his career. The artist's early, ruggedly realistic portraits often represent intimates, such as François Buron and his wife, who posed in 1769. One of David's earliest public successes, however, which was exhibited at the Salon of 1781 on his return from Rome, is the spectacular equestrian *Portrait of Count Potocki* (Warsaw, National Museum) (fig. 4), which anticipates the *Bonaparte Crossing the Alps*, executed almost twenty years later. Although painted for a private client, the grand style and ambitious scale revealed the genius of a history painter.[17] Indebted to both Rubens and Van Dyck, the *Portrait of Potocki* also illustrates David's painterly brio and propensity for the theatrical. It was, however, the vicissitudes of history itself—the French Revolution and the triumph of Napoleon—that provided the script for David's most inspired pieces of historical fiction: the lost *Portrait of Le Pelletier*, the *Death of Marat*, and *Bonaparte Crossing the Alps at Saint-Bernard*.

David's riveting *Death of Marat* (Brussels, Musées royaux des Beaux-Arts) (fig. 1) was commissioned by the Convention on 14 July 1793, the

Figure 3. Vigée LeBrun, *Marie Antoinette and Her Children*, 1787 (Versailles, Musée national du Château). Photo credit: Giraudon/Art Resource, New York.

Figure 4. J.-L. David *Portrait of Count Potocki*, 1781 (Warsaw, National Museum). Photo Giraudon reproduced by permission.

day after Marat's assassination, and completed in mid October, when it was exhibited as pendant to the *Portrait of Le Pelletier* on the President's tribunal.[18] The Convention also ordered engravings of the two martyrs' portraits: 1000 impressions were to be distributed to representatives of the people and the departments. David, an admirer of the detested and widely feared radical journalist, had visited Marat the day before the assassination and observed him at work in his bathtub.[19] It was this attitude that he selected for his commemorative portrait. In addition to painting Marat's official effigy, David organized the funeral ceremony and campaigned actively for the honors of the Pantheon that were briefly accorded to "l'ami du peuple."[20]

David's commemorative portrait is not a likeness in the ordinary sense. Contemporary accounts underline the physical debilities and *laideur* of Marat, which contributed to his cult as martyr and later provided a paradigm of the revolutionary dementia of the Terror.[21] The most reliable pictorial document is a representation of Marat writing, purportedly drawn from life by his friend Laplace in 1793 (Versailles, Musée Lambinet). Instead, David stresses drama and heightened emotion (traditional attributes of history painting) at the expense of objectivity and individual physiognomic peculiarities (defining characteristics of portraiture). The reasons for this theatricalization and amplification of the model are in this case rather transparent. In opting to portray Marat as a revolutionary martyr—in producing a veritable *pietà*—David turned to traditional religious iconography, specifically the death of Christ, and Caravaggesque lighting, as has frequently been noted. He may also have been influenced by the tableau of Marat's assassination on display in Curtius's Cabinet de Cire, which Mme Tussaud mentions in her memoirs.[22] In addition, there is a possible antique source for the composition.[23] David's painting of Marat was clearly intended to function as an *exemplum virtutis*, as the public display of the canvas and the commission for the engraving attest. The engraving does not duplicate the painting, however. Instead, it is based on David's dazzling pen and ink drawing of Marat's detached head (Versailles, Musée national du château) (fig. 5), which was also modeled in wax by Mme Tussaud. The disturbingly lifelike gaze seems to signal Marat's continued vigilance even after death.[24] The pure, almost childlike features of Marat, together with the asymmetrical gaze, the peculiar framing, and the mesmeric stippling and cross hatching effects, create an icon of extraordinary intensity.

The elaborate funeral ceremonies, like David's painted effigy, gave visual form to the myth and official sanction to the Marat cult. The victim was laid out on a triumphal bier in the Eglise des Cordeliers, surrounded by tricolor hangings along with two stones from the Bastille

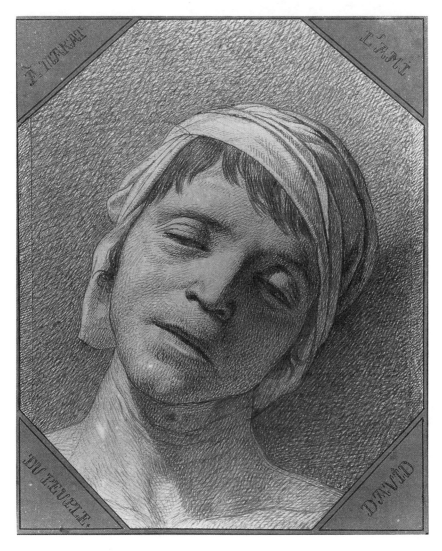

Figure 5. J.-L. David, *Head of Marat*, 1753 (Versailles, musée national du château).

inscribed "Marat" and "l'Ami du peuple"; his makeshift desk, the bathtub, and the inkwell were exhibited like instruments of the passion. The wound resembling Christ's (which David represented accurately), combined with Marat's gift of prophecy and the topos of self-sacrifice, further contributed to Marat's sanctification after his death.[25] But not even the flowers lovingly tossed on Marat's bier could disguise the rapid putrefaction of the corpse resulting from the heat and the diseased state of the deceased. The wound gaped; Marat's features soon became unrecognizable; and rumors of the plague began to circulate. The garish face and torso actually had to be whitened for the funeral procession, whose timing was unexpectedly advanced (Guilhaumou, 62-64). On 17 July Marat was buried in the garden of the Cordeliers; his heart, like those of French kings, was embalmed separately. At the funeral a painting depicting *Marat du séjour des Immortels aux Français* (of which no trace remains) was exhibited. The *mise en sublime* was now complete.[26]

In representing the *Death of Marat* David took a number of liberties, beginning with the room itself, which was actually wallpapered and furnished, not a dark, indeterminate hole. He also prominently displayed Charlotte Corday's second, undelivered letter, the one which appealed to Marat's mercy, and the *assignat* to be delivered to a mother of five. These attributes, together with the wooden crate and the ascetic surroundings, associated the revolutionary martyr with Christian charity, not a virtue for which he had been particularly noted in life.[27] Furthermore, David's verism functions selectively; the highly illusionistic treatment of details, such as the grain of the wood, the *trompe l'oeil* inscription, and the bloodied knife, seemingly guarantees the authenticity of the scene. Paradoxically, however, the verisimilitude of the objects also contributes to the picture's sacred aura or transcendence, functioning as a metaphysical springboard like Loyola's exercises in meditation. Finally, Marat's hideous features and unsightly illness have been painted out of the picture. The power of the image resides in its uneasy blend of the religious and the secular, violence and transfiguration, gruesome fact and cleansing fiction, as Baudelaire so aptly noted in 1846 when he referred to the appeasing role of death, which gives the work a tender, poignant quality. "Cruel like nature, this picture has all the perfume of the ideal" (225).[28]

Yet as Marie-Hélène Huet has suggested, the death of Marat was a complex chronicle of a death foretold in which victim and murderer became reversible when the events were restaged.[29] Several months before the assassination Marat had been tried and acquitted by the Revolutionary Tribunal, which effectively turned him into a "living martyr" and placed him outside the reach of the law.[30] The half dozen plays that reenacted the death of Marat (often ending with an apotheosis), like David's memorable painting, illustrated the impossiblity of forgetting and presented a double image of death and resurrection.[31] The three plays that celebrated Charlotte Corday's infamous act completed the cycle begun by the trial and execution of Louis XVI. On April 24, 1793, before the Tribunal, Marat had referred to himself as "martyr and apostle of liberty." David's bloody effigy, with its personalized funerary inscription, exemplifies the sublime or *écriture politique* in the Barthean sense—an *entelekheia* of the Revolutionary legend that required theatrical amplification and imposed a civic consecration of bloodshed.[32] Despite his distaste for its revolutionary subject, Delécluze hailed the *Death of Marat* as the first demonstration of the power and originality of David's talent (405-406). For Delécluze, David's *Marat* opened the way for his post-Revolutionary masterpieces, the *Sabines* and the *Coronation*.

The political case to be made in Napoleon's official portraits was more complex—the double problem was one of legitimation and consecration: how to provide a military opportunist with an imperial (preferably Roman) pedigree. The most blatant example is undoubtedly the *Bonaparte Crossing the Alps at Saint-Bernard*, 1800 (fig. 2), of which five versions exist. The equestrian portrait, commissioned by Charles IV of Spain, represents Napoleon in the Marengo costume, swathed in a swirling cape that was apparently invented by the artist.[33] Beginning with Delécluze (233), most scholars have attributed the idea behind the portrait to Napoleon himself, who supposedly told David that he wished to be represented icily mastering his fiery steed.[34] It is not known exactly when the artist and the future Emperor first met; however, they were certainly in contact by 1798.[35] After his victory at Marengo, Napoleon, then first consul, requested that David paint his portrait. David accepted with enthusiasm even though Bonaparte refused to pose, maintaining that portraits of great men ought to display their genius; physical resemblance was therefore of little consequence (Delécluze, 231-32). David had initially envisaged painting a grandiose portrait of Napoleon after the Battle of Castiglione with the treaty of Formio, accompanied by an attendant holding his horse. During the single three-hour sitting that he was accorded, David sketched Napoleon's head in the "Atelier of the *Horatii*"; modern history eclipsed the antique. This magnificent, thinly painted *ébauche* (Paris, Musée du Louvre) illustrates David's impassioned response to his new hero, whose head he rapturously described as "pur," "grand" and "beau comme l'antique" (Delécluze, 201-204).[36] A recently discovered preparatory sketch for the unrealized portrait represents the general standing before his horse, although there is no allusion to the Treaty of Formio (Schnapper, 378-80, plate 160). For reasons that are unclear, David abandoned the project.

Instead, in 1800 David painted *Bonaparte Crossing the Alps*. In this canvas David's political rhetoric reaches a feverish pitch. He represented the first consul as he wished to appear: sharply chiseled against the sublime backdrop of the Alps, coolly mastering his rearing horse with ranks of toy soldiers and a fluttering tricolor far below. Leading his troops across the Alps was unquestionably a brilliant tactical stroke; however, Bonaparte actually crossed the Alps on a mule, and most of the artillery had to be left behind.[37] The imperial legitimation motif is blatantly manifested by the names Bonaparte, Hannibal, and Charlemagne (in Latin) carved in the rocks below. The inclusion of Charlemagne is especially significant since it was the Carolingian historical precedent that would serve to legitimize Napoleon's imperial ambitions and which David himself invoked (Delécluze, 241). This highly propagandistic official portrait, painted in a hybrid romantic/classicizing style, is an elegant piece of historical fiction that embodies David's own limitless artistic ambitions.

In *Bonaparte Crossing the Alps* David returned to the equestrian motif that he had treated twenty years earlier in the *Portrait of Count Potocki* (fig. 4). There is also a pencil sketch of a man on a rearing horse that is annotated "first idea for the Bonaparte" (Schnapper, 386, plate 162). It is a generalized study of a nude rider and lacks the heroic gesture incorporated in the painting. The differences between the equestrian portraits of Potocki and Napoleon outweigh the similarities, however. The quasi sculptural representation of Napoleon and his plunging horse, poised precariously and battered by the elements, owes more to Falconet's superb equestrian statue of *Peter the Great* (fig. 6), a monument to enlightened despotism. Even the rocky pedestal, in which the names of Peter and Catherine are chiseled, is resurrected in David's painting. With his right hand Napoleon gestures upward, beyond the Alps to Italy and the Battle of Marengo that cemented his political fortunes (Lefebvre, 98). It is the French Revolution and a new conception of history that have intervened in David's art. The canvas effortlessly melds together prosaic detail and heightened emotion and rhetoric to create an historically invested but fictionalized representation of the modern hero. Napoleon has already taken his place on the stage of history. The next logical step was Napoleon's official consecration as emperor, which took place on 2 December 1804.

David recorded that moment in the oversized *Coronation of the Emperor and the Empress*, 1805-1807 (Paris, Musée du Louvre) (fig. 7). Pope Pius VII was summoned to Paris to provide a "fiction of Carolingian legitimacy" for the coronation.[38] David attended the lengthy coronation ceremony, took notes, and made sketches (in the finished painting, the artist is represented sketching in the second loge). In addition, he apparently had a maquette of the choir of Notre Dame constructed and fitted with costumed dolls in order to facilitate the composition of his immense tableau.[39] He also met with Degotti, the official scenic designer of the Paris Opera. Later, David exhaustively documented each courtier

David and Historical Fiction / 189

Figure 6. E.-M. Falconet *Monument to Peter the Great*, 1782 (Leningrad). Photo Lauros-Giraudon reproduced by permission.

and costume.[40] After establishing the pose from a model, David eventually sketched or painted the head from life. In addition, he had the costumes sent to his studio. The sketchbooks in the Fogg Art Museum, which are annotated with comments about color and costume and even the height of the sitter, attest to the artist's meticulous preparation.

Despite the overwhelming impression of verisimilitude, however, history was selectively rewritten in the *Coronation*. Characters who were

Figure 7. J. L. David, *The Coronation of the Emperor and the Empress*, 1805–1807 (Paris, Musée du Louvre). Photo Giraudon reproduced by permission.

not actually present (notably the emperor's mother) were included, and the scene itself was rearranged by the painter, who shifted his point of view to show the ceremony from the side. Even the central moment represented—that of the coronation—was selectively edited for posterity. Although Pope Pius VII was present, Napoleon actually crowned himself and then his empress. Rather than the controversial self-coronation portrayed repeatedly in the sketchbooks and in a preparatory study from 1805, David depicted the coronation of Josephine with the Pope making a gesture of benediction that was added at Napoleon's insistence in 1808. When the emperor saw the Pope's neutral pose, he reportedly remarked that he had not brought him to Paris to do nothing (Schnapper, 413).[41] David's principal preoccupation in recording the immense cast of characters present at the coronation was historical accuracy. Yet he was forced to modify certain portraits; in particular he considerably rejuvenated the tired features of the Empress Josephine. Nevertheless, it was David's faithfulness to visual appearances that struck critics and Napoleon himself when the immense canvas was finally unveiled to the court and the public. As the Emperor exclaimed: "Ce n'est pas une *peinture*, on marche dans ce tableau" (my emphasis).[42] The height of illusionism was attained when the members of the court viewed their lifesize portraits.

Yet despite David's painstaking attention to the individual portraits, this is a modern historical chronicle in which the sweep of history overshadows the individual actors, thus anticipating Hegel's philosophy of history and the great epic novels of Tolstoy and later nineteenth-century novelists. David has modified his *écriture* to suit the circumstances. Here he approaches a transparent style that seeks to efface itself behind the reality of the set and its glittering cast. The artist himself appears in a strangely rejuvenated portrait in the act of recording modern history. David referred to the *Coronation* as a *peinture-portrait* (Delécluze, 246), clearly indicating its hybrid nature—what I have been calling *historical fiction*. Yet there are artistic precedents, notably Rubens' *Coronation of Marie de Medici* (Paris, Musée du Louvre). In one of the sketchbooks in the Fogg Art Museum (1943–1815.12, fol. 1 recto), there is a study of a woman in profile copied from Rubens. Indeed the precedent could not have been more apropos since Marie de Medici, like Josephine, had been crowned and anointed at Saint Denis.[43] In Rubens' canvas, Henri IV, assassinated just after the queen's coronation, presides over the event from the tribune. Unlike the Medici series, however, with its abundant allegorical references, historical fiction for David is a human affair requiring no celestial extras or *deus ex machina* interventions. Nor did hereditary rank or political power make heroes and demigods of those who attended the coronation. It is this concept of history—a history of the masses, which resonated across Europe with the French Revolution and assumed literary definition in the historical novels of Sir Walter Scott—that Jacques-Louis David precociously painted into his official portraits. As Jacques-Emile Blanche, portraitist and chronicler of the Belle Epoque, perceptively remarked, "The entire history of the early nineteenth century can be read in David's portraits."[44]

NOTES

*I would like to thank the staff of the drawing room at the Fogg Art Museum for permitting me to see their David sketchbooks, as well as Agnes Mongan's forthcoming catalogue; I also wish to thank Richard Wendorf and Patricia Craddock for editorial comments.

1. Charles Baudelaire, "Salon de 1846," in *Oeuvres complètes*, ed. Marcel A. Ruff (Paris: Seuil, 1968), 248. For Baudelaire, David and Ingres were the leading proponents of the historical school of portraiture. The more poetic, or romantic, approach was exemplified by Rembrandt, Reynolds, and Lawrence. Baudelaire preferred the latter, in which imagination played a more important role. The poet also remarked that the novel is sometimes closer to the truth than history.
2. This is evident from both David's statements and correspondence and adheres to the hierarchy of the genres. See Léon Rosenthal, *Louis David* (Paris: Librairie de l'Art Ancien et Moderne, n.d.), 87, 127-29. Rosenthal points out that David was not classified as a portrait painter by his contemporaries, but Rosenthal overstates his case by arguing that David's portraits are devoid of any underlying design. In *Painting in Eighteenth-Century France* (Ithaca: Cornell University Press, 1981), Philip Conisbee conversely insists on the ideological dimension of all David's portraits whether created for a private or a public context (113).
3. Although most authors from Hautecoeur to Brookner and Schnapper discuss David's career chronologically, the portraits tend to be treated separately and have received far less attention than the history paintings. The recent elimination of a number of dubious paintings from the *oeuvre* has helped to provide a clearer picture of David's portrait-painting skills.
4. "David portraitiste," *Gazette des Beaux-Arts* 1 (1907): 306-30, especially 306-7. Many other authors have noted the realist/idealist split in David's art. In *David to Delacroix* (Cambridge, MA: Harvard University Press, 1977, orig. pub. 1955), however, Walter Friedlaender argues that the portraits supplement the body of David's other works (34).
5. On the *portrait historié*, see Conisbee, 122. In the portraiture chapter, he discusses allegorical portraits such as Dumont Le Romain's *Allegory of the Peace of Aix-la-Chapelle* (1761) and the *portrait historié* as practiced by

Raoux and Nattier. But David's portraits of Marat and Napoleon function in an almost antithetical manner.

6 Georg Lukács, *The Historical Novel*, trans. Hannah and Stanley Mitchell (London: Merlin Press, 1978; first English pub. 1962), especially chapter 1 on the classical form of the historical novel.

7 Thomas E. Crow, *Painters and Public Life in Eighteenth-Century Paris* (New Haven: Yale University Press, 1985), 258. Friedlaender more convincingly insists on the continuity between David's revolutionary and Napoleonic paintings.

8 See Conisbee, chapter 4, 111–42, and L. G. Baillet de Saint-Julien, *Réflexions et lettres* (Geneva: Minkoff Reprint, 1972), 109 ff. Saint-Julien called for nobility and taste in portraiture and praised the return to ordinary dress.

9 Cited in Lorne Campbell, *Renaissance Portraits* (New Haven: Yale University Press, 1990), 150. Campbell notes that Vasari avoided painting portraits.

10 *Réflexions sur quelques causes de l'état présent de la peinture en France* (La Haye: chez Jean Neaulme, 1747). Lafont mocked the pretensions of *portraits historiés*.

11 For eighteenth-century art criticism, see the *Deloynes Collection* (Paris: Bibliothèque Nationale, now on microfiche). The commercial success of portraiture made it suspect as an artistic genre. This also led to periodic attempts to adjust the prices of history painting.

12 On D'Angiviller's campaign to reinvigorate history painting, see Jean Locquin, *La Peinture d'histoire en France de 1747 à 1785* (Paris: Henri Laurens, 1912). On "les grands hommes," see Wend Graf Kalnein and Michael Levey, *Art and Architecture of the Eighteenth Century in France* (Harmondsworth: Penguin Books, 1972), 155–56.

13 *Marie Antoinette and Her Children*, 1787, is at Versailles. See Joseph Baillio, "Le Dossier d'un oeuvre d'actualité politique: Marie-Antoinette et ses enfants," *L'Oeil*, no. 310 (May 1981): 52–60, 90–91; *Elisabeth Louise Vigée LeBrun, 1755–1842* (Fort Worth: Kimbell Art Museum, 1982), 78–81. See also Simon Schama, *Citizens* (New York: Knopf, 1989), 220–27.

14 M. Miette de Villars, *Mémoires de David, peintre et député de la Convention* (Paris, 1850), 87–88, cited by Baillio, 90.

15 D'Angiviller refused permission to engrave the portrait for a volume on famous women that the royalist Ternisien d'Haudricourt wished to dedicate to the queen.

16 Max J. Friedländer, *Landscape. Portrait. Still-Life* (New York: Schocken Books, 1963), 230.

17 See Antoine Schnapper in the exhibition catalogue: *Jacques-Louis David, 1748–1825* (Paris: Editions de la Réunion des musées nationaux, 1989), 109–110. Schnapper cites the *Mémoires secrets de Bachaumont*. On the circumstances of the commission, see also A. Ryskiewicz, "Portrait équestre de Stanislas Kostka Potocki par Jacques-Louis David," *Bulletin du Musée national de Varsovie*, no. 3 (1963): 77–95. The portrait was apparently begun in Rome and finished in Paris.

18 The *Marat*, which was returned to David in 1795, remained in the artist's family and was donated to the Brussels Museum in 1886 by Jules David. The *Le Pelletier*, which was purchased by the model's royalist daughter, was presumably destroyed. The bibliography on David's *Marat* is extensive. See Schnapper, 282-85, for a good critical summary; see also Georges de Batz, "History, Truth and Art," *The Art Quarterly* 8 (Autumn 1945): 249-60. On the mythification of Marat, see *La Mort de Marat*, ed. Jean-Claude Bonnet (Paris: Flammarion, 1986), and Marie-Hélène Huet, *Rehearsing the Revolution: The Staging of Marat's Death, 1793-1797* (Berkeley: University of California Press, 1982). See also Jules Michelet, *Histoire de la Révolution Française*, 2 vols. (Paris: Bibliothèque de la Pléiade, 1952), 2:492-503.

19 Schnapper, 284; de Batz. Of greater interest is how David transposed and decontextualized the image of Marat. The Caravaggesque lighting he adopted, however, corresponds to the dramatic display of the body and the torchlight funerary procession. The abstract, stippled background recalls the preparatory drawing for the engraving.

20 Idem. See also *La Mort de Marat*, 103-104, 167-84, on the Marat cult. Marat was accorded the honors of the Pantheon on September 21, 1794, but de-Pantheonized on February 26, 1795. After Thermidor numerous busts were smashed and the Place du Carrousel Monument was destroyed. Marat himself was against Pantheonization.

21 See Eric Walter, "Vies et maladies du docteur Marat," in *La Mort de Marat*, 335-72. Jean-Claude Bonnet notes that despite official pressure Marat was often denounced, especially after Thermidor. See "Les Images négatives," in *La Mort de Marat*, 167-84.

22 *Madame Tussaud's Memoirs and Reminiscences of France*, ed. Francis Hervé (London: Saunders and Otley, 1838), 345. According to Mme Tussaud the tableau of Marat's assassination attracted crowds who lamented the loss of their idol. Robespierre apparently profited from his visit to harangue the crowd.

23 Hanno-Walter Kraft, "An antique model for David's 'Death of Marat,'" *Burlington Magazine* 125 (October, 1983): 605-607. The *Marat* (like *Le Pelletier*) also recalls David's dead classical hero in *The Grief of Andromache*, 1783.

24 Schnapper, 286, no. 119; the drawing was presumably executed from the corpse. On Mme Tussaud, see Hervé, 279 (who indicates that Mme Tussaud also took a cast of Charlotte Corday), and H. E. Hinman, "Jacques-Louis David and Madame Tussaud," *Gazette des Beaux-Arts* 66 (1965): 331-38. Both Hervé and Hinman indicate that David utilized Mme Tussaud's cast of Marat for his painting without offering conclusive proof.

25 See Jacques Guilhaumou, "La Mort de Marat à Paris," in *La Mort de Marat*, 62-72; see also Philippe Roger, "L'Homme du Sang," in *La Mort de Marat*, 149-58. Marat's bathtub was purchased by the Musée Grévin (late nineteenth century).

26 In his account of the funeral (72-78), Guilhaumou stresses the juxtaposition of the sublime and the disgusting, of death and its sublimation, which he links to the dynamics of the Revolution.
27 Schnapper, 285. Corday's letter was read at the Convention. See also Lise Andries, "Les Occasionnels et les Almanachs," in *La Mort de Marat*, 96. Andries points out that Marat's *grandeur d'âme*, demonstrated by Corday's letter, helped to assimilate him to Christ.
28 Baudelaire compared the picture to a novel by Balzac, in which the details are historic and real, but suffused with drama in all its lamentable horror.
29 The first play dealing with the death of Marat was actually written while he was still alive (although not performed until after his death).
30 Michelet, 2:318-19, cited and commented on by Huet. Michelet's cinematic account of Marat's triumph stresses the oddity of the cadaverous Marat covered with flowers, which anticipated his mortuary display in the Eglise des Cordeliers. The triumph was reenacted in the plays celebrating Marat's death and apotheosis.
31 Huet, 81. For example, *La Mort de Marat* (1794) included this cautionary notice: "Let them fear him still, he will live again in us." From this standpoint, David's Christ-like representation coincides with contemporary theatrical representations.
32 Roland Barthes, *Le Degré zéro de la littérature* (Paris: Editions du Seuil, 1972; orig. pub. 1952), 19-20. Barthes argues that the Revolution required a theatrical amplification of language in order to explain the singularity of the historical situation. Yet despite its apparent inflation, he insists that the revolutionary *écriture* is accurate and authentic. "L'écriture révolutionnaire fut comme l'entéléchie de la légende révolutionnaire: elle intimidait et imposait une consécration civique du Sang." David's *Death of Marat*, "created as if in a trance" as Delécluze noted, functioned in a similar manner (178-79).
33 Delécluze, 232-37; Schnapper, 384, 386. The versions vary; notably, the color of the horse and the cape differ. The Malmaison version is generally accepted as the original canvas commissioned by Charles IV. The other versions are at Versailles, Charlottenburg, and the Kunsthistorisches Museum, Vienna.
34 Napoleon's phrase is "calme sur un cheval fougueux."
35 Schnapper, 359. According to some historians David and Bonaparte met at an official reception in December 1797; others place the meeting at a public gathering at the Institute in January 1798. David asked to paint Bonaparte's portrait at a dinner given by J. J. Lagarde.
36 Although David remained faithful to the emperor and ended his life in political exile in Brussels, his relationship with Napoleon and his advisors was fraught with tension and constant financial wrangling. This is especially true of the most important commission that David received from the emperor—the four immense canvases representing the events of the coronation, only two of which were ever completed.
37 See Georges Lefebvre, *Napoleon, from 18 Brumaire to Tilsit, 1799-1807* (New York: Columbia University Press, 1969; orig. pub. in French, 1936), 98. The

crossing of the Grand Saint-Bernard began the night of 14-15 May and was completed on 23 May. Only ten cannons were dragged across the Alps. Later nineteenth-century artists represented Napoleon riding a mule.

38 On the *Coronation*, see Delécluze, 312-15; Schnapper, 399-420. Also of particular interest are the preparatory sketches in the Louvre sketchbooks and the two sketchbooks in the Fogg Art Museum (1943.1815.12, 13, Grenville L. Winthrop Bequest). The latter consist primarily of finished full-length studies of the principal figures in their definitive poses. See the forthcoming catalogue of the Fogg sketchbooks by Agnes Mongan, ms. p. 135.

39 Schnapper, 408, cited from *Affiches, Annonces et Avis divers* (7 December 1897); see also Mongan. As Schnapper points out, David's composition process remains mysterious. No painted sketches are known; the evidence suggests that David may have painted the heads directly on the canvas from life (410).

40 See Mongan, ms. pp. 136 ff. David sketched the Coronation and the principal groups from life during the ceremony and made notes on everything that he did not have time to draw.

41 It was supposedly Gérard who persuaded David to represent Napoleon crowning Josephine. Several studies in the Fogg sketchbooks illustrate David's hesitations about the final pose. See, in particular, fol. 2 verso (1943.1815.12), which shows Napoleon (nude) raising his right arm and clutching his sword with the inscription "dieu et mon épée," and fol. 52 recto (1943.1815.13), the definitive pose, with Napoleon raising the crown with both hands. There are also several studies of Napoleon crowning Josephine. According to the account in the *Monitor*, David wished to represent a single synthetic action.

42 Schnapper, 416-18; Delécluze, 312-15. The latter reports that David was criticized for making the empress the focus of the composition.

43 On the *Coronation of Marie de Medici*, see Susan Saward, *The Golden Age of Marie de Medici* (Ann Arbor: UMI Research Press, 1982), 97-98.

44 *Propos de peintre, de David à Degas* (Paris: Emile-Paul Frères, 1919), 183.

Swift and Patronage

DUSTIN GRIFFIN

In the seventy-five years between 1675 and 1750 the system of patronage, in which writers in England were sustained by wealthy peers and ultimately by the court, yielded to a system based on the booksellers and ultimately on the marketplace. But the pace of this great cultural change was by no means steady and uniform. Forms of patronage managed to survive well past 1750 — Johnson, after all, had a pension. And writers were variously affected, depending on their special circumstances. Swift, as an ordained Anglican, with friends in both church and state to help him, was inside the patronage system, and to some extent its beneficiary, in a way that his Catholic friend and younger contemporary Pope was not. As a man of some political influence, Swift was also empowered to act as a patron himself, and to smooth the way for younger writers and churchmen. Much good it did him. The irony is that Pope, the apparent outsider, in fact found more access to power and wealth than Swift, who had enough access to make him hungry and enough disappointment to make him bitter.

Biographers have made much of Swift's ambivalent relationship to the world of power. One constant theme, traceable to Swift's own favorite view of himself, is that, as a friend of great men, he prided himself on his equal standing, his independence, and his freedom to speak his mind. Another theme is his recurrent resentment that his would-be patrons —

from Sir William Temple to Robert Harley and the Queen herself—failed to help him as much as they might. Swift nursed that sense of resentment even as he established, in Ireland, a position of considerable authority. As Ehrenpreis has summarized, his "rewards were greater than his bitterness let him admit."[1] To some extent his resentful sense of injured merit must have been psychologically sustaining, but the costs may have been high. Johnson speaks both of Swift's "pleasure of complaining" and of "the rage of neglected pride, and the languishment of unsatisfied desire." His resentment was not enabling but ultimately disabling: Swift, says Johnson, "wasted life in discontent."[2]

Other observers have spotted additional ironies. David Nokes has shown that Swift thought the country owed its poets a living (this was the ideal under the old patronage system) and that even after he became the Hibernian Patriot, Swift still sought and would have accepted patronage in England in the late 1720s.[3] Another irony is that, as Ehrenpreis shows, Swift was more successful as a patron himself than as a client. "I can serve every body but my self," Swift complained in 1712, at the height of his access to power.[4] But the sharpest and most unkind irony comes from Johnson, who as a proud independent writer might have been expected to approve of Swift's manly bearing in the company of great men. What Swift and his admirers regarded as independence Johnson labels servility: "Much has been said of the equality and independence which he preserved in his conversation with the Ministers, of the frankness of his remonstrances, and the familiarity of his friendship. . . . No man, however, can pay a more servile tribute to the Great than by suffering his liberty in their presence to aggrandize him in his own esteem" (3:21).

Johnson invokes the principle of subordination—"between different ranks of the community there is necessarily some distance"—and suggests that any inferior who prides himself on his familiarity with a superior is fooling himself. For the inferior is present either on sufferance or because he is temporarily useful. Swift, he suspects, is guilty of "the pride of importance and the malice of inferiority" (3:22).[5] Swift at Harley's table was not displaying "magnanimity" or "greatness of soul." By encroaching on Harley's dignity, Swift in fact put himself in Harley's power, to be "repelled with helpless indignity, or endured by clemency and condescension" (3:61). One of Johnson's recurrent themes is the "power" of Swift as writer. But as Harley's client, Swift, as Johnson saw it, had no more power than did Gulliver, for all his self-importance, at the court of the King of Brobdingnag.

This is a severe and perhaps an unfair indictment. But there is some reason to believe that Swift would have recognized the picture Johnson drew. In a series of poems Swift himself drew pictures of the patron-client relationship he had known, especially with Harley. The poems have been read for evidence of Swift's friendships, self-conceptions, resentments, and anxieties. We can also see in them Swift's ambivalence about the system of patronage, his awareness that the client has access but no real power. But the poems are not just confessions of weakness. They also function as strategies (or fantasies) of retaliation, in which the client finds a way to upstage the patron.

Swift's imitation of the seventh epistle of Horace's first book, written in 1713, just after Swift was made Dean of St. Patrick's, casts Harley in the role of Maecenas. "My Lord" is "the nation's great support" (1), while Swift is just a poor priest. Harley takes him up and, for a jest, makes him a dean, promising a life of "plenty, power, and ease" (92). The poem laughs at Swift's impressionable naiveté—Swift the "gudgeon" takes Harley's bait (80)—and (in one common reading) conveys through its rallying tone of humorous grumbling the "intimacy" between clergyman and Lord Treasurer.[6] I would argue that the poem in fact implies some real resentment and reproach for Harley's callous "jest" (a term used three times—finally with an edge of bitterness). An Irish deanery was not what Swift wanted, and it quickly proved costly and vexing. Instead of ruling as a "tyrant" (90) over two dozen canons, Swift is obstructed and oppressed by tenants, farmers, and tithe collectors. His impotence is mocked by his patron's own commanding authority. In contrast to the hobbled dean, Harley need but speak, and his "summons" (73) is obeyed, by servant and by client alike.

But the poem does not leave Swift humiliated. It contrives, in fact, to turn the tables on the patron by re-asserting the client's own power. That power consists in just saying no. The poem begins with Swift's refusal to accept Harley's invitation to dinner, and concludes with his symbolic resignation: "And since you now have done your worst," he says to Harley, "Pray leave me where you found me first" (137-38). Just as Swift, before Harley found him, had "intended to retire" from the busy political world, so now he claims to control his own fate, and returns to his original plan. Although only symbolic, the resignation serves as a means of discharging any obligation or repudiating a debt (thanks for nothing!). Swift's strategy, in effect, is to deny that a patron-client relationship exists. Or rather, the relationship is displaced: Harley is the "patron" (l.23) of Erasmus Lewis, an Undersecretary of State, treated in the poem as Harley's "errand"-boy (l.24). Swift himself is not to be considered an ordinary parson, eager for preferment. He is "a clergyman of special note," and shuns his fellow clerics. *He* didn't approach Harley; Harley approached *him*. The money in Swift's pocket is not a gift but a loan.[7] The poem serves as a means for Swift to assert his own importance—Swift claims to go where he pleases and say what he thinks—but at the same time reveals that he shares Johnson's sense of the client's humble station. At Harley's table Swift "soon grows domestic" (77). The term suggests both that Swift is one of the family, and that he has become a mere household chaplain, or domestic servant.

"The Author Upon Himself" (1714) is another response to the collapse of Swift's political ambitions. Again his strategy is to deny his client status and to represent the removal to Ireland as a kind of retirement. As in the imitation of Horace, Swift avoids presenting himself as a clergyman seeking preferment. More a man of wit than a parson ("Nor showed the parson in his gait or face"—line 14), Swift displayed the kind of grace that got him invited to "the tables of the great" (16). Writing for Harley was not his idea. He is advised to do so by his friends, and submits to their "better judgements" (25). His allegiance is not to person or party but to principle. He wants to do what "friendship, justice, truth require" (73) and feels the obligation—fostered (as Swift knew, though he does not say) by scriptural parable—to employ his "talents" for "nobler ends" (24). He goes to court not to find a patron, but because he has been "invited" (28) by Harley. Once there he gains access and influence. Swift's tone combines pride and self-mockery—he is proud that he meets privately with Harley and St. John, and laughs at the rumors that exaggerate his importance. Swift's indirectness makes it difficult to decide how much power he actually lays claim to. It is said that Swift "oils many a spring which Harley moves" (40). As Rogers notes, the syntax makes it unclear whether Harley moves the spring oiled by Swift, or whether Swift oils the spring which then moves Harley.[8] Is Swift merely an understrapper or a manipulator of his master? He gains such influence as to become himself a patron, "caressed by candidate divines" (64) and solicited by the entire "Scottish nation" that he might "be their friend" (69-70).

But all comes to nought. Enemies maneuver and faction divides his "great contending friends" (72). Swift is reluctant to blame Harley and St. John, and conveys no sense that he himself was simply used by the ministers. His own importance is suggested by the magnitude of the forces allegedly mobilized to defeat him. The "old red-pate murdering hag," the "crazy prelate," and the "royal prude" (1-2) are larger-than-life villains, suitable for waylaying a heroic knight. The hag swears "vengeance" (53) on him and becomes a monster, her mouth filling with venom distilled from her red locks, and then instilled into the "royal ear" (56). Although a proclamation spread "through the realm" (59) puts a price on his head, he "scorns ignoble flight" (61) and determines to make a stand. At this point, however, Swift undercuts his heroic pose. He escapes not by resisting but because "his watchful friends preserve him by a sleight" (62) — that is, by covering up Swift's authorship of a libelous pamphlet — and he subsequently endures trials more embarrassing than chivalric, when the Treasurer of the Queen's Household "In Swift's ear thrusts half his powdered nose" (68). When Swift has done what he can, and what "friendship, justice, truth require" (73), he finally abandons the campaign: "What could he more, but decently retire?" (74).

The question is neatly self-enhancing. It makes the point that Swift's departure from court was voluntary. He leaves not as a disappointed suitor but as a veteran diplomat (like his old patron Temple) who decides to "retire" — perhaps to a life of rural leisure and contemplation. Swift does not say that he was holed up in Berkshire, or that — a full twelve months before the poem was written — he had already been inducted as Dean of St. Patrick's. Indeed, the pretense is that the poem is written in 1713 — the date assigned to the poem in its first appearance in print in the 1735 *Works* — when Swift was still a part of the court, and not in 1714, when his Irish fate was sealed.

The "Libel on the Reverend Dr. Delany" (1730) is couched in the form of cynical advice from a veteran of the political wars. Occasioned by an epistle from Delany, Swift's fellow churchman in Dublin, to Lord Carteret, Lord Lieutenant, the "Libel" is a way for Swift to laugh at Delany's deluded dreams of patronage, dreams that Swift himself once shared. But in the end the real joke is not on the client Delany, but on his would-be patron, Carteret, and ultimately on *his* masters, Walpole and the king himself.

Swift begins with a picture of the aspiring clients, welcomed by the great as companions for their table, and boasting of their access and their intimacy with men in power. It is Swift at Harley's table all over again. This time Swift makes it painfully clear that the intimacy is in fact one-sided: it is the great who "choose" their companions (2), and who "give leave" to let a client "sit when e'er you will" (4). If the client presumes on the familiarity to raise a matter of business, he "quite mistake[s] preferment's road" (12). Even Johnson's tart description of the self-important Swift in Harley's company pales beside Swift's own words, full of self-loathing, about the real relationship between patron and client:

> For, as their appetites to quench,
> Lords keep a pimp to bring a wench;
> So, men of wit are but a kind
> Of pandars to a vicious mind;
> Who proper objects must provide

To gratify their lust of pride.
(21-26)

Swift provides a series of examples of clients who either cynically complied with the lusts of great men (Congreve and Addison) or withdrew and starved (Steele and Gay). He notably omits his own case, and passes instead to Pope, who becomes the hero of the poem: "His heart too great, though fortune little,/ To lick a rascal statesman's spittle" (81-82). Pope can afford to despise slaves "that cringe for bread" (88) because he was "placed," with Homer's help, "above the reach of want." (Interestingly, Swift obscures the financial dimension of Pope's Homer project.[9] Though he resented the dependence on patrons, Swift did not admire writers who wrote for bread, and rarely accepted money for his own publications.)[10]

Turning to Delany's situation, Swift suspects that his friend will rise no higher than domestic chaplain, fit for flattering, carving at table, and showing his wit. But the real force of Swift's satire is turned on Carteret, who would, "*if he durst*, be more your friend" (114, emphasis added). The Viceroy, though he dispenses Irish patronage, is himself not a free agent. He serves at the pleasure of the Prime Minister, and must submit "To Walpole's more than royal will" (122). By an ironic reversal, the patron turns out to be but a dependent on a still greater man. Poor Carteret "must obey, or lose his place" (160). Clients then, from the deluded Delany to the unillusioned Swift, may take some comfort in the discomforts of dependence that plague their betters. Swift himself emerges as the second hero of the poem, able to "look on courts with stricter eyes" (175) and (in a stance that Pope was to find congenial in his own late satires) to base his judgment on "truth" (194). Walpole is no better than the monarch of hell, the viceroy but a "Viceroy devil" sent to do his bidding, and to spread "corruptions" through courts and senates as he passes (186-87). From Swift's almost-Olympian vantage, kings, ministers, viceroys, and their clients are all reduced to a single level.

With Swift's poems on patronage in mind, we can take a brief look at the famous "Verses on the Death of Dr. Swift" (1733), and read it too as an elaborate self-justifying fantasy and a denial that he ever sought patronage. Thus, the passive verb in "the Dean was never ill-received at Court" (308) both affirms that Swift had entree to the court and conceals that his footing there was that of a client on his own behalf or that of the Irish church. When he claims that "He never courted men in station" (325), Swift must mean not that he never worked with and for Harley and others—this would be too blatant a lie—but that he never stooped to "court" them. In Swift's self-preserving fiction, he was sought out by the great: it was they who "courted" him. In turn, he "never thought an honour done him,/ Because a duke was proud to own him" (319-20). Transferring pride from himself to the duke, Swift here answers in advance Johnson's charge that Swift valued himself the more for his association with the great. Even "with princes," says Swift, he "kept a due decorum,/ But never stood in awe before 'em:/ And to her Majesty, God bless her, / Would speak as free as to her dresser" (339-343). Again Swift seems to be implicitly observing Johnson's rule about subordination, and to speak freely with a sovereign just as Johnson himself was to do some thirty years later. Elsewhere, however, Swift reduces the queen from majesty to meanness. She had once promised to send him some "medals" and now forgets (or cancels) her promise (184). In explanatory footnotes, Swift makes clear that he sent her a "present" (apparently of Irish poplin) and later a piece of Indian plaid. In return Swift was to receive not payment but some "medals." Swift sees in the transaction not royal largesse promised and withdrawn, not an Irish merchant providing goods to the carriage trade, but (somewhat cheekily) an exchange of gifts between equals that one party has failed to fulfill.

If Swift had behaved prudently, he claims, he "might have rose like other men" (360). But he refused to spare his "tongue and pen" (359). And after laboring "to reconcile his friends in power" (370) — the phrase is little changed from its appearance twenty years earlier in "The Author upon Himself" — Swift "left the court in mere despair" (374). Once again, that is, Swift was not dismissed, but took his own leave. He gained nothing by leaving — in Ireland he met "continual persecution" (404) — but finally evens the score by turning patron himself. He left his estate to "public uses" (156), and "gave what little wealth he had,/ To build a house for fools and mad" (483-84). By becoming a donor rather than a recipient, he symbolically turns the tables on the patrons who — as he saw it — failed to support him and his church.

Swift had one card left to play. As client he was a dependent. But as clergyman charged with the care of souls, he had considerable power. Although all the evidence suggests that he performed his ecclesiastical duties scrupulously, he seems to have imagined, in some powerful fantasies left unpublished at his death, using his sacred authority to punish his enemies. The famous "Day of Judgement" may represent a dream of retaliation: sinners gather at the Last Judgment only to be told by an angry Jove (a stand-in for Swift himself) that it has all been a joke. More pertinent for my purposes is Swift's little poem on the "Sudden Drying up of St. Patrick's Well" (c. 1729). The "sacred well" (65), located near Trinity College, Dublin, was said to have healing properties and to have been produced by St. Patrick himself, Swift's symbolic predecessor as spiritual leader of Ireland, and namesake of his cathedral. In Swift's poem, St. Patrick speaks and laments the "fatal changes" (34) in Ireland since his time. The Irish are now drowned in vice and enslaved to the English. Aspiring clergymen must make slavish court to "foreign prelates," and for all their "sweat" can only "procure a mean support" (75-76). St. Patrick foretells worse yet, and closes by withdrawing his care: "I scorn thy spurious and degenerate line,/ And from this hour my patronage resign" (101-102). "Patronage" here means primarily the guardianship provided by saints, and in particular the guardianship by the patron saint of Ireland. But for the Dean of St. Patrick's the word has obvious links with the patronage or support he provided as champion of Irish rights, and the patronage he himself sought all his life. By speaking as St. Patrick and by "resigning his patronage," Swift gains a kind of fantasized revenge.

NOTES

1 Irvin Ehrenpreis, *Swift: The Man, His Works, and the Age*, 3 vols. (Cambridge: Harvard University Press, 1967), 2: xvii.
2 *Lives of the Poets*, ed. G. B. Hill, 3 vols. (Oxford: Oxford University Press, 1905), 3:61.
3 *Jonathan Swift: A Hypocrite Reversed* (Oxford: Oxford University Press, 1985). Swift's continuing search for patronage is a recurrent theme in the Nokes and Ehrenpreis biographies.
4 *Journal to Stella* for March 8, 1712. For an account of Swift's successful patronage on behalf of others, see Ehrenpreis, 2:607-618.
5 In the same passage, Johnson goes on to note that Swift's "better qualities" overpowered his "childish freedom."
6 See, for example, Timothy Keegan, "Swift's Self-Portraits in Verse," in *Augustan Studies*, ed. Douglas Patey and Timothy Keegan (Newark: University of Delaware Press, 1985), 129.
7 Swift once refused £50 from Harley because it would have put him "on a level with hired party scribblers." See Harold Williams, "Swift's Early Biographers," in *Pope and His Contemporaries*, ed. James Clifford and Louis Landa (Oxford: The Clarendon Press, 1942), 124, and *Journal to Stella*, March 7, 1711.
8 *Jonathan Swift: The Complete Poems*, ed. Pat Rogers (New Haven and London: Yale University Press, 1983), 670.
9 Unless we hear a slight sneer in Swift's hint that Pope "By Homer dead was taught to *thrive*" (85, emphasis added). Does "thrive" hint at Augustan suspi-

cions about the "art of thriving," as practiced by sharp new money-men and self-seekers?

10 "The taste of England is infamously corrupted by shoals of writers who write for their bread" (*Works*, ed. Herbert Davis [Oxford: Basil Blackwell, 1939-68], 17:398). G. B. Hill notes that Swift seems to have accepted money for his writings only twice (*Lives of the English Poets*, 3:50, note).

Nationality and Knowledge in Eighteenth-Century Italy

JAMES L. FUCHS

The dramatist Vittorio Alfieri received one of his more enthusiastic reviews from a highly infrequent, if not reluctant, playgoer and critic — Pasquale Paoli, the Corsican patriot and revolutionary. In a letter to a confidant, Paoli professed: "I read his tragedies over and over again and like them more each time, and they don't send me to sleep as always happens if I try to read the complete works of any other modern dramatist all through at a stretch. I feel sorry for those poor creatures [in Italy] because they lack the vitality to be in tune with the great passions which arouse and inspire this writer of tragedies."[1] Nor did Alfieri lack esteem for Paoli. He dedicated his *Timoleone* to him, considering him "eminently worthy to hear the accents of Timoleone as one who is fully able to understand and appreciate them."[2]

Somewhat ironically, but not inappropriately, Paoli came to admire Alfieri while the two men were in England: Alfieri was a guest, Paoli an exile. Since exile had reinforced both Paoli's patriotism and the egalitarian foundation of that patriotism, his praise of a poet who happened to have been a Piedmontese nobleman is revealing and striking. Though Paoli was himself a source of great patriotic inspiration, he nonetheless — like so many Italians of the Enlightenment — looked up to Alfieri as the spokesman, if not the epitome, of a pre-nascent Italian nationalism. No contemporary was concerned with, or impressed by, Alfieri's disclaimers regarding this role.

Alfieri's example as a patriotic poet was scarcely unprecedented or exceptional within Italian history and culture. Though, unlike his literary successor Gabriele D'Annunzio, he did not actually occupy a city in order to pursue his patriotic point, he was conscious that "Writing tragedies about freedom in a language of a people which is not free could perhaps rightly be considered mere foolishness," and he clearly perceived a corresponding relationship between Italian nationalism and the Italian language.[3]

The same point had been made equally dramatically, albeit not by a playwright, at the very beginning of the eighteenth century. Vincenzo Coronelli, a Franciscan Minister General and cartographer who was also the author of the first modern alphabetical encyclopedia in Italian, recognized in 1701 that the embattled state of the Italian Peninsula was paralleled in, and also linked to, the embattled state of the Italian language.[4] In other countries as well, vicissitudes of nationality have corresponded to those of language. Nonetheless, there were unique circumstances that fostered a national/linguistic relationship in seventeenth- and eighteenth-century Italy. The proponents of Ariosto's and Tasso's literary Italian had fought their battles as fiercely as the foreign powers that had carved up Italy. The conclusion of the many debates between the Accademia della Crusca and its rivals was a Tuscan triumph that was to remain both imperfect and incomplete. Coronelli, in the introduction to his encyclopedia, which he entitled the *Biblioteca universale sacroprofana,* lamented what he considered to be the barren state of the Italian language. He insisted that there was a dearth of vocabulary; and in publishing the first complete Italian encyclopedia, he envisioned himself as a "missionary of the Italian idiom."[5]

By attempting to enrich the Italian language through the vehicle of an encyclopedia, Coronelli was simultaneously pursuing other intellectual, and even social, goals. Intellectual and social motives became fused in his desire to disseminate encyclopedic knowledge to as broad an Italian audience as possible.

Coronelli noted that prior to his *Biblioteca universale*, Italians seeking encyclopedic knowledge had been compelled either to "borrow from the *biblioteche* and dictionaries of foreign tongues"; or to "sweat for a long time in researching dispersed [information]." Nor, in most cases, was it even possible to obtain "dispersed information" even when "sweating" for it, since so many books that were indispensable sources for a given subject were housed in private collections. Consequently, there was a need both "for reducing into a succinct epitome" a large number of otherwise inaccessible books, and for translating that "epitome" so that all Italians, or rather all those who knew Tuscan, would not be barred from encyclopedic knowledge.

By removing this language barrier, Coronelli was necessarily removing an intellectual and social one. Although Greek and Latin were standard fare for the well-to-do, the majority of Italians, humanism notwithstanding, had no training in these languages.[6] Without question, some of those who were not learned had considerable sums of money—enough, Coronelli presumed, to be able to afford the forty-five projected volumes of the *Biblioteca universale*. But most people who lacked a classical education did so at least partly because they did not have the means or leisure for it. Seeking to remedy their exclusion from encyclopedic knowledge, Coronelli specifically pointed out that he expected the *Biblioteca univerale* to benefit those to whom, he claimed, "Heaven had not been liberal." When making these remarks, he was alluding to inability to afford a large number of books, but he certainly had educational barriers in mind as well.

Coronelli thus aimed, through the *Biblioteca universale*, both to enlighten and unify. He would unify not simply by providing all Italians with the same body of information, but also by organizing that information in a way that emphasized precisely the unity he was attempting to instill within his readership. An alphabetical arrangement, he hoped, would make the search for information easier, rendering his encyclopedia more accessible than a topically-arranged work. He expected this accessibility to invite a broad and diverse core of readers. At the same time, an alphabetical, non-topical encyclopedia would produce a non-hierarchical treatment of the subject matter: thus it would parallel his campaign, in equally anti-hierarchical fashion, to make his work accessible to the layman and thereby expand its readership. As in Paoli's case, Coronelli's vision of unity was egalitarian in nature.

Coronelli argued that the organization of previous encyclopedic works had contributed as much to their unapproachability as the languages in which they had been written. There was no order, he asserted, in the non-alphabetical *biblioteche* that either he or any other reader could follow, which meant that these works were not really *biblioteche* at all. "The *biblioteche* without order," he claimed, "must rather be named labyrinths, where the mind, confounded, is lost; or . . . a chaos of materials, precious yes, but altered by confusion." As he then added in Latin, "A mass of bodies rude and undigested is neither ornamental nor of use."

Explaining the problem in more practical terms, he argued that any epistemological organization that forced people to plod through an entire work necessarily discouraged them from looking, and thus impeded the dissemination of knowledge. Then, once he began thinking that a method of organization could block the universal advancement of knowledge, he began to link previous encyclopedic arrangements to arrangements within Italian society that blocked both unity and mobility. In particular, he waged a campaign against both regionalism and hierarchy within his religious order, the Franciscan Order of Minori Conventuali.

As Minister General of the Order, Coronelli sought, within each convent, to promote *forestieri*—which, in this case, meant friars from other cities within Italy—whenever they in fact merited such promotions.[7] This was no easy task, since the "pan-Christian" sympathies that St. Francis had attempted to instill among his followers had yielded to regional loyalties long before the eighteenth century. Resistance to foreigners was particularly strong in Coronelli's native Venice, where all religious orders welcomed and actually solicited the Republic's intervention in their internal affairs, particularly when they sought legislation against the introduction of *forestieri* into their convents.

Both despite and because of the Venetians' adamant opposition to *forestieri*, Coronelli concentrated his campaign upon what was temporarily to become the "not so Serene Republic." He accordingly attempted to appoint as regents in the Venetian Convento degli Frari, Padre Maestro Allesandro Burgos of Messina, who was a poet, historian, and theologian; and Padre Maestro Giuseppe Platini, at that time regent of the Foggia convent. Later on, when the Frari brothers succeeded in blocking the appointments of both men, Coronelli persisted in his efforts to nominate foreigners and named Padre Giuseppe Frezzi of Viterbo instead. He also attempted to appoint *forestieri* to lectureships in the Paduan College of the Santo, but these efforts were also checked. Venice was once again "the Most Serene Republic."

The attempt to promote foreigners was at once a campaign against regionalism and privilege, but Coronelli's efforts against privilege within the Order of Minori Conventuali were not directed at one particular issue but at an entire "worldly" lifestyle. Among his other innovations at the Frari, Coronelli compelled everyone to abandon private kitchens and eat in the convent's refectory instead, even the guardian of the Frari. He also made certain that everyone received the same amounts of food as well as the same menu. The refectory thus became a *mensa comune* for the high and the low. Coronelli actually articulated the connection between his ecclesiastical reforms and his encyclopedic innovations in a metaphor in the preface to his *Biblioteca universale*. He compared his encyclopedia to a granary, which was available to all and from which all could take equally. How similar, then, in his own mind, was the *Biblioteca univer-*

sale to a *mensa comune*, at which the same portions were available to all, and upon which all had the equal right to draw in order to satisfy their needs.

Combining his efforts against hierarchies with his interest in unity and nationality, Coronelli used questionnaires to solicit as broad a contributorship as possible. He circulated these questionnaires *en masse*, and their language suggests the diverse audience that he was attempting to reach — both as contributors and as readers. The questionnaires asked for information "in vernacular idiom, and plain and concise style";[8] and Coronelli also found the need to stipulate to his potential collaborators that there not be even "minimum mutation or alteration" of information found in books or on monuments. Such a stipulation, combined with highly specific directions on how to collect, write, and send information, suggests that he was seeking contributors with little or no experience in such matters. He also made clear his expectation that contributors would become readers; and thus, in every aspect of the *Biblioteca universale*, Coronelli planned to bring together a large and broad group of Italians.

In many ways, Coronelli's questionnaires stressed notions of "peoplehood" and "nationality" by concentrating not simply upon geographical but also upon ethnographical information. Coronelli was interested in local customs, religion, and festivals. Although information about these subjects was necessarily regional, the compilation and combination of different observances, rites, and celebrations within one all-embracing Italian work tended to emphasize similarity and unity. Cultural unity is not infrequently a precondition of political unity; Coronelli's literary merging of Aquila, the Adriatic, Belluno, Bergamo, Bologna, Bolzano, Brescia, Brindisi, Calabria, the Campagna Romana, and — of particular importance for Venice — Candia, constituted in and of itself a step toward both cultural and political unity. Since many of these entries were replete with charts, synoptic tables, drawings of coats of arms, along with other materials and information that Coronelli's questionaires had yielded, this literary cohesion paralleled the unified efforts of contributors in all parts of Italy. Thanks also to these contributors' diverse social backgrounds, the foundation for this encyclopedic "*risorgimento*" was to be popular participation.

Coronelli obtained still more information about local customs from his own journeys; and especially in accounts of the Morea and Dalmatia, he explored the mores of people who were linked imperialistically, if not culturally, to Venice in particular and Italy in general.[9] He also described at length Venetian customs and festivals — within individual monographs such as his *Regatte di Venezia* (Venice: n.p., 1709) and in the *Biblioteca universale*.

In both his use of questionnaires and his general ethnographic concerns, Coronelli anticipated interests and developments of the later eighteenth century as well as of the early nineteenth century. During the 1770s, Alberto Fortis, also an Italian priest, likewise journeyed to Dalmatia, and he wrote an extremely elaborate account concerning the customs of the local "Morlacchi." Ludovico Antonio Muratori published in 1751—when he was librarian at the court of Modena—a series of essays on Italian antiquities; and albeit from a highly unsympathetic point of view, he described Italian popular traditions at considerable length.[10]

The revival of interest in popular tradition was also apparent in other parts of Europe, not least in Germany, which was as un-unified as Italy.[11] Both ethnography and patriotism were major themes for one of Coronelli's encyclopedic successors, Johann Heinrich Zedler, who published his 64-volume *Grosses vollständiges Universal Lexicon* between 1732 and 1750, and four supplementary volumes between 1751 and 1754.[12] Zedler appears to have been influenced by Coronelli's format as well, since he concluded his fourth supplemental volume with the word "Caq," just as Coronelli had concluded his final volume of the *Biblioteca universale* with the word "Caque." The editors of the 1740 edition of Moreri's *Grand Dictionnaire historique* similarly stressed the issue of ethnography,[13] although neither they nor Zedler concentrated upon the ethnographies of their own countries to the extent that Coronelli had.

Italians were thus somewhat unusual in their attitude toward national ethnography, because—thanks in no small part to Coronelli—popular customs had been a topic of interest since the beginning of the century. He had set the stage for Fortis, Muratori, and Giustina Renier Michiel, who was to write about Venetian festivals;[14] and in setting this stage, Coronelli had provided both an egalitarian and a nationalistic backdrop.

Coronelli had continually stressed the relationship between nationality and language. Thus even when dealing with customs that were peculiar to non-Italian cultures, he tended to use words associated with the language of the cultures in question. For example, his readings of Jewish tracts concerning the treatment of virgins spurred him to designate the Hebrew word "aalma" to head his entry on virgins.[15] He similarly recognized the importance of certain herbs and plants within Arabic traditions, and he accordingly used the Arabic words "abagar," "agak," and "abani" when writing about juniper, thistles, and the Matrubian herb "hairhound."

Coronelli correspondingly used Italian words to describe Italian customs, but the link that he established between the Italian people and the Italian language was far more profound. Because he was compiling an encyclopedia with the intention of attracting and edifying as many segments of the Italian population as possible, he provided, for the benefit of his more limited readers, fairly lengthy entries concerning some rather mundane Italian words. He devoted one and one-half columns to the words "abbottonare" (throw out) and "adolescenzia" and more than half a column each to "a baco" ("little by little"), "apice," and "a mano." The entry "adozione," which received four columns, is representative of hundreds of such words.

With similar motives, Coronelli also included a number of Italian expressions and words with sensational interest. He parceled out six-sevenths of a column to defining the verb "abbordellare"; his analysis of its etymology from the word "bordello, " and of its various meanings (literally, it means "to turn into a bordello" or "to profane") was painstaking. In similarly elaborate fashion, he provided examples of sentences in which the word has different uses and connotations. He allocated one and one-half columns to "bacio" ("kiss"); and having made that decision, he described for his readers' edification three types of kisses: the "osculum" (for a ruler or an old friend), the "basium" (for a family member), and the "suavium" (for a lover, or anyone else worthy of a kiss of "amore impudico . . . so called by its smoothness").[16] The word "bastardo" received four columns and a thorough etymology; "amare" (v.) nine columns; "amore" (n.) eight; and "amato" eight. "Adulterio," a subject for Franciscan sermons, but not usually for Franciscan encyclopedias, took up two and one-half columns.

These lengthy entries for mundane and risqué Italian words illustrate yet another way in which Coronelli's descriptions of both popular customs and popular expressions combined not infrequently with the alphabetical organization to reinforce the egalitarian nature of his enterprise. A cerebral scientific article could appear side by side with an etymological discussion of a vulgar expression, and he viewed both articles as important aspects of eighteenth-century Italian culture. Moreover, these combinations occurred once again in both an alphabetical context and an Italian linguistic context. This linguistic and social leveling and unity thus paralleled the practical and intellectual unity that he imposed upon his contributors/readers through his questionnaires and the articles that stemmed from them. The Italian language and the Italian people had been brought together from yet another perspective.

Coronelli's use of questionnaires to obtain local information was to prove more common in France than in Italy during the late eighteenth century; but early in the nineteenth century, a five-point questionnaire circulated in various parts of Italy, seeking information about customs, "prejudices and superstitions," and "so-called national songs."[17] Such a questionnaire could be used either for or against the goal of national unification. In 1818, an Italian official used it as a basis for a regional study,[18] but there was certainly material available for a more ambitious, and national, work. The unifying potential of ethnographic works was particularly apparent to Niccolò Tommaseo, the first major Italian folksong collector as well as an adamant opponent of Austrian domination of Italy.[19] Like Paoli, Tommaseo was to spend much of his life in exile.

In combining an alphabetical organization with considerable ethnographic material, Coronelli also anticipated by almost half a century Gianfrancesco Pivati's *Nuovo dizionario scientifico e curioso, sacroprofano*, the first fully completed modern alphabetical Italian encyclopedia. Pivati published the *Nuovo dizionario* in ten volumes between 1746 and 1751 (Venice: Benedetto Milocco).[20] Like Coronelli, he was a Venetian who had an established professional relationship with the Paduan *Reformatori dello studio*, the board of censors for the Republic of Venice. The *Riformatori* in fact appointed him to supervise the entire book censorship process.[21] More similar still, he devoted a considerable section of the *Nuovo dizionario* to the subjects of ethnography and popular culture, and again like Coronelli, he supplemented the articles on these subjects with numerous illustrations.

Pivati was not a member of a religious order; unconstrained by the clerical inhibitions that occasionally circumscribed Coronelli's efforts, he was perhaps more in a position to emphasize the religious practices of distant cultures. Yet the difference between the *Biblioteca universale* and the *Nuovo dizionario* concerning descriptions of such cultures was more one of nuance than of substance, since the censorship restrictions that Pivati faced in the 1740s equalled those imposed by the habit that Coronelli wore at the turn of the century. Still, Pivati did not hesitate to provide detailed, if not celebratory, discussions of non-Christian worship; and in a section on the Inca Indians, he included an elaborate set of sun-worshipping scenes, along with illustrations of the Inca marriage and funeral rites.

Pivati was concerned with depicting the daily life, as well as the folklore, of different cultures. Illustrations concerning the Laplanders, for example, vary from depicting the manner in which women carry babies to illustrating the traditional designs and structures that the men use in building huts. The pictures even chart their seasonal migrations. Folklore is also a theme of the *Nuovo dizionario* in articles that concern demon mythology, magical and astrological practices, and methods of folk healing. Along similar lines, Pivati compared Persian, Egyptian, Indian, Greek, and Chinese traditions concerning the Flood.

Despite his considerable interest in ethnography, Pivati did not particularly emphasize Italian folklore. He did not necessarily assume, as did some of his contemporaries as well as Coronelli, a correspondence between nationality and language. Nor was he likely to have concurred with, or even to have comprehended, the correlation that Coronelli drew between encyclopedic and hierarchical orders. Nonetheless, by completing an alphabetical Italian encyclopedia that treats ethnographic issues at considerable length, he realized in part Coronelli's ultimate objective. Moreover, although a less than perfect heir to Coronelli, he was still writing as the contemporary of Muratori.

Coronelli's *Biblioteca universale* also anticipated the encyclopedia that was to become the central publishing venture of the Enlightenment, the *Encyclopédie* of Diderot and d'Alembert.[22] In a manner not dissimilar to that of Coronelli, Diderot and his fellow *encyclopédistes* perceived a close connection between form and content—particularly when using cross-references to demonstrate inconsistancies and ironies vis-à-vis prevailing religious and political assumptions. By juxtaposing, through just such cross-references, two contradictory points of view, they undermined the authority of each one. By inserting a comic word such as "*capuchon*" (monk's head) after a "pompous eulogy" concerning the Franciscan order of the same name, they alerted their readers to their facetious intent.[23] Nor, having perceived the link between form and content, did the encyclopedists fail to grasp the implications of an alphabetical organization. In words reminiscent of Coronelli's, Diderot argued that an encyclopedia "must be clear and easy to grasp, not a tortuous maze in which one goes astray and never sees anything beyond the point where one stands."

An encyclopedia was accordingly alphabetical by definition,[24] and Diderot's analysis again echoed that of his encyclopedic predecessor: "It will be almost as convenient to search for some bit of truth concealed in nature as it will be to find it hidden away in an immense multitude of bound volumes." Such "hidden knowledge" was no more valuable than "a huge manuscript . . . carefully locked up in the King's library, hidden away from all other eyes but his." Once again, an encyclopedist was arguing that the dissemination of knowledge had social, and not simply intellectual, consequences.

As was the case with the *Biblioteca universale*, the *Encyclopédie*'s leveling of knowledge reinforced its unity of knowledge. The encyclopedists' goal was to unite the arts with the sciences, and they endeavored to do this by uniting the efforts of artisans and mechanics with those of intellectuals and nobles. More similar still to Coronelli, the encyclopedists brought the intellectual and the artisan alike into their enterprise by means of questionnaires. These questionnaires thus turned all the individuals who were sharing their knowledge into citizens of the world; but during the Enlightenment, being a citizen of the world often came to mean seeking to transform a particular part of the world.[25] Enlightenment led almost inexorably to nationalism, and the *Encyclopédie*, as the Enlightenment's central publishing venture, was part of the process. This was perhaps not the least of the reasons that it was highly popular, and frequently pirated, in Italy.[26]

Fifty years earlier, Coronelli, in all his innovations, had anticipated a variety of achievements that were to become associated with the mid and late eighteenth century. Muratori wrote his essays on Italian antiquities in 1751, and Fortis studied Dalmatia in the 1770s. Pivati began working on the *Nuovo dizionario* in 1746. Between 1751, the year in which Pivati completed his work, and 1765, Diderot and d'Alembert published the seventeen volumes of the *Encyclopédie*. Coronelli's religious innovations were also some half century ahead of their time. In 1758, Giovan Battista Costanza, a successor to Coronelli as Minister General of the Minori Conventuali, began a vigorous and extremely successful campaign in Venice to end discrimination in convents against foreigners and to eliminate private kitchens—in addition to seeking other reforms. Twelve years later, the Venetian *Provveditori e aggionto sopra monosteri* fully endorsed his program.

Coronelli was thus attuned to, and interested in, changes that were, or were about to be, in the air, and he capitalized upon them by incorporating them into his own projects. The unifying strands of these projects were an emphasis upon Italian and egalitarian unity, and an emphasis upon the Italian language as a vehicle of, and parallel to, that unity. As an encyclopedist, Coronelli had paved the way for Diderot and d'Alembert, and as an Italian he cleared the way for Paoli and Alfieri.

NOTES

1 Pasquale Paoli to Giuseppe Ottaviano Nobelli Savelli, 26 August 1785, in Franco Venturi, "Pasquale Paoli," *Illuministi italiani* (Milan: Ricciardi, 1965), 7:734–35; letter included in English translation in Venturi, *Italy and the Enlightenment: Studies in a Cosmopolitan Century*, ed. Stuart Woolf, trans. Susan Corsi (New York: New York University Press, 1972), 147.

2 Quoted in *Italy and the Enlightenment*, 146. According to Venturi, "Vittorio Alfieri dedicò a Paoli il suo *Timoleone*, parole in cui il significato politico specifico della esperienza isolana veniva ormai perdendosi per assurgere a simbolo di una impossibile virtù e perciò tanto più eroica" ("Pasquale Paoli," 734).

3 Venturi, *Italy and the Enlightenment*, 146.
4 On Coronelli, see James L. Fuchs, "Vincenzo Coronelli and the Organization of Knowledge: The Twilight of Seventeenth-Century Encyclopedism" (Ph.D. diss. Chicago, 1983).
5 Vincenzo Coronelli, "Al discreto lettore," *Biblioteca universale sacroprofana*, 7 vols. (1-5 Venice: Antonio Tivani, 1701-1705; 6 Venice: Giovanni Battista Tramontin, 1706; 7 Venice: n.p., 1707), l. All quotations from Coronelli are from this introduction, unless otherwise indicated.
6 Miriam Usher Chrisman's analysis of the close correlation between a classical education and social and economic privilege, particularly in Strasbourg, as well as the increasing influence of vernacular literature, in *Lay Culture, Learned Culture: Books and Social Change in Strasbourg, 1480-1599* (New Haven: Yale University Press, 1982), 192-230, is relevant to eighteenth-century Italy as well. Robert Darnton notes the striking growth of a popular readership for the *Encyclopédie* in France and abroad in *The Business of Enlightenment: A Publishing History of the Encyclopédie 1775-1800* (Cambridge, Mass.: Harvard University Press, 1979), 524-30.
7 See James L. Fuchs, "An Encyclopaedist among the Minori Conventuali: The Policy and Educational Reforms of Vincenzo Coronelli," *The Journal of Religious History* 14 (1986): 152-66.
8 S. Abate Giacinto Gimma, *Titoli delle opere di varie materie in idioma diversi composte, e stampate dall' anno MDCCIV* (Venice: Accademia degli Argonauti, 1708), 44-46. I did not find this request in any volumes of the *Biblioteca universale*, but its appearance in a publication of Coronelli's Accademia degli Argonauti suggests that Coronelli did send it out.
9 Coronelli published numerous editions of the *Memorie. . .della Morea*. The latest is Coronelli, *Memorie istoriografiche del Regno della Morea* (Venice: Giuseppe Ruinetti, 1688). In 1703, he published *Morea, Negroponte, e adiacenze* (Venice: P.V.). He wrote about Dalmatia in, among other publications, *Repubblica di Venezia* (Venice: n.p., c.1708). See also *Coronelli, Conquiste della serena Repubblica nella Dalmazia, Epiro, e Morea* (Venice: Laboratorio del p.m. Coronelli, 1696). The 1708 works contain considerable ethnographical information.
10 Alberto Fortis, *Viaggo in Dalmazia*, 2 vols. (Venice: Alvise Milocco, 1774), 1, 43f, cited in Peter Burke, *Popular Culture in Early Modern Europe* (New York: Harper & Row, 1978), 19, 291f. Ludovico Antonio Muratori, *Dissertazioni sopra le antichita italiane*, 3 vols. (Milan: G. Pasquali, 1751), also cited in Burke, 283-84, 328f.
11 Fritz Stern, *The Politics of Cultural Despair: A Study in the Rise of the German Ideology* (Berkeley and Los Angeles: University of California Press, 1961). Peter Burke discusses the Grimms and Herder along these lines in *Popular Culture*, 18-22.
12 *Grosses vollständiges Universal Lexicon aller Wissenschaften und Künste, welche bisshero durch menschlichen Verstand und Witz erfunden und verbessert worden*, 64 vols. in 63, vols. 19-64 ed. Carl Günther Ludovici (Halle and

Leipzig: Johann Heinrich Zedler, 1732-1750); *Nöthige Supplemente*, ed. Carl Gunther Ludovici, 4 vols. (Leipzig: Johann Heinrich Zedler, 1751-54).

13 See Arnold Miller, "Louis Moreri's *Grand dictionnaire historique*," in *Notable Encyclopedias of the Seventeenth and Eighteenth Centuries: Nine Predecessors of the Enyclopédie*, ed. Frank A. Kafker, *Studies on Voltaire and the Eighteenth Century* no. 194 (Oxford: The Voltaire Foundation, 1981), 32-37.

14 Giustina Renier Michiel, *Origine delle feste veneziane* (Venice: Alvisopoli, 1817), in Burke, 7, 288, 291.

15 *Biblioteca universale*, 1:cols. 27-28. The correct English translation of "aalma" is "young woman" rather than "virgin," but the Hebrew has been mistranslated since the first century.

16 *Biblioteca universale*, 4: cols.41-42.

17 Giovanni Tassoni, ed., *Arti e tradizione popolari: le inchiste Napoleoniche sui costumi e le tradizione nel Regno Italico* (Bellinzone: La Vesconta, 1900; rpt. 1973), in Burke, 15, 293.

18 Michele Placucci, *Usi e pregiudizi dei contadini di Romagna* (1818; rpt. Bologna: Lauriel, 1885; 1987). See also Burke (15, 293), who has consulted another edition of this work, under a different title (*Romagna tradizionale; usi e costumi, credenze e pregiuize*, ed. Paolo Toschi (Bologna: Capelli, 1952).

19 Burke, 12, 14, 16, 288.

20 See Silvano Garofalo, *L'enciclopedismo italiano: Gianfrancesco Pivati* (Ravenna: Longo, 1980). Garofalo summarizes much of this material, and frequently provides a direct English translation of the book, in his article "Gianfrancesco Pivati's *Nuovo dizionario*," which appears in Kafker, *Notable Encyclopedias*. A subject not treated at length in the article is Pivati's interest in electronic medicine (71-89).

21 Garofalo, *L'enciclopedismo italiano*, 24; "Gianfrancesco Pivati's *Nuovo dizionario*," 197.

22 Denis Diderot and Jean le Rond d'Alembert, *Encyclopédie ou dictionnaire raisonné des sciences, des arts et des lettres*, 17 vols. (Paris: Briasson, 1751-65). Between 1762 and 1772, eleven additional volumes of plates appeared as well.

23 "Encyclopédie," *L'Encyclopédie*, 5:633-39. For quotations, I have used the translation in Diderot, *Rameau's Nephew and Other Works*, trans. Jacques Barzun and Ralph H. Bowen (New York: Doubleday & Company, 1956; Indianapolis: The Bobbs-Merrill Company, 1964), 277-307.

24 "Let us assume that their extracts have been competently made, and that these have been arranged in alphabetical order and published in an orderly series of volumes by men of intelligence—you have an encyclopedia!" (300).

25 See Venturi, e.g. *Italy and the Enlightenment*, xix-xx.

26 See Darnton, 6, 19, 34-35, 37, 314-15.

From Clarens *to* Hollow Park, *Isabelle de Charrière's Quiet Revolution*

NADINE BÉRENGUIER

"Love is more pleasant than marriage for the reason that novels are more amusing than history."[1] In this lapidary maxim, Chamfort effectively captures what characterizes the plots of eighteenth-century novels. By placing novels on the side of love, this observer of eighteenth-century mores reminds us of the age-old dichotomy between love and marriage and underlines that, unlike love and the novel, the novel and marriage do not make a good match. What happens, then, when such a golden rule is transgressed and the intruder, that is, marriage, becomes the major topic of a novel? What is the impact of such a break with tradition on the ideological content of the novel? Such questions are raised by *Lettres de Mistriss Henley*, initially published in 1784, in which Isabelle de Charrière departs radically from the novelistic tradition of her time.[2] This break did not escape the attention of the first public reviewers who gave a critical reading of *Lettres de Mistriss Henley* with Samuel de Constant's *Le mari sentimental*, published together (anonymously) in the 1785 Paris edition.[3] In *Le Mercure de France*, the review began thus: "Le fond de ce double roman, dont la forme est assez singulière, a le mérite d'être absolument neuf."[4] [The content of this double novel, whose form is quite remarkable, has the advantage of being absolutely new.] It pointed out that the authors had left the beaten tracks of French prose-fiction by omitting "aventure merveilleuse, amants persécutés, dispersés, réunis;

... ces intrigues filées, promenées d'obstacles en obstacles ... Amants, passions amoureuses" (186) [unreal adventure, persecuted, separated, and reunited lovers; ... these endless plots meandering from obstacles to obstacles ... Lovers, amorous passions]. These remarks were echoed by the *Année littéraire*: "Ce roman, monsieur a une marche différente de celle des autres. La plupart renferment des intrigues amoureuses qui se terminent par le mariage; celui-ci, ou ceux-ci (car il y en a deux) commencent là où les autres finissent. On n'imagine guère que deux personnes mariées soient capables d'exciter un intérêt bien vif."[5] [This novel, Sir, takes a different path from the others. Most of them have amorous plots which end in marriage. This one (or these for they are two) begins where the others end. It is difficult to imagine that two married persons can arouse such great interest.] It seems that even at the end of the century Chamfort's remark was still accurate. Nevertheless, both reviewers praised this attempt to provide insight into a matter previously ignored by novels: the (mal)functioning of conjugal unions. The *Mercure de France* in particular displayed an unambiguous enthusiasm: "Cette tentative a déjà été faite au théâtre; mais nous croyons que c'est la première fois qu'elle ait été risquée dans un roman: il nous semble cependant qu'elle pourrait être répétée avec succès, et même infiniment étendue" (186). [Such an attempt has already been made in the theater; but we believe that it is the first time that it has been risked in a novel: it seems nonetheless that it could be repeated successfully, and even infinitely extended.] Novels, in order to fulfill their edifying mission, should not leave any aspect of life unexplored but should rather "tracer les tableaux de la vie, afin que parmi ceux qui se rapprochent le plus des circonstances qui nous entourent, nous choisissions la route que nous devons suivre, les écueils que nous devons éviter" (187) [draw pictures of life, so that among those which are closest to the circumstances familiar to us, we can choose the path that we must follow and the obstacles that we must avoid]. As suggested by the format of the 1785 Parisian edition, the two novels were perceived as inseparable parts of a diptych. In *Le mari sentimental*, M. Bompré is led to commit suicide by the selfish behavior and insensitivity of his wife, while in *Mistriss Henley*, Mrs. Henley is disenchanted by the excessively rational attitude of her husband.[6] In their haste to acclaim the uniqueness of this double plot, both reviewers privileged the issues raised by the controversy between *Le mari sentimental* and *Mistriss Henley* and forgot to mention a prior attempt to include married life in a novel: Jean-Jacques Rousseau's *Julie ou la Nouvelle Héloïse* (1761).

Le mari sentimental is explicitly inscribed (as we shall see) in *Mistriss Henley*, but the dialogue does not stop with the companion text. Too many allusions to be ignored point, in *Mistress Henley*, to *Julie*. It is unnecessary to recall at length the impact of *Julie* on the public of the period or to document the fact that Charrière had read Rousseau's work.[7] In the Second Preface to *Julie*, Rousseau, an ardent detractor of contemporary novels, proposes to break with the literary conventions of his day and to revolutionize prose-fiction in France by focusing on married life and domestic concerns.[8] Charrière does not voice her own claims in such an outspoken way, but her deliberate choice to deal exclusively with the bare matter of married life and domesticity constitutes in itself another radical departure. Unlike Mary Wollstonecraft, who very explicitly responds to Rousseau in her *Vindication of the Rights of Woman*, Charrière answers implicitly but in fictional terms; she offers a serious and significant contribution to discussions about marriage and the family through a critical rewriting of the marriage ideology displayed in *Julie*.

I suggest with Nancy K. Miller that "Learning to read women's writing entails not only a particular attentiveness to the marks of signature that [she has] called 'overreading'; it also involves 'reading in pairs (or, in Naomi Schor's coinage, 'intersextually'). By this [Miller] mean[s] looking at the literature of men's and women's writing side by side to perceive at their points of intersection the differentiated lines of a 'bi-cultural' production of the novel—Persian *and* Peruvian—more complicated than the familiar, national history of its tropes."[9] I do not propose *Mistriss Henley* for an exercise in overreading, but for "reading in pairs," taking *Julie* as a grid through which to read *Mistriss Henley*, and vice versa. This method does not mean that I will look at the influence of Rousseau on Charrière. Rather, I will examine Charrière's fictional treatment of Rousseau's marriage narrative and of its consequences for women. *Mistriss Henley* fully explores the new paths opened by *Julie* and, I will argue, more radically than *Julie*. Charrière's novel departs from narrative tradition in areas where Rousseau fell short of doing so. In fact, Rousseau preserved major rules of the genre he despised so much, a feature of *Julie* widely acknowledged by scholars studying his fiction.[10] For her part, in *Mistriss Henley*, Charrière abandons all the conventions still favored by Rousseau and simultaneously provides a veiled ironic comment on *Julie* by giving a very different outlook on marriage as an institution, marital relationships, and domestic affairs (e. g., running a household, education and child-rearing, social functions).

Why did the first reviewers and later critics ignore a precedent as well-known as *Julie*? On the one hand, Rousseau's status and legacy might explain this silence. Rousseau was not considered merely a novelist, but rather a *philosophe* (in the general sense), concerned with various political and social issues (such as the passage from a state of nature to civil society, the birth of property, the role of arts and sciences in society). Therefore, the characters, relationships, and situations in Rousseau's successful novel could be perceived as part of a wider system representative of his opinions and principles. The "didactic" side of *Julie* was commented upon by Rousseau's contemporaries, such as Duclos, d'Alembert, and Madame Necker, and has been examined by more recent critics, such as Jean-Louis Lecercle: "He could not avoid entrusting his characters with themes which obsessed him, to the extent that this book has been called a synthesis of his thought."[11] The short and bare format of the *Mari sentimental/Mistriss Henley* duet seems far removed from the all-encompassing project of *Julie*. Because of their focus on the severed relationship between two spouses, the critics perceived the new novels as very topical works whose perspective was limited to the psychoemotional and the private. Such a view could conveniently accommodate the biographical reading of *Mistriss Henley* initiated by Philippe Godet, Charrière's first major biographer, who qualified it as "insignificant" despite its interest as a reflection of "the moral state of the author during this period of her life.[12] Though an autobiographical view is historically justified, it is regrettably likely to hide other possible implications of her departure from novelistic convention.[13] Both the polemic and the autobiographical approaches reduce Charrière's innovation to a mere emotional reaction, be it to another novel, or to her own experience. In short, the difference of status between *Julie* and *Mistriss Henley* can account for the failure of literary critics to establish a connection between them.

Both the polemic and autobiographical elements that have prevailed among the novel's readers are actually embedded in the first page of *Mistriss Henley*. The reader is immediately invited by the protagonist to see her writing as a response to a "cruel et charmant petit livre" [cruel and charming little book] (*Le mari sentimental*) that has tormented her ever since she read it. A reading of the novel to her husband and his reaction to it are decisive in prompting her "confessions" to a silent "confidante." Hoping that her husband will perceive differences between their situation and that of Bompré in *Le mari*, she is distressed to sense his perception of similarities and his tendency to identify with the unfortunate husband:

> Quand j'ai lu tout cela à mon mari, au lieu de sentir encore mieux que moi ces différences, comme je m'en étais flattée en commençant la lecture, ou de ne point sentir du tout cette manière de ressemblance, je l'ai vu tantôt sourire, tantôt soupirer; il a dit quelques mots, il a caressé son chien et regardé l'ancienne place du portrait. Ma chère amie, ils se croiront tous des MM. Bompré, et seront surpris d'avoir pu supporter si patiemment la vie (101). [When I read all of this to my husband, instead

of feeling these differences more than I did, as I had flattered myself he would when I started, or not feeling this sort of resemblance at all, I saw him sometimes smile, sometimes sigh; he said a few words, petted his dog and looked at the former place of the portrait. My dear friend, they will all think themselves Bomprés, and are surprised that they have been able to endure life so patiently.]

Besides identifying itself as a party in a controversy, the novel introduces the question of the influence of fiction on "real" life. By affording them a comparison with their own experience, *Le mari sentimental* becomes part and parcel of the conjugal difficulties encountered by the Henleys. After interpreting Constant's novel according to her own experience, Mrs. Henley tries to decipher its negative impact on her husband's behavior: "Il vivait et me jugeait, pour ainsi dire, au jour la journée, jusqu'à ce que M. et Mme Bompré le soient venus rendre plus content de lui et plus mécontent de moi. J'ai eu bien du chagrin depuis ma dernière lettre" (108). [He was living and judging me, so to speak, on a day-by-day basis, until Mr. and Mrs. Bompré made him more content with himself and less satisfied with me. I have had much sorrow since I last wrote to you.] Fiction and personal experience fuse and become confused, as fiction becomes so palpable that it intensifies the pain inflicted by life.

The well-established belief that novels had an impact on readers' taste and behavior was central to the debate that raged in the eighteenth century regarding this relatively new genre.[14] Because of the preeminence of love in their plots, novels were accused of corrupting the morals of their readers, especially of young women. In *Mistriss Henley*, Charrière reformulates the relationship between the effects of fiction and its content and gives it a completely new turn. Even when fiction promotes a "serious" topic—and marriage is one—it can be harmful. Even "good" models—devoid of seduction, adultery, abduction, disobedience, and life-theatening conflicts—do not guarantee a beneficial effect of fiction on readers who might still have to pay an emotional price, contrary to what one might deduce from *Julie*'s Second Preface: "Si les romans n'offraient à leurs lecteurs que des tableaux d'objets qui les environnent, que des devoirs qu'ils peuvent remplir, que des plaisirs de leur condition, les romans ne les rendraient point fous, ils les rendraient sages" (22). [If novels offered to their readers only depictions of objects that surround them, duties that can be fulfilled, the pleasures of their conditions, novels would not render them insane, they would render them reasonable.] As it refutes this point, Charrière's "insignificant" novel begins to take a radical stand.

A comparison of prefatory remarks in the Second Preface of *Julie* and the first letter of *Mistriss Henley* illustrates a novel's possible effects on readers who identify with their characters. Both novelists innovate by targeting not individuals, but married couples. However, each sheds a very different light on this enterprise. In *Julie*'s Second Preface, in the dialogue between R and N, R attributes to the depiction of a domestic life the power to reform mores in general and regenerate conjugal relations in particular:

> J'aime à me figurer deux époux lisant ce recueil ensemble, y puisant un nouveau courage pour supporter leurs travaux communs, et peut-être de nouvelles vues pour les rendre utiles. Comment pourraient-ils y contempler le tableau d'un ménage heureux, sans vouloir imiter un si doux modèle? Comment s'attendriront-ils sur le charme de l'union conjugale, même privé de celui de l'amour, sans que la leur se resserre et s'affermisse? (23) [I like to imagine husband and wife reading this collection of letters together, drawing from it new courage to endure their common tasks, and perhaps gaining new views to render these tasks useful. How could they contemplate the picture of this happy household, without wishing to imitate such a pleasing model? How can they be moved by the charm of the conjugal bond, even deprived of the charm of love, without seeing their own union tightened and strengthened?]

In this passage, Rousseau presents his novel as a conduct-book that prescribes a new way of life (centered upon the home and the family) and that should inspire married readers to have more harmonious unions.

In the first page of *Mistriss Henley*, we see Mrs. Henley practicing what R advocates: that is, reading novels with her husband; ironically, however, she reads not *Julie*, but *Le mari sentimental*. Far from providing a model to be imitated by both spouses (like *Julie*, in Rousseau's opinion), this novel creates a split between husband and wife, who read it very differently. The lack of harmony between them is underscored by the purpose suggested by Mrs. Henley for the publication of her own letters. From a reader she turns into a writer:

> Si ma lettre ou mes lettres ont quelque justesse et vous paraissent propres à exciter quelque intérêt, seulement assez pour se faire lire, traduisez-les en changeant les noms, en omettant ce qui vous paraîtra ennuyeux ou inutile. Je crois que beaucoup de femmes sont dans le même cas que moi. Je voudrais, sinon corriger, du moins avertir les maris (102). [If my letter or my letters are in any way correct and seem to you likely to trigger any interest, if only enough to be read, translate them, changing the names and suppressing whatever seems to you boring or useless. I believe that many women are in a situation similar to mine. I would like, if not to reform, at least to alert husbands.]

If Charrière makes her (male) readers reconsider their own attitudes, it is through a warning and not through a positive model. The prefatory material built into the novel's body bears witness to the urgency of the situation and finds itself in stern contrast with *Julie*'s elaborate dialogued preface (also entitled "Ecrit sur les romans") in which Rousseau indicates the objectives of his novel and debates the laws of the genre. Both novelists, eager to see reforms implemented in the mores of their contemporaries, are innovative in aiming at married readers, but this common effort reveals opposite attitudes on their part: on Rousseau's, a propensity to idealize situations; on Charrière's an attempt to scrutinize them as lucidly as possible, and lay them as bare as possible.[15] This contrast emerges through their use (or neglect) of certain traditional plot elements. In what follows, I will compare Julie's and Mrs. Henley's fates as married heroines and mention a few aspects of Rousseau's fidelity to novelistic tradition, not in order to lessen the impact of his enterprise, but to highlight more clearly Charrière's narrative boldness in *Mistriss Henley*.

In eighteenth-century France, marriage, as social historians Jean-Louis Flandrin and James Traer have documented, was central to strategies of alliances ensuring the transmission, redistribution or acquisition of property, the continuation of a lineage, and the improvement of social status.[16] Such conclusions, based on the study of family documents, are also found in the writings of social critics of the period, who claimed that as long as marriages were based on transactions between families rather than on individual agreements, no personal satisfaction could come from married life. Montesquieu, Diderot, collaborators in the *Encyclopédie*, as well as Rousseau himself, did not question the institution of marriage so much as the custom of arranged marriages, and they favored freedom in the choice of a partner, combined with the right to divorce (except Rousseau), as the solution to conjugal misery.[17] In turn, fiction often dealt with obligatory arranged marriage; *Julie* was no exception. Like many other novels of the period, the first half of *Julie* stages an amorous passion between two young protagonists (Julie and Saint-Preux) and the stubborn opposition of Julie's father to their union. Under such circumstances, marriage is treated as a transaction upsetting the familial stability and as a source of conflict between generations. Family relationships crystallize and intensify around the prohibition of Julie's union with Saint-Preux and then, around the arrangement of Julie's marriage to Wolmar. Seen from this angle, Julie's situation resembles that of other novels' heroines, adolescents who have reached a marriageable age and struggle with the difficulties generated by the critical transition from childhood to adulthood. Thus marriage becomes a source of conflict between generations and the focus of parent/child power dynamics.[18]

In *Mistriss Henley*, the period directly preceding marriage, central to many eighteenth-century novels, is practically discarded. Mrs. Henley does not use any pretext to linger on her past. When she announces to her correspondent in a rhetorical question: "Voulez-vous, ma chère amie, que je vous fasse l'histoire de mon mariage, du temps qui l'a précédé, et que je vous peigne ma vie telle qu'elle est aujourd'hui?" (102) [Do you want, my dear friend, to hear the story of my marriage, of the time which preceded it, do you want me to describe my life as it is nowadays?], one would expect her to focus on "the time that preceded it," as is customary in a fair number of eighteenth-century novels.[19] Instead, Mrs. Henley briefly summarizes those years: an orphan raised by a loving aunt who treated her like a daughter, she was promised to Lord Alesford (the heir of her aunt's husband) at a very young age, and both quietly waited for their future union. Sent on a tour of Europe, the young lord died in Italy after being unfaithful to his beloved.[20] This period is narrated very hastily, her sorrow remembered in a few lines: "Je ne vous dirai point tout ce que je souffris alors, tout ce que j'avais déjà souffert pendant plusieurs mois. Vous vîtes à Montpellier les traces que le chagrin avait laissées dans mon humeur" (102). [I shall not tell you how much I suffered then, how much I had already suffered for several months. You saw in Montpellier the traces that my sorrow had left in my temper.] The ellipsis, underscored by the "I shall not tell you," supposes the reader well enough equipped to fill in the gaps of the narrative. Of course, no more details are necessary for a correspondent whom she met at the time of her affliction, just as they are superfluous for any reader familiar with the deceived lovers populating the fiction of the time. She can thus concentrate on her "life as it is nowadays"; this focus is signalled by the absence of her maiden name, which precludes any other identity.

The circumstances more directly surrounding their marriages also create a contrast between Julie and Mrs. Henley. Given by her authoritative father to an aging husband, Julie is again submitted to the fate of many heroines who are denied a say in the choice of a spouse and must marry according to family interests (or not marry at all and enter a convent). Fundamentally, in regard to their situation as women, both Julie and Mrs. Henley have an obligation to marry, and no other option is offered to either of them (as non-Catholics, not even the convent). Julie, whose brother is dead, is responsible, among other things, for continuing the family blood-line, which is threatened with extinction. As she will inherit very little money from her aunt, the future Mrs. Henley must find a husband in order to enjoy financial security. However, in contrast to Julie, Charrière's heroine is given a choice of possible partners, which she perceives as extreme freedom.[21] Far from rejoicing over this widely praised freedom, Mrs. Henley expresses ambivalent feelings toward it and in retrospect she regrets having been given the right to prefer Mr. Henley, a man of the gentry, over a merchant returned rich from India (whom she calls the "Nabab"):

> Si un père tyrannique m'eût obligée à épouser le Nabab, je me serais fait peut-être un devoir d'obéir; et m'étourdissant sur l'origine de ma fortune par l'usage que je me serais promis d'en faire, "les bénédictions des indigents d'Europe détourneront," me serais-je dit, "les malédictions de l'Inde." En un mot, forcée d'être heureuse d'une manière vulgaire, je le serais devenue sans honte et peut-être avec plaisir; mais me donner moi-même de mon choix, contre des diamants, des perles, des tapis, des parfums, des mousselines brodées d'or, des soupers, des fêtes, je ne pouvais m'y résoudre, et je promis ma main à Mr. Henley (103-104). [If a tyrannical father had obliged me to marry the Nabob, I probably would have made a point of obeying; and in an attempt to forget the origin of my fortune through the use I made of it, "the blessings of the needy of Europe will divert," I would have told myself, "the maledictions of India." In a word, forced to be happy in a vulgar manner, I would have become so shamelessly and perhaps with pleasure; but I could not decide on my own to exchange myself freely for diamonds, pearls, carpets, perfumes, gold embroidered muslins, suppers, feasts, and I promised my hand to Mr. Henley.]

Irony pervades this passage, in which the character is creating her own fiction on the basis of traditional narratives and providing a defense of forced marriages. This ironic tone fits the paradox of her situation: she perceives her relative freedom as an unbearable burden and regrets the absence of a severe and impervious father who would have imposed his will (as Julie's father did). She could have been sold by her father (or her aunt, for that matter), but does not feel entitled to be herself the performer of the exchange as well as its object. This passage lucidly analyzes the unexpected consequences of the freedom to choose a husband. As Elisabeth de Fontenay argues in an article on the invention of "ménage" by Rousseau, "companionate marriage, [on the other hand], subjects the woman because it transforms the patriarchal contract between families into a conjugal and inter-individual bond deprived of any socio-political dimension. In making this bond private, one excludes women from public life and one condemns them exclusively to domestic life."[22] In refusing to marry primarily for money (she does not marry for love either), Mrs. Henley seals an inter-personal agreement with the man whom she has elected as her husband.

This type of conjugal bond introduces the protagonist into a private and enclosed world, limited to the family and domestic duties. The absence of a father's strong coercion is symptomatic of the absence of external causes for the failed relationship: "Je suis d'autant plus malheureuse qu'il n'y a rien à quoi je puisse m'en prendre, que je n'ai aucun changement à demander, aucun reproche à faire, que je me blâme et me méprise d'être malheureuse" (107). [I am all the more unhappy that there is nothing which I can blame, no change I can request, no reproach I can make, and that I blame myself and despise myself for being unhappy.] Again, this predicament is linked to the double role that she has had to perform: as a woman giving herself, she does not feel entitled to place responsibility outside herself. The focus on marriage as a private relationship between two individuals rather than as a function of external principles, as in *Julie*, is a revolt against *Mistriss Henley*'s predecessor. The married couple, exposed as an internally fragile unit when stripped of external threats, becomes a newly-constituted literary character through Charrière's innovation.

While in other novels of the period, married life eludes narration as if its privacy had to be kept from indiscreet readers, or rather, as if it were unlikely to provide an acceptable plot line, in *Julie* as in *Mistriss Henley*, the marriage ceremony does not constitute a happy and hasty conclusion.[23] In both novels, marriage opens a new era for the protagonists, and married life is the object of much attention. *Julie*, one might add, is the first novel published in France in which the heroine leads her married life in the country, cares about the success of her marriage, has children and is involved in their education. The "révolution soudaine" [sudden revolution] that strikes her during the wedding ceremony constitutes the best symbol of the power of marriage, inaugurating simultaneously a new life for the character and a new theme for novelistic fiction. However, Julie's wedding is powerfully described as a sacrifice through which she undoes the violation of her sexual integrity: "Je fus menée au temple comme une victime impure qui souille le sacrifice où l'on va l'immoler" (353; III, 18). [I was brought to the temple as an impure victim that sullies the sacrifice where she is going to be immolated.] Her devotion to married life appears as a way to expiate her premature loss of virginity: "Douce et consolante vertu, je la [la vie] recommence pour toi; c'est toi qui me la rendras chère; c'est à toi que je la veux consacrer" (355; III, 18). [Sweet and consoling virtue, I recommence it (my life) for you; you will make it dear to me; I want to devote it to you.] Julie's past and her "fault" justify her mystical devotion to domesticity and give her marriage to Wolmar all the characteristics of an expiation for her illicit relationship with Saint-Preux. This suffices to make the Wolmars an exception to the rule asserted by the reviewer of the *Année littéraire* ("It is difficult to imagine that two married persons can arouse such great interest"); they are likely to interest readers greatly.

Only a brief sentence inaugurates Mrs. Henley's career as a wife, her wedding being the object of no detailed description. "Nos noces furent charmantes" (104) [Our wedding was charming] says it all, because the frustrated wife wants to introduce without any further delay the central issue of the novel, that is, her relationship with her husband. She portrays him thus: "Spirituel, élégant, décent, délicat, affectueux, M. Henley enchantait tout le monde; c'était un mari de roman; il me semblait quelquefois un peu trop parfait; mes fantaisies, mes humeurs, mes impatiences trouvaient toujours *sa raison et sa modération* en leur chemin" (104; my emphasis). [Witty, elegant, decent, delicate, affectionate, Mr. Henley enchanted everyone; he looked like a story-book husband and sometimes appeared too perfect; my fancies, my moods, my irritations always found his reason and his temperance in their way.] Strangely enough, though, the expression "mari de roman" can hardly mean "husbands as novels portray them," since husbands are rarely given a positive role in the plot of French novels.[24] "Mari de roman," thus, might refer to prospective husbands, "prince charmings" who fight abusive fathers and (sometimes) defeat them at the end of the story. However, there is one exception to this rule, the perfect "mari de roman" identified in *Julie*: M. de Wolmar.

Mr. Henley is a younger and more seductive version of M. de Wolmar. Describing their husbands, both wives mention reason and moderation as the men's fundamental traits. Julie introduces him to Saint-Preux: "Sa physionomie est noble et prévenante, son abord simple et ouvert, ses manières sont plus honnêtes qu'empressées; il parle peu et d'un grand sens, mais sans affecter ni précision ni sentence. Il est le même pour tout le monde, ne cherche et ne fuit personne, et *n'a jamais d'autres préférences que celles de la raison*" (369; III, 20; my emphasis). [His physiognomy is noble and welcoming, his demeanor simple and open, his manners more honest than zealous; he talks little and with logic, but does not pretend to precision or sententiousness. He is the same for everybody, seeks nobody and avoids nobody, and has no other preferences than those dictated by reason.] Henley's position as Wolmar's heir is all the more interesting in that their reasonable behaviors have very different outcomes. Wolmar is a "mari de roman" of a new kind. Like any other novelistic husband he has not been chosen, but unlike most of them, he is highly praised and admired by his young wife. Unlike Mrs. Henley, Julie does not hint at the difficulties likely to result from daily intercourse with such a controlled personality. This reign of reason in their relationship, executed by Wolmar, is yet another manifestation of Julie's urge to expiate her passionate past. The perfection that Julie claims for her union with M. de Wolmar is best explained by her attempt to compensate for her haunting love of Saint-Preux. When Wolmar invites Saint-Preux to join them at Clarens, the past illicit love is reenforced by its possible resurgence under the guise of adultery. In that respect, Rousseau remains faithful to the tradition according to which married life serves as a background for the analysis of illicit love, and more precisely of the feminine struggle against adultery or its temptation.[25] Wolmar's initiative regarding Saint-Preux, moreover, shows the limits of his reasonable behavior as he takes perverse pleasure at the triangular situation with which he experiments and tests his wife: "Il prend plaisir à la confiance qu'il me témoigne" (498; IV, 12) [He takes pleasure in the trust that he shows me], Julie comments to Claire.[26] Their relationship is shaped by a mediation which allows Rousseau to glorify simultaneously a married couple and an irresistible illicit passion, as if he made his innovations more admissible through the pervasive use of more traditional novelistic elements. This is at the same time the strength of his project and possibly the limit of his transgressive fiction.

Such traditional elements, though suggested briefly, are never carried out in *Mistriss Henley*, and no underlying passion counterbalances the reason incarnated by Mr. Henley. Mrs. Henley fantasizes about adultery as a device to arouse her husband's jealousy and modify his cool behavior towards her. At a ball, she has made the acquaintance of a young woman and her brother whom she has invited to dinner. She makes a point of telling her husband of this man's resemblance to her first fiancé, Lord Alesford, but to no avail. No titillating effect is obtained. Her attempt is immediately dismissed as irrelevant by Mr. Henley who declares, smiling: "Heureusement je ne suis pas jaloux" (116). [Fortunately, I am not jealous.] Reacting vehemently to what she perceives as indifference, she draws the portrait of a paradoxical "husband of her dreams": " 'Oui!' ai-je ajouté, excité à la fois par ma propre vivacité et par son sang-froid inaltérable, 'les injustices d'un jaloux, les emportements d'un brutal, seraient moins fâcheux que le flegme et l'aridité d'un sage'" (116). ['Yes!' I added, irritated as much by my own outburst of temper as by his unfailing self-control, 'the injustice of a jealous man, the anger of a brute would be less of a nuisance than the phlegm and the dullness of a wise man.'] Not only does she allude once more to another possible novelistic institution (the abusive husband), but she also reveals her mistrust of rationality and her delusion regarding the ability of reasonable behavior to operate in all realms of human endeavor. In a letter written after this outburst, she addresses her husband in these terms: "Vous avez pourtant eu un tort: vous m'avez fait trop d'honneur en m'épousant. Vous avez cru — et qui ne l'aurait cru? — que trouvant dans son mari tout ce qui peut rendre un homme aimable et estimable, et dans sa situation tous les plaisirs honnêtes, l'opulence et la considération, une femme raisonnable ne pouvait manquer d'être heureuse. Mais je ne suis pas une femme raisonnable, vous et moi l'avons vu trop tard" (117). [You are however wrong on one account: you honored me too much by marrying me. You believed—and who would not have believed it?—that, finding in her husband all that can make a man lovable and estimable, and in her situation all honest pleasures, opulence and consideration, a reasonable woman could not fail to be happy: but I am no reasonable woman; you and I have realized it too late.]

The link established between marriage and happiness corresponds to a modern notion of the married couple. In her striving to perfection, Mrs. Henley is a very modern wife. Just before leaving London to settle with her husband in the country, she had dreamed of becoming "la meilleure femme, la plus tendre belle-mère, la plus digne maîtresse de maison que l'on eût jamais vue" (104) [the best wife, the most tender step-mother, the most worthy housewife that was ever seen]. Because this marriage is of her own doing, she sees it not only as the functional association of two persons in order to procreate, to continue the lineage, and to transmit wealth, but also as a strong affective bond, with its own dynamics that suppose a dedicated contribution of the individual to the benefit of the relationship. As a consequence, Mrs. Henley's affective energy is centered on her rapport with her husband. As the young Mrs. Henley has placed high expectations on married life as a source of personal success and happiness, she perceives its failure as a traumatic experience, all the more poignant in that no external factor (such as arranged marriage or love for another man still found in *Julie*) can be held accountable for it. While Rousseau still uses external elements to undermine the Wolmar couple, Charrière demystifies Rousseau's ideal pair by planting the seeds of its destruction inside the private conjugal walls.

Since no paternal constraint, no past illicit passion, no jealousy, no threat of adultery endangers their relationship, what exactly imperils the Henleys' marriage? Mrs. Henley indirectly answers this question at the beginning of her fourth letter: "Je vous entretiens ma chère amie, de choses bien peu intéressantes, et avec une longueur, un détail!—mais c'est comme cela qu'elles sont dans ma tête; et je croirais ne vous rien dire, si je ne vous disais pas tout. Ce sont de petites choses qui m'affligent ou m'impatientent, et me font avoir tort. Ecoutez donc encore un tas de petites choses" (112). [I talk to you, my dear friend, about things without interest, at too great a length and with too many details!—but so they are in my head; and I would feel as if I said nothing if I did not tell you everything. It is small things which afflict or irritate me, and put me in the wrong. Listen then to a heap of small things.] Their relationship is endangered by "a heap of small things." Aware of the lack of diversion in her life, she admits to focusing too much on domestic affairs, such as the education of her step-daughter, the replacement of wallpaper and furniture, the unfortunate acquisition of a cat, the affair of her chambermaid with a neighboring farmer, the argument about a dress that she wears at a ball. With regard to Mrs. Henley's personal story, these incidents illustrate her incompatibility with Mr. Henley, and their accumulation expresses the emptiness of her life. More importantly for my purpose, these episodes engage problems of education and mothering that greatly preoccupied Rousseau. In order to complete the assessment of Charrière's critique of *Julie*'s seemingly perfect world, I shall consider not so much the filiation of ideas as the way these issues are incorporated into *Mistriss Henley*'s plot.

While Rousseau makes education and parenting the topic of a single enlightened conversation among Julie, Wolmar and Saint-Preux (who narrates it in letter 3 of part V), Charrière stages the issue in a series of short quarrels between husband and wife, concerning the clothes suited for her step-daughter, the teaching of La Fontaine fables, their diverging views on the future of their unborn child, and maternal breast-feeding. In *Julie*, the pages devoted to education are didactic and summarize major principles developed at length in *Emile*. Consequently, Julie's and Wolmar's ideas on the education of their sons are in full harmony. She will take care of them until they reach the age to leave the "gynécée" and come under the guidance of their father and Saint-Preux, their future tutor. Regarding the education of Henriette (Claire's daughter, whom Julie considers her daughter), Wolmar has nothing to say, since men cannot be involved in girls' education, and this discussion is absent from Julie insofar as "les principes en sont si différents qu'ils méritent un entretien à part" (585; V, 3). [Its principles are so different that they deserve a separate discussion.] In *Julie*, education is a segregated activity according to the children's age and sex, while in *Mistriss Henley*, all aspects of child-rearing (of male and female children) concern both parents, and constitute a potentially problematic endeavor as a source of conflict between them.[27]

What unifies the Wolmars divides the Henleys. A case in point is provided by La Fontaine's *Fables*. On this topic, Julie peacefully expresses ideas that have Wolmar's full approbation: "Et convaincue que les fables sont faites pour les hommes, mais qu'il faut toujours dire la vérité nue aux enfants, je supprimai La Fontaine . . . . Je veux aussi l'habituer de bonne heure à nourrir sa tête d'idées et non de mots: c'est pourquoi je ne lui fais rien apprendre par cœur" (581–82; V, 3). [And convinced that fables are meant for adults but that one must always tell the naked truth to children, I suppressed La Fontaine . . . . I also want to get him into the habit of feeding his mind with ideas and not with words: this is why I never have him learn anything by heart.][28] In *Mistriss Henley*, the same topic is the pretext for a dispute between Mrs. Henley and her husband. As a good Rousseauian father (although he does not strictly go by the book on Rousseau's principles regarding geography and history), Mr. Henley condemns the teaching of the fable "Le Chêne et le Roseau": " 'Elle récite à merveille,' dit M. Henley; 'mais comprend-elle ce qu'elle dit? Il vaudrait mieux peut-être mettre dans sa tête des vérités avant d'y mettre des fictions: l'histoire, la géographie . . . ' " (105). ['She recites beautifully,' said Mr. Henley, 'but does she understand what she is saying? Maybe it would be better to teach her truths before teaching her fictions: history, geography . . . .'] The short exchange that ensues so baffles Mrs. Henley that she leaves the room in tears. Unlike M. de Wolmar, who considers Julie as a disciple,[29] Mr. Henley does not share his philosophical maxims with his wife and instead utters snap judgments at specific moments. Such patterns govern all their discussions, including those on education, in which he preaches modesty and simplicity in realms as disparate as clothing suited for girls and moral principles instilled in children. These animated confrontations are a far cry from the Wolmars' serene tone in their hour-long conversation, during which they appear to be less than literary characters, mere conduits for the philosophy of their author. In contrast, by weaving the topic of education into the plot of the novel, Charrière not only gives an account of how a couple comes to grip with new concerns, but also denounces the possible shortcomings of the models presented by Rousseau in his didactic novel.

As spokesmen of reason and philosophy, both Wolmar and Mr. Henley show interest in the pregnancy of their wives. Talking about her first pregnancy, Julie valorizes the *philosophe* in her husband: "Durant ma première grossesse, effrayée de tous mes devoirs et des soins que j'aurais bientôt à remplir, j'en parlais souvent à M. de Wolmar avec inquiétude. Quel meilleur guide pouvais-je prendre en cela qu'un observateur éclairé qui joignait à l'intérêt d'un père le sang-froid d'un *philosophe*?" (561; V, 3). [During my first pregnancy, in fear of all the duties I would have to fulfill and of all the care I would have to give, I often imparted my worries to M. de Wolmar. What better guide could I take for this matter than an enlightened observer who reconciled the concern of a father with the controlled attitude of a *philosophe*?] As a disciple of her husband, Julie harmonizes both roles (husband and *philosophe*) and attributes to the *philosophe* the ability to know what is best for women. Pregnancy, as a particular moment in the life of a woman, is not discussed, but rather what follows it. At stake is the larger issue of the rearing of men, and not the specific preoccupations and needs of the expectant mother. Her concerns — maternal "duties" and "care" for the infant — reflect those of male *philosophes* and their thoughts on the role to be played by women in the educational process. Mrs. Henley has a very different position on the question, as illustrated by the discussion on breast-feeding.

During her pregnancy, ridden by anxieties about nursing, Mrs. Henley focuses on female physicality, and especially on the physicality of motherhood, to address sexuality and reproduction from the woman's point of view. She debates within herself whether or not to breast-feed her child and (rationally) considers the pros and cons: against it, the burden and fatigue involved and the damage to a woman's figure, and in its favor, the pleasure of bonding with the child and above all, her sense of duty joined to the "humiliation d'être regardée comme incapable et indigne de remplir ce devoir" (119) [humiliation of being considered unable and unworthy to fulfill this duty]. She feels that her body escapes her control through the moral pressure placed on mothers for the well-being of their children. Her attempt to hold a dialogue with her husband leads to a sermon, which once more reinforces her fears and hurts her more than it comforts her:

> A son avis, rien au monde ne pouvait dispenser une mère du premier et du plus sacré de ses devoirs, que le danger de nuire à son enfant par un vice de tempérament ou des défauts de caractère, et il me dit que son intention était de consulter le docteur M. son ami, pour savoir si mon extrême vivacité et mes fréquentes impatiences devaient faire préférer une étrangère. De moi, de ma santé, de mon plaisir, pas un mot. (120) [According to him nothing in the world could excuse a mother from the first and most sacred of her duties, except the danger of harm to her child through a defect in her temperament or in her personality, and he told me that his intention was to take the advice of his friend, doctor M., in order to know whether my extreme liveliness and my frequent impatience would justify choosing a wet-nurse. Not a single word about me, about my health, about my pleasure.]

As physiocrats and *philosophes* warned against a decline in the population, a new valorization of children's lives (also preached by doctors[30]) engendered in large part the doctrine of motherhood that prevailed in the second half of the eighteenth century. Rousseau made it readily available to those reading literature, particularly in passages of *Emile*.[31] Mrs. Henley fully measures the consequences of the double-edged argument borrowed from Rousseau, who valorized motherhood at the expense of the woman's other needs (emotional, physical, etc.). It is precisely because her role was seen as so crucial that a woman was considered unable to fulfill it alone and had to be placed under a competent authority.[32] Mrs.

Henley's new responsibility as the mother of a priceless child, so well delineated by her husband, is accompanied by a loss of self-esteem. In correlating Mr. Henley with a *philosophe* who seeks the advice of his ally, the doctor, Charrière expresses serious doubts regarding the benefits for women of these recently introduced educational principles that deprived them of control over their own bodies. Such discussions, in presenting the Rousseauian model as a possible source of anxiety for women and of tension in a family, make the harmony of Clarens suspect and unveil its dark side. Ultimately, what threatens the Henleys' relationship is the Rousseauian philosophy.

Through its terrifying perfection, Hollow Park appears as a territory of strangeness that underscores Mrs. Henley's alienation: "Je ne vous parlerai pas non plus de tout ce que je fais pour me rendre la campagne intéressante. Ce séjour est comme son maître, tout y est trop bien; il n'y a rien à changer, rien qui demande mon activité ni mes soins" (118). [I will not talk to you any more about everything I did to make the country interesting for me. This dwelling is like its master, everything is too nice; there is nothing to change, nothing requiring my activity or my care.] As a woman from the city, she is a stranger in a rural environment which she does not understand and where she feels out of place. Any attempt on her part to contribute to her new environment leads to unfortunate events. Even her chambermaid disturbs the status quo by attracting the attention of a young farmer and breaking up his marriage to the daughter of Hollow Park's housekeeper. The moving about of old furniture and the removal of the portrait of the first Mrs. Henley from her room bear witness to her effort not to be a stranger any more in what should be her house: "Je ne dois pas être une étrangère jusque dans ma chambre" (106). [I must not be a stranger in my own room.] She fails in this endeavor, and in her last letter, concedes that her estrangement from her husband has reached its apex. After another excruciating conversation during which he announces his refusal of a prestigious position at court and in the parliament, Mrs. Henley admits to being torn between "l'estime que m'arrachait tant de modération, de raison, de droiture dans mon mari et l'horreur de me voir étrangère à ses sentiments, si fort exclue de ses pensées, si inutile, si isolée" (122) [the esteem forced from me by so much moderation, reason, right-mindedness in my husband and the horror of feeling so estranged from his feelings, so excluded from his thoughts, so useless, so isolated]. The destructive power of their marriage leads to the dissolution of her self, inscribed in the fainting fit that follows this moment of unbearable internal tension.

Her growing awareness of being a stranger is paralleled by her inability to secure a stable position in the privacy of her home. Her correspondence opens with a fear of being identified by her husband with *Le mari sentimental*'s selfish Mme Bompré, a sign that her self-image rests on very unstable grounds. Subsequently, she becomes haunted by images of other women with whom she compares herself, only to reinforce her sense of failure and displacement. In the privacy of her home, she replaces Mr. Henley's first wife, whose portrait hangs in her bedroom, and is very conscious of her inadequacy as a substitute mother. In her social circle, she feels an absolute misfit in the presence of Lady Bridgewater, magnificent through her elegance and simplicity, and of Miss Clairville, a young and modest country woman to whom her husband pays much attention. Their seemingly superior company subjects her to a vertigo of comparison which casts her into a well of self-loathing. The ball scene, during which Mr. Henley criticizes the dress her aunt sent from London, attests to her identity crisis: "Je me déplaisais, j'étais mal à mon aise" (115). [I disliked myself, I felt uneasy.]

Under these circumstances, Mrs. Henley's correspondence appears as the only means to break her solitude and her silence while scrutinizing the causes of her alienation. The confession of absolute loneliness, "Je suis seule, personne ne sent avec moi" (107) [I am alone, nobody feels with me], echoes Claire's situation at the end of *Julie*: "Je suis seule au milieu de tout le monde" (744; VI, 13) [I am alone amid everyone], allowing "a glimpse [here] of the unspeakable solitude at the heart of all relationships that every other page of the book has worked to transcend or conceal or deny," to quote Tony Tanner.[33] Through this line written from Claire to Saint-Preux after Julie's death, Tanner explicates a fundamental component of Rousseau's novel: idealization. In Charrière's novel, denial and concealment (through idealized situations and characters) give way to a lucid confrontation with the belief that only family life will bring back order and happiness. The utopia of the perfect husband in the perfect home is replaced by a rigorous observation of the cruel absence of communication in the family. She achieves this through a plot that leaves no room for complacency, and by the same token, is deprived of a major characteristic used (by men) to describe women's fiction: the use of imagination. Repeating a truism about women's talents in fiction writing, Choderlos de Laclos writes in a famous epistolary exchange with Marie-Jeanne Riccoboni:

> Peut-être alors, conviendront-ils [les lecteurs] que c'est aux femmes seules qu'appartiennent cette sensibilité précieuse, cette imagination facile et riante qui embellit tout ce qu'elle touche, et crée les objets tels qu'ils devraient être; mais que les hommes condamnés à un travail plus sévère, ont toujours suffisamment bien fait quand ils ont rendu la nature avec exactitude et fidélité. [Perhaps then, will they agree that

women alone possess this precious sensibility, this easy and cheerful imagination that embellishes everything it touches, and creates objects as they should be; but men, who are condemned to a harsher labor, have always acquitted themselves when they have rendered nature exactly and faithfully.][34]

On the contrary, Charrière refuses to play with imagination or to embellish her story. It is not fortuitous that Clarens crumbles to give way to Hollow Park. Testing Rousseau's ideals in a hypothetical marriage, Charrière cannot protect the woman against the negative impact of doctrinaire self-control. After all, being human involves uncontrollable emotions.[35] In contrast to Rousseau, who idealizes reason and self control in *Julie*'s marriage narrative while creating imaginary models and situations, Charrière condemns reason by paradoxically discarding from her novel's plot anything that would cater to readers' imaginations.

Even Mrs. Henley's attempt to dissect and question her lack of control — her correspondence — comes to an end. Witness to her deep identity crisis, her last letter simultaneously announces her prospect of giving life and repeatedly hints at her possible death. As an apparently open-ended conclusion to the novel, this ultimate message leaves us with the bitter-sweet taste of a puzzling alternative: "Je ne suis qu'une femme, je ne m'ôterai pas la vie, je n'en aurai pas le courage; si je deviens mère, je souhaite de n'en avoir jamais la volonté; mais le chagrin tue aussi. Dans un an, dans deux ans, vous apprendrez, je l'espère que je suis raisonnable et heureuse, ou que je ne suis plus" (122). [I am only a woman and I will not take my life, I will not be courageous enough; if I become a mother, I hope not to want death; but sorrow also kills. In one year, in two years, you will hear, I hope, that I am reasonable and happy, or that I am no more.] If the alternative to death is happiness (based on reason), happiness becomes a simulacre, and acquires a macabre flavor. This is not surprising since the novel emphasizes the inadequacy of reasonable behavior and its inability to secure satisfactory relationships, particularly in the private realm of the family. Mrs. Henley's acceptance of self-control, through the permanent suppression of affects and emotions, will only confirm the erasure of her self, by annihilating her ability to quietly challenge her husband's order. In *Mistriss Henley,* neither disease nor accident nor death-bed scene is necessary to signify the death of a woman. Charrière resorts to no external devices, and relies on the internal dynamics of the Henley family. Susan Lanser is right to state that the alternative "marriage *or* death" gives way to the collusion "marriage as death" (53) and that "*Mistriss Henley*'s apparent 'open' ending is not open at all. Mistriss Henley the character and *Mistriss Henley* the text, court death in order to make utterly clear that marriage in Mr. Henley's patriarchal terms—the terms of the heroine's text—is no life at all" (54).[36] Mrs. Henley's death—symbolic or "real"—prepared in the quiet, confined, and smothering atmosphere of Hollow Park sparks fundamental questions regarding what might be gained by women from the reforms suggested by Rousseau and other men in the preceding decades of the century. Heiress of Enlightenment ideas and ideals, Chaière participates in the ongoing debate about such issues as the extent of freedom in the choice of a spouse, the conditions of a harmonious married life, and the education of children: regarding marriage matters, freedom of choice is no panacea, and in domestic affairs "reason" surely cannot claim victory.

As a polemical novel, *Mistriss Henley* entered a much wider debate than its framing publication (*Le mari sentimental*) suggests. Reading in pairs (through a parallel with Julie's marriage narrative) proves rewarding as it highlights the far-reaching implications of the novel. In taking readers into a field of scrutiny that French novels (by women and men) had neglected until Rousseau and in radicalizing this new option (through the centrality of marriage as a personal relationship between two individuals and the integration of issues dear to Rousseau in this "trivial" plot), Charrière denounces the pretense of happiness implied by Julie's conjugal practices and shows the possible fallacies of Julie's idealized model of private relationships. The price exerted by idealization is tragic: the sacrifice of the woman's self. Remarkably, though confined to the domestic realm, the novel opens outward on a public debate concerning women's private role and status. Far from being limiting, Charrière's choice of such an intimate plot in *Lettres de Mistriss Henley* vindicates the right of the private woman to enact a quiet, but pervasive, revolution.

NOTES

1 Nicolas Sébastien Roch de Chamfort, *Products of Perfected Civilization*, trans. W. S. Merwin (San Francisco: North Point Press, 1984).

2 Isabelle de Charrière, *Lettres de Mistriss Henley*, œuvres complètes 8 (Amsterdam: Van Oorschot; Genève: Slatkine Reprints, 1980). All references in the text come from this edition. Except where otherwise indicated, translations are mine. The term "tradition" refers not so much to the novel's form (epistolary and "monovocal," quite frequent in the period) as to its plot.

3 A history of its publication can be found in the introduction to the above edition. Following a first publication in Geneva in 1784, the Parisian edition appeared without her authorization in 1785 and, in the *Journal de Paris* of

May 1786, she disavowed more particularly the apocryphal "Justification de M. Henley," in which Mr. Henley expresses remorse about the death of his wife subsequent to childbirth. The Parisian edition is anonymous and none of the reviewers seems very much concerned with the identity of the author(s). The *Année littéraire* does not raise the question. In the *Mercure de France*, the novelists are differentiated, since the reviewer refers to the author of *Le mari sentimental* as the author of *Camille, ou Lettres de deux filles de ce siècle* (without mentioning any name) and attributes *Lettres de Mistriss Henley* to Mme de C. . . . de Z. Even recently, the confusion about authorship has led Béatrice Didier to attribute both novels to Isabelle de Charrière in *L'écriture-femme* (Paris: P. U. F., 1981).

4 *Mercure de France*, no. 16 (22 avril 1786), 186 (republished by Slatkine Reprints, 1974).

5 *Année littéraire* 8, lettre VII (1785): 270.

6 The polemical aspect of the relationship between the two novels recalls legal briefs called "factums" written by lawyers in defense of their clients. They were usually presented in pairs to the judge, since each, representing a different party, gave a very different version of the facts. The judicial metaphor is also suggested by Marie-Paule Laden, who sees *Mistriss Henley* as a self trial: " 'Quel aimable et cruel petit livre': Madame de Charrière's *Mistriss Henley*," *French Forum* 11 (September, 1986): 287–99.

7 In 1790, Charrière published an *Eloge de Jean-Jacques Rousseau* that was first written for a literary competition organized by the Académie française; she was involved with her friend DuPeyrou in the polemic surrounding the publication of the second part of *The Confessions*. Throughout her correspondence there are numerous references to Rousseau's works.

8 "Les gens du bel air, les femmes à la mode, les grands, les militaires: voilà les acteurs de tous vos romans. Le raffinement du goût des villes, les maximes de la cour, l'appareil du luxe, la morale épicurienne: voilà les leçons qu'ils prêchent, et les préceptes qu'ils donnent." *Julie ou la Nouvelle Héloïse*, Seconde Préface (Paris: Bibl. de la Pléiade, Gallimard, 1961), 2:19. All references in the text come from this edition. [People of high rank, fashionable women, nobility, military men: here are the protagonists of all your novels. The affectedness of city taste, maxims of the court, luxury, epicurian morals: here are the lessons that they preach and the precepts that they convey.] All translations of *Julie* are mine. The only modern translation is abridged: *Julie or the New Eloise*, trans. and abridged by Judith H. McDowell (University Park: Pennsylvania State University Press, 1968).

9 Nancy K. Miller, "Men's Reading, Women's Writing: Gender and the Rise of the Novel," *Yale French Studies* 75 (1988): 48–49. In this article, Nancy Miller discusses canon formation using Françoise de Graffigny's *Lettres d'une Péruvienne* as a paradigm for the way literary historians have treated women's writing.

10 Among others, Gagnebin and Raymond, in notes of the Pléiade edition of Rousseau's œuvres complètes, Joseph Boone in *Tradition Counter Tradition*

(Chicago: University of Chicago Press, 1987), 43-45, and Jean-Louis Lecercle in *Rousseau et l'art du roman* (Paris: Armand Colin, 1969), chapter 3.

11 "Il n'a pas pu éviter de confier à ses personnages les thèmes qui l'obsédaient, à tel point que ce livre a pu être qualifié de synthèse de sa pensée." *Rousseau et l'art du roman*, 73, with a reference to M. B. Ellis, *Julie or La Nouvelle Héloïse: A Synthesis of Rousseau's Thought* (Toronto: University of Toronto Press, 1949). For reactions of Rousseau's contemporaries to *Julie*, see Lecercle, 72.

12 "Quant à l'autre roman [*Mistriss Henley*], insignifiant comme peinture de mœurs et comme intrigue, il reflète d'une façon intéressante l'état moral de l'auteur à cette époque de sa vie. *Mistriss Henley ou la femme sentimentale* n'est guère autre chose que la plainte de son âme endolorie. On ne peut comprendre *Mistriss Henley* que si l'on a lu le *Mari sentimental* de Samuel de Constant, dont elle est en quelque sorte la contre-partie." *Madame de Charrière et ses amis*, abridged edition (Paris: Attinger, 1927), 149 (two-volume original 1905). Other perspectives have been offered more recently in doctoral dissertations by Teresa Lluch Myintoo (Berkeley, 1980), Christabel Braunrot (Yale, 1973), and Sigyn Minier-Birk (Connecticut, 1977), and most recently by Susan S. Lanser in "Courting Death: *Roman*, *romantisme*, and *Mistress Henley*'s Narrative Practices," *Eighteenth Century Life* 13, n.s. 1 (February 1989). Lanser's article, which reads *Mistriss Henley* in relation to Charrière's *Caliste ou lettres écrites de Lausanne*, provides an excellent reading of both novels.

13 Laden points out that "Charrière's fiction falls chronologically between two important bodies of correspondence—with Constant d'Hermenches, which ends in 1775, and subsequently with his nephew Benjamin Constant, whom she met during a trip in Paris in 1786—it is as if her fictional output relieved her need to confide in her friends" (290).

14 The most thorough treatment of this question can be found in Georges May's *Le dilemme du roman au dix-huitième siècle* (Paris: P. U. F., 1963).

15 This aspect of Charrière's prose-fiction has been widely recognized, as is clear from the titles of articles such as: Suzanne Muhlemann, "Madame de Charrière ou un regard lucide," *Documentatieblad* 27-29 (June 1975): 141-57, or S. Dresden, "Madame de Charrière et le goût du témoin," *Neophilologus* 45 (October 1961): 261-78.

16 Jean-Louis Flandrin, *Familles. Parenté, maison, sexualité dans l'ancienne société* (1976; reprint, Paris: Seuil, 1984); James Traer, *Marriage and the Family in Eighteenth-Century France* (Ithaca: Cornell University Press, 1980).

17 In spite of slight divergences, the freedom of choice of a partner remains one of the major claims of male Enlightenment thinkers regarding marriage.

18 Numerous variations on themes such as the absolute and abusive authority of parents opposed to their daughter's marriage with the man of her choice, as well as the arranged and forced marriage with a man of their choice and consequential illicit love, are discussed in Pierre Fauchery's monumental thesis, *La destinée féminine dans le roman européen du dix-huitième siècle*.

1713-1807. Essai de gynécomythie romanesque (Paris: Armand Colin, 1972), 132-38.

19 Marivaux's *Vie de Marianne* constitutes an extreme example, since the narrative is interrupted as soon as a suitor proposes marriage to Marianne.

20 She compares the traveling lord with Rousseau's Lord John from *Emile*, Book V (Pléiade, 4:853-54; Bloom translation, 470-71). This explicit reference in the early pages of the novel substantiates Charrière's unnoticed dialogue with the *philosophe*.

21 The fact that the novel is set in England may not be fortuitous, since continental observers contended that the English enjoyed more freedom in marriage matters. Lawrence Stone points out that "foreign visitors in the mid- and late eighteenth century were unanimous in their conviction that the English enjoyed a greater freedom of choice of a marriage partner and greater companionship in marriage than on the Continent." *The Family, Sex, and Marriage in England 1500-1800*, abridged ed. (New York: Harper and Row, 1979), 214.

22 "Le mariage de convenance, en revanche, assujettit la femme puisqu'il transforme le contrat entre familles, de type patriarcal, en un lien conjugal interindividuel, et dénué de toute dimension socio-politique. En privatisant ce lien, on rejette la femme hors de la vie publique et on la condamne exclusivement à la vie domestique"—Elisabeth de Fontenay, "Pour Emile et par Emile, Sophie ou l'invention du ménage," *Les temps modernes* 358 (1976): 1792. Erica Harth, in "The Virtue of Love: Lord Hardwicke's Marriage Act," similarly questions the progressive status of love-based marriage and concludes that it entails dependency for the woman. *Cultural Critique* 9 (Spring 1988): 3123-54.

23 In *Lettres de Madame de Sancerre*, despite many comments on unsuccessful unions, Marie-Jeanne Riccoboni summarizes the happy ending of her novel in one sentence: "Malgré la différence de leurs caractères, ces deux aimables femmes rendirent leurs maris également heureux"—*Œuvres complètes* (Paris: 1786), 6:338. [In spite of their different personalities, these two lovable women made their husbands equally happy.]

24 See Fauchery, 378-396.

25 In the section "Le mariage dix-huitième siècle" (368-69), Fauchery presents adultery as a French specialty in fiction. Madame de Clèves in Lafayette's *La princesse de Clèves*, the Marquise in Crébillon fils' *Lettres de la marquise de M*****, the Presidente de Tourvel in *Liaisons dangereuses* all provide vivid examples of attempts to resist adultery.

26 Put differently by Jean Starobinski: "*La Nouvelle Héloïse* is an 'ideological' novel. Happily for the work, however, the quest for a moral synthesis does not prevent constant slippage into passional ambivalence. It is highly significant that the success of Wolmar, the novel's rational character, is threatened by psychological ambiguities that Rousseau constantly finds in himself and that are represented in the novel by Saint-Preux and Julie. Thus the enticement of failure counterbalances the aspiration to happiness, and desire for

punishment coexists with the will to justification"—*Jean-Jacques Rousseau. Transparency and Obstruction*, trans. Arthur Goldhammer (Chicago and London: University of Chicago Press, 1988), 115.

27 From the outset, we know that Mr. Henley is looking for a mother for his five-year-old daughter: "Il me parla de sa fille et du désir qu'il avait de lui donner, non une gouvernante, non une belle-mère, mais une mère" (103). [He told me about his daughter and about his desire to give her not a governess, not a stepmother, but a mother.]

28 This issue is treated extensively in *Emile*, Book II (Pléiade, 4: 351–57; Bloom's translation, 112–16).

29 In the letter on education, Julie insists that "je ne fais que suivre de point en point le système de M. de Wolmar; et plus j'avance, plus j'éprouve combien il est excellent et juste, et combien il s'accorde avec le mien" (437; V, 3). [I only follow scrupulously M. de Wolmar's system; and the further I go, the more I feel how excellent and just it is, and how much it matches my own system.]

30 Tissot in *Avis au peuple sur la santé* (1761), Raulin in *De la conservation des enfants* (1767), and Buchan in *Médecine domestique* (1775) combined medical and hygienic advice with educational principles. Much information can be found in the chapter "The Preservation of Children" in Jacques Donzelot's *The Policing of Families* (New York: Pantheon Books, 1979).

31 In the first book of *Emile*, Rousseau contributes to the age-old debate about the advantages and drawbacks of maternal breast-feeding. He defends the old idea that milk can transmit passions to the child and therefore prefers a healthy nurse to a spoiled mother (4:257; Bloom, 45). But from a moral point of view, however, no hesitation is possible: "Mais que les mères dignent nourrir leurs enfants, les mœurs vont se réformer d'elles-mêmes, les sentiments de la nature se réveiller dans tous les cœurs, l'Etat va se repeupler; ce premier point, ce point seul va tout réunir" (4:258). [But let mothers deign to nurse their children, morals will reform themselves, nature's sentiments will be awakened in every heart, the state will be repeopled. This first point, this point alone will bring everything back together (Bloom, 46).]

32 In *Emile*, the competent authority is not a doctor but the narrator-governor: "Au nouveau-né il faut une nourrice. Si la mère consent à remplir son devoir, à la bonne heure; on lui donnera ses directions par écrit: car cet avantage a son contrepoids et tient le gouverneur un peu plus éloigné de son élève (4:272). [For the newly born a nurse is required. If the mother consents to perform her duty, very well. She will be given written instructions, for this advantage has its counterpoise and keeps the governor at something more of a distance from his pupil (Bloom, 56).]

33 *Adultery in the Novel. Contract and Transgression* (Baltimore: The Johns Hopkins University Press, 1979), 178.

34 "Correspondance entre Mme Riccoboni et M. de Laclos," *Œuvres complètes* (Paris: Bibl. de la Pléiade, Gallimard, 1951), 759. I use Nancy Miller's translation of this passage (50).

35 In *Emile*, Rousseau's approval of the rational husband is spelled out in the

governor's stand on virtue through self-control: "Qu'est-ce donc que l'homme vertueux? C'est celui qui sait vaincre ses affections. Car alors il suit sa raison, sa conscience, il fait son devoir, il se tient dans l'ordre et rien ne l'en peut écarter . . . . Maintenant sois libre en effet; apprends à devenir ton propre maître; commande à ton cœur, ô Emile, et tu seras vertueux" (4:818). [Who then is the virtuous man? It is he who knows how to conquer his affections; for then he follows his reason and his conscience; he does his duty; he keeps himself in order, and nothing can make him deviate from it. . . . Now be really free. Learn to become your own master. Command your heart, Emile, and you will be virtuous (Bloom, 445).]

36 In the alternative death/marriage one can recognize the categories "dysphoric"/"euphoric" used by Nancy Miller in *The Heroine's Text* to characterize female destinies in eighteenth-century male fiction. Charrière's "unfinished" novels were criticized by Germaine de Stael in a letter to Charriére dated "27 août 1793" (*OEuvres complètes* 4:162-63). The "openness" of her novels and tales has been reassessed by feminist critics who have challenged the idea that open-ended narratives fail. See Susan K. Jackson, "The Novels of Isabelle de Charrière, or, a Woman's Work is Never Done," *Studies in Eighteenth-Century Culture* 14 (1985): 299-306, and Elizabeth MacArthur, "Devious Narratives: Refusal of Closure in Two Eighteenth-Century Epistolary Novels," *Eighteenth Century Studies* 21 (1987): 1-20.

The Origins and Significance of Gossip about Princess Augusta and Lord Bute, 1755-1756

JOHN L. BULLION

Where two or three gather in faith, St. Paul informed us, there is the church. When men in business meet, warned Adam Smith, a conspiracy in restraint of trade is a distinct possibility. And when politicians conversed or corresponded in eighteenth-century Britain, they frequently gossiped.[1] Their observations on a speech in Parliament, of a smile or a frown from royalty at a drawing room or from a minister at a levee, of business and pleasure at court, of meetings between people who should (or should not) have been together, were the grist of a gossip that was endlessly fascinating to them. Moreover, their interpretations of what these observations meant for the present and future seemed enormously significant at the time. Thus gossip fills their papers.

The phenomenon of gossip has proved to be equally fascinating to scholars in a number of diverse disciplines.[2] In eighteenth-century studies, Patricia Meyer Spacks, in particular, has drawn upon these findings and her own wide-ranging and sensitive knowledge of the literature of the period to produce a remarkable and suggestive study.[3] Historians of eighteenth-century British politics, however, are exceptions to this rule. By and large, they have not yet either explored the role of gossip or investigated particular episodes in which it played a major part.[4] Political gossip is a potentially promising area of inquiry for a number of reasons. The gossip of politicians can yield interesting insights into the behavior of their fellows at court and in Parliament. It can reveal the personalities and characters of the gossips themselves. Finally, the mere fact that some people were gossiped about in certain ways at specific moments could change the historical events of their time.

In this essay, I will discuss one of the most important of those moments. I will examine the origins of rumors about the relationship between the earl of Bute and Augusta, Dowager Princess of Wales. Then I will call attention to the effect that the rapidly spreading conviction that they were lovers had on British politics during the 1750s and 1760s.

Both of these subjects have been hitherto overlooked by historians. I think there are two explanations for this. First, scholars have assumed that the rumors about Augusta and Bute had no real historical significance during the 1750s. According to the prevailing wisdom, if this talk about an affair had any importance at all, it did so because it contributed to Bute's unpopularity during the early years of George III's reign. Studying the gossip during the 1750s in much detail thus would divert one's attention from more central issues. Second, historians have without exception dismissed the rumors as almost certainly false. To the extent that they have examined them at all, they have busied themselves in amassing circumstantial evidence that—to their minds at least—substantiates that assumption.[5] This preconception about the significance of the gossip before George II's death, and the focus on "proving" that Augusta and Bute were not lovers, have caused historians to neglect other areas of inquiry. Even a matter as basic to historical research as determining the chronology of an event has remained unexplored. *When* did the rumors about the princess and her friend begin? No one has as yet pinpointed that time. It is no wonder that, having failed to inquire about such an obvious point, historians have not understood one of the most important consequences of those rumors. As we shall see, establishing that they began during the late summer and early fall of 1755 raises interesting questions about their origins. Even more important, it yields a crucial clue to their significance for the intense and momentous friendship between Bute and the future George III.

Historians have also failed to recognize the strengths and weaknesses of the sources of the gossip about Augusta and Bute, and to use that knowledge to inform an analysis of both the rumors and their relationship. Spacks's shrewd comments (65, 101–13, 153, 181–82) about what made the eighteenth century "a great age of gossip"—the minute attention to detail and the penchant for interpreting character on the basis of those observed details of behavior—have not informed their analyses. As a result, scholars have not fully credited how keenly and carefully observant eighteenth-century politicians were of the words and actions of those around them. Two examples will illustrate this trait and its significance.

The editors of the political journal of George Bubb Dodington note that his words are the records of "the day-to-day work of a man whose object and political training it was to be accurate about the affairs that interested him."[6] What was true of Dodington was true of others as well. Men who hoped to establish their careers at Westminster, Whitehall, and particularly the king's court at St. James or the princess's at Leicester House soon learned that it was crucial to observe the behavior of their superiors carefully and to describe it accurately. The accounts left by many politicians are often striking in the density and specificity of physical and conversational detail their descriptions provide.

An example is Princess Augusta's account, as recorded by her friend Dodington, of the flirtation of her sister-in-law, Princess Amelia, with the earl of Chesterfield. Augusta began by criticizing Amelia's gambling for high stakes in public at Bath. When Dodington asked with whom, she seized the chance to tell him "It was prodigious the work she made with Lord Chesterfield." "When he was in Court," she recalled, Amelia "would hardly speak to him; at least as little as was possible to a man of his rank." But now, "she sent to enquire of his coming before he arriv'd; when he came sent her compliments and that she expected he should be of all her parties at play; that he should sit by her always in the public rooms, that he might be sure of a warm place, etc."[7] Notice how closely Augusta and her informants had observed Amelia at St. James and in Bath, how carefully they listened to her, and how quickly they noticed differences in her behavior vis-a-vis the earl. Whether or not one believes, as Augusta did, that this flirtation was improper and might well indicate the potential, if not the actuality, of an affair, the description of Amelia at play with games of chance and Chesterfield is vivid and convincing.

Another example is Horace Walpole's account of a wit telling a joke about Bute and the princess. "George Selwyn," wrote Walpole, "hearing some people at Arthur's t'other night lamenting the distracted state of this country joined in the discourse with the whites of his eyes and his prim mouth, and fetching a sigh, said, 'Yes, to be sure it is terrible! There is the Duke of Newcastle's faction, and there is [Henry] Fox's faction, and there is Leicester House! Between two factions and one fuction, we are torn to pieces!"[8] The joke itself is feeble; what sticks in the mind is Walpole's sketch from life of Selwyn's mannerisms, timing, and delivery. As was the case with Dodington's account of Augusta's censure of Amelia, the description of the event in question is persuasive, whatever one thinks about the principal message of the passage. An eye for the telling detail, and the capacity to communicate it effectively—these abilities were shared by the Princess, Dodington, Walpole, and other contemporaries.

An understanding of why they watched so closely and wrote so carefully reveals why historians should respect their descriptions of behavior. Eighteenth-century men and women constantly observed and communicated others' acts because they believed that outward behavior provided the only reliable clues to inner human motives. In so doing, they adopted a remarkably legalistic way of assessing intent, and it is not surprising that the most precise statements of their criterion of assessment may be found in opinions from the bench. "We must judge of a man's motives," declared Lord Kenyon, "from his overt acts." Mr. Justice Willis elaborated on this point: "What passes in the mind of man is not scrutable by any human tribunal; it is only to be collected from his acts."[9] Those who traded in political and social gossip used the same standard of judgment. This may be clearly seen in the following discussion by Lord Hervey of the relationship between Frederick, the Prince of Wales, and Lady Archibald Hamilton during the 1730s. "There are always some people," Hervey noted, "who doubt of the most notorious intrigues." So some thought, or pretended to think, that the "commerce between Lady Archibald Hamilton and the Prince was merely platonic." But "stronger symptoms of an *affaire faite* never appeared on any pair than were to be seen between this couple," Harvey claims in rebuttal of such views. And here is the evidence: Frederick often saw her at her house; he often met her at her sister's; he walked with her "day after day for hours together tête-à-tête in a morning in St. James Park; and whenever she was at the drawing-room (which was pretty frequently), his behavior was so remarkable that his nose and her ear were inseparable, whilst, without discontinuing, he would talk to her as if he had rather been relating than conversing from the time he came into the room to the moment he left it, and then seemed to be rather interrupted than to have finished."[10] To Hervey, this was proof positive they were lovers.

Is it, though? The evidence of his senses was enough for Hervey, but historians need not accept his conclusions. In fact, some have doubted that there was any sexual liaison between the prince and Lady Hamilton.[11] We cannot be certain, for the affair, if there was one, was not openly acknowledged by the participants, as was the liaison between George II and the countess of Yarmouth. The best rule of thumb for assessing eighteenth-century gossip is to keep the distinction between observation and interpretation firmly in mind. One should regard descriptions of observed acts by politicians who were practiced at watching the people around them as basically accurate, unless, of course, there is factual information that contradicts their narratives of events, or convincing reasons to believe that biases about the people involved or preconceptions about the audience hearing the story distorted their accounts. One may also, I think, rely on people at court to notice and to describe carefully behavior that was out of the ordinary in political or social interaction. As the preceding examples demonstrate, contemporaries were keenly alert to unusual displays of interest between men and women. Their explanations of what these acts revealed is more problematical, however. They were obviously quicker to see lust in operation and an affair in progress than to view an emotional reaction between a man and a woman as friendship, affection, or some socially acceptable form of love. Historians should not rush to the same judgment in the absence of compelling supporting evidence. In my analysis of the gossip about the princess and Bute, I have tried to keep observation and interpretation separate, and to give the former the credit it deserves while recognizing the limitations of the latter.

I.

During the summer of 1755, reports began to circulate about Augusta's reactions to the crisis in relations with France and her political intentions. Dodington, who paid close attention to the political gossip of London's coffee houses, soon heard them, and shared what he had discovered with the princess in early August. She expressed surprise, protesting that she was not involved in any schemes to oppose the government, and pointing out that certainly "nobody could stand clearer than she; that everyone must know everybody that she saw, and when." Dodington laughed at this, and joked that he "had some thoughts of writing her life and transactions, as I pick them up, and presenting it to her, of which, I was persuaded, that she knew nothing at all." Augusta "seem'd mightily pleas'd with the idea, and after laughing, took serious pains to convince me that she had no fix'd settlement, or connexions, at all."[12] It is unlikely that Dodington would have attempted such a joke if he had heard any rumor about an "intrigue" between the princess and Bute at that time; the possibility for embarrassment and loss of her favor would have been too great. Yet no more than six weeks after his conversation with her, that talk had begun. Within a week after his return from Hanover on 16 September, George II had received from Earl Waldegrave, the governor of the Prince of Wales, "thorough information" about the political plans of Leicester House. And, though Waldegrave discreetly avoided any direct comment on this subject in his *Memoirs*, it seems likely he also informed the king of his conviction that Augusta and Bute were lovers.[13] Certainly by early October, the countess of Yarmouth, Newcastle, and Newcastle's closest friend, the earl of Hardwicke, had heard the story. All of them apparently believed it.[14] They did not remain alone in that belief. The news passed quickly through court, and then on to the wider world of London. Soon the story about an "intrigue" at Leicester House was widely known and commonly believed.

Why did these rumors spread so rapidly? In part, they did because a liaison with the princess helped to explain Bute's role in arranging an alliance between Leicester House and William Pitt in opposition to the government.[15] For example, the countess of Yarmouth discounted hopes that Augusta would remain aloof from opposition politics by reminding Newcastle that the princess " 'is in the hands of those who will not permit that' and then [added] with a smile, 'we both know what we mean, though neither of us will speak' " (Newcastle to Hardwicke, 2:251). Moreover, as Spacks has observed, sex was the most popular subject of gossip at the time, with the possible exception of money (68). Reports of sexual misconduct by Augusta appealed to what Sir Horace Mann singled out as characteristic of "the greatest gossips," "[they] are always . . . fond of the marvelous."[16] That the dowager princess of Wales would take a lover fit Samuel Johnson's definition of "the marvelous" as "wonderful," meaning a "surprise caused by something unusual or unexpected" (*The Dictionary*). Her friends and enemies unanimously regarded her as a prudent woman, one who was discreet and cautious, who weighed alternatives carefully and had the ability to discern and follow the most politic and profitable course of action. By 1752, according to Dodington, she "had establish'd a character for prudence"; in 1755, Waldegrave recalled that she "was reputed by those who knew her imperfectly a Woman of excellent Sense and extraordinary Prudence."[17] Thus the possibility that she would discard caution, reject morality, and risk reputation by yielding to an illicit passion fascinated people in the political and social worlds that orbited around the court. Their fascination with the difference between public reputation and private reality, plus the political import of the "intrigue," sped the rumors on their way.

What were the origins of these rumors? What first aroused the suspicions of observers at Leicester House? The answer must be that during the summer of 1755 Augusta's behavior toward Bute dramatically changed. She had known the earl since the late 1740s, and no scandal had been attached to their relationship, even though gossips later speculated that an affair between them might have begun then.[18] The changes that happened in 1755 have been detailed by Walpole in his *Memoirs of the Reign of King George II*. Drawing upon conversations with his friend Waldegrave, he recalled that "the eagerness of the pages of the backstairs to let her know whenever Lord Bute arrived, a mellowness in her German accent as often as she spoke to him, and that was often and long, and a more than usual swimmingness in her eyes, contributed to dispel the ideas that had been conceived of the rigour of her widowhood."[19] This was clearly conduct well out of the ordinary for the usually discreet, prudent Augusta. Any observant person—and Waldegrave certainly was one—could not have missed it. Bute's responses attracted his notice as well. "The favoured personage," continued Walpole, "naturally ostentatious of his person and of haughty carriage, seemed by no means desirous of concealing his conquest. His bows grew more theatric, his graces contracted some meaning, and the beauty of his leg was constantly displayed in the eyes of the poor captivated Princess."[20]

As these passages indicate, Waldegrave believed that the Princess's obvious enchantment with Bute was the outward manifestation of a powerful sexual attraction to him. He could think of nothing else. The earl had no respect for Bute's intelligence, learning, or political acumen. To the contrary: his contacts with "the favoured personage" at court caused him to dismiss Bute as a pompous lightweight, a man deserving to be called *Bombastus Vigorosus* by more discerning persons. Waldegrave conceded, however, that Bute was a physically striking man. "He was above the middle size, had broad shoulders, great muscular strength, and remarkable fine legs." "Those bodily perfections. . .," Waldegrave later observed with bitter sarcasm, "sometimes may have attracted vulgar widows" (163-64; 229). In 1755, he felt no animus toward Augusta, and certainly did not regard her as a "vulgar widow." Even so, he was certain during that summer that she was susceptible to Bute's physical grace and beauty. Perhaps he recalled, as did Walpole, that "the nice observers of the court thermometer, who often foresee a change of weather before it actually happens, had long thought her Royal Highness was likely to choose younger ministers than [her two advisers,] that formal piece of empty mystery, [James] Cresset; or the matron-like decorum of Sir George Lee." After all, "her eyes had often twinkled intelligibly enough at her countryman Prince Lobkowitz" (*Memoirs*, 2:151). Whether or not Waldegrave heard and credited the same gossip, he clearly believed that her friend's appearance and mannerisms had transfixed the Princess. To him, it was obvious that she was either helpless, or did not try, to conceal her passionate fascination.

Waldegrave was equally sure that the two were actually having an affair. The basis for his confidence was his knowledge that they had created ample opportunities for themselves to consummate and continue a sexual relationship. The earl evidently heard on the authority of "three old Ladys, one Gentleman Usher, and two Pages of the Back Stairs" that Augusta and Bute were together alone for lengthy periods of time, either walking in the gardens at Kew and Carlton House, or meeting in her private apartments at Leicester House.[21] Walpole translated walking into a metaphor for sexual relations, his own contribution to the gossip about the princess and her friend. "As soon as [Prince Frederick] was dead," he archly noted, the Princess and Bute "walked more and more in honour of his memory" (*Memoirs* 2:251). His conviction that these private meetings were more devoted to lovemaking than to more innocent activities was shared by Waldegrave and many others. Even when they learned—perhaps from the same servants who informed them about the meetings between the princess and Bute—that he at least occasionally saw the prince, they did not change their minds. These encounters, they were sure, "were less addressed to the Prince of Wales than to his mother" (Walpole *Memoirs*, 2:251). Indeed, to Waldegrave, what he saw and heard admitted of only one explanation: the two were lovers who through foolishness and arrogance had thrown caution to the winds. He carefully noted the details that convinced him in his interviews with the king and the ministers, and later in conversations with friends such as Walpole. Those details, plus Waldegrave's reputation for being both sagacious about politics and worldly-wise about society, persuaded them as well about the reality of an intrigue between Augusta and Bute.[22]

II.

Historians have been far less impressed by Waldegrave's testimony. They have not been persuaded by his certainty that the Princess and Bute were lovers, and they have been unconcerned about his description of their behavior. Yet Waldegrave's observations are worthy of attention and explanation. They were the products of an experienced observer and judge of both political and social behavior, whose description and interpretation of the events at Leicester House during the summer of 1755 were uncolored by malice. To be sure, he never liked Bute, and a year later, after he learned in June 1756 that he would not be Groom of the Stole for the Prince of Wales, that dislike widened to include Augusta and deepened into hatred for them both. But until that disappointment, Waldegrave recalled later, "the Princess and her Son seem'd fully satisfied with my Zeal, diligence, and faithful Services; and I was treated with so much Civility, that sometimes I thought myself almost a Favorite" (177). As Clark points out in his introduction to Waldegrave's memoirs (78), the earl had reason to believe that he and young George were on good terms even as late as June 1756. Waldegrave, enjoying as he did a pleasant relationship with Augusta, and heartened by the prospect of preferment and power in the next reign, had no reason to exaggerate or distort the evidence of his eyes and ears. He did, however, have a duty to the sovereign he respected, George II, to report fully and precisely on events at Leicester House. An intimate connection—be it political or personal—forged between Augusta and anyone could have a significant impact on relations between her court and the king's, and on the balance of power between the forces of government and opposition in Parliament. Waldegrave was therefore obliged to bring his observations of the conduct of the princess and Bute, and the conclusions he drew from them, to the king's attention. That duty he fulfilled as loyally and conscientiously as he did other responsibilities during his tenure as governor to the Prince of Wales.[23]

But one need not merely rely on Waldegrave's reputed powers of observation and his fidelity to George II to substantiate the accuracy of his description of changes in Augusta's behavior toward Bute and the intensity of her attachment to him. A comparison of reactions at court to her relationship with Dodington with her responses to Bute in 1755 reveals that Waldegrave had indeed seen an unmistakable change in her usual conduct and attitudes toward her friends. The princess frequently spent time alone with Dodington. His discussions of his meetings with her during 1752-1755 are peppered with notations that they walked together for two or three hours in the garden, that they met in private, and that he was shown immediately by her pages to her chambers when he saw only her, and, on occasion, her children. When together, they shared "much talk upon all matter of private subjects, serious and ludicrous."[24] In particular, Augusta was remarkably candid in discussing her concerns about her son's development and education with Dodington. The two also had a number of guarded but reasonably frank exchanges about political events and prospects. She liked and trusted Dodington. This was no secret at court. So, why were there no rumors about a possible sexual involvement, given their private meetings, their obvious rapport, and Dodington's reputation as a veteran of affairs of the heart?[25]

Part of the answer must be his appearance. Unlike Bute, Dodington was "short, dumpy . . . comically fat and ugly, with an absurd uptilted nose, large mouth, protruding eyes, and pudgy hands." He affected the manners and dress of his youth, a style which had been out of fashion for thirty years.[26] If Augusta had a fondness, as observers claimed, for younger, graceful, handsome men, she would have found nothing in this friend to tickle her fancy. But more to the point, Augusta never displayed in public any trace of an intense emotional attachment or commitment to Dodington. (Nor did she show any such commitment in private. There is not the least hint of any sexual attraction or deeply affectionate connection between the two in his notes on their meetings.) Observers of them in public concluded—correctly—that theirs was a friendship that both found frequently useful, occasionally amusing, and nothing more. That speculation sprang up that her attachment to Bute was of a very different nature gives us ample reason to believe that Waldegrave in fact did see something unprecedented in Augusta's behavior during the summer of 1755. Private meetings that no one thought worthy of remark when she saw Dodington were regarded as occasions for adultery in the case of Bute. The princess's obvious excitement and eagerness when she greeted the earl unquestionably revealed feelings for him that were far stronger than for her other friend, feelings too powerful to conceal from alert, knowing eyes.

Conceding that Waldegrave first recognized, then accurately described Augusta's powerful attachment to Bute does not mean, however, that we are compelled to agree with his interpretations of what he saw. Were the two lovers? Conclusive evidence of a sexual affair was lacking at the time, and none has been unearthed since. Indeed, to the extent that Waldegrave's confidence was based on his conviction that they had ample opportunities for lovemaking during the long periods of time they spent together alone, it rested on an uncertain foundation. What seemed to him to be suggestive and suspicious behavior with Bute may with equal plausibility be explained as another example of the way Augusta usually behaved with trusted political and personal friends. Besides, asking whether they were lovers is, in important ways, following the scent of a red herring. It was so for contemporaries, as we shall see; it has been for historians for too long. That question has distracted us from asking what caused the princess's conduct toward Bute to change so suddenly and dramatically during the summer of 1755. Waldegrave and Walpole believed that sexual desire was the principal, if not the sole, explanation. We need not accept this, even though the earl was practiced at assessing attractions between men and women. He overlooked a persuasive alternative explanation for the princess's obvious affection for Bute. And the fact that he failed to consider this possibility had a significant impact on the history of his time.

III.

Augusta herself once said that "nobody but God could judge of the heart" (Dodington, 301), and, insofar as her relationship with Bute was concerned, only she and the Almighty ever completely knew for sure about its nature. Still, there was one passion in Augusta's life that we can be sure of, for she freely confessed to it. "She could," the princess told Dodington, "have nothing so much at heart as to see [George] do well [as king], and make the nation happy." She knew, however, that he was not doing well preparing himself for the monarchy. She was pleased that he was "a very honest boy," but she also wished when he was fourteen that "he were a little more forward, and less childish, at his age" (Dodington, 178, 180). Augusta hoped that as George learned more from his tutors, he would mature. Unfortunately, in May 1755, when he was nearly seventeen, she lamented to Dodington that "his education had given her much pain." "His book-learning," she continued, "she was no judge of, [but] suppos'd it small, or useless." She had "hop'd he might have been instructed in the general course of things," and Waldegrave had disappointed her even in this modest expectation (Dodington, 318).

Still, the passage of time had convinced the princess that the fault was not wholly the pupil's. In 1752, she had despairingly said to Dodington that he knew George "as well as she did" (180). By 1755, she felt she knew her son's qualities. "He was not," according to her, "a wild, dissipated boy, but good natur'd, and cheerful, but with a serious cast, in the whole." Waldegrave and his tutors, she scornfully observed to Dodington, "knew him no more than if they had never seen him: . . . he was not quick, but with those he was acquainted with, applicable and intelligent." Her friend soon had proof of this. Perhaps inspired by Augusta's remarks, Dodington "afterwards [had] much talk with the Prince about funding, etc., and other serious things, [which he] seem'd to hear with attention and satisfaction" (318).

Dodington's experience with George indicated, in a small way, how sensible was a desire the princess had expressed to him almost a year earlier. Then she had "wish'd he had acquaintance older than himself" to instruct him. At that time, she could not intervene by placing appropriate men around the prince to guide him. She "durst not recommend," she recognized, "for fear of offence: while he had governors etc., [and] was under immediate inspection, all that they did not direct, would be imputed to her" (Dodington, 217). Such charges, she also knew, could be dangerous. In 1752, Augusta had discerned that some political opponents were trying to intervene in the prince's education and "by taking him from the people now about him . . . by degrees, consequently, from her." Part of their plot, she believed, was "to get the Prince to their side, and then, by their behaviour, to throw her off from her temper and so make their complaint to the King stronger and make her disoblige him, in defending the accus'd." They were certain, she was further convinced, that "if they could force her into any indiscreet warmth" when she supported George's present instructors, they would make "so plausible a story to the King as might have compass'd their ends" by convincing him that he should move his grandson to Kensington Palace (192-93). She had evaded this effort to trick her into appearing to interfere with the prince's education, and she had every intention of resisting the temptation to intervene in reality. At present, she could do nothing. She consoled herself, however, with the belief that "in a year or two, [the prince] must be thought to have a will of his own, and then he would, she hop'd, act accordingly" (271).

After one of those two years passed, Augusta decided to act. During the summer of 1755, she asked Bute to begin tutoring her son in secret.[27] Two reasons probably determined her choice. She regarded the earl as the only one of Prince Frederick's former associates who had always been loyal to her.[28] Such loyalty was essential in this situation; if Waldegrave, the ministers, or George II got wind of the princess's intervention, they certainly would try to remove Bute. That removal would take the form of separating George from his mother and placing him within the king's household. As she told Dodington in May 1755, "there were a hundred good reasons that tied her hands from interfering with the king," emphasizing "those about her children, [which] were obvious enough." "If she was to stir," she continued, "it would make things worse" (299). The events of 1752 had stayed fresh in her memory. Who educated the next king, and what they taught him, could quickly become politically controversial issues. The raising of such questions that year had eventuated in the removal of Lord Harcourt and the bishop of Norwich from their posts as Governor and Preceptor of the prince, and threatened the careers of even such eminent men as William Murray, a famous attorney and important politician, and Andrew Stone, the duke of Newcastle's secretary. At that time, the princess had grown "quite weary" of hearing "such an outcry at [Harcourt and the bishop's] leaving them, as if they were the most considerable men in the nation."[29] That outcry, she could anticipate, would be even louder and the consequences more dire for her, should news leak out that she was decisively intervening on her own initiative in her son's education. She had to proceed with the utmost secrecy. Therefore she could call upon only the most reliable friend. Moreover, Bute's views on personal and political morality corresponded to hers. Unlike Dodington, who was convinced the prince needed to be more frequently with people his own age and doubted the usefulness of much book learning, Augusta held strong opinions about "the universal profligacy . . . of the young people of distinction" and had a high regard for formal education.[30] Bute shared these convictions. On the grounds of prudence, morality, and pedagogy, he was the obvious, if not the only, choice.

Delighted by Augusta's proposal, Bute eagerly accepted. For obvious reasons: not only did this role appeal to his sense of himself and his duty, but also, if he were successful, he would become the most powerful politician in the realm when George succeeded his grandfather. His private letter of thanks to her after he began instructing the prince is the effusive written equivalent of the noticeably and unusually dramatic — even for the normally theatrical Bute — bows he made to her in public during that summer. "How great the confidence she is pleased to place in him," he wrote, in the third person. "How immense the obligation laid upon him. . . . He feels her favor as he ought, he has a heart that can feel it, it will palliate a thousand other ills, nor shall he easily repine at anything but at those bounded faculties so little suited to the great trust reposed in him. What is however wanting in talents shall be supplied with industry and the great business of his life shall while the Princess pleases point to that one center." This flow of language ultimately roused even Bute's concern that it might seem too grateful. "Let not Her Royal Highness," he hastily added, "think that these are words of course or affected phrases, 'tis the language of his heart."[31] Judging from the vigor with which Bute conducted the education of the prince, the flowery language expressed honest sentiments and truly arose from powerful emotions.

Nor is there any reason to question how pleased Augusta was by the earl's taking up the challenge, and how moved she was when it became clear he was succeeding. Bute evidently preserved only one of the princess's letters to him; it is not surprising that he kept this one. "I cannot express the joy I feel to see he has gained the confidence and friendship of my son. Pursu my worthy friend those instructions you have begun, and imprint your great sentiments in him, thos will make my son and his mother happy. Ld. Bute forbids his best friend to speak what she feels, but he must allow her to be grateful."[32] The gratitude and affection she felt for a friend who was bringing toward reality her ambitions for her son are obvious in this letter. Even though Bute forbade "his best friend to speak what she feels," her feelings compelled her to disobey. They were equally compelling on public occasion. She did not conceal them in the drawing rooms and in front of servants. Always alert for changes in relationships at court, Waldegrave and others heard and saw her indiscreet words and acts. Moreover, these observers were not wrong: Augusta's behavior did betray a passionate attachment to Bute. But they did not intuit what the princess identified as the most important component in that friendship. Waldegrave never perceived that he was seeing the visible expressions of a mutual joy and gratefulness that a very difficult and supremely important task—the preparation of George for the throne—was going very well. That failure had important consequences.

IV.

By now, the significance of the talk about an intrigue involving the princess and Bute that began during the late summer of 1755 should be clear. That confident interpretation of their behavior in public prevented some usually acute observers from realizing the truth about Bute and the Prince of Wales.

So "fond of the marvelous," and thus so certain that the earl and the princess were involved in an affair were observers that no one divined that (at least some of) Bute's trips up the back stairs ended in tutoring sessions with George, and that many long hours when the earl was in the royal gardens and chambers were spent with the heir to the throne, not Augusta. The court knew that Bute was sometimes with the prince, but this was seen as incidental to, and perhaps an excuse for, his being with the princess. During 1755–1756, according to Walpole, it was "whispered that the assiduity of Lord Bute at Leicester House, and his still more frequent attendance in the gardens at Kew and Carlton House, were less addressed to the Prince of Wales than to his mother."[33] In fact, the reverse was true. Had Waldegrave realized this, he would have informed the king, and thereby set in motion a chain of events very different from what did occur. George II had no respect for Bute, and in any case wished to remove his grandson from the princess's court.[34] News about the earl's secret usurpation, with Augusta's approval and assistance, of the role of the prince's governor would have inspired the monarch and his ministers to make serious efforts to take George away from his mother and her friend. But neither Waldegrave nor anyone else discerned what was going on behind closed doors and garden walls. They were stunned to discover when George came of age in June 1756 that he wanted his "dearest friend" to be his Groom of the Stole and ultimately to become "the minister" when he took the throne. Compelling a minor to change palaces and friends would have been politically difficult enough, but it might have been managed. Forcing a young man who would reign when his grandfather died, who would not be dependent on a council of regency, to drop his firmest commitments, soon proved impossible. George II and his ministers had to yield, and Bute became a powerful man, one who would have to be reckoned with in the present and future (Waldegrave, 177–83).

Why did no one suspect that Bute was forging an intimate relationship with the prince? It was partly the result of the contempt Waldegrave and others had for the princess's friend. They simply could not believe that his pompous, stilted words and mannerisms would attract the notoriously withdrawn George. That he would succeed where better men had failed obviously never occurred to them. In their eyes, Bute was a sententious yet insignificant player in the politics of the court. But their misreading of the earl seems minor indeed compared to their underestimation of the princess. Neither Waldegrave, nor George II, nor anyone else at court except Bute, who was necessarily privy to her secret, knew how attached Augusta was to the future king, and how determined she was to fulfill her wish that he be "great and happy for [his] own sake."[35] Thus they did not anticipate the lengths she would go, and the risks she would run, for her son. That she would look for a different tutor for him, find one she judged loyal, intellectually capable, and morally sound, arrange secret meetings between them, and conceal many of the sessions by providing the misleading appearance that the prince's new mentor was meeting her—these suspicions never crossed their minds. Yet that was the plan her concern for her son caused her to conceive and to execute.

Of course, we know now that Augusta was risking not only discovery of her plot, which did not happen, but scandalous whispers about her morality, which did. Did that possibility ever occur to her? Did she decide to put her reputation at jeopardy as well? If she did, it was an extraordinary act of maternal love and courage. As Spacks has emphasized in *Gossip,* eighteenth-century women depended completely on their reputations for sexual virtue, and had no means of effectively refuting any scandals that put their good names in doubt or of retaliating against their persecutors (31–32).[36] There is no sure way of ascertaining whether Augusta was aware of this danger, but the possibility cannot be dismissed entirely. The princess certainly was aware, as she told Dodington, "that everyone must know everybody she saw and when" (316–17). She also knew that those at court watched the behavior of men and women together closely for signs of impropriety. Augusta herself avidly played the game of assessing the potential for lust and adultery on occasion, and seems to have been as quick as anyone else to conclude sexual misconduct was occurring and to gossip about it (e.g., Dodington, 174). From this, she might have guessed that her good name could be jeopardized. Still, her knowledge of and her participation in the realities and rituals of life at court do not prove that she consciously risked her own reputation. Barring the discovery of other evidence, that must remain unknown.

When the prince first heard the rumors, his determination not to be separated from his mother and his mentor was strengthened. "I will ever remember," he vowed, "the insults done to my mother, and never will forgive anyone who shall offer to speak disrespectfully of her." And "in the same solemn manner" he resolved, "I will defend my Friend . . . and will more and more show to the world the great friendship I have for him, and all the malice that can be invented against him shall only bind me the stronger to him."[37] Ironically, George never realized how crucial the blackening of their reputations had been for him and Bute. It provided a necessary protective coloration, and thus permitted the germination and flowering of that intense friendship that so strongly influenced events in Britain, Europe, and the empire during the 1760s.[38]

NOTES

1 I have borrowed this introduction from J. H. Hexter, *Doing History* (Bloomington: Indiana University Press, 1971), 85. In his version, the gossips are historians, not eighteenth-century politicians.
2 For an excellent bibliography of studies of gossip as a social phenomenon, see Edith B. Gelles, "Gossip: An Eighteenth-Century Case," *Journal of Social History* 22 (1989): 679, n. 4.
3 Patricia Meyer Spacks, *Gossip* (New York: Knopf, 1985). For Spacks's comments about studies of gossip by social scientists, see p. 34.
4 As Gelles's bibliographical notes make clear, those eighteenth-century historians who have most frequently studied gossip are social historians. Gelles's own article, for example, deals with the role of gossip in determining an appropriate husband for Abigail Adams Junior, the daughter of John and Abigail Adams. The role of gossip in polities has remained unexamined.
5 For examples of the tendencies described above—all of them in solid studies of the period—see John Brewer, "The Misfortunes of Lord Bute: A Case-Study in Eighteenth-Century Political Argument and Public Opinion," *The Historical Journal* 16 (1973): 3-4, and Brewer's book, *Party Ideology and Popular Politics at the Accession of George III* (Cambridge: Harvard University Press, 1973), 152-53, 294n; Frank O'Gorman, "The Myth of Lord Bute's secret influence," in *Lord Bute: Essays in Re-interpretation*, ed. Karl W. Schweizer (Leicester: Leicester University Press, 1988), 59-60; and John Brooke, *King George III* (London: Constable, 1972), 48-49.
6 The quotation is from the introduction by John Carswell and Lewis Arnold Dralle, eds., *The Political Journal of George Bubb Dodington* (Oxford: Oxford University Press, 1965), xxiv. For examples of the special care

Dodington took in recording conversations and describing facial expressions, see 180, 198, 244, 399.
7 Dodington, 174. As this conversation reveals, Augusta did not mind telling Dodington about her personal reactions to people. She was much more cautious in discussing political events with him. Dodington had been a follower of her late husband Prince Frederick, and kept in close contact with her after his death in 1751. Because of her frankness with him, especially about her sons, and because of his skill as an observer, his *Journal* is the most reliable source for her opinion on personal matters during the early 1750s.
8 *The Yale Edition of Horace Walpole's Correspondence*, 48 vols. (New Haven: Yale, 1937-1983), 9:202. Leicester House was Augusta's official residence in London. Its name was used as a shorthand reference to the faction which supported her interests in policies. As John Cannon observed, Selwyn's humor, "so greatly admired in his lifetime, seems to have depended for its effect upon a mock-serious delivery: in print, it appears laboured." See Cannon's entry on Selwyn in Sir Lewis Namier and John Brooke, eds., *The History of Parliament: The House of Commons, 1754-1790*, 3 vols. (London: Oxford University Press, 1964), 3:421.
9 I owe this point, and the quotations illustrating it, to J. C. D. Clark, *The Dynamics of Change: The crisis of the 1750s and English party systems* (Cambridge: Cambridge University Press, 1982), 19. For a similar comment by Dodington, see 301.
10 Lord Hervey, *Memoirs*, ed. Romney Sedgwick (London: W. Kimber, 1952), 138-39. An "intrigue" in eighteenth-century usage was a clandestine illicit intimacy between a man and a woman.
11 For example, Sir George Young, *Poor Fred: The People's Prince* (Oxford: Oxford University Press, 1937), 79-80, 169.
12 Dodington, 316-17. In fact, Augusta had commissioned Bute to negotiate with William Pitt, a political alliance that she took pains to conceal from Dodington. Dodington believed her on this occasion, but at other times he suspected, rightly, that the princess withheld political intelligence from him. See, for example, 227. It must be emphasized that while Dodington's *Journal* is an invaluable source for Augusta's personal opinions, historians should use it very carefully on matters political.
13 "Memoirs of 1754-1757," in *The Memoirs and Speeches of James, 2nd Earl Waldegrave*, ed. J. C. D. Clark (Cambridge: Cambridge University Press, 1988), 169-71. See also Clark's introduction to this splendid edition, 76-79, for a judicious discussion of Waldegrave's possible role in the spread of rumors about the princess and Bute. Clark argues that the evidence for Waldegrave's role is not conclusive, yet he himself notes (169, n. 110) that "the clear implication" of passages in the *Memoirs* "is that Waldegrave himself told George II everything that happened at Leicester House." As the earl later told the prince of Wales, "I was accountable to his Majesty, and it was my Duty to give Informations as to some particulars, when he required it: or supposing it had been my Intention to deceive the King, even in that case it would have

been absurd to have denied those things, which might be seen at every Drawing room, and were the subject of conversation at every Coffee House" (181). Waldegrave's reference to "every Drawing room" is crucial to an understanding of this passage. In contemporary usage, a "drawing room" referred to the formal levee, a reception held in the morning, by a member of the royal family or a person of rank. The earl was pointing out that he and others had observed unmistakably suggestive behavior between Augusta and Bute at her levees, and that he had discussed those observations with George II.

14 The duke of Newcastle to the earl of Hardwicke, October 4, 1755, and Hardwicke to Newcastle, October 13, 1755, in Philip C. Yorke, *The Life and Correspondence of Philip Yorke, Earl of Hardwicke, Lord High Chancellor of Great Britain*, 3 vols. (Cambridge: Cambridge University Press, 1913), 2: 250-52.

15 Sir John Pringle, the queen's physician after 1761, and Horace Walpole believed that there was another political consideration that helped explain the speed with which the rumor circulated. Both asserted that powerful men at the king's court broadcast the story in an effort to discredit Augusta and to prevent Bute from becoming the preeminent politician in the kingdom during the next reign. The two differed on one significant detail. Sir John was convinced "a party of the great people" had concocted the rumor themselves with those ends in mind. Walpole knew the real source of the story (i.e., Waldegrave), believed in the purity of his motives and the accuracy of his observations, and therefore was absolutely certain that the princess and Bute were lovers. To him, the role of the great men—specifically Hardwicke—was confined to spreading the news in the expectation it would serve them politically. No evidence has been found in the extant papers of prominent politicians during the 1750s that supports either version of events. For Pringle's and Walpole's accounts, see Clark's introduction to Waldegrave, 77-78, with n. 251; see also *The Yale Edition of Horace Walpole's Memoirs of King George II*, ed. John Brooke, 3 vols. (New Haven: Yale University Press, 1985), 2: 160-61.

16 Sir Horace Mann to Walpole, October 25, 1755, *Walpole Correspondence*, 20:505.

17 Dodington, 180; Waldegrave, 159. Even Horace Walpole, who held no brief for Augusta, praised "the quiet inoffensive good sense of the Princess (who had never said a foolish thing, or done a disobliging one since her arrival [in England], though in very difficult situations . . .)" in his account of 1751. *Memoirs*, 1:53.

18 For speculation that the affair started sooner than 1755, see Walpole, *Memoirs*, 2:151; and Waldegrave, "An Allegory of Leicester House," 229.

19 *Memoirs*, 2:151. Brooke (2: 251-52n) and Clark (introduction, Waldegrave, 78) are certain that Waldegrave was the source of Walpole's information about Leicester House. Their assumptions are justified; with this passage compare Waldegrave's memoirs, particularly his revealing and bitter "An Allegory of Leicester House," 163-64, 229-231, 233. Thanks to Brooke, we

know that Walpole wrote this section between August 6 and October 6, 1758. Since this was before he had access to Waldegrave's papers, he must have relied on conversations with the earl.

20 *Memoirs*, 2:151. John Brooke helpfully supplies in his notes different versions of this passage. In an earlier draft, Walpole described Bute's actions thus: "the veins in the calf of his leg were constantly displayed in the eyes of the poor captivated Princess, and of a court who maliciously affected to wonder that they preserved so much roundness." Though Walpole's dislike of Bute is obvious in these passages, one should not conclude that the description in them of the earl's figure and mannerisms was inaccurate. Alan Ramsay's portrait of Bute, which was done in 1758 at the order of the prince of Wales, is visual confirmation of the words of Walpole and Waldegrave. As he posed, Bute carefully gathered his robe in his right hand in order to display his legs. He also crossed them in such a way that the observer's eye is drawn to them. The general effect is of a man proudly conscious of his physical attributes, and practiced at presenting himself in such a way as to call attention to them and to heighten their attractiveness. Owned by the present marquess of Bute, this portrait is on loan to the National Galleries of Scotland. Scholars may see an unfortunately dim reproduction of it, with comments, in John Brewer, "The Faces of Lord Bute: A Visual Contribution to Anglo-American Political Ideology," *Perspectives in American History* 6 (1972): 96-97.

21 "An Allegory of Leicester House," Waldegrave, *Memoirs*, 231; Walpole, *Memoirs*, 2:151. Servants at Leicester House continued to supply tidbits of information about the behavior of Bute and members of the royal family to interested politicians during the early years of George III's reign. See, for example, the duke of Devonshire's diary, November 2, 1761, in *The Devonshire Diary: William Cavendish, Fourth Duke of Devonshire, Memoranda on State of Affairs, 1759-1762*, ed. Peter D. Brown and Karl W. Schweizer, Camden, 4th ser. 27 (London: Royal Historical Society, 1982), 147.

22 For Waldegrave's knowledge about politics and society, see Clark's excellent account of his life in his introduction to Waldegrave's memoirs, especially 41-64. The earl's description so completely persuaded Walpole that during the 1780s he told John Pinkerton, the antiquary and historian, "I am as much convinced of an amorous connection between B[ute] and the P[rincess] D[owager] as if I had seen them together." *Correspondence*, 12:262n.

23 On Waldegrave's punctilious performance of his duties as governor, see Clark and the earl's own comments, 57-64, 71-76, 169-71, 176-83.

24 Dodington, pp. 164, 173 (for the quotation), 189, 202, 197, 227, 240, 243, 245, 249, 263, 271-72.

25 For Dodington's reputation as a lover, see Walpole's "Brief Account of George Bubb Dodington, Lord Melcombe," an appendix to *Memoirs*, 3: 160-61.

26 The description of Dodington is from Carswell and Dralle's introduction, xii-xiii. Their description is borne out by Lord Townshend's caricature of Dodington, which is reproduced in their frontispiece.

27 The beginning of Bute's efforts to educate the prince of Wales may be dated by a letter from the prince to Bute (July 1, 1756), in which he observed, "I have had the pleasure of your friendship during the space of a year." *Letters from George III to Lord Bute*, 1756-66, ed. Romney Sedgwick (London: Macmillan, 1939), 2.

28 James Lee McKelvey, *George III and Lord Bute: The Leicester House Years* (Durham: Duke University Press, 1973), 21.

29 For an account of the controversy over the prince's education in 1752, see Brooke, *George III*, 35-39. The princess's views may be found in Dodington, 189-195 (quotation 190).

30 Dodington, 300. For Dodington's views on education, see 178. Augusta had never hesitated to talk to Dodington about her dissatisfaction with George's progress. Nor did she hide the fact that she blamed it on his governor Waldegrave and his tutors. She had even hinted on May 29, 1754, that she might in the future look for someone to assume control of her son's education. But her habitual caution when discussing political issues with Dodington asserted itself once she settled on Bute. She never told him about her decision.

31 Bute to Augusta [summer 1755], in *Letters from George III to Bute*, li-lii.

32 Augusta to Bute, [1755?], *Letters from George III to Bute*, 4n.

33 Walpole, *Memoirs*, 2:151.

34 Waldegrave told Augusta in 1756 that whenever he mentioned the possibility of Bute's being appointed the prince's Groom of the Stole to George II, he "never obtain'd a serious Answer; and . . . as often as I touched on the Subject, [the king] immediately laugh'd in my Face" (182). He also recalled that before 1756 George II had "already declared his opinion, by speaking of the Princess's Favorite, and of her Partiality towards him, with the greatest Contempt" (178). For the king's intention to move the prince away from his mother to Kensington Palace, see Brooke, *George III*, 50-51.

35 Bute to the prince [1755], *Letters from George III to Bute*, liii-liv.

36 For other penetrating comments about the importance of women's sexual reputations in the eighteenth century, see Lawrence Stone, *The Family, Sex, and Marriage in England, 1500-1800* (London: Harper and Row, 1977), 501-507.

37 July 1, 1756, *Letters from George III to Bute*, 3. George apparently never forgave Waldegrave for what he believed was the earl's role in creating and spreading these rumors. In 1804, he described Waldegrave as "a depraved worthless man." See Clark, introduction to Waldegrave, *Memoirs*, 53. Gossip about his mother and his "dearest friend" may have also taught George to be more aware of how servants could initiate stories and cause mischief. When he heard the first news about his grandfather's death, he "order'd all the servants that were out to be silent about what had passed as they value their employments." Later, he insisted that his bride-to-be limit the number of servants she would bring with her from Mecklenburg-Strelitz. "The utmost she can bring is one or two Femes de Chambres, which I own I hope will be quiet people, for

by my own experience I have seen these women meddle much more than they ought to do" (*Letters from George III to Bute*, 48, 58).

38 The impact of George's and Bute's friendship has been analyzed many times. In particular, see John Brewer, "The Misfortunes of Lord Bute: A Case-Study in Eighteenth-Century Political Argument and Public Opinion," *The Historical Journal* 16 (1973): 3–43; and *Lord Bute: Essays in Re-interpretation*, the collection cited above, n. 5.

Presidential Address: Did Minnesota Have an Eighteenth Century And If So, When?

PAUL ALKON

During the years that I taught at Minnesota the winters made a deep impression. I often recalled and at last understood Jack London's powerful story "To Build a Fire." Annually I wrote to the English department chairman at the University of Hawaii asking whether anyone there wanted to change places with me, preferably during winter quarter, to use Minnesota's excellent library while I went to Honolulu to find what I needed for my own research. No one ever did, although remarkably polite answers arrived each year conveying the bad news. As winters passed in daydreams of Waikiki Beach and with anxious attention to the health of my furnace and car heater, I often marveled that people had survived in such a climate before the machine age. Of course as a loyal member of the American Society for Eighteenth-Century Studies I especially wondered what it was like to live in Minnesota during the eighteenth century. But I never pursued this question.

Finally I have an ideal occasion for describing life in Minnesota in the eighteenth century. Unfortunately there is an embarrassing ontological obstacle: during what we call the eighteenth century there was, after all, no such entity as "Minnesota." And if Minnesota did not exist in the eighteenth century, it is hardly possible to address you on what life was like there then. Other ontological obstacles are equally daunting. Although one may project the present borders of Minnesota back through all past time to define what we mean by "there," and thus hope to escape the disappointment of finding as Gertrude Stein did of Oakland that there was no "there" there, it is not so easy to delineate for life within those imaginary boundaries a stable eighteenth century.

Does one resort with our more latitudinarian colleagues to the "long eighteenth century" defined as the interval from 1660 to 1837 or even 1850? This is now becoming a favorite parameter for eighteenth-century studies, adopted for example in excellent recent books by Roy Porter and Dianne Dugaw.[1] Does one follow the middle way chosen by J. H. Plumb for a book entitled *England in the Eighteenth Century (1714-1815)*? Or does one adhere with the strict constructionists to an eighteenth century defined less imperialistically as merely the interval from 1700 to 1800? If so, do we measure by the old style Julian calendar or the new style Gregorian calendar that was not adopted in Great Britain and its American colonies until 1752?[2] Usually the latter, but all of these measures applied to America impose a Eurocentric definition of era upon a diversely populated region whose native inhabitants had no such measure of time. It therefore appears alarmingly possible that, at least in an absolute sense, there was for Minnesota no then, there.

Moreover, if we set aside ethnocentric anachronistic concepts of space, the idea of a stable, clearly delineated "there" also disintegrates. Boundaries proliferated, shifted, and overlapped according to when they were seen and who saw them. "Minnesota in the eighteenth century" is thus even more problematic than Oakland in Gertrude Stein's day: there was no there there, and there was no then then. It takes no deconstructionist to see these difficulties. Surely you sympathize with my dilemma. It is impossible to address you today on the best of all possible topics: life in Minnesota in the eighteenth century. What to do?

I

When in doubt one should turn to the available evidence. In this case the *locus classicus* is Jonathan Carver's *Travels Through the Interior Parts of North America in the Years 1766, 1767, and 1768*. The first part recounts his journey from Fort Michilimackinac to the Falls of St. Anthony in quest of the elusive Northwest Passage. The second part is a description of local plants and animals together with a long section entitled "Of the Origin, Manners, Customs, Religion and Language of the Indians."

Illustrations include what might anachronistically be called the first picture of Minneapolis: a plate entitled "The Falls of St. Anthony in the

Figure 1. "The Falls of St. Anthony," Jonathan Carver, *Travels Through the Interior Parts of North America* (London, 1778).

River Mississippi, near 2400 Miles from its entrance into the Gulf of Mexico" (Figure 1).[3] This title specifies the scene's enormous exotic distance from all European and even most North American readers while nevertheless giving the waterfall a name that appropriates it for their culture if not for their country. In the text Carver describes with admiration the piety of "a young prince of the Winnebago Indians" who set aside other plans and eagerly accompanied the expedition to St. Anthony's Falls, of which he had often heard from his chiefs, for the purpose of performing there elaborate religious ceremonies honoring the Great Spirit. But whether the Indians ever had their own name for such evidently holy ground Carver does not say, reporting only that the falls had been named in the 1680s by Father Hennepin (66–69).

Dramatic emphasis on the falling and foaming water is a nice instance of what Barbara Stafford has shown to be a Newtonian "propensity of eighteenth-century travellers for interpreting the fume of waterfalls as barely visible yet acutely sensible signs of matter's physical powers."[4] Dynamism of the water is echoed and reinforced by remarkably large birds in flight against a vast background of cloudy sky. All this movement is further emphasized by contrast with the stasis of surrounding fields and heavily wooded islands. Two Indians carrying a canoe in the

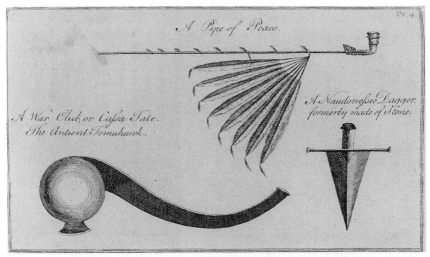

Figure 2. Peace pipe, dagger, and "The Antient Tomahawk," Jonathan Carver, *Travels Through the Interior Parts of North America* (London, 1778).

right foreground serve primarily to establish scale. Other canoes above the falls as well as a whole village of tepees in the far distance also dwindle to insignificance by comparison with their sublime setting. The natives and their artifacts are included here mainly to enhance the exotic appeal of what the book's index describes as a "picturesque view."

Other illustrations concentrate more on Indian life. Taken out of context to float in abstract space are a peace pipe, an old-model stone dagger, and "The Antient Tomahawk" (figure 2). "A Man and Woman of the Ottigaumies" are shown together with a child against a background of fields, curiously proportioned trees, and a hut (figure 3). The ancient tomahawk has given way here to the warrior's musket and hatchet which imply contact and trade with European settlers. "A Man & Woman of the Naudowessie" are shown with their child against a background of trees, fields, tepees, and indistinct figures of other villagers passing the tepee at far right (figure 4). This warrior's bow and arrows imply the scene's greater remoteness from European culture. Carver's text does not mention that "Naudowessie" is a Chippewa term meaning roughly "snake in the grass." It was given by the Chippewa to their enemies the Dakota, picked up by the French, and given widest currency in the pluralized francophone form "Sioux" as a convenient though alienated and alienating way of describing various Dakota tribes that in Carver's lifetime were being driven away from the Great Lakes region by the Chippewa but who eventually gave a better account of themselves against another enemy at

Eighteenth-Century Minnesota? / 271

Figure 3. "A Man and Woman of the Ottigaumies," Jonathan Carver, *Travels Through the Interior Parts of North America* (London, 1778).

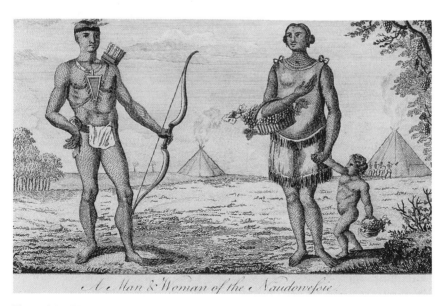

Figure 4. "A Man and Woman of the Naudowessie," Jonathan Carver, *Travels Through the Interior Parts of North America* (London, 1778).

Little Big Horn.[5] This political development was beyond Carver's capacity to describe, requiring as it does for comprehension more knowledge than he had or wanted to have of Indian history and also requiring a twentieth-century vantage-point allowing definition of what might be called a very long eighteenth century.

Colorized versions of the Indian pictures, though not of St. Anthony's Falls, appeared in the 1781 edition of Carver's *Travels*. The peace pipe, dagger, and tomahawk primarily gain in verisimilitude by this transformation. For the family scenes the colorizer leaves backgrounds untouched to concentrate upon human figures, whose costumes become more strikingly exotic than in the uncolored versions, and whose more conspicuously dark skin must have created for most readers a sense of even greater cultural distance between themselves and the Indian life depicted in Carver's book.

These pictures and others to which I will soon turn enjoyed very wide circulation. First published in London in 1778 (new style), Carver's *Travels* gained immediate popularity and lasting fame as the most appealing early account of the region including what is now called Minnesota. By 1800 (new style) no less than twelve editions in English were supplemented by French, Dutch, and German translations as well as a widely distributed German abridgment designed for young readers. Swedish and Greek translations followed along with many more editions in English.[6] Here then, we may hope, is solid ground: an undeniably eighteenth-century artifact well known *during* the period, representative *of* the period, and embellished with pictures of people, places and things encountered *in* the period. Though Minnesota did not then exist, Carver's book certainly did. Moreover it still exists. Those of you who attended the Bell Library's reception for ASECS saw it with your own eyes. And seeing is believing, is it not?

Certainly not, as we all know, and least of all in this case. Carver's plagiarisms earned him prominent mention among the rogues' gallery so nicely analyzed in *Travelers and Travel Liars 1660–1800* by Percy G. Adams, who characterizes Carver as "finally, the most notorious of these, at least among Englishmen." Adams notes of Carver that "In one breath he maligned Lahontan, Hennepin, Adair, and Charlevoix and in the next breath took here a chapter on Indian marriage ceremonies from Lahontan, there a passage on war from Charlevoix, here a description of Indian lacrosse from Adair, and there 'a short Vocabulary of the Chipeway Language' from 'La Hontan's Dictionary of the Algonquion Language.'" Even the famous funeral speech which Schiller rewrote from Carver as the universally admired *Nadowessiers Todtenlied* was itself a rewriting of one in Lahontan."[7] Carver's *Travels* thus poses its own ontological problems.

John Parker's superb 1976 edition of Carver's journals, which had remained unpublished for over two centuries, has to some extent recuperated Carver's reputation by establishing that he did indeed go to St. Anthony's falls pretty much as he narrates the trip in the first Part of his *Travels*, producing en route reasonably accurate maps important for cartography of the region, thereby adding to knowledge of its geography. Unacknowledged borrowings are largely confined to the account of Indians in part two. And these plagiarisms may be ascribed to an anonymous editor whom Carver calls "the reviser" in a journal page granting permission to add "any thing that the reviser shall see fit to add to embellish or give better sence [sic] to the journal."[8] Perhaps such help came from Carver's friend and physician Dr. John Lettsom, trying his hand at a little literary malpractice. More likely, as John Parker argues, Carver's anonymous collaborator was an obscure Grub Street writer named Alexander Bucknell.[9]

In any case, modern scholarship has shown in its spoil-sport way that Carver was neither the only nor the major author of *Travels Through the Interior Parts of North America*. Modern scholarship has shown too that the text is in its second part largely a kind of Whitman's Sampler of delectable morsels about Indian life taken from the most delicious though not necessarily the most truthful parts of works by Carver's predecessors: unhealthy fare for the would-be Minnesota historian, whose gloom at these findings may verge on incurable melancholy.

Postmodern critical theory, however, dispels such vapors by teaching us that although readers live the Author is dead, thus rendering irrelevant all worries about authorship. "Carver" may be alluded to as I shall henceforward do with the understanding that this name in connection with authorship of the *Travels* refers only to a convenient fiction. Postmodern critical theory also teaches us that the condition of all literature is intertextual dialogism. Seen from this happy perspective, Carver's *Travels* offers more advantages than liabilities.

To postmodern eyes, its hitherto deplorable plagiarisms are a highly revealing case of conspicuous intertextuality inviting explication. Its hitherto deplorably jumbled passages about Indian life lifted from Hennepin, Lahontan, Adair and others are a cultural treasure-trove summing up in one place for convenient recovery a vast range of crucial attitudes held consciously or unconsciously about North America. Because of its popularity Carver's *Travels* powerfully shaped as well as expressed European imaginings of first encounters in the region to which we have traveled for our 1990 meeting. On the cover of our program the conference theme is proclaimed as "Frontiers in the Eighteenth Century: Imaginary and Real." For this topic Carver's *Travels* is an archetypal text. In it fantasy and reality combine to delineate relationships between physical and temporal frontiers in ways that I want now to outline before concluding with what I believe to be the moral of Carver's tale for us.

II

Consider "Carver" as he was presented in the posthumous 1781 edition of his *Travels*. Here strong reassurance is provided by an imposing authorial figure in a frontispiece entitled "Captain Jonathan Carver from the original Picture in the Possession of J. C. Lettsom M. D." (figure 5). For this edition Lettsom also attested the narrative's credibility by providing in addition to the portrait an affecting biography of Carver telling of his religious piety, implying honesty; of his brave service as a Captain in the French and Indian war; of his arduous explorations; and of his pathetic death of starvation after subsequent struggles to support a new family during a decade in London where he failed to get further government employment or adequate recompense for past services. Lettsom does not vary the panegyric tone of his account by any allusion to the incongruous fact that in addition to a London wife and two small children Carver at his death also had in North America a living wife and five more children. If this information makes Captain Carver look to us like some more portly but equally unreliable version of Captain Macheath, there is little doubt that for eighteenth-century readers the credibility of Carver's book was only enhanced by its association with Lettsom, who was eminently respectable as a trustworthy promoter of genuinely important medical projects.[10]

In profile with arms rigidly by his side as though standing at attention awaiting his majesty's next commands, Captain Carver is neatly groomed, nicely bewigged, well-dressed and well-fed to the point of a certain double-chinned though pleasing plumpness. His somewhat inscrutable expression might be described as expectant. Ignoring alike the artist and beholders of the portrait, he stares in wide-eyed but calm absorption at something off in the distance that readers cannot see. Perhaps caught in one of his prophetic moods, Carver may be contemplating with satisfaction that Eurocentric mid-western utopia he so eloquently predicted by emphatically insisting early in *his* preface that "There is no doubt but that at some future period, mighty kingdoms will emerge from these wildernesses, and stately palaces and solemn temples, with gilded spires reaching the skies, supplant the Indian huts, whose

Figure 5. Frontispiece, Jonathan Carver, *Travels Through the Interior Parts of North America* (London, 1781).

only decorations are the barbarous trophies of their vanquished enemies" (viii). For many there was doubtless comfort in this assurance that despite all those grisly scalp-poles on unsightly Indian lodges scattered throughout the interior parts of North America, what really mattered was not that present landscape but its glorious urban future.

To Carver—and perhaps to most of his eighteenth-century readers—native life around the Falls of St. Anthony was only a passing phase of transient interest. Such emphasis on the future in Carver's preface allows his entire ensuing description of Indian customs, manners, religion, and language at the terminus of his journey to be taken, as it were, under erasure. Thus when readers proceed to contemplate Carver's maps, they have already been encouraged by the utopian vision of his preface to regard geographical realities of the frontier as a stable basis of future cultural developments that will displace and render obsolete most of the demographic and political features delineated on these same maps. In this respect, of course, Carver's *Travels* is altogether typical of European views of the new world, notable mainly for its explicit orientation toward the future.

Carver's "New Map of North America" (figure 6) shows frontier regions thickly studded with Indian names that give a rough idea of tribal boundaries, whereas Indian nomenclature has all but vanished from Eastern areas dominated by Europeans. The "Plan of Captain Carver's Travels in the Interior Parts of North America in 1766 and 1767" (figure 7) provides a close-up political anatomy of a frontier landscape that includes regions prominently named the Chipeway Territories, Winnebago Land, Ottigaumies Land, Naudowessie Country, and Naudowessie of the Plains. These terms written in capital letters vie in prominence with such purely geographical features as "Lake Superiour" and Lake Michigan.

Smaller print includes Indian place-names and purely physical information like a notation on the South shore of Lake Superior that "about here is Plenty of Virgin Copper." There are some combinations of cultural and physical facts as in the notation just north of the lake at bottom left that "In these Mountains are large Quaries of Red Marble where the Neiboring [sic] Nations resort to get their Calemates of Peace" (i.e. their peace pipes). Most of the small print deals with politics, although the changing fortunes of intertribal warfare are only glanced at in one notation remarking of land to the Southwest of Lake Superior that "This vast Extent of Country is now possess'd by the Chipeways." Its former owners are not specified. Other notations merely describe current political geography as in the comment printed to the south of White Bear Lake and Red Lake that "This is the Road of War between the Nadowessie and

Figure 6. "A New Map of North America," Jonathan Carver, *Travels Through the Interior Parts of North America* (London, 1778).

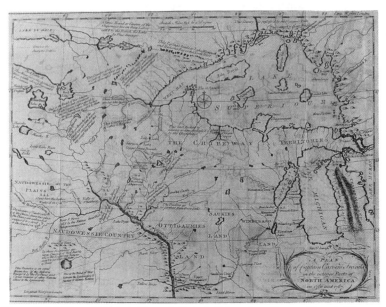

Figure 7. "A Plan of Captain Carver's Travels," Jonathan Carver, *Travels Through the Interior Parts of North America* (London, 1778).

Assiniboils." Carver adds here an ungrammatical explanation that "All Country's [sic] not posses'd by any one Nation where War Parties are often passing is call'd by them the Road of War." Many other warpaths are also indicated. The "Plan of Captain Carver's Travels" is a vivid snapshot of Indian political relationships around Lake Superior and Lake Michigan dated 1766-67 without, however, any clarification of prior developments or explicit prediction of future relationships among all the tribes alluded to and between them and Europeans likely to follow Carver's path into their territories.

One familiar vision of that future is implicit in Carver's preceding "New Map of North America" showing that European place-names had supplanted Indian names as settlements proceeded westward. The likely continuation of this process in the future was hardly a matter that had to be made explicit, or that allowed convenient representation on a map. But the ever-helpful Dr. Lettsom provided an exemplary scenario showing how with dream-like ease the land might be cleared of troublesome Indians to create the utopian future that Carver invites readers to imagine.

Lettsom included in his biography of Carver a hitherto unpublished text purportedly of a deed dated May 1, 1767, signed with the marks of Sioux chiefs improbably named Hawnopawjatin and Otohtongoomlisheaw, granting to Carver a very large portion of what is now Minnesota and Wisconsin, including the entire present site of St. Paul (figure 8). Even by Southern California standards the value of all this real estate can only be called awesome. And so it certainly seemed to Carver's descendants from both his wives along with a large cast of other greedy characters who pursued what they claimed as their inherited or purchased portions of this fabulous grant well into the nineteen twenties, greatly vexing Minnesota officials after there was a Minnesota.[11]

Although a version of the deed in Carver's hand has recently been discovered, its terms have not enhanced acceptance of its authenticity as a record of an actual event. Among other implausibilities is the bothersome detail that all the land so lavishly given to Carver by his Sioux friends actually belonged to their implacable enemies the Chippewa. If Hawnopawjatin and Otohtongoomlisheaw really offered land to Carver they were certainly having their little joke and deserve special eminence in the annals of American confidence men.[12] Authorship of the printed version of the deed is uncertain: perhaps Carver, perhaps Lettsom. Indians queried about the grant in 1817 denied that chiefs named Hawnopawjatin and Otohtongoomlisheaw ever existed. These marvelously generous Noble Savages are apparently figments of the European

[14]
" cave, May the firſt, one thouſand ſeven
" hundred and ſixty-ſeven."

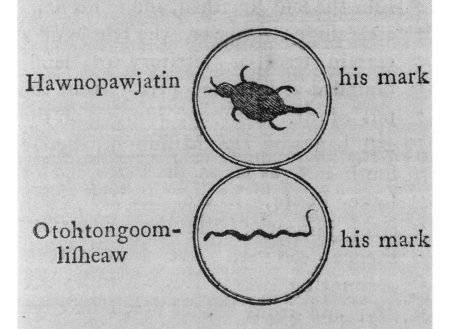

Soon after the above period, our author concluded to return to Boſton, where he arrived in 1768, having been abſent two years and five months, during which time

Figure 8. Indian signatures on the grant printed in Jonathan Carver, *Travels Through the Interior Parts of North America*. (London, 1781)

imagination dreaming of an already utopian frontier where the paleface has only to arrive to acquire title peacefully to land that will establish a prosperous future from which Indians have not only withdrawn voluntarily but have thereby themselves erased all signs of their own present and past.

This fantasy of a tranquil future devoid of bothersome scalp-hunters would have been especially appealing to land-starved armchair travelers reading Carver's book in the old world and day-dreaming with its help of owning country estates beautifully situated around St. Anthony's Falls. After perusing Lettsom's preface, many of Carver's readers must have looked again at the illustration of that landmark in Carver's *Travels* (figure 1), with something other than disinterested appreciation of its sublime power, including surely all those readers who actually fell for the ensuing swindle and bought shares in the imaginary deed so obligingly signed by Hawnopawjatin and Otohtongoomlisheaw. That picture of St. Anthony's Falls may anachronistically but not altogether inaccurately be regarded as the first Minnesota real estate advertisement.

After perusing Carver's account of the Indians attentive readers also had available another way of interpreting the maps and regarding the illustrations of Indian life because Carver suggests that his journey was a trip through time as well as through space: in progressing westward he encountered tribes "that have held but little communications with the provinces" and therefore "preserved their manners or their customs in their original purity" (221-22). Previous travelers had no such luck, according to Carver, who emphatically insists that he is "able to give a more just account of the customs and manners of the Indians, in their ancient purity, than any that has been hitherto published" (222). However dubious the accuracy of this boastful comparison, which so blithely ignores the cornucopia of unacknowledged borrowings in the *Travels*, the remark creates for readers proceeding through its text a strong sense of backward motion in time.

To read his maps from east to west is to see not only the ground of a utopian future, but a progression from present to past, from eastern settlements exemplifying eighteenth-century civilization to western territories where Indians can be found living just as they did in ancient days. To follow Carver in the mind's eye from Fort Michilimackinac to the Falls of St. Anthony is in imagination to boldly go back to an earlier era where no paleface has gone before. To go from the picture of an Ottigaumy warrior with a musket signifying cultural contamination of his tribe's "ancient purity" of customs to the picture of such Naudowessie implements as "the ancient tomahawk" and to the picture of a Naudowessie warrior with bow and arrows is to journey through an intermediate past era back to the truly ancient days. Readers thus become time-travelers performing along with Carver the imaginative feat of leaving their own eighteenth century to encounter Indians as they lived in "ancient" days.

How ancient? What is the final destination of Carver's bibliographical time machine? He provides no explicit answer to these questions but his lengthy survey of theories about Indian origins certainly implies a very great leap backward. Although himself adhering to the plausible notion that North America was populated via the Bering Straight at some indeterminate past time which he describes only as "in the earliest ages" (202), Carver notes that population of the continent must have been "completed at different periods" (182). He then gives ample consideration to competing theories that argued for Norwegian Vikings; for Spaniards "more than two thousand years ago" (186); for the Carthaginians; for the Phoenicians; for "the Israelites, either whilst they were a maritime power, or soon after their general captivity" (203); and for "the Scythians or Tartars . . . soon after the dispersion of Noah's grandsons" (184). About possibilities for such migration in Noah's era Carver seems to agree with Charlevoix, who stoutly argued that "Navigation . . . might possibly have been more perfect in those early ages than at this day" because he found it impossible to doubt "That the builder and pilot of the largest ship that ever was . . . should be ignorant of, or should not have communicated to . . . his descendants . . . the art of sailing upon an ocean" (198). Carver also cites with approval George De Hornn's conviction that America could not "have been peopled before the flood, considering the short space of time which elapsed between the creation of the world and that memorable event" (189). The *terminus ad quem* of Carver's *Travels* is thus the Flood.

Indians encountered in what Carver describes as "their original purity" and "their ancient purity" are accordingly envisioned as residing in a kind of mythic time specified in relationship to the Flood rather than by specific years during or before the Christian era. Of course there had been various contradictory attempts to date the Flood, but Carver never alludes to such speculations. Consequently he leaves readers with an impression that Indians around St. Anthony's Falls and westward live not only outside the eighteenth century but also outside the entire realm of secular history where events can with any assurance be specified by dates. As in his vision of the future, this idea of a living past eternally recurring in one region of the present shows Carver's utopian imagination at work inasmuch as one of the most conspicuous features of utopian literature from Sir Thomas More onward is presentation of travelers who encounter a remarkably changeless society.

By seeing at his destination around the Falls of St. Anthony only what he imagined to be Indians still living exactly as they had in ancient days, Carver turned a blind eye while also blinding his readers to the implications of such momentous political developments as displacement of the Dakota by the Chippewa. Warpaths are simply a perennial but ultimately insignificant feature of the landscape Carver maps. That landscape has no history, only a perpetual present of time past. The natives will always fight but nothing will essentially change for them because unless they are disturbed by Europeans they will go on living exactly as in ancient days. In this view only Europeans have history: it is another of their gifts to the red man. In this view native politics do not count, because change from past to present to future, and thus history itself, is only induced by relationships between natives and outsiders.

In its treatment of those relationships Carver's *Travels* affords a classic instance of the process described by Johannes Fabian: informants occupying the same time as the observer are relegated to another and earlier time-stream by anthropologists who characterize native society as primitive and thus by virtue of its alien temporality regard its inhabitants as Other.[13] By consigning the Indians to a mythic time of the ancients, Carver denies them equal temporal status as fellow residents of the eighteenth century or indeed of historical time. He views them through the wrong end of what another eighteenth-century book calls Time's Telescope. They are seen at maximum temporal as well as physical and cultural distance rather than brought closer. Despite all the information supplied in his *Travels* its readers are therefore not much encouraged to identify with the Indians or attempt to see the world as they might see it.

Carver's journals do contain one fascinating picture of a safe-conduct drawn by Carver's Indian pilot showing how some things including white men and the passage of time looked through Indian eyes (figure 9). On the left is "A Naudowessie chief delivering a belt of wampum with a speech" to (on the right) a Chippewa chief depicted "according to their customs . . . in form of a deer, receiving the belt and speech." Englishmen in the canoes are identified by hats, a Frenchman by a handkerchief around his head, and "Six tents or houses signify that six days passed" or else (Carver is not sure) that six encampments had requested safe passage for his expedition (*Journals*, 143). But this picture was suppressed. No engraving was made from it for Carver's *Travels*. It was published only some two centuries later by John Parker in his 1976 edition of Carver's *Journals*.

Carver's only attempt to convey in print a sense of how Indians themselves might have regarded their location in time is a short section reporting that the Indians "count their years by winters" or "by moons" and

Figure 9. "A Naudowessie chief delivering a belt of wampum with a speech," from Jonathan Carver's manuscript journals (British Museum Additional Manuscripts 8949 and 8950) as published in *The Journals of Jonathan Carver*, ed. John Parker (St. Paul: Minnesota Historical Society Press, 1976).

giving what he took to be Indian names for the various months: "April is termed by them the month of Plants. May, the Month of Flowers. June, the Hot Moon. July, the Buck Moon. . . . August, the Sturgeon Moon. . . September the Corn Moon" and so on (250-51). In fairness to Carver (and his reviser) on this point, however, it must be said that even now there is scant evidence concerning calendric systems of Dakota Indians, although there were such systems. Iron Shell's winter count starting in the year we call 1807 has survived.[14] Also available is Lone Dog's more famous winter count starting in the winter that we call 1799-1800, shown here as published in 1877 by Captain Mallery with numbers added to the facsimile for convenience in referring to the symbols (figures 10 and 11).[15] The tracing was made from a drawing done by Lone Dog on a buffalo robe.

Years are distinguished by events rather than vice versa. The thirty black lines of item one, for example, represent thirty Dakotas killed by Crow Indians in the first year of Lone Dog's calendar. The second year is marked by an outbreak of smallpox whose "symbol is the head and body of a man, covered with red blotches" (11). The circle accompanied by two stars at upper left (number 70) represents a year denoted by an eclipse of the sun. The flag (number 68) represents a year of significant meetings with United States peace commissioners that eventually resulted in a treaty.

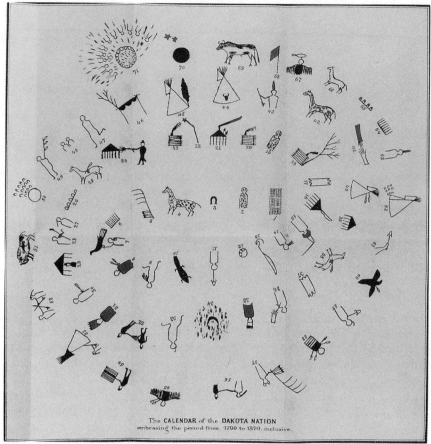

Figure 10. Lone Dog's winter count, from the facsimile published in *Bulletin of the United States Geological and Geographical Survey of the Territories* 3, no. 1. (April, 1877).

III

I want now to end with some observations on the confrontation I have described between people holding attitudes toward time and the other exemplified by Carver's *Travels* and people who recorded time in the manner of Lone Dog's calendar. Such winter counts imply a relativistic rather than absolute notion of time. Paradoxically, they share this feature with the majority of pre-Enlightenment historical writing. And they share it too with Carver's *Travels*, which in its dating of Indian life mainly with vague reference to ancient days defined in terms of the Flood is itself significantly relativistic.

Eighteenth-Century Minnesota? / 285

Figure 11. Lone Dog's Winter Count: detail.

In a remarkable book that I hope will be widely read, Donald J. Wilcox reminds us that

> the concept of centuries did not come into widespread use before Newton's time. Not until after the seventeenth century did most literate contemporaries identify the epoch in which they lived as their 'century,' and only in the course of the Enlightenment did the term take on the epochal significance we now attach to it. . . . For historians before Newton the time frame did not include a group of events; a group of events contained a time frame. This perspective led them to use a variety

of relative dating systems, none of which had an absolute temporal significance apart from the group of events that gave it meaning.[16]

Wilcox persuasively argues that with physics and literature now so much influenced by notions of relativity, historians should consider the virtues of pre-and also post-Newtonian systems of dating events without exclusive reliance on absolute time-scales. Attention to old and new systems of relativistic dating certainly highlights a great irony in the confrontation between Carver and Indians in what is now Minnesota: neither they nor he saw the encounter as an eighteenth-century event. Whether they included his arrival in any winter count is not known, but if so it could hardly have been with reference to "the eighteenth century." Nor as we have seen did Carver include them in his eighteenth century except as examples of life in ancient days. It is only *we* who see this encounter on an absolute time-scale as primarily an eighteenth-century event. Minnesota only has an eighteenth century in retrospect, *now*, thanks to people like us and organizations like our Society.

We ought to give more thought to the way we create such eighteenth centuries. The American Society for Eighteenth-Century Studies was founded twenty-one years ago to encourage a multi-disciplinary approach to *the* eighteenth century. Its goal was to regard that presumably single though complex object from many different perspectives. Looking backward over our history I think we may claim great success. Let me close by suggesting that while maintaining our indispensable variety of perspectives as an interdisciplinary group we should now also pluralize our object of study. We need not change our name. But we should be more aware that there are many eighteenth centuries of our devising defined with respect to various relative chronologies established more by significant events than by dates. We should also be more aware that some eighteenth centuries, like Carver's eighteenth century, intersected with other streams of human time that are also relevant to our studies though impossible to define only by absolute time-scales or to confine within our period. Increasing popularity of various long eighteenth centuries should be our cue. This movement toward application of variable time-frames ought to be accelerated. Our province is all the eighteenth centuries, and our most challenging task now is to find them.

NOTES

1 Roy Porter, *Health for Sale: Quackery in England, 1660–1860* (Manchester: Manchester University Press, 1989); Dianne Dugaw, *Warrior Women and*

Popular Balladry, 1650-1850 (Cambridge: Cambridge University Press, 1989).
2 See Paul Alkon, "Changing the Calendar," *Eighteenth-Century Life* 7, no. 2 (January 1982): 1-18.
3 Illustrations are from Jonathan Carver, *Travels Through the Interior Parts of North America, in the Years 1766, 1767, and 1768* (London, 1778), and Jonathan Carver, *Travels Through the Interior Parts of North America* (3rd. ed., London, 1781) as noted on the figures. For permission to reproduce these illustrations and the facsimile of Lone Dog's winter count in figures 10 and 11 (see note 15 below), I am grateful to the Huntington Library, San Marino, California. Quotations from Carver's *Travels* are taken from the 1781 edition and will be cited parenthetically in my text.
4 Barbara Maria Stafford, *Voyage into Substance: Art, Science, Nature, and the Illustrated Travel Account, 1760-1840* (Cambridge, MA and London: The MIT Press, 1984), 210.
5 See Royal B. Hassrick in collaboration with Dorothy Maxwell and Cile M. Bach, *The Sioux: Life and Customs of a Warrior Society* (Norman: University of Oklahoma Press, 1964); Robert W. Meyer, *History of the Santee Sioux: United States Indian Policy on Trial* (Lincoln: University of Nebraska Press, 1967); and Edmund Jefferson Danziger, Jr., *The Chippewas of Lake Superior* (Norman: University of Oklahoma Press, 1978).
6 On the publishing history of Carver's *Travels* see the Introduction and Appendix Three, "A Bibliography of Jonathan Carver's *Travels*," in *The Journals of Jonathan Carver and Related Documents, 1766-1770*, ed. John Parker (St. Paul: Minnesota Historical Society Press, 1976).
7 Percy G. Adams, *Travel and Travel Liars 1660-1800* (Berkeley and Los Angeles: University of California Press, 1962), 83-84.
8 Carver, *The Journals of Jonathan Carver*, 143.
9 Parker, "Introduction," *The Journals of Jonathan Carver*, 31-32.
10 See James Johnston Abraham, *Lettsom: His Life, Times, Friends, and Descendants* (London: William Heineman Medical Books Ltd., 1933).
11 See Theodore C. Blegen, *Minnesota: A History of the State, With a New Concluding Chapter by Russell W. Fridley*, 2nd. ed. (Minneapolis: University of Minnesota Press, 1975; rpt. 1985), 67-70.
12 For a facsimile of the grant in Carver's hand and discussion of it see John Parker, "New Light on Jonathan Carver," *The American Magazine and Historical Chronicle* 2 (Spring-Summer 1986): 4-17. Parker rejects the idea that the Naudowessie were playing a joke on Carver and their enemies the Chippewa, arguing persuasively instead that after forging the grant as a desperate scheme to raise money "Carver realized its weaknesses, which explains why he never included it in his journal or his *Travels*." On the key point of why "if he was to fabricate a grant of land from the Western Sioux" he did not have them "place it in their territory," Parker responds: "Because he was keenly aware that as of 1763 the land west of the Mississippi belonged to Spain. He mentions this in his journal. Such land was hardly a good prospect for sale in

London in 1775. Why not create a grant from the Chippewa, since it was their land he was claiming? He had no occasion among the Chippewa for a conference comparable to the May 1, 1767, meeting with the Western Sioux at the great cave. His wintering among the Sioux gave him the opportunity to create the appearance at least of an obligation on their part by which a grant of land might be justified. Also, any Chippewa grant would likely have been made to Captain James Tute, who was in command of the expedition as it moved northward through their territory. Carver was its only member who wintered among the Western Sioux" (10–11).

13 Johannes Fabian, *Time and the Other: How Anthropology Makes its Object* (New York: Columbia University Press, 1983).

14 See "Appendix A: Iron Shell's Winter Count" in Hassrick, *The Sioux*, 346–51.

15 Garrick Mallery, "A Calendar of the Dakota Nation," *Bulletin of the United States Geological and Geographical Survey of the Territories* 3 (April 1877): 3–25.

16 Donald J. Wilcox, *The Measure of Times Past: Pre-Newtonian Chronologies and the Rhetoric of Relative Time* (Chicago and London: University of Chicago Press, 1987), 9.

Contributors to Volume 21

PAUL ALKON, Leo S. Bing Professor of English Literature at the University of Southern California, is author of *Samuel Johnson and Moral Discipline*, *Defoe and Fictional Time*, and *Origins of Futuristic Fiction*.

NADINE BÉRENGUIER is Assistant Professor of French at Harvard University. She has written articles on Barthes, Diderot, and the question of adultery. She is working on the representation of the family in eighteenth-century novels. Her research interests also include the relations between literature and law in eighteenth-century France.

JOHN L. BULLION is Professor of History at the University of Missouri-Columbia. He has published extensively on British politicians and the origins of the American Revolution and is currently working on a study tentatively titled *George III and the American Revolution, 1756-1783*. His essay was initially presented at the 1990 ASECS conference.

ROBERT DARNTON is Shelby Cullom Davis Professor of European History at Princeton University. Among his publications relevant to the Clifford Lecture presented here are *The Business of Enlightenment: A Publishing History of the Encyclopèdie* and *The Literary Underground of the Old Regime*, as well as *Revolution in Print: the Press in France, 1775-1800* (co-edited with Daniel Roche).

STEVEN M. DWORETZ teaches political science at Wheaton College (Massachusetts). He is the author of *The Unvarnished Doctrine: Locke, Liberalism, and the American Revolution*. He presented his paper on a panel celebrating the tercentenary of the publication of three of John Locke's works, at the 1990 ASECS conference in Minneapolis.

JACOB FUCHS, Professor of English at California State University, Hayward, is the author of *Reading Pope's Imitations of Horace*. The article published here, first presented at the 1990 meeting of WSECS, is part of a larger project on English mock-epic poetry.

JAMES L. FUCHS is Assistant Professor of History at Earlham College. He has published on Coronelli in the *Journal of Religious History* and is completing a book on the history of encyclopedism. The present paper was presented at the 1988 meeting of MWASECS.

DUSTIN GRIFFIN, Professor of English at New York University, has published widely on Milton and on eighteenth-century poetry and satire. He is currently at work on a book on patronage in the eighteenth century. His essay was first presented at ASECS in Minneapolis, 1990.

CHARLES H. HINNANT is Professor of English at the University of Missouri-Columbia. He is the author of books on *Gulliver's Travels* and Samuel Johnson and is currently at work on a book-length critical study of the poetry of Anne Finch, the Countess of Winchilsea.

KATHLEEN HOLCOMB is Professor of English at Angelo State University, San Antonio, Texas. She is currently working on an edition of the contributions of Thomas Reid to the Aberdeen Philosophical Society and the Literary Society of Glasgow. This paper was read at the ASECS meeting in New Orleans in 1989.

ALAN T. MCKENZIE is Professor of English and Director of Graduate Studies at Purdue University. He is the author of *Certain Lively Episodes: The Articulation of Passion in Eighteenth-Century Prose* (Georgia, 1990). He came to Chesterfield by way of the *Dictionary of Literary Biography*, for which he wrote the Chesterfield entry. The present paper was given at the WSECS meeting in Colorado Springs, February 1990.

HEATHER MCPHERSON is Associate Professor of Art History at the University of Alabama at Birmingham. Her research focuses on French painting. She has published essays and exhibition catalogues on Greuze, David, Manet, portraiture in the Age of Proust, and Marie Laurencin, and is currently preparing a series of studies dealing with portraiture after the advent of photography.

KATHARINE M. ROGERS, Research Professor of Literature at the American University, has published several books on eighteenth-century women authors, including *Feminism in Eighteenth-Century England* (1982) and *Frances Burney: The World of "Female Difficulties"* (1990). She has just completed an anthology of early American woman authors.

JON ROWLAND is a doctoral candidate in English at the University of Montreal. Under the supervision of William Kinsley, he is currently completing his dissertation on aspects of panegyric in Marvell and Swift, parts of which have been presented at conferences in Canada and the United States. He was named a "Graduate Scholar" by the ECASECS in 1989.

MARGARET OLOFSON THICKSTUN, who teaches English at Hamilton College, studies Puritan literature and seventeenth-century English and American women's religious experience. Her book, *Fictions of the Feminine: Puritan Doctrine and the Representation of Women*, was published by Cornell in 1988.

HANS-PETER WAGNER, Associate Professor of English at Eichstätt University (Germany), presented his essay at the 1990 ASECS conference. He is the author of *Erotica of the Enlightenment in England and America* (1988) and the editor of *Erotica and the Enlightenment* (1990).

Executive Board, 1990–91

President: ARAM VARTANIAN, William R. Kenan Professor of French, University of Virginia

Past President: PAUL ALKON, Leo S. Bing Professor of English, University of Southern California

First Vice-President: JANE PERRY-CAMP, Professor of Music, Florida State University

Second Vice-President: PAULA R. BACKSCHEIDER, Professor of English, University of Rochester

Executive Secretary: EDWARD P. HARRIS, Professor of Germanic Languages and Literatures, University of Cincinnati

Treasurer: BARBARA BRANDON SCHNORRENBERG, History, Birmingham, Alabama

Members-at-Large: DANIEL HEARTZ, Professor of Music, University of California, Berkeley (1991)
DAVID CARRITHERS, Adolph Ochs Professor of Government, University of Tennessee, Chattanooga (1991)
JOSEPH M. LEVINE, Professor of History, Syracuse University (1992)
SUSAN ROSA, History of Ideas, Healdsburg, California (1992)
CHRISTOPHER FOX, Professor of English, University of Notre Dame (1993)
JOHN W. YOLTON, Professor of Philosophy, Rutgers University (1993)

Business Manager: DONNA L. HILL-HARRISS, University of Cincinnati

Institutional Members
of the American Society
for Eighteenth-Century Studies

American Antiquarian Society
National Library of Australia
Brown University
University of Calgary
University of California, Irvine
University of California, Los Angeles / William Andrews Clark Memorial Library
University of California, San Diego
Carleton University
Case Western Reserve University
Claremont Graduate School
Colonial Williamsburg Foundation
Dalhousie University
Dartmouth College
Emory University
University of Evansville
Florida State University
Folger Institute of Renaissance and Eighteenth-Century Studies
Fordham University
Georgia Institute of Technology
Hamilton College
Herzog August Bibliothek, Wolfenbüttel
Institute of Early American History and Culture
The Johns Hopkins University
University of Kansas
University of Kentucky
University of Michigan, Ann Arbor
University of Minnesota
City University of New York
State University of New York, Binghamton
University of North Carolina, Chapel Hill
Northern Illinois University
Northwestern University
University of Pennsylvania
University of Rochester
Rutgers University
Smith College
Smithsonian Institute
University of Southern California
University of Southern Mississippi
Stanford University
Swarthmore College
Sweet Briar College
University of Tennessee
Texas Tech University
Towson State University
Tulane University
University of Tulsa
University of Utrecht
Institute of Comparative and General Literature
University of Victoria
Washington University, St. Louis
The Henry Francis du Pont Winterthur Museum
University of Wisconsin, Milwaukee
Yale Center for British Art
Yale University
York University

Sponsoring Members

of the American Society for Eighteenth-Century Studies

Paul Alkon
Wye Jamison Allanbrook
Lillian H. Andon-Milligan
Anonymous
Paula R. Backscheider
Joel H. Baer
Chinmoy Banerjee
Carol Barash
Richard Barney
James L. Battersby
Jerry C. Beasley
Pamela J. Bennett
L. J. Bianchi
David Blewett
Thomas E. Blom
Carol Blum
Peter Boerner
Arnd Bohm
Thomas F. Bonnell
Martha F. Bowden
George C. Branam
Rudolph L. Brathwaite
Leo Braudy
Gwen W. Brewer
Elizabeth Brophy
Anthony E. Brown
Stephen N. Brown
Morris R. Brownell
Martine Watson Brownley
Martha L. Brunson
John L. Bullion
James H. Bunn
Max Byrd
Joseph A. Byrnes
Jill Campbell
Filisha Campbell Camara-Norman
Rocco Lawrence Capraro
Marilyn Carbonell
Guillermo Carnero
W. B. Carnochan
Vincent Carretta

David W. Carrithers
Michael T. Cartwright
Ralph Cohen
Judith Colton
Thomas M. Columbus
Elizabeth Colwill
Syndy M. Conger
Michael J. Conlon
Edward W. Copeland
Brian Corman
Peter Cosgrove
Howard J. Coughlin Jr.
Rosemary E. Cowler
Richard A. Cox
Patricia B. Craddock
James Cruise
John B. Dalsant
Marlies K. Danziger
Charles G. Davis
Robert Adams Day
Robert DeMaria
Alix S. Deguise
Pierre Deguise
Charles W. Dewees Jr.
Suellen Diaconoff
Richard J. Dircks
John Dowling
Joyce E. East
William F. Edmiston
Jolynn Edwards
Donald G. Eisen
A. C. Elias Jr.
Lee Andrew Elioseff
Antoinette Emch-Deriaz
John C. English
Lincoln B. Faller
Jan Fergus
Charles N. Fifer
John Irwin Fischer
Laurie Fitzgerald
Carol Houlihan Flynn

Alexander M. Forbes
Antonia Forster
Bernadette Fort
Christopher Fox
Roderick S French
Jack Fruchtman. Jr.
Henry L. Fulton
Gordon Fulton
P. Gabriner
Anne Barbeau Gardiner
James Garrett
James D. Garrison
Byron Gassman
Morris Golden
Peter B. Goldman
Ruth Graham
John E. Grant
Michael K. Green
Mary Elizabeth Green
Josephine Grieder
Hanns Gross
Walter Grossmann
Leon M. Guilhamet
Diana Guiragossian-Carr
Phyllis J. Guskin
Madelyn Gutwirth
George Haggerty
H. George Hahn
Roger Hahn
Karsten Harries
Frances Harrold
Phillip Harth
R. G. Harvey
Donald M. Hassler
Daniel Heartz
Patrick Henry
Kinzo Higuchi
Emita B. Hill
Charles H. Hinnant
Kathleen Holcomb
Claudine Hunting
Adrienne D. Hytier
Paul Ilie
Malcolm Jack
David Jackel
Wallace Jackson
Paul Jacob
Thomas Jemielity
Loftus Townshend Jestin

Denis Jonnes
Frank A. Kafker
Madeleine Kahn
Martin I. Kallich
Carol Kay
Frederick M. Keener
Robert E. Kelley
Ann Cline Kelly
Shirley Strum Kenny
Oscar Kenshur
William Kinsley
Lawrence E. Klein
Charles A. Knight
Philip Koch
Gwin J. Kolb
J. M. Konczacki
Yvonne Korshak
Patricia Koster
Carl R. Kropf
Mary N Kudarauskas
Colby H. Kullman
Catherine LaFarge
Guy Laprevotte
John E. Larkin, Jr.
I. Leonard Leeb
J. A. Levine
Joanna Lipking
Lawrence Lipking
Herbert Livingston
F. P. Lock
April London
Ada Long
Richard C. Lounsbury
Gregory Ludlow
Albert M. Lyles
Mark Samuel Madoff
Masaharu Maeda
Joseph T. Malloy
David D. Mann
Thomas E. Maresca
Robert Markley
Jean I. Marsden
Carol G. Marsh
Masafumi Masubuchi
Georges May
Gita May
John A. McCarthy
J. A. E. McEachern
Robert McHenry

Sponsoring Members / 297

Alan T. McKenzie
David McNeil
Roy W. Menninger
Robert G. Meeker
Jeffrey Merrick
Ann Messenger
Ellen Messer-Davidow
Paul H. Meyer
Patricia Howell Michaelson
Earl Miner
Michael Mooney
Judith Moore
Dewey F. Mosby
Karen Mulhallen
Maureen Mulvihill
W. W. Mynhardt
Daisuke Nagashima
Nicolas H. Nelson
Melvyn New
Matthew S. Novak
Sheryl O'Donnell
Mary Ann O'Donnell
John H. O'Neill
Hal N. Opperman
Hugh Ormsby-Lennon
Douglas Lane Patey
Ronald Paulson
Harry C. Payne
Virginia J. Peacock
Stuart Peterfreund
Carl A. Peterson
Joni Webb Petschauer
Peter Petschauer
Mary Sue Ply
J. G. A. Pocock
George W. Poe
R.S. Porter
Irwin Primer
Richard E. Quaintance, Jr.
Katherine Quinsey
Ruben D. Quintero
J. Karen Ray
R B Reaves
Thomas J. Regan
Cedric D. Reverand II
Vincent L. Remillard
Walter E. Rex
John Richetti
John Rieder

John Riely
Frances Mayhew Rippy
Albert J. Rivero
Betty Rizzo
Raymond Rizzo
Bruce Robertson
Trevor Ross
Eric Rothstein
Valerie C. Rudolph
Treadwell Ruml II
Peter Sabor
Takeshi Sakamoto
Mona Scheuermann
Beverly Schneller
Barbara Brandon Schnorrenberg
Gordon J. Schochet
William C. Schrader
Richard B. Schwartz
Robert Schwartz
Helen E. Searing
Joanne Sears
Peter Seary
Stuart Sherman
Charles E. Shields III
Totaro Shimamura
Michael Shugrue
Ann B. Shteir
D. T. Siebert
William Sievert
Oliver F. Sigworth
Geoffrey M. Sill
Sarah Simmons
Elaine Sisman
Jeffrey Smitten
Henry L. Snyder
Alex A. Sokalski
Robert Donald Spector
Martin S. Staum
Edna L. Steeves
Joan Koster Stemmler
Joan Hinde Stewart
Philip Stewart
R. A. Stephanson
Damie Stillman
Ann T. Straulman
Albrecht B. Strauss
Florian Stuber
Felicia Sturzer
Zenzo Suzuki

298 / *Sponsoring Members*

Amie G. Tannenbaum
Janice Thaddeus
Madeleine Therrien
Claudia Thomas
Diana M. Thomas
James Thompson
Connie C. Thorson
James L. Thorson
James Edward Tierney
Edward Tomarken
Betty Perry Townsend
Daniel Townsend
Linda Veronika Troost
Randolph Trumbach
Gordon Turnbull
Jack Undank
David L. Vander Meulen
Aram Vartanian

David F. Venturo
Thomas A. Vogler
John O. Voll
Morris Wachs
Rene Waldinger
Helmut L. Watzlawick
Shawncey Webb
D. H. Weinglass
Kathleen Wellman
Byron R. Wells
Richard Wendorf
Gretchen A. Wheelock
Dora Wiebenson
Roger L. Williams
James Woolley
John P. Wright
Elizabeth V. Young
Rose Zimbardo

Patrons

*of the American Society
for Eighteenth-Century Studies*

Mark S. Auburn
Lawrence G. Blackmon
T. E. D. Braun
Patricia Brückmann
Richard G. Carrott
Chester Chapin
Louis Cornell
Margaret Anne Doody
Frank H. Ellis
Roger L. Emerson
John E. Grant
Mary Lynn Johnson Grant
Dustin H. Griffin
Basil Guy
Diether H. Haenicke
Martha Hamilton-Phillips
Edward P. Harris
Marilyn Harris
Alfred W. Hesse
Stephen Holliday
Robert H. Hopkins
J. Paul Hunter
Kathryn Montgomery Hunter
Margaret C. Jacob
Annibel Jenkins
Judith Keig
Paul J. Korshin
Paul LeClerc
J. Patrick Lee
Maynard Mack
Robert P. MacCubbin
Geoffrey Marshall
H. W. Matalene
Helen L. McGuffie

Donald C. Mell, Jr.
John H. Middendorf
Felicity Nussbaum
Jane Perry-Camp
Leland D. Peterson
R. G. Peterson
James Pollak
John Valdimir Price
Jack Richtman
Edgar V. Roberts
Ronald C. Rosbottom
Lawrence A. Ruff
Harold Schiffman
Elaine C. Showalter
English Showalter
Jacqueline Smalley
Patricia Meyer Spacks
Susan Staves
Elizabeth Stewart
Keith Stewart
Mary Margaret Stewart
J. E. Stockwell, Jr.
Rebecca Stockwell
Debra Thomas
Connie C. Thorson
James L. Thorson
Teri Noel Towe
Robert W. Uphaus
Tara Ghoshal Wallace
Howard D. Weinbrot
James A. Winn
Calhoun Winton
John W. Yolton

Index

Adair, James, 272, 273
Adams, John, 110, 117, 126
Adams, Percy G., 272, 287
Adams, Randolph G., 109
Adams, Samuel, 109, 124
Addison, Joseph, 34, 37, 40, 169, 202
Alfieri, Vittorio, 207, 208, 216
Alkon, Paul, 267-289
Allen, John, 108
Amelia, Princess Sophia Eleonora, 247
Ames, Dianne S., 43
Anderson, John, 95, 100
Antal, Frederic, 70
Aristotle, 40, 55, 65, 72, 79, 136, 143, 147, 169
Arthur, Archibald, 95, 99
Astell, Mary, 149-157
Augusta, Dowager Princess of Wales, 245-260
Austen, Jane, 27

Bacon, Francis, 169
Bailyn, Bernard, 123
Barbauld, Anna, 27-41
Barbauld, Rochemont, 39
Barker, Ernest, 109
Barnett, Richard L., 129
Baudelaire, Charles, 177, 186, 192, 194
Beattie, James, 92, 94-96
Becker, Carl, 115, 116
Bentley, Richard, 139
Bérenguier, Nadine, 219-243, 289
Blanche, Jacques-Emile, 191
Boas, George, 86
Bolingbroke, Henry St. John, Viscount, 166, 167, 173, 174
Borges, Jorge Luis, 130

Bossuet, Bishop Jacques-Bénigne, 80
Boucher, François, 60
Bouilhet, Louis-Hyacinthe, 135
Bourdieu, Pierre, 22, 85
Boyle, Robert, 138
Bretonne, Restif de la, 11
Bucknell, Alexander, 273
Bullion, John L., 245-265, 289
Bunyan, John, 62
Burgos, Allesandro, 210
Burney, Frances, 40
Buron, François, 181

Calonne, Etienne de, 14
Campbell, George, 90, 98
Campbell, Lorne, 178, 193
Caroline, Queen of England, 164, 174
Carteret, John, Lord, Earl Granville, 166, 173, 202
Carver, Jonathan, 283
Cato, 103, 106, 121
Chamfort, Nicolas Sébastien Roch de, 219, 220
Champion, Judah, 22, 87
Charlemagne, 187
Charles IV, King of Spain, 187
Charlevoix, 272, 281
Charrière, Isabelle de, 219-238
Charteris, Francis, 67-69
Chesterfield, Philip Dormer Stanhope, fourth Earl of, 159-172
Clarendon, Edward Hyde, Earl of, 169
Colman, George, the younger, 38
Congreve, William, 202
Corday, Charlotte, 186, 194
Corneille, Pierre, 23
Coronelli, Vincenzo, 208-217, 289

Costanza, Giovan Battista, 216
Courthope, William John, 175
Cowley, Robert L.S., 74
Cresset, James, 251
Curti, Merle, 101, 120

d'Alembert, Jean le Rond, 18, 25, 215, 216, 218, 222
D'Annunzio, Gabriele, 208
d'Herbois, Collot, 15
Dabydeen, David, 58, 73
Darnton, Robert, 3-26, 217, 218, 289
David, Jacques-Louis, 177-194
Day, Geoffrey, 39
Day, Robert Adams, 139, 147
de la Tour, Quentin, 178
de Man, Paul, 25
de Staël, Germaine, 33, 40
Defoe, Daniel, 29, 43, 55, 78, 289
Delafaye, Charles, 162
Delany, Patrick, 201, 202
Derrida, Jacques, 25
Desmoulins, Camille, 15, 18, 19
Dickinson, John, 106, 107, 122-124
Diderot, Denis, 12, 22 24, 215, 216, 218, 225, 289
Diggins, John Patrick, 103, 126
Dodington, George Bubb, 247-250, 253-256, 259-264
Donne, John, 131
Dorbec, Prosper, 177
Downer, Silas, 111
Dryden, John, 142, 146, 169
Duclos, Charles Pinot, 222
Dugaw, Dianne, 268, 287
Dulany, Daniel, 114-116
Dunbar, James, 92
Dunn, John, 102, 114, 115, 121, 122
Dunton, John, 138-141, 147
Duval, Jamerey, 11
Dworetz, Steven M., 101, 289

Earle, John, 169
Ehrenpreis, Irvin, 43, 50, 198, 204
Elizabeth I, Queen of England, 130
Esculapius, 165

Fabian, Johannes, 80, 282, 288
Fabre d'Eglantine, 16

Fell, Margaret, 149-158
Ferguson, Adam, 79
Ferguson, James, 92
Fielding, Henry, 28-30, 32, 37, 38, 41, 55, 74
Fiorenza, Elizabeth Schussler, 155, 158
Flandrin, Jean-Louis, 224, 240
Flaubert, Gustave, 135
Fontenay, Elizabeth de, 227, 241
Fortis, Alberto, 212, 216, 217
Foulis, Andrew, 95, 99
Fox, Henry, 247
Frangonard, Jean-Honoré, 60
Francis of Assisi, 210
Frederick, Prince of Wales, 248, 249, 252, 253, 256, 258, 261, 263, 264
Freud, Sigmund, 25
Frezzi, Guiseppe, 210
Friedlaender, Walter, 178, 192
Frye, Roland M., 82
Fuchs, Jacob, 43-51, 289
Fuchs, James L., 207-218, 289
Fuseli, Henry, 70, 74

Galloway, Joseph, 119
Gay, John, 43-51, 66, 202
Genette, Gérard, 129-148
George I, King of England, 165, 167, 173
George II, King of England, 163, 167, 170, 173, 174, 246, 248-250, 253, 256, 258, 259, 261, 262, 264
George III, King of England, 246, 260, 263-265, 289
Gerard, Alexander, 91, 92, 99
Gibbon, Edward, 33
Gillray, James, 70, 74
Godet, Philippe, 222
Gordon, Thomas, 91, 98, 121
Gordon, William, 105
Greenblatt, Stephen, 175
Greenough, Chester Noyes, 169, 175
Gregory, John, v, 91, 92, 99
Grierson, Herbert, 131, 147
Griffin, Dustin, 197-205, 289
Grotius, Hugo, 115, 116, 125
Gubar, Susan, 50

Hall, Joseph, 18, 123, 169
Hamilton, Lady Archibald, 99, 248, 290
Handlin, Oscar and Lilian, 120
Hannibal, 187
Harley, Robert, first Earl of Oxford, 198-201, 203, 204
Hawley, Joseph, 124
Hegel, George Wilhelm Friedrich, 191
Herodotus, 82, 134
Hervey, John, 164, 174, 175, 248, 261
Hicks, William, 107, 123
Hinnant, Charles H., 75-88, 289
Hitchcock, Gad, 105
Hobbes, Thomas, 80, 103
Holcomb, Kathleen, 89-100, 290
Home, Henry, Lord Kames, 79, 85-89, 91, 98
Homer, 132, 202, 205
Horace, 169, 173, 199, 200, 247, 250, 261, 262, 289
Hudson, Winthrop S., 72, 73, 121
Huet, Marie-Hélène, 186, 193, 195
Hume, David, 92

Inchbald, Elizabeth, 36, 38

Jenyns, Soame, 113, 114
Johnson, Samuel, 27, 44, 175, 176, 250, 289
Jones, Malcolm, 73
Jonson, Ben, 131, 169
Josephine, Empress of France, 191, 196
Joyce, Lester Douglas, 40, 126
Junius Americanus (Arthur Lee), 112, 116, 124
Justamond, J.O., 173
Juvenal, 53, 72

Katz, Stanley, 101, 121
Knox, Vicesimus, 28

La Bruyère, Jean de, 170, 171, 176
La Harpe, Jean-François de, 18
La Porte, Joseph de, 4, 5, 11, 12
Laclos, Choderlos de, 236, 242
Laetius, Johannes, 82
Landa, Louis, 84, 204

Lanser, Susan, 237, 240
Lathrop, John, 105, 108
Lebrun, Vigée, 181, 193
Lecercle, Jean-Louis, 222, 239, 240
Lecouvreur, Adrienne, 22
Lee, George, 116, 124, 251, 264
Leonard, Daniel, 124
Lessing, Gotthold Ephraim, 181
Lettsom, John, 273, 274, 278, 280, 287
Lewis, Erasmus, 199
Lewis, Theodore B., 125
Lichtenberg, Georg-Christoph, 53, 57, 69, 72
Locke, John, 80, 101-123, 125-127, 289
Louis XIV, King of France, 18, 23, 24, 26
Louis XVI, King of France, 19, 186
Lovejoy, A. O., 86, 87
Lucian, 134
Lukács, Georg, 178, 192
Lutz, Donald, 121, 122, 124
Lyle, Guy R., 130, 147

Machiavelli, Niccolo Di Bernardo Dei, 104, 120
MacPherson, C. B., 103, 121
Mander, Karel van, 178
Mann, Horace, 250, 262
Marat, Jean-Paul, 15, 177, 178, 181, 184-186, 192-195
Marie Antoinette, Queen of France, 181, 193
Marvell, Andrew, 129-147, 290
Mayhew, Jonathan, 117, 126
Mazarin, 165
McKenzie, Alan T., 159-176, 290
McPherson, Heather, 177-196, 290
Medici, Marie de, 191, 196
Mercier, Louis-Sebastien, 5, 15
Michelangelo, 178
Michiel, Guistina Renier, 212, 218
Millar, John, 79, 95, 96, 99
Miller, John C., 101, 120
Miller, Nancy K., 221
Milton, John, 72, 121, 289
Molière, Jean-Baptiste Poquelin, 3, 17-21, 24-26

304 / Index

Monboddo, James Burnett, Lord, 79
Montagu, Charles, first Earl of Halifax, 169
Moor, James, 95, 99
Moore, Catherine E., 40
Moore, Edward, 39
More, Sir Thomas, 282
Muratori, Ludovico Antonio, 212, 215–217

Namier, Sir Lewis, 174, 261
Napoleon I, Emperor of France, 177–196
Necker, Madame Suzanne Churchod, 222
Newton, Isaac, 70, 74, 92, 286
Nisbet, Robert, 80, 87
Nokes, David, 198, 204
Novak, Maximillian, 83, 88
Nussbaum, Felicity, 72, 74

Ogée, Frédéric, 65, 74
Ogilvie, William, 91, 92
Otis, James, 115–117, 125, 126
Overbury, Thomas, 169
Ovid, 44, 53, 72

Paoli, Pasquale, 207, 209, 214, 216
Parker, John, 273, 283, 287, 288
Parker, Matthew, 132
Parker, Samuel, 132
Parrington, Vernon, 101, 120
Paulson, Ronald, 60, 65, 67, 72–74, 138
Pelham, Thomas, Duke of Newcastle, 160–164, 167, 171, 173–175, 247, 250, 256, 262
Perry, Ruth, 150
Pitt, William, first Earl of Chatham, 101, 123, 166, 172–174, 250, 261
Pius VII, 188, 189
Pivati, Gianfrancesco, 214, 216, 218
Platini, Guiseppe, 210
Plato, 79
Plautus, 134
Plumb, J. H., 268
Pocock, J. G. A., 101–104, 120, 122
Pollak, Ellen, 46, 47, 50, 51

Pope, Alexander, 43, 45, 49, 50, 62, 74, 77, 165, 169, 197, 202
Porter, Roy, 268
Potocki, Stanislas Kostka, 181, 188, 193
Pratt, Charles, 108
Pufendorf, Samuel, 80, 115
Pulteney, William, 166, 173, 174
Pye, Henry, 28

Quintilian, 143

Raphael, 181
Reeve, Clara, 27–29, 32, 40
Reid, Thomas, 90–100
Reynolds, Joshua, 178, 192
Riccoboni, Marie-Jeanne, 236, 241, 242
Richards, I. A., 133
Richardson, Samuel, 28–34, 37–41
Richelieu, Armand, Duc de, 165
Riley, Patrick, 125
Rivarol, Antoine, 12–19, 21
Robespierre, François-Maximilien-Joseph De, 15, 20, 21, 26, 194
Rochester, John Wilmot, second Earl of, 62, 63
Rogers, Katherine, 27–41, 51, 150, 290
Rosa, Guimaraes, 130
Rossiter, Clinton, 104, 105, 122, 126
Rousseau, Jean-Jacques, 17–22, 24–26, 115, 220–222, 224, 225, 227, 230, 231, 232–234, 236–242
Rowland, John, 129–148, 290
Rowlandson, Thomas, 70, 74
Rubens, Peter Paul, 181, 191

Saint-Yenne, Lafont de, 178
Scarborough, Richard, Earl of, 164–167, 173, 174
Schiller, Friedrich von, 272
Schlesinger, Arthur M., 124
Schor, Naomi, 221
Scott, Sir Walter, 191
Selwyn, George, 247, 261
Shakespeare, William, 28, 33, 40, 72, 175
Shapin, Steven, 92, 93, 99

Sherbo, Arthur, 43, 50
Sheridan, Frances, 35, 37
Shklar, Judith N., 104, 121
Sieyès, L'abbé Emmanuel-Joseph, 15, 19
Skene, David, 91–93, 98, 99
Smith, Adam, 79, 94, 95, 100, 245
Smith, Charlotte, 36
Smith, Hilda, 149
Smollett, Tobias, 29, 39, 174
Spacks, Patricia Meyer, 44, 50, 245, 246, 250, 259, 260
Steele, Richard, 202
Stein, Gertrude, 268
Steuert, James, 95
Stiles, Ezra, 122
Stone, Andrew, 256
Stone, Lawrence, 241, 264
Strauss, Leo, 103, 121
Stuart, John, third Earl of Bute, 245–260
Suffolk, Lady, 170
Swift, Jonathan, 37, 43, 48–51, 53, 55, 66, 72, 74–88, 129, 131, 132, 134, 137–147, 197–205, 290

Tacitus, 169
Tanner, Tony, 236
Temple, Sir William, 80, 164, 198, 201
Terence, 169
Theophrastus, 169, 170, 175
Thickstun, Margaret Olofson, 149–158, 290
Thomson, Alexander, 93, 98, 99
Tolstoy, Leo, 191
Tommaseo, Niccolò, 214
Tonson, Jacob, 142
Townshend, Charles, 167, 168, 264
Traer, James, 225, 240
Traill, Robert, 92
Tucker, John, 110, 111

Tussaud, Madame, 184, 194

Ulman, Lewis, 92, 99

Valente, Luiz Fernando, 130, 147
Van Dyck, Sir Anthony, 181
Varro, Marcus Terentius, 79, 86, 88
Venette, Nicolas, 55, 73
Villiers, Barbara, Duchess of Cleveland, 142
Virgil, 44, 48, 51
Voltaire, 12, 14–17, 21–26, 180, 218

Wagner, Hans-Peter, 53–74, 290
Waldegrave, James, second Earl, 249–259, 261–264
Walpole, Horace, 247, 248, 250–252, 254, 258, 261–264
Walpole, Sir Robert, 162, 165, 166, 173, 201, 202
Warren, Joseph, 110
Washington, George, 180
Weinglass, David H., 74
Wesley, John, 85, 88
Whately, Thomas, 113
Wheatley, Henry B., 130, 142, 147
Wilcox, Donald J., 286, 288
Wilkes, John, 124
Williams, Carolyn D., 51
Williams, Kathleen, 76
Willis, Justice, 248
Wilson, Alexander, 94, 99
Winckelmann, Johann Joachim, 181
Wollstonecraft, Mary, 221
Wright, Benjamin, 115, 125

Yorke, Philip, first Earl of Hardwicke, 164, 166, 250, 262

Zedler, Johann Heinrich, 212, 218